COASTAL
FISHES

of the PACIFIC NORTHWEST

REVISED AND EXPANDED SECOND EDITION

COASTAL FISHES

of the PACIFIC NORTHWEST

ANDY LAMB and PHIL EDGELL

Photography by Phil Edgell

HARBOUR PUBLISHING

*This book is dedicated to the establishment
of a network of No-Take Marine Protected Areas
throughout the Pacific Northwest.*

Harbour Publishing Co. Ltd.
P.O. Box 219, Madeira Park, BC, V0N 2H0
www.harbourpublishing.com

Edited by Peter Robson
Text design by Martin Nichols
Map by Roger Handling
Additional image captions: front cover, Wolf-eel; back cover, Tiger Rockfish; spine, Yelloweye Rockfish; title page, Decorated Warbonnet, spawning Sockeye Salmon (Danny Kent photograph) and Kelp Greenling; page 16, diver with Lingcod.
Printed in Canada on chlorine free paper made with 10% post-consumer waste using soy-based inks.

Harbour Publishing acknowledges financial support from the Government of Canada through the Canada Book Fund and the Canada Council for the Arts, and from the Province of British Columbia through the BC Arts Council and the Book Publishing Tax Credit.

Library and Archives Canada Cataloguing in Publication

Lamb, Andy, 1947–

   Coastal fishes of the Pacific Northwest / by Andy Lamb; photographs by Phil Edgell.
   —2nd ed., rev. and updated

   Includes bibliographical references and index.
   ISBN 978-1-55017-471-7

1. Marine fishes—British Columbia—Pacific Coast—Identification. 2. Marine fishes—Pacific Coast (U.S.)—Identification. 3. Marine fishes—British Columbia—Pacific Coast—Pictorial works. 4. Marine fishes—Pacific Coast (U.S.)—Pictorial works.
I. Edgell, Phil, 1951- II. Title.

QL623.4.L35 2010   597.177'43   C2010-900389-6

CONTENTS

INTRODUCTION 10

FISH FOR THE FUTURE: A Personal Perspective on Conservation 11

HOW TO USE THIS BOOK 12

HAGFISHES (Family Myxinidae) 17
1 species

LAMPREYS (Family Petromyzontidae) 18
2 species

COW SHARKS (Family Hexanchidae) 21
2 species

CATSHARKS (Family Scyliorhinidae) 23
1 species

MACKEREL SHARKS (Family Lamnidae) 25
3 species

SLEEPER SHARKS (Family Somniosidae) 27
1 species

REQUIEM SHARKS (Family Carcharhinidae) 27
1 species

BASKING SHARKS (Family Cetorhinidae) 28
1 species

DOGFISH SHARKS (Family Squalidae) 29
1 species

HOUND SHARKS (Family Triakidae) 30
2 species

THRESHER SHARKS (Family Alopiidae) 31
1 species

ANGEL SHARKS (Family Squatinidae) 32
1 species

SKATES (Family Rajidae) 33
3 species

ELECTRIC RAYS (Family Torpedinidae) 37
1 species

EAGLE RAYS (Family Myliobatidae) 39
1 species

MANTAS (Family Mobulidae) 39
1 species

STINGRAYS (Family Dasyatidae) 40
1 species

SHORTNOSE CHIMAERAS (Family Chimaeridae) 40
1 species

STURGEONS (Family Acipenseridae) 43
2 species

HERRINGS (Family Clupeidae) 45
3 species

ANCHOVIES (Family Engraulidae) 48
1 species

SMELTS (Family Osmeridae) 49
5 species

SAND LANCES (Family Ammodytidae) 53
1 species

SALMON AND TROUT (Subfamily Salmoninae) 55
9 species

CODS (Family Gadidae) 71
4 species

MERLUCCID HAKES (Family Merlucciidae) 76
1 species

VIVIPAROUS BROTULAS (Family Bythitidae) 77
1 species

CUSK-EELS (Family Ophidiidae) 79
1 species

EELPOUTS (Family Zoarcidae) 79
5 species

SILVERSIDES (Family Atherinopsidae) 82
2 species

LIZARDFISHES (Family Synodontidae) 83
1 species

BARRACUDAS (Family Sphyraenidae) 83
1 species

LANCETFISHES (Family Alepisauridae) 84
1 species

RIBBONFISHES (Family Trachipteridae) 84
1 species

STICKLEBACKS (Family Gasterosteidae) 85
1 species

TUBESNOUTS (Family Aulorhynchidae) 87
1 species

PIPEFISHES (Family Syngnathidae) 88
1 species

SANDFISHES (Family Trichodontidae) 89
1 species

SURFPERCHES (Family Embiotocidae) 90
9 species

SEA CHUBS (Family Kyphosidae) 98
1 species

TILEFISHES (Family Malacanthidae) 98
1 species

DRUMS AND CROAKERS (Family Sciaenidae) 99
2 species

MEDUSAFISHES (Family Centrolophidae) 99
1 species

BUTTERFISHES (Family Stromateidae) 99
1 species

RAGFISHES (Family Icosteidae) 100
1 species

POMFRETS (Family Bramidae) 100
1 species

OPAHS (Family Lamprididae) 100
1 species

MOLAS (Family Molidae) 101
1 species

ARMORHEADS (Family Pentacerotidae) 101
1 species

GOBIES (Family Gobiidae) 102
3 species

RONQUILS (Family Bathymasteridae) 106
3 species

KELP BLENNIES (Family Clinidae) 109
3 species

PRICKLEBACKS (Family Stichaeidae) 112
15 species

GUNNELS (Family Pholidae) 126
6 species

WOLFFISHES (Family Anarhichadidae) 133
1 species

WRYMOUTHS (Family Cryptacanthodidae) 136
2 species

QUILLFISHES (Family Ptilichthyidae) 138
1 species

GRAVELDIVERS (Family Scytalinidae) 139
1 species

PROWFISHES (Family Zaproridae) 140
1 species

JACKS (Family Carangidae) 142
2 species

MACKERELS (Family Scombridae) 143
4 species

DOLPHINFISHES (Family Coryphaenidae) 145
1 species

TRIGGERFISHES (Family Balistidae) 145
1 species

TEMPERATE BASSES (Family Percichthyidae) 146
1 species

SEA BASSES AND GROUPERS (Family Serranidae) 146
1 species

ROCKFISHES AND OTHER SCORPIONFISHES
(Family Scorpaenidae) 147
26 species

SABLEFISHES (Family Anoplopomatidae) 184
2 species

GREENLINGS (Family Hexagrammidae) 186
8 species

SCULPINS (Superfamily Cottoidea) 200
46 species

TOADFISHES (Family Batrachoididae) 252
1 species

POACHERS (Family Agonidae) 255
13 species

SNAILFISHES (Family Liparidae) 270
8 species

LUMPSUCKERS (Family Cyclopteridae) 280
1 species

CLINGFISHES (Family Gobiesocidae) 283
2 species

SAND FLOUNDERS (Family Paralichthyidae) 287
3 species

TONGUEFISHES (Family Cynoglossidae) 290
1 species

RIGHTEYE FLOUNDERS (Family Pleuronectidae) 291
16 species

ACKNOWLEDGEMENTS 309

APPENDIX Aquaria: Public Viewing Opportunities
for Pacific Northwest Fishes 311

SELECTED BIBLIOGRAPHY 313

INDEX 314

INTRODUCTION

When people first began to study fishes along the Pacific shores of North America, many amateur naturalists worked side by side with professional biologists. Together, they slowly and steadily developed an understanding of the fishes living in the region. However, as technology increased, a gulf unfortunately developed between career ichthyologists (people who study fishes) and curious lay people. Technical jargon, complex mathematical interpretations and other factors tended to isolate the many interested amateurs from the sophisticated professionals.

Fortunately, other technology such as scuba, relatively inexpensive underwater photographic equipment and computer wizardry is providing new opportunities for these two groups to collaborate. *Coastal Fishes of the Pacific Northwest: Second Edition* is an attempt to assist all interested parties in identifying fish quickly and accurately while using a minimum of technical terminology. Its target audience is the amateur fish observer, including the recreational angler, diver, commercial fisherman, beachcomber, dockside stroller and seafood fancier. Hopefully, it will also assist the professional.

The First Edition: A Glance Back

As enthusiastic fish watchers since our youth, we knew that a user-friendly guidebook focusing on the inshore species of the Pacific Northwest (which we define as the area between northern California and the Gulf of Alaska) would be helpful to folks who interact with these fascinating creatures. As young staffers at the Vancouver Aquarium, we literally became immersed in the subject and were surrounded by great opportunities to soak up interactions with these fishes.

During the 1970s, we brazenly decided to "write a book on local fish" and boldly began assembling photographs to go with our concept. Fortunately, many of our colleagues, dive buddies and other friends encouraged these efforts—assistance vital to the project's completion. Together with Howard White of Harbour Publishing, we moved forward to create Coastal Fishes of the Pacific Northwest, which appeared in 1986. Over the years since then, the book has remained a popular resource and we continue to receive positive feedback from its users.

The Second Edition: Finning Forward

While species of fishes living throughout the Pacific Northwest have remained virtually the same, almost everything about human relationships with them has changed, often with dire consequences.

Naturalists and scientists continue to learn more about them. Evolving technologies increase and enhance the knowledge database, providing more access through advanced observation techniques. Integrating the appropriate new information into another edition is long overdue and hopefully has resulted in a quality, up-to-date reference.

As authors and observers, we personally have learned much over the years since *Coastal Fishes of the Pacific Northwest* was first delivered to the printers. Certainly we have continued to be fascinated by these creatures and understand more about their lives. But perhaps even more importantly, we have interacted with many readers of the first edition and found the feedback enlightening. Happily, most of it has been positive and instructive. Consequently, we have made changes while maintaining the basic foundation that created so many enthusiastic readers. The following preamble attempts to summarize this approach.

—Andy Lamb and Phil Edgell

FISH FOR THE FUTURE A Personal Perspective on Conservation

During our time on this planet, we have witnessed a dramatic change in how the marine environment is perceived. In our youth, the oceans were thought to be able to provide an endless supply of food for an expanding world population. Now, as seniors, we are routinely informed, by all manner of media, of looming and actual fishery collapses worldwide. A total reversal within fifty years or so!

What happened? What does the future hold? Can mankind adjust and positively address the issue?

These are very important questions. Understanding the history of the first then grappling with possible answers to the second and third is critical to the future of the planet.

Fortunately, thanks in part to the media, the alarm is being sounded and there is a growing realization that the oceans alone cannot sustain the world's human population and that many species have been overfished and may never recover. An informed motivated citizenry, provided with opportunity, is the best hope to resolve the crisis. Around the world, an increasing number of conservation-oriented organizations offer empowerment. There is cause to hope that we can positively affect the future.

A Case for No-Take Marine Protected Areas

One beautifully simple and greatly effective option to address the over-exploitation of the world's marine resources is to establish a network of No-Take Marine Protected Areas. This process is already well underway as an ever-increasing number of countries continue to set aside sections of their coastlines for this purpose—and they are being rewarded by proven evidence of its success.

A No-Take Marine Protected Area is a very simple concept. It is actually an adaptation of the terrestrial park model that has been so successfully used for many years the world over. In such a zone, consumptive uses within its boundaries are forbidden, while non-consumptive activities are permitted and even encouraged. In essence, a No-Take Marine Protected Area is a policy that ensures the future of living marine resources. Within its boundary, all organisms are immune from harvesting and complete ecosystems operate without human consumptive interference.

Likely nearing 90 years of age and carrying perhaps a million tiny young, this very pregnant Yelloweye Rockfish is the ultimate representative for No-Take Marine Protected Areas.

The holistic approach of the No-Take Marine Protected Area strategy ensures that long-established food webs remain, providing feeding and breeding opportunities for all organisms within. Protecting individual species such as the killer whales or various rockfish via narrowly focussed regulations or fishing closures, while admirable, misses the point. If these targeted species do not have enough food or breeding opportunities, such well-meaning efforts will be ineffective.

Numerous excellent references exist that detail the many benefits of No-Take Marine Protected Areas and we encourage this readership to avail themselves of their collective wisdom. One in particular stands out because it is easily read and takes a common-sense approach. *Marine Reserves for New Zealand*, by Dr. Bill Ballantine, University of Auckland, Leigh Laboratory Bulletin #25, 1991, remains perhaps the best introduction to the topic, and its author is the father of the No-Take Marine Protected Area movement. It may be difficult to find, but it is absolutely the best reference.

No-Take Marine Protected Areas and the Pacific Northwest

A large number of maritime nations have successfully adopted the No-Take Marine Protected Area approach and are now benefiting from its many positive outcomes. Despite a growing volume of positive evidence generated from many other countries around the world, the governments of both Canada and the USA in the Pacific Northwest (with the exception of California)—have yet to act.

The only No-Take Marine Protected Areas established so far—at Brackett's Landing in Edmonds, Washington, and Porteau Cove and Whytecliff Park near Vancouver in British Columbia—came about as a result of small, community initiatives and despite their success, they have not spurred significant national or international action.

As this guide went to press, government bureaucrats remained mired in endless consultative processes and seem powerless to establish even a single No-Take Marine Protected Area. The time to act is long overdue. Our dwindling marine resources of the Pacific Northwest desperately need No-Take Marine Protected Areas.

The authors invite readers to help with the establishment of No-Take Marine Protected Areas in the Pacific Northwest. You can contact us either by mail at P.O. Box 16-2, Thetis Island, BC, V0R 2Y0 or electronically at notakempas@telus.net.

HOW TO USE THIS BOOK

The primary purpose of *Coastal Fishes of the Pacific Northwest: Second Edition* is to help readers identify fish. The following steps are provided to help guide the reader.

If unfamiliar with the various fish families of the Pacific Northwest, start with the Table of Contents. Find and examine the silhouette(s) that closest resembles the fish you are trying to identify. This will steer you to one or more family groups where more detailed information and photos are found.

Look through the associated species pages for that family (or families) until you find one (or more) that could be the fish you are trying to identify. Incidentally, for fish families that feature many species, similar-looking fish are grouped together to assist the process.

Using both the colour photograph(s) and the labelled, shaded drawing(s), attempt to make a final choice. This step may be more involved if there are similar-looking species to choose from. For most fishes, several colour images are included, which will help account for species variation. For optimal results, it is important to use both the colour images and the drawings in tandem.

Within the text for each species, additional information is presented, including distribution, size, behaviour and natural history details, to help confirm the identification.

The order of appearance of the various fish families is based upon a traditional approach employed by the majority of marine life identification guides. It is generally termed a *phylogenetic* ordering. Simply put, this system begins with those groups considered more primitive and progresses through to the most advanced. Unfortunately, such an approach is the subject of continual debate among scholars, resulting in variable interpretations of "advanced" versus "primitive." However, a phylogenetic scheme functions reasonably well and seems the best choice for this publication.

The American Fisheries Society based in Bethesda, Maryland has a standing committee that officially deals with nomenclatorial issues and changes. *Common and Scientific Names of Fishes from the United States, Canada and Mexico, 6th Edition*, 2004, is the latest summary of this work. The common and scientific names used in this guide are presented in accordance with this authority.

Auxiliary Species. Numerous species that primarily range outside the north/south extremes of the Pacific Northwest are encountered sporadically or infrequently. To address this issue, the descriptions for these "auxiliary" fishes are presented in short paragraph form with an accompanying photograph, as opposed to the full descriptions given for most species. These "auxiliaries" are placed according to the established "modified phylogenetic" system of categorizing families and species. Some are included as part of the appropriate existing family sections while others are presented within new family headings.

Which Species? When considering which species to include in this edition, we decided to be as inclusive as possible. However, even by stretching the definition of "coastal" (nearshore or inshore), a line had to be drawn. Many species of deepwater fishes that could be considered Pacific Northwest species by other interpretations were not included, as only certain commercial fisherman harvesting in generally inaccessible areas might encounter them. The list includes approximately 21 eelpouts, 21 rockfishes, 18 snailfishes, 6 sculpins, 3 righteyed flounders and 2 skates.

Common Name. The common name represents the current English-language term assigned to each fish and the name designated by an international committee of ichthyologists (see above).

Scientific Name. When first encountered by most people, scientific names such as the graveldiver's *Scytalina cerdale* appear baffling, strange and perhaps unnecessary. However, scientific names are, in fact, the best and most universal system for defining fishes and may be pronounced simply by using routine English language phonetics: *Scytalina cerdale*, for example, sounds like *sky-tal-eena sur-da-lee*.

Scientific names prove most useful when someone is communicating to people speaking another language because these scientific names are universal and eliminate completely the vagaries of regional variations. These definitive binomials, usually derived from Greek or Latin, correspond to names of ordinary people. The first element in the scientific set equates with the personal family name, and the second element with the given name. For example, *Scytalina cerdale* equates with Smith, John. Readers are encouraged to become familiar with the scientific names because one can always find information concerning a certain species under that creature's scientific name that otherwise might be unavailable under its common name(s).

Other Common Names. Unfortunately, due to cultural, geographic and historical reasons, a fish may have more than one common name. Even more confusing is that two different species may have the same popular name. The alternate names listed appear in order of "relative" acceptability. Those prefixed with "Incorrect" are just that.

Maximum Recorded Size. This information represents the best documentation available. Many species, particularly those that are economically significant, have received more intense statistical scrutiny.

Distribution. The geographic limits provided indicate the current documented extremes of each species' range.

Habitat. This information will help the scuba diver, snorkeler, angler, commercial fisherman and shoreside naturalist identify where the species can be found—whether noticed underwater, accessed from the surface, via a boat or while strolling the intertidal zone.

Comments. This section provides an assortment of information about the species and may include life cycle/biology, angling tips, commercial fishing history and recipes.

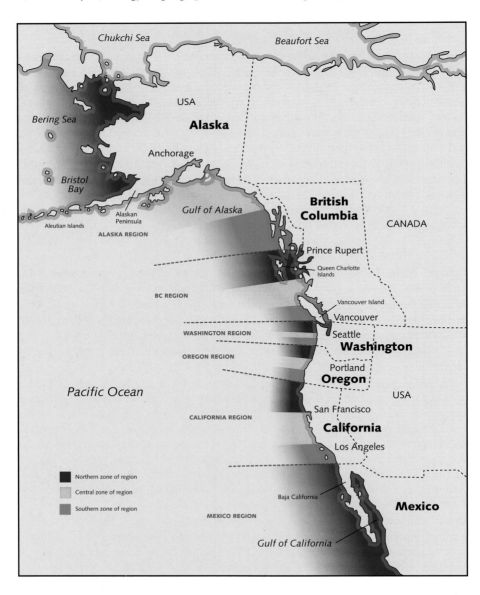

Icons

Within the information given for each species are usually one or more small icons that contain silhouette symbols for the angler, the diver, the beachcomber, the commercial fisherman and the seafood fancier. They serve as a quick reference to identify the type of material provided within that species' Habitat and Comments section and to identify for whom this information will be most relevant. Each icon also serves to highlight which user group might most likely encounter that species.

The angling icon shows the entry contains fishing techniques, bait and tackle for the recreational angler. This book does not make value judgments concerning the species angled for, but rather focuses on the factors affecting successful fishing experiences. Please help ensure future opportunities for all by following the angling rules and regulations set out by appropriate government agencies.

The scuba-diving icon shows the entry contains information on where to look for that species, at what depth, and any special behavioural characteristics. Most entries are based on finding the species at depths to 36 m (120 ft)—these depths generally represent safe recreational diving limits. However, with special training and proper equipment, increasing numbers of technical divers may now safely explore deeper territory. The recent availability of good quality, compact and reasonably priced underwater photographic equipment allows keen observers the chance to take underwater images. Such photographs can confirm species identification and document noteworthy behaviour. Spearfishing devotees and other consumptive users should adhere to a good conservation ethic and abide by official government harvest limits.

The commercial fishing icon shows the entry contains information about the commercial fishing industry's historical and contemporary relationship with that species.

The surface-bound naturalist icon shows the entry includes information about above-the-surface viewing opportunities for that species—whether the person is a strolling beachcomber, a wharf-bound observer or a curious boat passenger. In the name of conservation, please show good beach etiquette by replacing overturned rocks to their original position. Take photographs and leave fish and their habitat on the beach.

The seafood-fancier icon means the entry includes information concerning a species' edibility, often with a recipe suggestion. With the influx of many cultures to the Pacific Northwest, an increasing array of local fish species are being used as seafood. Many fish, once considered far from gourmet, are now popular for both the restaurant scene and the family dinner table.

Eco-aware seafood consumers can positively impact the overharvesting of Pacific Northwest fish species. Programs such as the Seafood Watch, sponsored by the Monterey Bay Aquarium, and Oceanwise, promoted by the Vancouver Aquarium, provide assistance to consumers about what species are being harvested in a sustainable, environmentally friendly way.

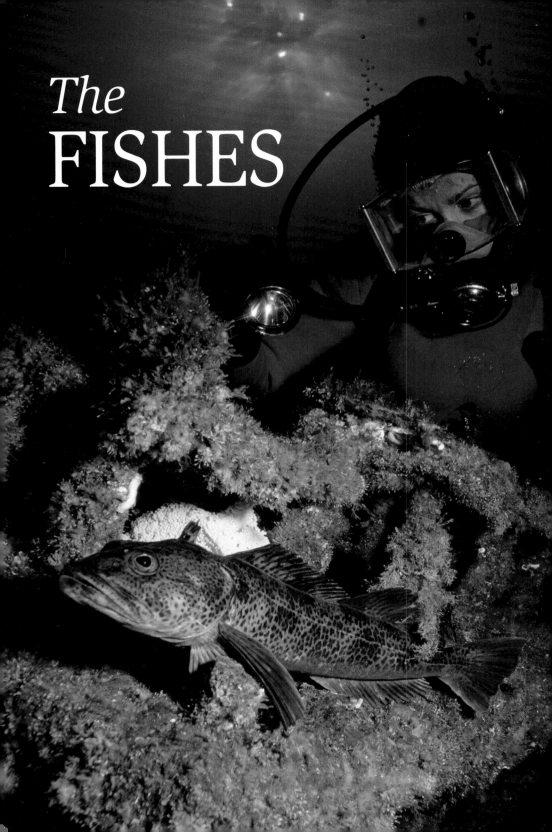

The
FISHES

THE **HAGFISHES** (Family Myxinidae)

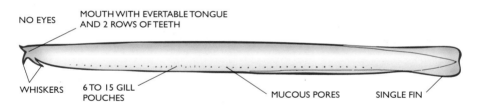

NO EYES

MOUTH WITH EVERTABLE TONGUE
AND 2 ROWS OF TEETH

WHISKERS

6 TO 15 GILL
POUCHES

MUCOUS PORES

SINGLE FIN

The hagfishes, scientifically known as Myxinidae, comprise a family of fishes containing approximately 60 living species. Blind, scale-less and jawless, the largest of these elongate creatures may attain lengths of 80 cm (32 in). Most dwell in deep, largely inaccessible haunts among sandy or muddy substrates of the continental shelf.

They are among only a few fishes that truly qualify as scavengers. Using their keen sense of smell, hagfishes seek out dead or dying fish that lie almost motionless on the sea floor. After burrowing inside the bodies of their prey, these lethargic fish reduce the carcasses literally to skin and bone. If disturbed, particularly while feeding, hagfish may produce amazing amounts of thick, viscous, toxic slime that adheres to virtually anything.

Among present-day fishes, the hagfishes—lacking paired fins—relate most closely to the somewhat similar lampreys.

There are two Pacific Northwest species: the Pacific Hagfish and the Black Hagfish. The latter, *Eptatretus deani*, is not included in this guide because it lives in such deep water that it is seldom seen.

Pacific Hagfish

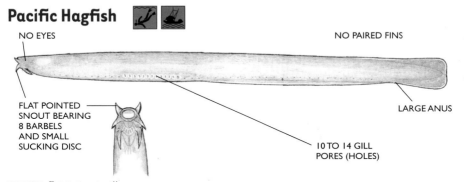

NO EYES

NO PAIRED FINS

FLAT POINTED
SNOUT BEARING
8 BARBELS
AND SMALL
SUCKING DISC

LARGE ANUS

10 TO 14 GILL
PORES (HOLES)

SPECIES: *Eptatretus stoutii*
OTHER COMMON NAMES: California hagfish, common hagfish, hagfish, hag-fish, hag. Incorrect: slime eel

C. Egg cases.
Bernard P. Hanby photograph

MAXIMUM RECORDED SIZE: 63.5 cm (25 in)
DISTRIBUTION: Central Baja California, Mexico, to Vancouver Island, southern British Columbia (southeastern Alaska reports undocumented)
HABITAT: Scuba divers may find Pacific Hagfish at depths greater than 16 m (54 ft) resting on silt bottoms coiled in a figure eight or a tight circular pattern.

COMMENTS: Pacific Hagfish are dubbed "slime eels" by many commercial trawl fishermen, mainly in California and Oregon, whose nets they occasionally foul. The Pacific Hagfish is exported to Korea for its flesh and skin.

THE **LAMPREYS** (Family Petromyzontidae)

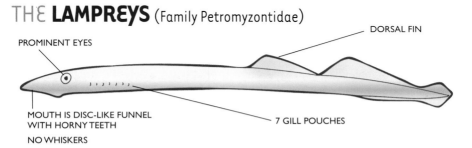

PROMINENT EYES

DORSAL FIN

MOUTH IS DISC-LIKE FUNNEL WITH HORNY TEETH

NO WHISKERS

7 GILL POUCHES

Approximately 40 known living species of lampreys form the Petromyzontidae, the "stone suckers." All lampreys reside in the cool temperate or frigid boreal waters of the world. Although some frequent both fresh and saltwater during different life-cycle stages, others, such as the Pacific Northwest's Western Brook Lamprey, *Lampetra richardsoni*, live their lives entirely in freshwater habitats. No strictly marine petromyzontids exist, however, as all species ascend rivers or streams to spawn.

Two anadromous (fishes that migrate into rivers or streams to breed) species exist within the Pacific Northwest: the Pacific Lamprey and the River Lamprey. As adults, they migrate from the sea to freshwater to spawn, and upon entering streams, pair up and build nests by moving small rocks with their mouths, hence the name "stone suckers." Soon after hatching, tiny larval lampreys, termed ammocoetes, burrow into muddy or silty river bottoms and remain there for some months, staying inactive while extracting nourishment from the surrounding ooze. When the tiny ammocoetes transform into miniature adults, they emerge from the mud and, in the case of saltwater species, make their way seaward to forage actively. Lampreys are fast enough to overtake primary prey such as herring and salmon. Once they locate prey, petromyzontids sink their tooth-studded sucking-disc mouths onto the victim's bodies and begin to rasp holes through skin or scales. Although few lampreys attain lengths of 92 cm (36 in), they attack many varieties of large fishes and even whales. The swift-moving lampreys relate most closely to the more sluggish hagfishes because both lack jaws, paired fins and scales, though they have different feeding behaviours.

Early European and North American cultures highly regarded petromyzontids as food and considered them delicacies. However, lamprey does not appear in contemporary seafood markets.

Pacific Lamprey

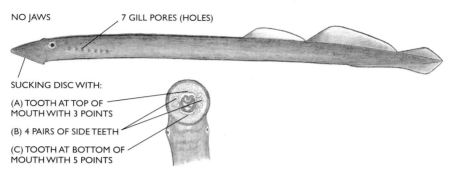

NO JAWS   7 GILL PORES (HOLES)

SUCKING DISC WITH:

(A) TOOTH AT TOP OF MOUTH WITH 3 POINTS

(B) 4 PAIRS OF SIDE TEETH

(C) TOOTH AT BOTTOM OF MOUTH WITH 5 POINTS

SPECIES: *Lampetra tridentata.* Formerly *Lampetra tridentatus*

OTHER COMMON NAMES: Pacific sea-lamprey, three-toothed lamprey, tridentate lamprey, sea lamprey

MAXIMUM RECORDED SIZE: 76 cm (30 in) and 0.5 kg (1 lb)

DISTRIBUTION: Northern Baja California, Mexico, to the Bering Sea coast of Alaska; also the Commander Islands, Kamchatka, Russia and Hokkaido, Japan

HABITAT: Because it dwells at depths below those accessible to scuba divers, it would be rare to see an active Pacific Lamprey. Shorebound naturalists never spot this species in shallow waters.

COMMENTS: Sport fishermen may occasionally find a Pacific Lamprey dangling from a hooked salmon or other gamefish. More likely though, a circular scar on salmon, Pacific Hake, Sablefish or Arrowtooth Flounder will indicate a former attack.

Working together as mated pairs from April to July, Pacific Lamprey construct gravel nests stone by stone with their suctorial mouths.

Some folks eagerly eat fried, broiled, or baked Pacific Lamprey, while others prefer it smoked.

B. Ammocoete of an undetermined Pacific Northwest lamprey species. *Jackie Hildering photograph*

River Lamprey

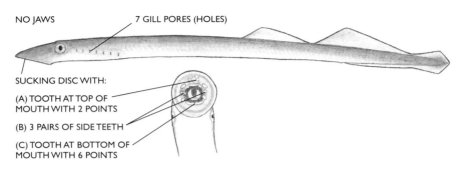

NO JAWS   7 GILL PORES (HOLES)

SUCKING DISC WITH:

(A) TOOTH AT TOP OF
MOUTH WITH 2 POINTS

(B) 3 PAIRS OF SIDE TEETH

(C) TOOTH AT BOTTOM OF
MOUTH WITH 6 POINTS

SPECIES: *Lampetra ayresii*. Formerly *Lampetra ayresi*

OTHER COMMON NAMES: western river lamprey, American river lamprey, parasitic river lamprey, western brook lamprey, western lamprey

MAXIMUM RECORDED SIZE: 31 cm (12.2 in)

DISTRIBUTION: Central California coast to southeastern Alaska

HABITAT: The Pacific Herring is the favourite prey of the River Lamprey and attacks may be fairly common near the surface from June to September in some locales. This is about the only time a diver may see this mostly open-water species. The feeding River Lamprey might attack an unsuspecting herring, young salmon, or anchovy adjacent to a wharf or jetty where the naturalist could conceivably observe the entire episode.

COMMENTS: Usually this lamprey fastens along the upper side of the host between the victim's head and tail. While larger, stronger salmon may survive these attacks, often receiving circular scars, the smaller Pacific Herring is usually completely devoured. Like its anadromous prey the salmon, the River Lamprey migrates to fresh water for intricate courtship and spawning activities.

    Throughout the world, cultures feast upon the delicate flesh of lampreys. Skin and try it—any recipe for eel will do. Smoked or fresh, the River Lamprey offers potentially fine eating.

THE **COW SHARKS** (Family Hexanchidae)

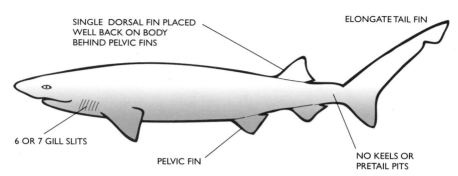

SINGLE DORSAL FIN PLACED WELL BACK ON BODY BEHIND PELVIC FINS

ELONGATE TAIL FIN

6 OR 7 GILL SLITS

PELVIC FIN

NO KEELS OR PRETAIL PITS

The Hexanchidae, popularly known as the cow sharks, contains only four species known to exist today. They range widely, with some, including the Pacific Northwest's Bluntnose Sixgill Shark, distributed almost worldwide in temperate and tropical regions. Cow sharks live only in the marine environment and when in tropical latitudes, they seek out deep, dark, cool waters. They are sluggish creatures that swim slowly along the bottom and may rest upon the sea floor.

Cow sharks possess either six or seven pairs of gill slits, instead of the usual five sets prevalent upon most other living sharks. As a result they are believed to be among the most primitive of existing species, exhibiting little change over the past 150 million years.

Reports from natural history expeditions of the 1800s document the largest cow shark at 5.6 m (18 ft) long and 771 kg (1,700 lb) in weight.

The reproductive capacity of cow sharks is also amazing: a large, prolific female may give birth to as many as 108 fully-formed pups at once, each measuring up to 40 cm (16 in).

Broadnose Sevengill Shark

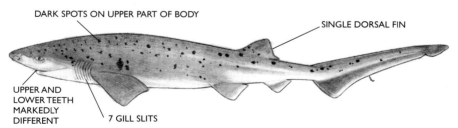

DARK SPOTS ON UPPER PART OF BODY

SINGLE DORSAL FIN

UPPER AND LOWER TEETH MARKEDLY DIFFERENT

7 GILL SLITS

SPECIES: *Notorynchus cepedianus.* Formerly *Notorynchus maculatus* (for eastern Pacific form)
OTHER COMMON NAMES: seven-gill shark, spotted cow shark
MAXIMUM RECORDED SIZE: 2.9 m (9.5 ft) and at least 107 kg (235 lb)
DISTRIBUTION: Throughout the world's temperate seas. Along the Pacific coast of North America, from the Gulf of California, northern Mexico, to northern British Columbia. Records for southeastern Alaska are unconfirmed.
HABITAT: The Broadnose Sevengill Shark is infrequently encountered by sport divers in California. It is apparently common in shallow estuarine bays farther north but a search is not advisable as visibility is likely to be poor. Reportedly aggressive, this shark feeds upon fish, marine mammals (seals) and carcasses.

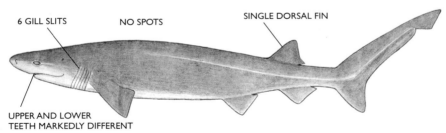

COMMENTS: Although seldom seen, the Broadnose Sevengill Shark is easily recognized by its seven pairs of gill slits and spotted body. In summer, pregnant females may give birth to as many as 83 young measuring between 35 and 45 cm (14 to 18 in).

B. Cindy Hanson photograph

Prior to the Second World War and the development of synthetic products, the Broadnose Sevengill Shark was harvested for the oil from its liver. Its flesh was rendered to meal.

Bluntnose Sixgill Shark

6 GILL SLITS   NO SPOTS   SINGLE DORSAL FIN

UPPER AND LOWER
TEETH MARKEDLY DIFFERENT

SPECIES: *Hexanchus griseus*

OTHER COMMON NAMES: six-gill shark, six-gilled shark, six-gill cowshark, shovelnose shark, mud shark

MAXIMUM RECORDED SIZE: 4.8 m (15.8 ft) and 590 kg (1,300 lb); reports of much larger specimens have proved false

DISTRIBUTION: Throughout the world's temperate seas (also cold, deep tropical waters); along the Pacific coast of North America from northern Baja California, Mexico, to south of the Aleutian Island chain, Alaska

HABITAT: Especially in British Columbia and Washington State, the bulky Bluntnose Sixgill Shark may drift past delighted divers—most often in summer. Sightings have increased over the years, perhaps due to the creature's population growing after years of reduced commercial fishing pressure, more recreational diving activity or a combination of these factors. Look and enjoy, but don't touch. Its powerful, tooth-filled jaws are potentially very dangerous.

COMMENTS: Development of synthetic oil before the Second World War eliminated the targeted set-line fishery for the Bluntnose Sixgill Shark. This fish is still incidentally caught by longliners and trawlers.
   Bluntnose Sixgill Shark flesh is soft but tasty and occasionally appears in restaurants.

THE **CATSHARKS** (Family Scyliorhinidae)

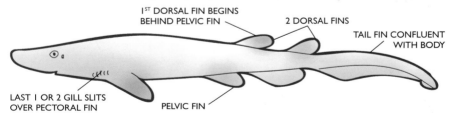

1ST DORSAL FIN BEGINS BEHIND PELVIC FIN

2 DORSAL FINS

TAIL FIN CONFLUENT WITH BODY

LAST 1 OR 2 GILL SLITS OVER PECTORAL FIN

PELVIC FIN

The Scyliorhinidae, popularly known as the catshark family, contains nearly 60 known living species. The catsharks live throughout the world's temperate and tropical seas, flourishing particularly in the Indo-Pacific region. Few grow to more than a modest size: 122 cm (48 in). Most catsharks inhabit shallow inshore waters, swimming sluggishly near the bottom and taking frequent rest intervals. Only a few species populate deep-water haunts: one is the Brown Catshark. Among the vast array of present-day sharks and rays, the slow-moving and bottom-dwelling nurse sharks most closely relate to the scyliorhinids.

Brown Catshark

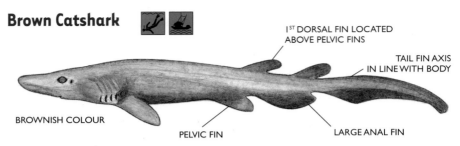

1ST DORSAL FIN LOCATED ABOVE PELVIC FINS

TAIL FIN AXIS IN LINE WITH BODY

BROWNISH COLOUR

PELVIC FIN

LARGE ANAL FIN

SPECIES: *Apristurus brunneus*
OTHER COMMON NAMES: brown cat shark, catshark. Incorrect: brown shark
MAXIMUM RECORDED SIZE: 69 cm (27 in)
DISTRIBUTION: Panama to southeastern Alaska
HABITAT: The Brown Catshark's minimum depth record is 33 m (109 ft), so the casual diver should not expect to see many specimens. A determined technical diver, though, may find it an intriguing subject to look for. For scuba divers, this shark's 5 cm (2 in) long egg case, with string-like tendrils at each corner, is a noteworthy find.
COMMENTS: Several months after mating, a female Brown Catshark deposits several horny egg cases containing developing young on the sea floor. These rectangular packets are species-specific in shape and most often have curly tendrils at their corners that act as anchors. After weeks of developing into miniature sharks, the young squirm free of their egg cases and immediately begin to search for food.

Commercial trawlers are known to take many Brown Catsharks when dragging nets over sandy, muddy bottoms at depths to 1,190 m (3,900 ft) and occasionally, deep mid-water sweeps capture specimens well off the bottom. This soft, flabby species is of no direct commercial value.

C. Egg case.

THE **MACKEREL SHARKS** (Family Lamnidae)

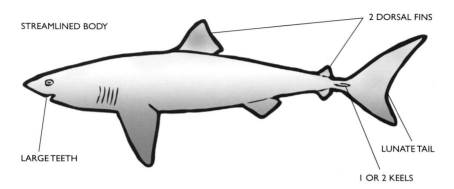

STREAMLINED BODY

2 DORSAL FINS

LARGE TEETH

LUNATE TAIL

I OR 2 KEELS

Perhaps representing the classic vision of sharks, the mackerel shark family, or Lamnidae, contains five sleek, active species. Warm-blooded, they prey variously upon swift-swimming fish and mammals. As predators, the mackerel sharks' efficiency is much enhanced by being warm blooded via specialized circulatory systems. These formidable fish are traditionally classified to varying degrees as dangerous to man.

Of the three species recorded in the Pacific Northwest and appearing below, only the Salmon Shark is a year-round resident.

Salmon Shark

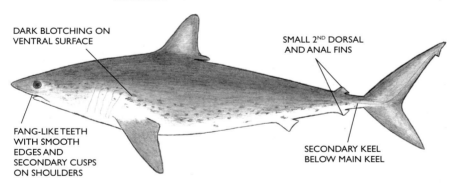

DARK BLOTCHING ON
VENTRAL SURFACE

SMALL 2ND DORSAL
AND ANAL FINS

FANG-LIKE TEETH
WITH SMOOTH
EDGES AND
SECONDARY CUSPS
ON SHOULDERS

SECONDARY KEEL
BELOW MAIN KEEL

SPECIES: *Lamna ditropis*
OTHER COMMON NAMES: mackerel shark
MAXIMUM RECORDED SIZE: 3 m (10 ft)
DISTRIBUTION: Southern Baja California, Mexico, to both Bering Sea coasts and south to Korea and Japan
HABITAT: The Salmon Shark is a fast-swimming pelagic species found both on the high seas and in coastal waters. It feeds upon smaller fishes that share its habitat. A diver spotting one is very unlikely. Organized cage diving represents the only real opportunity for serious underwater viewing of the Salmon Shark.
COMMENTS: Traditionally an incidental sport catch throughout its range, the Salmon Shark is the object of a targeted recreational fishery in Prince William Sound, Alaska, during the annual salmon migration. The Salmon Shark has not been a commercially important species.

Salmon Sharks are sometimes stranded on beaches. Kim Musgrove photograph

(Great) White Shark

Carcharodon carcharias
Often in El Niño years, Great White Sharks move north along the Pacific Northwest coast. A few of the largest specimens ever recorded have been washed up on the exposed shores of British Columbia's Queen Charlotte Islands. This heavy-set shark has prominent, triangular serrated teeth and a dorsal fin originating primarily behind the pectoral fins. It grows to a length of at least 6 m (19.5 ft). This species' official name is White Shark.

Ib Hansen photograph

Shortfin Mako

Isurus oxyrinchus
Very occasionally the Shortfin Mako ventures into Pacific Northwest waters during the summer in warm-water years. Seldom, though, does this species venture near shore and provide casual viewing opportunities. A slender conical snout and prominent long, curved pointed teeth are distinctive. This shark attains a length of at least 3.9 m (12.9 ft).

Marty Snyderman photograph

THE **SLEEPER SHARKS**
(Family Somniosidae. Formerly Dalatiidae)

Pacific Sleeper Shark

Somniosus pacificus
The Pacific Sleeper Shark possesses two small, spineless dorsal fins and has no anal fin. It grows to a length of 6 m (20 ft). This remarkable photograph was taken via a robotic submersible as part of the activities of the Monterey Bay Aquarium Research Institute.

MBARI photograph

THE **REQUIEM SHARKS** (Family Carcharhinidae)

Blue Shark

Prionace glauca
The Blue Shark routinely moves north into the Pacific Northwest during spring and summer with warm-water events. During these periods, it can be a nuisance bycatch for various commercial enterprises and an occasional sighting for recreational divers. Notice its bright blue colour, long pointed snout and long pectoral fins. It grows to a length of at least 3.8 m (12.5 ft).

Marc Chamberlain photograph

THE **BASKING SHARKS** (Family Cetorhinidae)

The Cetorhinidae contains only one living species, the Basking Shark featured below. This family, therefore, is termed monotypic. This shark uses its large gill rakers (extensions of the stiff gill support structure) to strain its planktonic prey. These filtering structures are shed in the winter when plankton populations are reduced. Off the coast of Britain, where populations are significant and stable, the Basking Shark is a valuable resource and is the focus of educational shark-watching tours. Here in the Pacific Northwest, having exterminated our stocks, such a marvelous opportunity has vanished. Imagine a Basking Shark-watching industry similar to the popular whale and other marine mammal-watching activities we have today.

Basking Shark

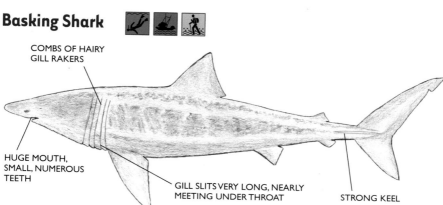

COMBS OF HAIRY
GILL RAKERS

HUGE MOUTH,
SMALL, NUMEROUS
TEETH

GILL SLITS VERY LONG, NEARLY
MEETING UNDER THROAT

STRONG KEEL

SPECIES: *Cetorhinus maximus*
OTHER COMMON NAMES: bone shark (Atlantic)
MAXIMUM RECORDED SIZE: 9.8 m (32.2 ft)
DISTRIBUTION: Worldwide in cool temperate seas. In the North Pacific, from the Gulf of California, northern Mexico to the Gulf of Alaska and perhaps the Aleutian Island chain. Also off Siberia, Japan and Korea
HABITAT: The slow, surface-dwelling Basking Shark—the second-largest marine fish in the world—is a very rare sighting along the Pacific Northwest coast.
COMMENTS: From the Second World War to the late 1960s, commercial fishing interests in British Columbia deemed this large docile creature a scourge. Thousands died, tangled in nets or slaughtered with harpoons. Canada's Fisheries Department even armed one of its patrol boats with a large steel blade and used it to cruelly slice these sharks in two. By the 1970s, the Basking Shark population had crashed and only a few tiny remnants remained. One of the last of these groups mysteriously disappeared from Clayoquot Sound, Vancouver Island, in the early 1990s. For a detailed account of this sad story, we highly recommend *Basking Sharks: The Slaughter of BC's Gentle Giants,* by Scott Wallace and Brian Gisborne, New Star Books 2006.

Chris Gotschalk photograph

THE **DOGFISH SHARKS** (Family Squalidae)

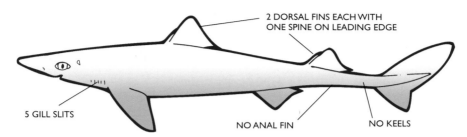

2 DORSAL FINS EACH WITH
ONE SPINE ON LEADING EDGE

5 GILL SLITS

NO ANAL FIN

NO KEELS

Each of the 47 living species of dogfish sharks (Squalidae) possesses a spine at the front of each dorsal fin but does not possess an anal fin. Dogfish sharks attain only modest maximum lengths. The Pacific Spiny Dogfish, featured below, is one of the largest.

The various dogfish sharks live throughout the temperate latitudes of the world in a great variety of habitats, from inshore shallows to abyssal offshore haunts. The majority of squalid sharks, including those with luminescent organs, swim at great depths. The tiny light sources that dot the bodies of some deepwater dogfish sharks undoubtedly aid social interaction at almost lightless depths.

Pacific Spiny Dogfish

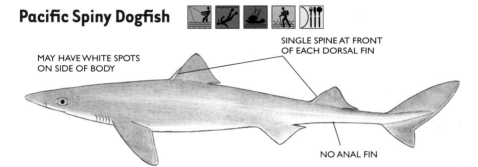

SINGLE SPINE AT FRONT
OF EACH DORSAL FIN

MAY HAVE WHITE SPOTS
ON SIDE OF BODY

NO ANAL FIN

SPECIES: *Squalus suckleyi* (formerly Spiny Dogfish, *Squalus acanthias*)
OTHER COMMON NAMES: Pacific dogfish, piked dogfish, Pacific grayfish, grayfish, spurdog, mud shark. Incorrect: sand shark, salmon shark
MAXIMUM RECORDED SIZE: 160 cm (63 in) and 9.1 kg (20 lb)
DISTRIBUTION: Throughout much of the North Atlantic Ocean and Mediterranean Sea, as well as the Pacific from the Gulf of California, northern Mexico, to the Bering Sea coast of Alaska and eastern Chukchi Sea

HABITAT: Sporadically the Pacific Spiny Dogfish becomes a schooling fish and an active companion for the diver. Such encounters may be somewhat unnerving because these small but fierce-looking animals may quickly dart toward the diver. The active Pacific Spiny Dogfish frequently swims at the surface, finning or thrashing in pursuit of plankton, herring or other small fish and may be seen from shore, wharf or boat.

COMMENTS: The Pacific Spiny Dogfish is commonly caught by fishermen pursuing more popular quarry such as salmon and rockfish. If caught, this writhing catch should be handled carefully. Avoid its snapping jaws and its sharp dorsal fin spines.

In addition to its edible flesh, at one time the Pacific Spiny Dogfish provided sandpaper from its skin and oil and vitamins from its large liver. Throughout history, however, commercial fishermen have alternately reviled and actively harvested this shark.

After correct pre-cooking preparation to rid its flesh of ammonia contamination, it's surprisingly delicious. In England, it is a prime choice for traditional fish and chips.

THE **HOUND SHARKS** (Family Triakidae)

Tope (Soupfin Shark)

Galeorhinus galeus

Historically somewhat common in the Pacific Northwest, the Tope was a targeted commercial species. Recently, its distribution appears more sporadic, with captures being incidental or recreational. A large terminal lobe on the upper tail fin and a small second dorsal fin distinguish this shark. The Tope grows to a length of almost 2 m (6.5 ft).

Mick McMurray photograph/SeaPics

Leopard Shark

Triakis semifasciata

The distinctively marked Leopard Shark is a southern species and only recorded as far north as northern Washington. It lives in shallow coastal waters and may form wandering schools. The Leopard Shark reaches a length of 2.1 m (7 ft). Dark spotting and saddle markings distinguish this species.

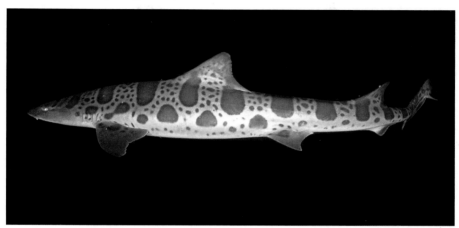

Cindy Hansen photograph

THE **THRESHER SHARKS** (Family Alopiidae)

Common Thresher Shark

Alopias vulpinus

A seasonal summer migrant, the Common Thresher Shark is infrequently a bycatch for both commercial and recreational fisheries in the Pacific Northwest. This shark's very long upper tail lobe makes it easy to identify. The Common Thresher Shark reaches a length of at least 5.2 m (17.2 ft).

Ann Greening photograph/Monterey Bay Aquarium

THE **ANGEL SHARKS** (Family Squatinidae)

Pacific Angel Shark

Squatina californica

Rare north of California, the flattened Pacific Angel Shark was documented in Puget Sound, Washington, in 1933. Via an unverified report, scientists mentioned a small specimen from southeastern Alaska in 1907. In 1991, one was very likely spotted in Howe Sound, British Columbia. This shark grows to a length of 1.5 m (5 ft).

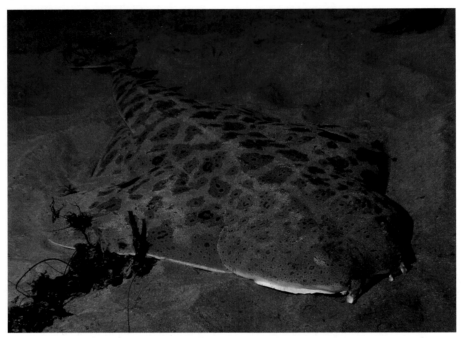

Chris Grossman photograph

THE **SKATES** (Family Rajidae)

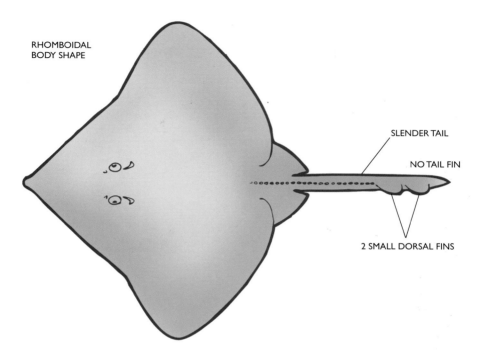

RHOMBOIDAL
BODY SHAPE

SLENDER TAIL

NO TAIL FIN

2 SMALL DORSAL FINS

The large family of skates, scientifically termed Rajidae, contains 288 valid living species and at least 50 more yet to be officially described. The skates are believed to have evolved more than 63 million years ago. These broad, thin creatures include the world's largest, the Big Skate of the Pacific Northwest. Most skates dwell in coastal regions of the continental shelves in cool northern or temperate seas. Except for a few species that occasionally wander into brackish waters, the skates are strictly marine.

When not cruising just off the bottom with graceful sweeping strokes of their immense pectoral fins, or "wings," rajids rest upon the substrate. They may frequently bury in gravel, sand or silt to conceal themselves from both predator and prey. Seasonal spawning periods bring mature male and female rajids together for breeding behaviour that culminates in copulation. Soon after the female is fertilized, special glands secrete a chitinous, horny envelope, called an egg case, around one or more of her large, yolky fertile eggs. Several months pass before the mother skate deposits the distinctive egg cases onto the sea floor. For several weeks each baby skate lives off an ever-dwindling yolk supply. Ultimately, the young skates, miniature replicas of the adult, wriggle free of their weakened egg cases and begin to explore their new environment.

Although plentiful and excellent to eat, skates are seldom pursued by commercial fishermen. Some seafood restaurateurs use cookie cutters to slice skate wings into round pieces and pass them off as scallops.

Two northern species, the Alaska Skate, *Bathyraja parmifera*, and the Aleutian Skate, *Bathyraja aleutica*, dwell in southeastern Alaska.

Longnose Skate

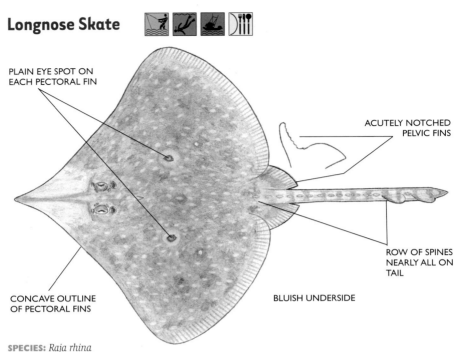

PLAIN EYE SPOT ON
EACH PECTORAL FIN

ACUTELY NOTCHED
PELVIC FINS

ROW OF SPINES
NEARLY ALL ON
TAIL

CONCAVE OUTLINE
OF PECTORAL FINS

BLUISH UNDERSIDE

SPECIES: *Raja rhina*

OTHER COMMON NAMES: long-nose skate

MAXIMUM RECORDED SIZE: 137 cm (54 in)

DISTRIBUTION: Northern Baja California, Mexico, to southeastern Bering Sea, Alaska

HABITAT: Scuba divers cruising along sandy, silty bottoms at depths greater than 20 m (66 ft) should look closely for the Longnose Skate. It habitually rests partially or completely buried and its sandy-coloured body is usually difficult to see. Watch also for the Longnose Skate's 8–12 cm (3–5 in) long egg cases upon the sea floor.

COMMENTS: The Longnose Skate is often incidentally taken by trawlers and set-line harvesters, although relatively few find their way to market. For some truly fine eating, remove and skin the large pectoral fins or "wings" from the Longnose Skate then pan-fry them in butter.

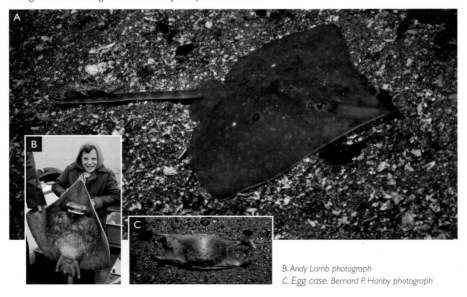

B. Andy Lamb photograph

C. Egg case. Bernard P. Hanby photograph

Big Skate

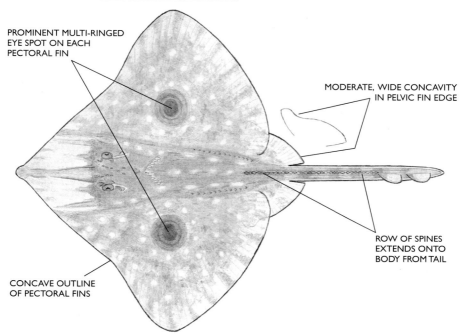

PROMINENT MULTI-RINGED EYE SPOT ON EACH PECTORAL FIN

MODERATE, WIDE CONCAVITY IN PELVIC FIN EDGE

ROW OF SPINES EXTENDS ONTO BODY FROM TAIL

CONCAVE OUTLINE OF PECTORAL FINS

SPECIES: *Raja binoculata*

OTHER COMMON NAMES: Pacific great skate, Pacific barndoor skate. Incorrect: barndoor skate, barn-door skate

MAXIMUM RECORDED SIZE: 2.4 m (8 ft) and 91 kg (200 lb)

DISTRIBUTION: Northern Baja California, Mexico, to the eastern Bering Sea and the Aleutian Island chain, Alaska

A

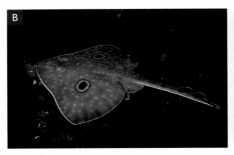
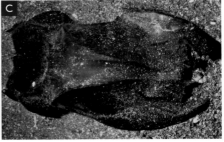

B. *Juvenile. Bernard P. Hanby photograph*   *C. Egg case.*

HABITAT: Although the broad Big Skate inhabits shallow, easily-explored depths, it is well camouflaged against grey sandy or muddy bottoms. Scuba divers look closely! When observed while slowly gliding by, it is a special dive memory. Rather than spotting the Big Skate itself, the beachcomber or dockside watcher will more likely find its large, empty "mermaid's purses" or egg cases washed ashore.

COMMENTS: Because it inhabits depths to within a few metres of the surface, the Big Skate is the skate most often caught by sport fishermen as a surprising and novel catch. The Big Skate may seize baits such as clams, shrimp, marine worms and fish offered over sandy, nearly level bottoms. Irregular flashing of shiny jigs or lures may also attract this skate.

    An incidental catch during many commercial harvesting activities, the Big Skate sporadically finds its way to the marketplace. Newborns are particularly susceptible as trawl bycatch. As "skate wings," it appears as a tasty, relatively inexpensive buy. For a real taste treat, boil the skinned pectoral fins or "wings" of the Big Skate in water with a bit of vinegar or in a court-bouillon; its boneless flesh has a flavour not unlike scallop.

Sandpaper Skate

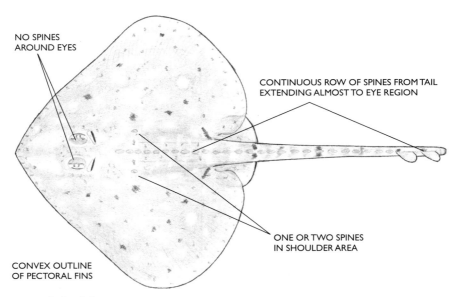

NO SPINES
AROUND EYES

CONTINUOUS ROW OF SPINES FROM TAIL
EXTENDING ALMOST TO EYE REGION

ONE OR TWO SPINES
IN SHOULDER AREA

CONVEX OUTLINE
OF PECTORAL FINS

SPECIES: *Bathyraja interrupta*
OTHER COMMON NAMES: black skate
MAXIMUM RECORDED SIZE: 86 cm (34 in)
DISTRIBUTION: Southern California to the eastern Bering Sea and the Aleutian Island chain, Alaska
HABITAT: The Sandpaper Skate lives at depths of 60 to 1,500 m (200 to 5,000 ft) and upon muddy or sandy bottoms. This is deeper than most sport divers would descend, though intrigued technical divers might.

COMMENTS: Commercial trawlers and shrimpers frequently capture the Sandpaper Skate incidentally. Seldom do they market this small skate; instead they usually discard it at sea. Small quantities of Sandpaper Skate occasionally have been rendered to produce mink feed or fertilizer.

A large Sandpaper Skate is definitely worth eating. Remove and retain the broad, wing-like pectoral fins and discard the remaining carcass. The flesh is flavourful and has a crab-like texture. Try skate *au gratin*, or make fritters from the carefully hoarded livers.

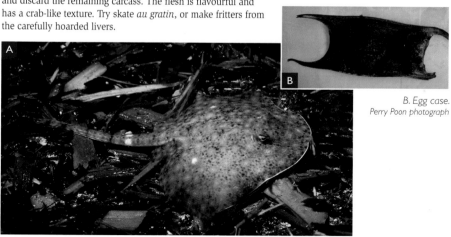

B. Egg case.
Perry Poon photograph

THE **ELECTRIC RAYS** (Family Torpedinidae)

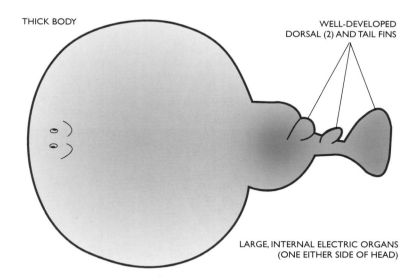

THICK BODY

WELL-DEVELOPED
DORSAL (2) AND TAIL FINS

LARGE, INTERNAL ELECTRIC ORGANS
(ONE EITHER SIDE OF HEAD)

Approximately 88 living species make up the Torpedinidae, or electric ray family. Most are warm-water denizens and the group is represented throughout the world's seas.

As the name suggests, these flattened fish are capable of generating a significant electric current from internal, kidney-shaped organs located at the base of each pectoral fin. These specialized organs assist in prey capture and help deter predation. While being photographed, the Pacific Electric Ray featured next continually discharged its organs and repeatedly set off co-author Phil Edgell's underwater strobe.

Pacific Electric Ray

ROUND, DEPRESSED FORM

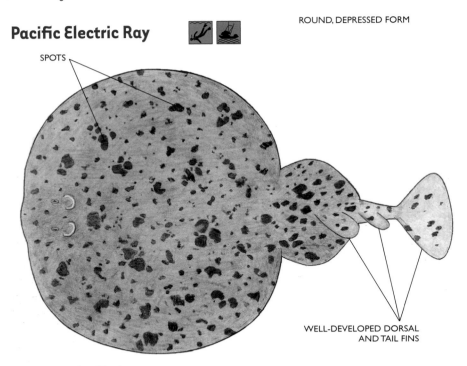

SPOTS

WELL-DEVELOPED DORSAL
AND TAIL FINS

SPECIES: *Torpedo californica*
OTHER COMMON NAMES: Pacific torpedo ray, electric ray
MAXIMUM RECORDED SIZE: 1.4 m (4.6 ft) and 23 kg (50 lb)
DISTRIBUTION: Central Baja California, Mexico to northern British Columbia
HABITAT: Reasonably often encountered by recreational divers in California, the Pacific Electric Ray essentially remains unobserved by Pacific Northwest aficionados. If you encounter one, enjoy such a rare event. However, be aware that this amazing fish can deliver a strong electrical shock if touched or provoked.
COMMENTS: Bottom trawlers operating in British Columbia sporadically capture the unwanted Pacific Electric Ray. For example, a shrimp trawler in Barkley Sound caught the photographed specimen.

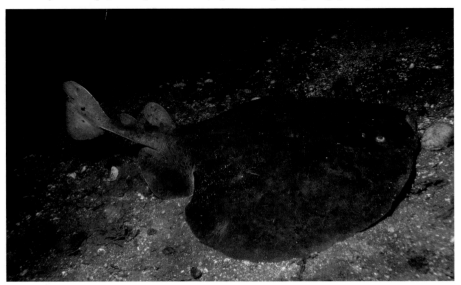

THE **EAGLE RAYS** (Family Myliobatidae)

Bat Ray

Myliobatis californica

Rarely found as far north as Oregon, the strange-looking Bat Ray lives on sandy or muddy substrates, but often near rocky outcrops. Divers may encounter it resting on the sea floor or swimming actively. A big bulbous head and large, almost triangular pectoral fins are noteworthy characteristics for this fish. It may be solitary or form schools. The Bat Ray grows to a length of 1.8 m (6 ft).

Chris Grossman photograph

THE **MANTAS (DEVIL RAYS)** (Family Mobulidae)

Ib Hansen photograph

Giant Manta

Manta birostris

The spectacular Giant Manta has a circum-tropical distribution and its mention here represents a fascinating observation. In 1985, Alaska Department of Fish and Game biologists reported seeing several in the waters off the Columbia Glacier, central Alaska. Apparently no photographic verification or captured specimens resulted. This distinctive fish, with scoop-like cephalic lobes at the front of its large head, attains a width of 7.2 m (22 ft).

THE **STINGRAYS** (Family Dasyatidae)

Pelagic Stingray

Pteroplatytrygon violacea

Apparently very rare visitors to the Pacific Northwest, several Pelagic Stingrays were inadvertently hooked by salmon trollers off Kyuquot Sound, on the west coast of Vancouver Island, British Columbia. These encounters represent the northernmost reports for this species. The Pelagic Stingray reaches a length of 1.6 m (5.3 ft). It is distinguished by a rounded front profile and a very long, thin tail.

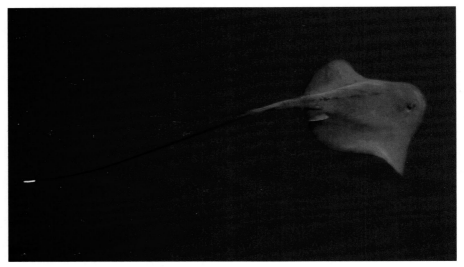

Marc Chamberlain photograph

THE **SHORTNOSE CHIMAERAS** (Family Chimaeridae)

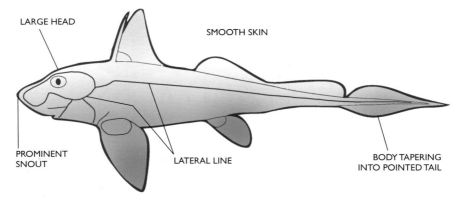

LARGE HEAD

SMOOTH SKIN

PROMINENT SNOUT

LATERAL LINE

BODY TAPERING INTO POINTED TAIL

The shortnose chimaeras make up a small family of grotesque fishes, scientifically termed Chimaeridae, of which approximately 25 present-day species have been described. All live in the marine environment and flourish mostly in the Pacific and Atlantic oceans. Only one of the known species, the Spotted Ratfish, resides in the Pacific Northwest.

Although a few chimaerids live in shallow coastal habitats, most inhabit deep and dark offshore haunts. These species seem to become more bizarre as the depth increases. Slow, graceful swimmers, all reside near the sea floor, including the largest species, the Atlantic Ratfish, *Chimaera monstrosa*, a North Atlantic resident that may attain 152 cm (60 in) in length.

The name chimaera suggests the monsters of Greek mythology; indeed, these fishes are as ludicrously absurd as anything real or imaginary. They have long, rat-like tails and bulbous heads with round or pointed snouts, but almost rabbit-like mouths—a form that looks as though its tail end does not match its front end. Swimming as if they are slow-flying birds, their huge eyes often shine emerald green from scale-less "metallic" bodies that shimmer silver and bronze. Paleontologists trace the chimaerid ancestors back 345 million years.

Before the discovery of new artificially manufactured products, chimaerid livers were processed to make fine oils for lubricating guns.

Spotted Ratfish

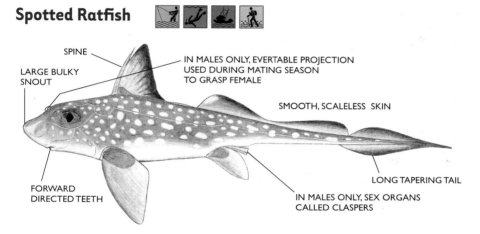

SPINE

LARGE BULKY SNOUT

IN MALES ONLY, EVERTABLE PROJECTION USED DURING MATING SEASON TO GRASP FEMALE

SMOOTH, SCALELESS SKIN

LONG TAPERING TAIL

FORWARD DIRECTED TEETH

IN MALES ONLY, SEX ORGANS CALLED CLASPERS

SPECIES: *Hydrolagus colliei*
OTHER COMMON NAMES: ratfish, rat-fish, chimaera, rabbitfish, spookfish, elephant-fish, goatfish, water hare
MAXIMUM RECORDED SIZE: 97 cm (38 in)

A

DISTRIBUTION: Central Baja California, Mexico, to the Gulf of Alaska; also an isolated population at Isla Tiburon, in the upper Gulf of California, Mexico

HABITAT: When viewed underwater, particularly at night, the spectacular Spotted Ratfish immediately attracts the diver's attention. A shimmering silver and bronze form glides slowly over the bottom, propelled by bird-like sweeps of its pectoral fins. Both young and adults may swarm over sandy bottoms in shallow water. Empty egg cases—spindle-shaped and often black—commonly rest upon the sea floor.

At night, Spotted Ratfish sometimes swim toward wharf or dock-mounted lights and may be seen by the shorebound naturalist.

COMMENTS: Anglers, who sometimes catch the Spotted Ratfish incidentally, have an entirely different perspective than a scuba diver. This fish is often a bycatch for various commercial fishing activities. Wriggling at the end of fishing line, it is usually disdainfully called "ugly" or "bizarre." Be careful to avoid the large dorsal spine as it can inflict a nasty wound!

B. Mating pair.
Takuji Oyama photograph
C. Female laying egg cases.
D. Juvenile.

THE **STURGEONS** (Family Acipenseridae)

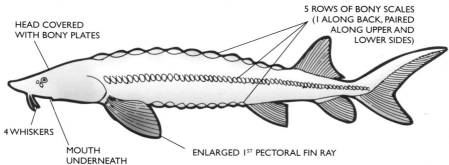

HEAD COVERED WITH BONY PLATES

5 ROWS OF BONY SCALES (I ALONG BACK, PAIRED ALONG UPPER AND LOWER SIDES)

4 WHISKERS

MOUTH UNDERNEATH

ENLARGED IST PECTORAL FIN RAY

A simple glance at the heavily armoured, shark-like form of a sturgeon clearly shows the primitive nature of the Acipenseridae. Only 25 known species still exist and all are restricted to the cool waters of the northern hemisphere.

For at least some portion of their life cycles, all acipenserids live in fresh water, and most species spend their entire lives in large silty-bottomed rivers or lakes. A few types, though, are anadromous—they may migrate to sea as adult fish and return to fresh water to spawn.

Because they live primarily in very murky water, their sight assists little in locating bottom-dwelling prey. The tiny-eyed acipenserids compensate for poor visibility with external taste buds located on the long whisker-like barbels that precede their mouths. By dragging these sensitive barbels along the bottom, the sturgeon locates small animals such as shrimp, worms and clams before sucking them up into their protrusible, tube-like mouths.

Early literature notes some truly gargantuan sturgeons. Indeed, the world's largest freshwater fish is an acipenserid—the Beluga of northern Asia that may attain a length of 8.5 m (28 ft) and a weight of 1,360 kg (3,000 lb)!

White Sturgeon

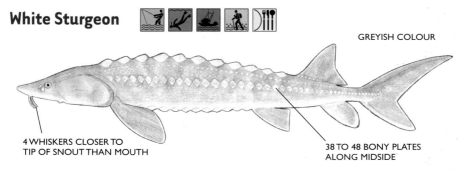

GREYISH COLOUR

4 WHISKERS CLOSER TO TIP OF SNOUT THAN MOUTH

38 TO 48 BONY PLATES ALONG MIDSIDE

SPECIES: *Acipenser transmontanus*
OTHER COMMON NAMES: Pacific sturgeon, Oregon sturgeon, Columbia sturgeon, Sacramento sturgeon
MAXIMUM RECORDED SIZE: 6.1 m (20 ft) and 816 kg (1,800 lb)
DISTRIBUTION: Northern Baja California, Mexico, to the Gulf of Alaska
HABITAT: Few divers venture into turbid, current-swept rivers or estuaries where the White Sturgeon is most plentiful but where viewing conditions are extremely poor. Only when a disturbed White Sturgeon leaps clear of the very silty waters of a river or estuary is the shorebound naturalist likely to observe it.

COMMENTS: Severe population declines have occurred throughout the Pacific Northwest in recent years. This disturbing trend has stimulated major conservation efforts, including mandatory catch and release in almost all jurisdictions. Greatly reduced bag limits and size restrictions are in force, if retention is allowed at all. Be sure to check local regulations.

Marine anglers who troll or still-fish near estuaries occasionally capture the strong White Sturgeon, which puts up a tough, long battle, sometimes with aerial acrobatics. Special heavy tackle is needed to catch large specimens. Bait fishing along the banks of large rivers, such as the Fraser and Columbia, accounts for the bulk of the White Sturgeon sport fishery. Historical commercial fishing involvement with the White Sturgeon is now passé and its future availability as a farmed species holds promise for the seafood gourmet.

Fine dining awaits anyone who samples the White Sturgeon. Its flaky white flesh contains virtually no bones and cuts beautifully into portion-sized steaks. Marinate them in oil, lemon juice, paprika and spices. Try curried sturgeon. Or why not stuff it with truffles, marinate it in brandy, and poach in champagne?

Green Sturgeon

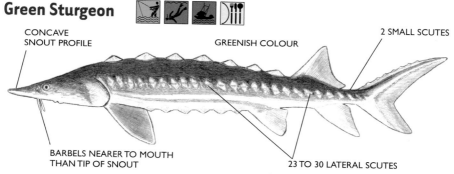

CONCAVE SNOUT PROFILE

GREENISH COLOUR

2 SMALL SCUTES

BARBELS NEARER TO MOUTH THAN TIP OF SNOUT

23 TO 30 LATERAL SCUTES

SPECIES: *Acipenser medirostris*
MAXIMUM RECORDED SIZE: 2.1 m (7 ft) and at least 159 kg (350 lb)
DISTRIBUTION: Northern Baja California, Mexico, to southeastern Alaska
HABITAT: In spite of reputedly being the more marine of the two Pacific Northwest species, the Green Sturgeon very rarely, if ever, swims within view of recreational divers. It moves slowly along sandy or silty bottoms, with its taste-sensitive barbels touching the surface in search of food.
COMMENTS: Bait fishing in the lower stretches and estuaries of the major Pacific Northwest river systems sometimes produces Green Sturgeon catches. Large specimens can provide considerable sport and heavy tackle is recommended. Recently, however, coastwide populations of Green Sturgeon have dwindled to extremely low levels and in most jurisdictions, this species is subject to either fishing moratoria or mandatory catch and release.

Daniel W. Gotshall photograph

THE **HERRINGS** (Family Clupeidae)

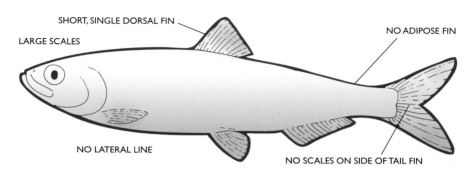

SHORT, SINGLE DORSAL FIN

LARGE SCALES

NO ADIPOSE FIN

NO LATERAL LINE

NO SCALES ON SIDE OF TAIL FIN

The large herring family, scientifically termed Clupeidae, includes the schooling shads, alewives, menhaden, sardines and herrings. Except for the frigid polar regions, the seas of the world contain more than 180 known species. Most are harboured in tropical regions such as the vast expanse of the Indo-Pacific.

Although certain varieties tolerate brackish water at some point during their life cycles, there are very few species of strictly freshwater herrings. These silvery fishes, most of which attain lengths less than 46 cm (18 in), school in open shallow regions or in mid-water over deeper haunts. It is not uncommon for herring to gather in immense shoals that cover many square kilometers of ocean.

Economies of many nations, both directly and indirectly, depend very significantly on the various existing herring fisheries of the world.

Pacific Herring

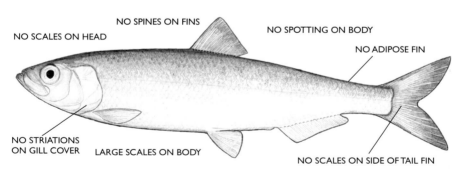

NO SPINES ON FINS

NO SCALES ON HEAD

NO SPOTTING ON BODY

NO ADIPOSE FIN

NO STRIATIONS ON GILL COVER

LARGE SCALES ON BODY

NO SCALES ON SIDE OF TAIL FIN

SPECIES: *Clupea pallasii.* Formerly designated a subspecies *Clupea harengus pallasi*
OTHER COMMON NAMES: herring
MAXIMUM RECORDED SIZE: 46 cm (18 in)
DISTRIBUTION: Northern Baja California, Mexico, to the Bering Sea and northeast to Bathurst in the Beaufort Sea; along the Asian coast from the Lena River in the Arctic Ocean, through the Bering Sea to Korea and Ibaraki, central Japan
HABITAT: In the Pacific Northwest, the small silvery fish "flipping" or leaping clear of the water and turning on its side under the surface, creating a silvery flash, is nearly always the Pacific Herring. Large schools of Pacific Herring, particularly juveniles, crowd into shallow bays or along shores that are popular spots for divers. Look up into the greenish open water to see a school. The silvery mass will move as if it were one animal until your startling approach temporarily scatters the group.

COMMENTS: The foremost baitfish in the Pacific Northwest, the Pacific Herring is particularly valuable to salmon anglers, who fillet it into strips for trolling and casting, use it whole for trolling, or use it alive for a type of still-fishing called mooching. Resourceful sport fishermen often capture their own Pacific Herring by raking or jigging their various bare-hooked or sharp-pronged instruments.

Just after the Second World War, an immense seine fishery for Pacific Herring developed in the Pacific Northwest. While the bulk of this catch was formerly reduced to meal, other more profitable products such as kippers, bloaters, rollmops, and canned and dry-salted herring still remain popular. Most recently, the major Pacific Herring fishery focuses on lucrative roe products. Many commercially important fish feed very heavily upon the Pacific Herring.

A multi-purpose seafood, the Pacific Herring is delicious fresh. It is also very popular as a pickled product. Try poaching herring roe; add a bit of vinegar or lemon juice.

Pacific Sardine

SPINDLE-SHAPED BODY   ROW OF DARK SPOTS

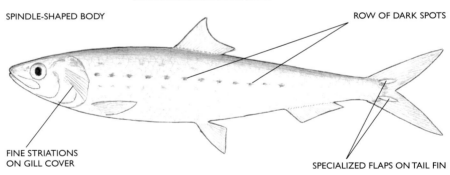

FINE STRIATIONS
ON GILL COVER

SPECIALIZED FLAPS ON TAIL FIN

SPECIES: *Sardinops sagax*
OTHER COMMON NAMES: California pilchard, pilchard
MAXIMUM RECORDED SIZE: 41 cm (16.3 in)

Chris Grossman photograph

DISTRIBUTION: Gulf of California and Baja California, northern Mexico, to southeastern Alaska. In the Asian Pacific, from Siberia to south of Japan. Also Peru, Chile and southern Africa

HABITAT: Wharves, docks and breakwaters provide fine viewing platforms to see schools of Pacific Sardine. Its distinctive black spots are often visible from the surface. California sport divers routinely see large schools of Pacific Sardines. There, this spotted species often forms mixed schools with other small silvery fish. With increasing populations of

Pacific Sardine throughout the Pacific Northwest, local divers will likely encounter this fish more in the future.

COMMENTS: The Pacific Sardine is a potential baitfish for various Pacific Northwest game fish, but it has not been readily available along this coast for many years.

A huge purse seine fishery for the Pacific Sardine existed before World War II, when a stable supply of fish existed. The catch was used for reduction to oil and fishmeal. Subsequently, its population crashed in the Pacific Northwest and the species became economically extinct. There is speculation about why this has happened but there is no definitive answer. With a recent rebound in its numbers, the Pacific Sardine is again being caught commercially and its economic significance is re-emerging.

The Pacific Sardine rates as an excellent ingredient for seafood recipes requiring a somewhat oily fish.

American Shad

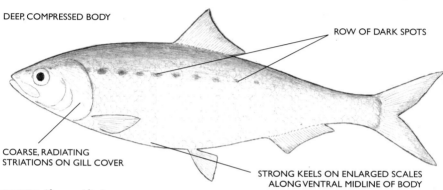

DEEP, COMPRESSED BODY

ROW OF DARK SPOTS

COARSE, RADIATING
STRIATIONS ON GILL COVER

STRONG KEELS ON ENLARGED SCALES
ALONG VENTRAL MIDLINE OF BODY

SPECIES: *Alosa sapidissima*
OTHER COMMON NAMES: shad
MAXIMUM RECORDED SIZE: 76 cm (30 in) and 6.8 kg (15 lb)
DISTRIBUTION: Central Baja California, Mexico, to the southeastern Bering Sea coast of Alaska and Siberia. Successfully introduced in the early 1870s to the Sacramento River from the east coast of North America.
HABITAT: For most of the year, the American Shad lives in the pelagic waters of the open sea, but migrates inshore in spring on its journey to spawn in fresh water. Commercial net fishermen sporadically take it at this time. Since its introduction, this fish has successfully established populations throughout the Pacific Northwest.
COMMENTS: In spring, anglers gather along the lower reaches of major Pacific Northwest river systems to cast for American Shad. This annual light tackle opportunity coincides with this species' spawning migration and is significant in the Columbia River.

The American Shad is considered gourmet on the eastern seaboard where major fisheries supply its flavourful flesh. Try consulting an east coast cookbook or the internet for some assistance with preparation.

THE **ANCHOVIES** (Family Engraulidae)

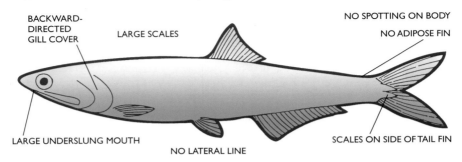

BACKWARD-DIRECTED GILL COVER

LARGE SCALES

NO SPOTTING ON BODY

NO ADIPOSE FIN

LARGE UNDERSLUNG MOUTH

NO LATERAL LINE

SCALES ON SIDE OF TAIL FIN

Approximately 140 known living species form a large family of fishes called the Engraulidae, or anchovies. These streamlined, silvery fish actively gather in surface and midwater habitats, often forming truly immense schools to feed, breed and migrate en masse.

An anchovy feeds by grazing plankton—tiny floating algae and animals—from oceanic pastures. After gulping a large amount of plankton-containing water, an anchovy, by means of long, thin, close-packed gill rakers, strains the food from the water as it passes through the gills and out the gill openings, or opercula. Paleontologists believe ancestral anchovies existed as long as 60 million years ago.

In many regions, harvesting very significant anchovy populations not only directly supplies protein for human consumption, but also provides valuable bait for other important fisheries. When processed into pellets, anchovies are a major source of feed for farmed fish. Even more noteworthy, though, engraulids are food for countless other creatures and therefore vital to the ecology of tropical seas in particular.

Indo-Pacific and southern Atlantic regions possess a wealth of anchovy species, but only one, the Northern Anchovy, a veritable giant at 24.8 cm (9.8 in), lives in the Pacific Northwest.

Northern Anchovy

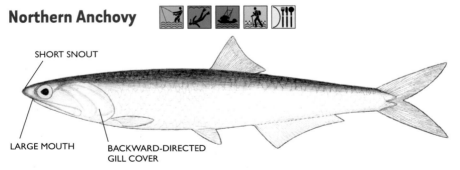

SHORT SNOUT

LARGE MOUTH

BACKWARD-DIRECTED GILL COVER

SPECIES: *Engraulis mordax.* Formerly designated a subspecies *Engraulis mordax mordax*
OTHER COMMON NAMES: plain anchovy, California anchovy, anchovy
MAXIMUM RECORDED SIZE: 24.8 cm (9.8 in)
DISTRIBUTION: Gulf of California, around the tip of Baja California, Mexico, and north to the central Gulf of Alaska
HABITAT: The Northern Anchovy occurs sporadically in large schools around wharves. Watch a specimen as it feeds and see it open its large mouth to seize planktonic morsels. During feeding, the fish's lower jaw drops and its head seems almost to fall apart—a spectacular sight when an entire school is foraging in unison.

In California, huge schools of Northern Anchovy often swarm in popular dive sites. Cameras mounted on submersibles have filmed this anchovy at depths as great as 310 m (1,023 ft).

COMMENTS: Along the Californian and Mexican coasts, party boat anglers extensively use the Northern Anchovy as bait, or even as "chum" for game fish, to encourage them to remain nearby. In the Pacific Northwest, salmon fishermen use it as bait.

A Northern Anchovy fishery in California, harvested by purse seiners, periodically fuels a "boom-bust" reduction industry. A small part of this take is selected for human consumption, either canned or fresh. Lampara seine nets capture a sizable bait-take for the recreational angling market.

Canned Northern Anchovy has a fine, delicate flavour. Fresh-cooked specimens compare favourably with delicious juvenile Pacific Herring. Fry in olive oil.

THE **SMELTS** (Family Osmeridae)

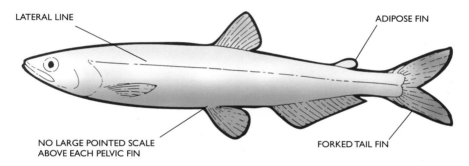

LATERAL LINE

ADIPOSE FIN

NO LARGE POINTED SCALE
ABOVE EACH PELVIC FIN

FORKED TAIL FIN

A small family of approximately 15 known living species, the Osmeridae, contains the smelts, the Capelin and the Eulachon. These fishes swim in the temperate and boreal waters of the world. Some forms reside in the Arctic and Atlantic oceans. Most osmerids attain less than 30 cm (12 in) in length, swim in surface or mid-water layers and usually form schools. While most live out their entire lives in shallow coastal marine habitats, a few more adaptable osmerids, such as the Eulachon, are anadromous. After the fertilized eggs of these anadromous species develop and hatch in rivers, the tiny, weak-swimming transparent larvae are swept downstream to sea where they begin to feed and grow rapidly.

Salmon and trout relate most closely to the osmerids: members of both families possess adipose fins and several noticeable skeletal similarities.

Modest, locally significant commercial fisheries harvest some of the larger varieties of smelt, typically coinciding with spawning seasons when these fish congregate along shallow beaches or in rivers and estuaries. As significant prey for many larger animals such as marine mammals, seabirds and fish, osmerids fill a vital niche in the marine ecosystem.

While present in the Pacific Northwest, the Whitebait Smelt, *Allosmerus elongatus*, is not often encountered by anglers, divers, or naturalists and therefore is not featured here.

Longfin Smelt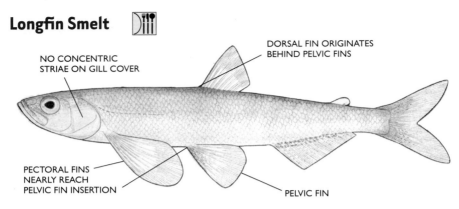

DORSAL FIN ORIGINATES
BEHIND PELVIC FINS

NO CONCENTRIC
STRIAE ON GILL COVER

PECTORAL FINS
NEARLY REACH
PELVIC FIN INSERTION

PELVIC FIN

SPECIES: *Spirinchus thaleichthys*

OTHER COMMON NAMES: long-finned smelt, Puget Sound smelt, Pacific smelt

MAXIMUM RECORDED SIZE: 20 cm (8 in)

DISTRIBUTION: Central California coast to the Gulf of Alaska. Isolated populations also flourish in freshwater localities such as Harrison Lake, British Columbia, and Lake Washington, Washington.

HABITAT: In autumn, the Longfin Smelt moves into shallow beach locales, but with turbidity problems in this habitat, scuba diving observations are unlikely. Blessed with clear water, the beachcomber or dockside observer might catch a fleeting glimpse of the Longfin Smelt—but likely not sufficient for a positive identification.

COMMENTS: An important food source for many fish, this smelt matures and spawns at two years of age, with very few surviving to breed again the following season. There are a number of ways to prepare Longfin Smelt for eating. Soak in milk, coat with flour and deep fry. Eat them right away or marinate 12 hours in vinegar with onion, thyme and bay leaf. Try it shish kebab. Smelt require salt.

NOTE: The Night Smelt, *Spirinchus starksi*—a fish very similar to the Longfin Smelt, but possessing shorter pectoral fins— has a nearly identical distribution. For some reason, though, the Night Smelt is seldom encountered.

Eulachon

CONCENTRIC STRIAE OR
LINES ON GILL COVER

DORSAL FIN ORIGINATES
BEHIND PELVIC FINS

FATTY ADIPOSE FIN

LARGE MOUTH

PELVIC FIN

SPECIES: *Thaleichthys pacificus*

OTHER COMMON NAMES: Columbia River smelt, candlefish, oilfish, fathom fish, salvation fish, small fish, yshuh, swaive, chucka and numerous spelling or phonetic variants of Eulachon: oolakon, oolachon, oolichan, oulachon, oulachan, oulacon, ulchen, uthlecan

MAXIMUM RECORDED SIZE: 25.4 cm (10 in)
DISTRIBUTION: Central California coast to Bristol Bay, Bering Sea, and the Aleutian Island chain, Alaska
HABITAT: Only when the anadromous Eulachon makes its spring spawning migration to large silty rivers does it inhabit depths suitable for scuba divers. Unfortunately, turbidity usually obscures this schooling fish from view.
COMMENTS: Spring finds the Eulachon migrating up large river systems, such as the Fraser or Columbia, to spawn. Historically, the Eulachon was intensely gillnetted during spawning migrations. Recent population crashes—and no one knows exactly why—are very disturbing and may have long-term negative effects on other species that prey on the Eulachon.

Historically, resourceful folks used to harvest dying spawned-out specimens as they drifted downstream. Because of its high oil content, First Nations peoples living along large rivers have trapped, raked or netted the highly prized Eulachon for centuries. This fish was vital to the aboriginal economy not only because it represented food and fat, but also because it was an item of barter along the "grease trail" trade route to the interior of the Pacific Northwest.

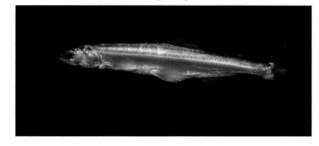

Within the recent past, the modern version of this tradition has faded due to a severe drop in the numbers of migrating Eulachon, but a high value for the grease remains.

When populations were strong, many Pacific Northwest-erners actively sought the popular Eulachon for frying in butter.

Surf Smelt

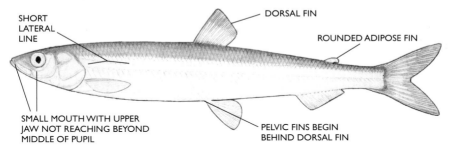

SHORT
LATERAL
LINE

DORSAL FIN

ROUNDED ADIPOSE FIN

SMALL MOUTH WITH UPPER
JAW NOT REACHING BEYOND
MIDDLE OF PUPIL

PELVIC FINS BEGIN
BEHIND DORSAL FIN

SPECIES: *Hypomesus pretiosus.* Formerly designated a subspecies *Hypomesus pretiosus pretiosus*
OTHER COMMON NAMES: silver smelt, smelt
MAXIMUM RECORDED SIZE: 30.5 cm (12 in)
DISTRIBUTION: Southern California to the Alaskan Peninsula and the Gulf of Alaska
HABITAT: Even a very observant diver seldom sees the Surf Smelt because it frequents the murky waters of shallow beaches.

In summers past, when the spawning Surf Smelt swarmed to sandy beaches, enthusiastic amateur "smelters" did the same, gathering the tasty fish with gillnets or dip-nets, rakes and buckets. Twilight hours just before a high tide was considered prime time for such "smelting." With recent and severe declines in Surf Smelt populations, this popular pastime has practically disappeared.
COMMENTS: In some localities, the recreational angler catches Surf Smelt from wharves or piers with a "smelt jig," a line from which dangles a series of shiny, bare hooks. La Conner, Washington, has sponsored an annual smelt derby on the first Saturday of February. Unfortunately, due to low Surf Smelt population levels, this event has now become more of an action-packed family festival than a smelt derby.

Formerly, commercial fishermen took the Surf Smelt with gillnets or seine nets set from sandy beaches and primarily marketed it fresh. Optimal harvesting occurred during summer in British Columbia and Washington and the catch was modest and localized.

American First Nations, such as the Quileutes on the outer coast of the Olympic Peninsula, welcome the seasonal appearance of the Surf Smelt, and much tribal lore focuses on these schooling fish that are so easy to gather.

Most aficionados fry flour-covered Surf Smelt in butter, either gutted or whole. Beach parties, especially those with open fire cookery, truly enhance Surf Smelt collecting trips. The Quileutes dried these white-fleshed fish on cedar bark.

Capelin

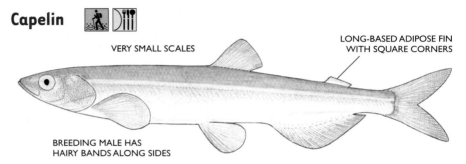

VERY SMALL SCALES

LONG-BASED ADIPOSE FIN WITH SQUARE CORNERS

BREEDING MALE HAS HAIRY BANDS ALONG SIDES

SPECIES: *Mallotus villosus*
OTHER COMMON NAMES: Pacific capelin, lode
MAXIMUM RECORDED SIZE: 25.4 cm (10 in) (in the Pacific Ocean)
DISTRIBUTION: Southern British Columbia to Arctic Alaska and along the Asian Pacific coast, from Siberia to northern Japan and Korea. In the Atlantic Ocean, from Labrador to Greenland, Iceland, Norway and Russia
HABITAT: Except for a few weeks in autumn, this small smelt lives in deep waters. However, an opportunity for Pacific Northwest divers to view the seldom-seen Capelin arrives during September and October when it swarms inshore to spawn along certain shallow, gravelly beaches. Try night diving at high tide when the moon is full.

By the light of a full moon, dedicated enthusiasts also eagerly gather along selected beaches to witness the spawning Capelin. When these swarming smelt actually wriggle out of the water to spawn among the pebbles and sand, collectors scoop them up with buckets, rakes, screening or nets. In recent years, declining Capelin populations in the Pacific Northwest have curtailed such activities.

COMMENTS: Each two- or three-year-old female Capelin may deposit up to 6,000 tiny adhesive eggs that stick to the gravel before being buried by waves. The young develop and are ready to hatch at the next equally high tidal sequence in about two weeks. Beautiful biological timing!

Capelin is a chief dietary staple for many fish.

Capelin fans fry their catches whole, often right on the beach over a bonfire.

Rainbow Smelt

Osmerus mordax

The Rainbow Smelt is a boreal species, found in many cold Arctic seas around the globe to a depth of 150 m (500 ft). An important forage species, it is anadromous, migrating up river systems to spawn. Somewhat difficult to distinguish from other smelt, this one has a relatively large mouth and more prominent teeth. It reaches a maximum recorded size of 35.6 cm (14 in).

Dr. Catherine Mecklenburg photograph

Although sightings are documented as far south as southern British Columbia, the Rainbow Smelt is an unlikely observation for most Pacific Northwest naturalists because of its far northern range.

THE **SAND LANCES** (Family Ammodytidae)

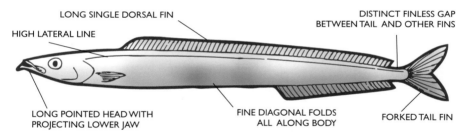

LONG SINGLE DORSAL FIN

DISTINCT FINLESS GAP BETWEEN TAIL AND OTHER FINS

HIGH LATERAL LINE

LONG POINTED HEAD WITH PROJECTING LOWER JAW

FINE DIAGONAL FOLDS ALL ALONG BODY

FORKED TAIL FIN

The sand lances comprise a small, very distinct family of fishes containing approximately 18 recognizable present-day species. Most grow to less than 30 cm (12 in). Members of this strictly marine family are distributed widely and fairly evenly throughout the world's oceans and seas, with representative species in tropical, temperate and even boreal latitudes.

Members of this group are extremely important forage species for large predatory fishes as well as many seabirds and marine mammals. By hiding in the sand, sand lances are able to temporarily avoid many of their predators. Upon emerging, sand lances feed on a variety of small planktonic animals.

Sand lances are thought to have existed at least 25 million years ago. The Ammodytidae is a very distinct group, not closely related to any other.

Pacific Sand Lance

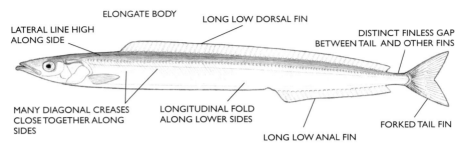

LATERAL LINE HIGH
ALONG SIDE

ELONGATE BODY

LONG LOW DORSAL FIN

DISTINCT FINLESS GAP
BETWEEN TAIL AND OTHER FINS

MANY DIAGONAL CREASES
CLOSE TOGETHER ALONG
SIDES

LONGITUDINAL FOLD
ALONG LOWER SIDES

FORKED TAIL FIN

LONG LOW ANAL FIN

SPECIES: *Ammodytes hexapterus*

OTHER COMMON NAMES: stout sand lance, Arctic sandlance, sand-lance, sandlaunce, needlefish

MAXIMUM RECORDED SIZE: 28 cm (11 in)

DISTRIBUTION: Southern California to the Aleutian Island chain, the Bering Sea, and east along the Arctic Ocean shore to Hudson Bay. Also south along the Asian shore to the Sea of Japan

HABITAT: In spring, adult Pacific Sand Lance swim free of sandy bottoms to breed and may form large densely packed schools near wharves and pilings. In summer, divers swimming near the surface often encounter schools of Pacific Sand Lance near shore. They often form mixed schools with juvenile Pacific Herring.

While strolling along a sandy shore at low tide, barefooted beachcombers may be startled to find specimens squirming out of the sediment. At night, when attracted by a beam of light, these swarming creatures may be easily scooped up with a long-handled dip-net.

COMMENTS: The pencil-thin Pacific Sand Lance is a very important prey for many large inshore fishes and is therefore indirectly but vitally important to various commercial and recreational fisheries. An amazing event for a lucky scuba diver is to see hundreds, even thousands of these fish either disappearing into, or emerging from (or both simultaneously) the sea floor.

For a delicious, crunchy snack or hors d'oeuvre, gather fresh Pacific Sand Lance, coat them with flour and fry them whole in butter.

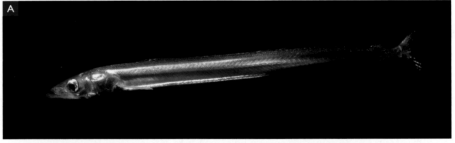

B. Jon Gross photograph

THE **SALMON AND TROUT** (Subfamily: Salmoninae)

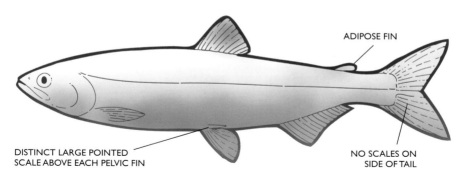

ADIPOSE FIN

DISTINCT LARGE POINTED
SCALE ABOVE EACH PELVIC FIN

NO SCALES ON
SIDE OF TAIL

The classification, or scientific ordering, of plants and animals constantly changes. Since the first edition of this guide, taxonomists have decided that salmon, trout and char deserve a subfamily category rather than a family status. Within the still-existing family Salmonidae, all the species are now sorted into three distinct subfamilies: the whitefishes, Coregoninae; the graylings, Thymallinae; and the Salmoninae, containing salmon, trout and chars. Therefore, while salmon, trout and char can still be referred to as salmonids, they are more precisely salmonins.

Active fishes that often school, the approximately 30 known living species of salmon, trout and char may occur in salt or fresh water, with some species spending at least part of their lives in each environment. These adaptable species that, as adults, migrate from the sea back to rivers and streams to spawn, are anadromous and include eight Pacific Northwest species. Although many salmon and trout live only in fresh water throughout their lives, no completely marine species exist.

Originally, the boreal and temperate waters of the northern hemisphere contained all of the world's salmon and trout, but man has extensively transplanted many of these popular fishes into nearly all waters of the globe. For example, the hardy Rainbow Trout, native to North America, flourishes today in virtually every freshwater corner of the world. Much to fishermen's delight, many salmonins attain impressive sizes, with the Pacific Northwest's Chinook Salmon topping the list at 160 cm (63 in).

Prehistoric ancestors of present-day salmon and trout lived at least 40 million years ago. The various smelts, which also possess adipose fins, are among the closest living relatives of the salmon and trout.

World renowned as gamefish and food sources, salmonins represent a most significant economic factor in many countries. Commercial and recreational interests lobby so intensely that governments annually spend millions of dollars to maintain or increase wild salmon and trout stocks. Canada's ambitious Salmonid Enhancement Program is perhaps the most sophisticated of these efforts.

Spawning salmon and trout are all seasonally present in freshwater systems throughout the Pacific Northwest. Government salmonid enhancement projects are often optimal sites for watching. (Consult official websites to find these seasonal opportunities.)

Salmon farming in the Pacific Northwest has become a major industry and produces more salmon than the wild commercial harvest. It also provides much-needed employment to the region. However, there is intense debate about how it is done and its effects on the marine environment. While salmon farming is no doubt here to stay, it must continue to evolve and become an environmentally good corporate entity.

One non-resident trout that was introduced into the Pacific Northwest has not yet established marine migrating populations. The Brown Trout, *Salmo trutta*, a golden-brown fish with dark spots surrounded by light halos, exists in some coastal British Columbia stream headwaters and is not featured here.

Pink Salmon

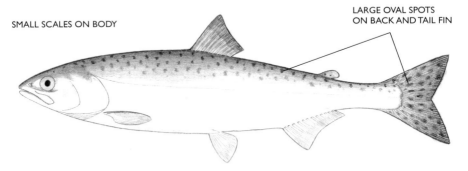

SMALL SCALES ON BODY

LARGE OVAL SPOTS
ON BACK AND TAIL FIN

SPECIES: *Oncorhynchus gorbuscha*
OTHER COMMON NAMES: humpback salmon, pink, humpie. The Russian name for this fish is *gorbuscha*.
MAXIMUM RECORDED SIZE: 76 cm (30 in) and 6.8 kg (15 lb)
DISTRIBUTION: Southern California to the Bering Sea and the Canadian Arctic to the Mackenzie River; along the Asian coast from the Lena River, Arctic Ocean, through the Bering Sea to Korea, and southern Japan. Introductions have been made throughout North America and the Kola Peninsula, northern Europe, but populations have only successfully established themselves in the Great Lakes.
HABITAT: The elusive Pink Salmon adult easily avoids most divers, and an aquanaut noticing a specimen usually only has a fleeting glimpse of it. Along shorelines in April through June, however, tiny ocean-bound fry school to feed at the surface where both divers and snorkelers easily find them.

Large schools of tiny, blue-backed Pink Salmon fry congregate along rocky shores and adjacent to wharves or jetties, but unfortunately the topside observer will find it difficult to distinguish this species from the very similar but parr-marked Chum Salmon fry.

Adult Pink Salmon, with prominent "humped backs" (particularly the males), can be observed in many freshwater rivers and streams during their fall spawning migration.

A

COMMENTS: In some northern locales, the smallish Pink Salmon is popular with spincasters using buzz bombs or sting sildas in late summer. It is also taken by trollers who drag plugs and dodger spoon rigs. While commercial gillnetters and purse seiners take most of the large Pink Salmon catch for canning, the troller fleet supplies small quantities for the fresh market. Both recreational and commercial harvest occurs as this species returns to spawn at the end of its two-year life cycle.

Although the Pink Salmon has historically rated low in comparison with other salmon, it is unquestionably a fine eating fish and when used promptly, worthy of a chef's best efforts; its light pink-coloured flesh bakes, broils, fries or boils very well, suiting virtually any fish recipe. Try a salmon soufflé.

B. Catherine Statham photograph
C. Spawning pair.
D. Fry.

Chum Salmon

NO DISTINCT
BLACK MARKINGS

GAP BETWEEN TAIL FIN AND
OTHER FINS IS SLENDER

DARK EDGES ON FINS

CUT-AWAY OF GILL COVER
SHOWING 1ST GILL ARCH
WITH 18–26 SHORT STUBBY
GILL RAKERS

SPECIES: *Oncorhynchus keta*

OTHER COMMON NAMES: dog salmon, fall salmon, keta salmon, calico salmon, chum, qualla. *Keta* is the popular name in Kamchatka, Russia.

MAXIMUM RECORDED SIZE: 109 cm (43 in) and 20.8 kg (45.8 lb)

DISTRIBUTION: Southern California to the Bering Sea through to the Mackenzie River, in the Canadian Arctic; along the Asian coasts from the Lena River, Arctic Ocean, through the Bering Sea to Korea and southern Japan. Transplants to Hudson and James Bays met with poor results.

HABITAT: After leaving their streams of birth in schools, tiny parr-marked Chum Salmon fry swarm along the seashore on their way to the open ocean. The pier-side naturalist or shorebound stroller will have difficulty in distinguishing them from the non-parred pinks. While divers seldom get close enough for even a fleeting glimpse of an adult Chum Salmon, in spring, schools of fry swim at the surface where they can be observed by both divers and snorkelers.

Adult Chum Salmon, with prominent horizontal purplish bars along their sides, can be observed in many freshwater rivers and streams during their fall spawning migration.

COMMENTS: Infrequently sought by traditional, action-seeking sport fishermen, the Chum Salmon occasionally strikes the angler's line. A buzz bomb, herring strip or double dodger rig trailing a hook wrapped with yellow yarn particularly fascinates this fish when on its autumn approach to spawning streams—after three to five years at sea. A large specimen can provide a good scrap!

This species is very important in Asia where the resourceful Japanese can or salt the flesh and pickle the roe as *sujiko*.

Of the five Pacific species, the Chum Salmon smokes best because of its high oil content. It is also excellent cooked fresh.

B. Catherine Statham photograph
C. Spawning pair.
D. Fry.

Sockeye Salmon

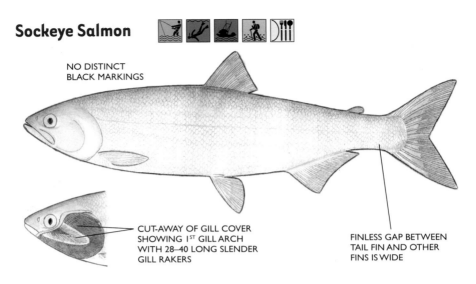

NO DISTINCT
BLACK MARKINGS

CUT-AWAY OF GILL COVER
SHOWING 1ST GILL ARCH
WITH 28–40 LONG SLENDER
GILL RAKERS

FINLESS GAP BETWEEN
TAIL FIN AND OTHER
FINS IS WIDE

SPECIES: *Oncorhynchus nerka*

OTHER COMMON NAMES: red salmon, blueback salmon, sockeye, blue back. *Nerka* is the popular name for this fish in Russia.

MAXIMUM RECORDED SIZE: 84 cm (33 in) and 7 kg (17 lb)

DISTRIBUTION: Southern California to the Bering Sea and north to Bathurst Inlet, on the Canadian Arctic coast; also along the Asian Pacific coast from Siberia to northern Japan. Introductions to some locales, such as the Great Lakes, have been attempted.

HABITAT: Both adult and juvenile Sockeye Salmon swim swiftly and so elusively that divers very seldom see them. Beachcombers or pier-side naturalists never see the sleek and silvery Sockeye Salmon alive. Alas, they must settle for a glimpse of a recently dead one when a sport fisherman comes alongside a wharf, a commercial vessel heaves-to, or in a fish market.

Bright red adult Sockeye Salmon, with their green heads and tails, can be observed in many freshwater rivers and streams during their fall spawning migration.

COMMENTS: Sockeye Salmon readily take a sport lure, and most of those that do, seize squid-like hoochies, or hooks wrapped with red cotton to simulate small planktonic prey.

B. Spawning pair of Sockeye Salmon.
Danny Kent photograph

Without doubt, the Sockeye Salmon has ranked as the most important commercial fish in the Pacific Northwest. Commercial seiners and gillnetters harvest Sockeye along coastal channels and at river mouths as they return to complete their four-year life cycle. Although most of the total catch is canned, trollers also tow egg spoons, feathered lures and hoochies on many lines to supply Sockeye Salmon for the fresh fish market.

This species is likely most at risk due to the effects of climate change, particularly warming of spawning rivers, because their tolerance to higher temperatures appears to be low. Although the Sockeye Salmon's bright red flesh is world renowned, it attracts the most attention from seafood lovers in the Pacific Northwest.

C. Catherine Statham photograph
D. Spawning pair.
Cora Moret photograph
E. Fry.

Chinook Salmon

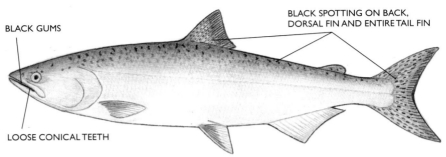

BLACK SPOTTING ON BACK, DORSAL FIN AND ENTIRE TAIL FIN

BLACK GUMS

LOOSE CONICAL TEETH

SPECIES: *Oncorhynchus tshawytscha*

OTHER COMMON NAMES: spring salmon, king salmon, blackmouth salmon, quinnat salmon, chub salmon, Sacramento River salmon, Columbia River salmon, chinook, spring, king, quinnat, hookbill, tyee for specimens of 14 kg (30 lb) and over. The name for this fish in Kamchatka, Russia is *tshawytscha*.

MAXIMUM RECORDED SIZE: 160 cm (63 in) and 61.2 kg (136 lb).

DISTRIBUTION: Southern California to the Bering Sea, and Coppermine in the Canadian Arctic; along the Asian Pacific coast from Siberia to northern Japan. The many worldwide transplants attempted have as yet only established viable, reproducing populations in the Great Lakes, New Zealand and Chile.

HABITAT: Occasionally divers may see a Chinook Salmon cruising above them in the clear green water, particularly at the edge of kelp beds. Looking upward is required, though. Rarely do shorebound naturalists see the fast-swimming Chinook Salmon as an adult, and they can see it only slightly more often as a juvenile.

Adult Chinook Salmon can be observed in many freshwater rivers and streams during their fall spawning migration.

COMMENTS: Significant numbers of Chinook Salmon spend the saltwater phase of their two-to-eight-year life cycle along coastal waters and are therefore available year-round to Pacific Northwest harvesting interests. Sport fishermen eagerly seek the mighty Chinook Salmon—the acknowledged "heavyweight champ" of the Pacific Northwest—by trolling and mooching. Using herring, either whole or as "strip," or artificial lures such as hoochies and plugs during dawn or dusk hours, anglers will most likely catch trophy-sized specimens. Jacks, or jack springs—small, precocious males that mature a year earlier than

A

"normal," as well as moderate-sized Chinook Salmon, bite readily throughout daylight hours. Using numerous hook-and-line rigs, commercial trollers harvest many Chinook Salmon for the fresh fish trade, while gillnetters and seiners generally supply their catch for canning or freezing. An ever-increasing number of major hatcheries propagate this valuable species, both in Canada and the USA, but the numbers of fish produced from these efforts has persistently decreased in the new millennium.

Whether red or white-fleshed, Chinook Salmon is excellent eating. Try stuffing a whole fish with your favourite dressing and then barbecuing or baking it for a real taste treat. Possessing very pale flesh, likely due to hereditary and dietary factors, "white spring" is reportedly best for smoking.

B. Catherine Statham photograph
C. Spawning pair.
D. Fry.

Coho Salmon

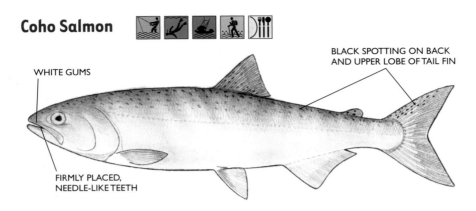

WHITE GUMS

BLACK SPOTTING ON BACK
AND UPPER LOBE OF TAIL FIN

FIRMLY PLACED,
NEEDLE-LIKE TEETH

SPECIES: *Oncorhynchus kisutch*

OTHER COMMON NAMES: silver salmon, coho, silver, hooknose, blueback (young only). The name for the fish in Kamchatka, Russia, is *kisutch*. Incorrect: dog salmon, jack salmon, sea trout

MAXIMUM RECORDED SIZE: 108 cm (42.5 in) and 17.7 kg (38.9 lb)

DISTRIBUTION: Northern Baja California, Mexico, to the Bering Sea, the Aleutian Island chain and the Beaufort Sea, Alaska; along the Pacific Asian coast from Siberia to northern Korea and northern Japan. Transplants to Argentina, New Hampshire, Maine, Maryland, Chile, Alberta, Lake Michigan and Lake Superior have as yet established viable populations only in the last four regions.

HABITAT: During the summer, divers who look up into the green water above may see the silhouettes of adult Coho Salmon cruising by, particularly if herring are schooling in the area. In spring and summer, young orange-tinged, parr-marked Coho Salmon dart quickly through shallow water near shore or around jetties and piers.

Adult Coho Salmon can be observed in many freshwater rivers and streams during their fall spawning migration.

COMMENTS: Aerial acrobatics performed by battling Coho Salmon give it top billing as a Pacific Northwest gamefish. Any of a wide variety of tackle and techniques, such as flies, jigs, plugs, spoons, whole juvenile herring or herring strip when trolling near the surface, live herring while mooching, or herring strip for strip

casting, may be used to catch this aggressive fish. Early in Coho Salmon season, April to June, "Blue-backs"—young specimens of only a few kilograms—bite readily, but these same fish, if released, may grow to 10 kg (22 lb) by August or September the same year.

Towing many lines, each with numerous hooks, commercial trollers take Coho Salmon and sell them fresh or frozen. Historically, gillnetters and seiners have caught large numbers for canning, smoking or freezing.

With its bright red flesh and rich flavour, the Coho Salmon is a seafood lover's dream. Coat a Coho steak in egg and breadcrumbs with a touch of tarragon and fry in butter.

B. Catherine Statham photograph
C. Spawning pair.
D. Fry.

Coho and Chinook: a guide for anglers. Coho above, Chinook below. Note the white gums of the Coho Salmon (upper right) and the black gums of the Chinook Salmon (lower right). *Catherine Statham photographs*

Steelhead (Rainbow Trout)

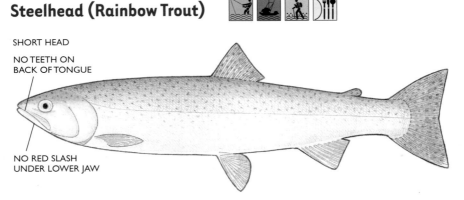

SHORT HEAD

NO TEETH ON BACK OF TONGUE

NO RED SLASH UNDER LOWER JAW

SPECIES: *Oncorhynchus mykiss.* Formerly *Salmo gairdneri*

OTHER COMMON NAMES: steelhead trout, coastal rainbow trout, Gairdner's salmon, salmon trout, hardhead, metalhead, ironhead, halfpounder

MAXIMUM RECORDED SIZE: 122 cm (48 in) and 23.6 kg (51.9 lb)

DISTRIBUTION: Northern Baja California, Mexico, to Bristol Bay on the Bering Sea coast of Alaska and the Aleutian Island chain. The rainbow trout, of which the steelhead is a sea-run race, has been successfully transplanted throughout the world.

HABITAT: Divers frequenting clear rivers and estuaries might see the sleek, fast Steelhead; usually, though, turbid water drastically decreases sighting possibilities. The swift open-ocean Steelhead is only accessible to shorebound naturalists when it moves into spawning streams where, unfortunately, turbidity often obscures it.

COMMENTS: The Steelhead is a sea-going form of the species known as Rainbow Trout and as such spends two or three years on the high seas before returning to its native river to spawn. Unlike Pacific salmon, it does not necessarily die after spawning. Often, it migrates back to the ocean for another term before returning to spawn again—perhaps repeating the process a third time.

There is an immense volume of literature and folklore concerning the joys of "steelheading" in rivers and streams, where legions of anglers avidly pursue this legendary fighter. However, most anglers fishing in salt water rarely expect to catch a Steelhead. In a few specific beach locales, however, some do take it casting bobbers or salmon spoons. To enhance this world-famous fish, governments annually spend considerable sums on hatcheries and habitat protection—although budgetary issues have recently decreased such expenditures.

A rift between sport anglers and commercial fishermen over the valuable Steelhead periodically flares. While gillnetting, purse seining, or trolling for the various Pacific salmon, professional harvesters take varying quantities of this fish as an incidental catch while the covetous angler condemns any such exploitation. Governments have attempted mediation via temporary closures as well as catch and release.

Seafood lovers extol the delights of feasting on Steelhead; its rich flesh is particularly tempting when baked or barbecued. Try canning some too!

B. *Spawning female.*
C. *Spawning male.*
D. *David Murphy photograph*
E. *Juvenile.*

Cutthroat Trout

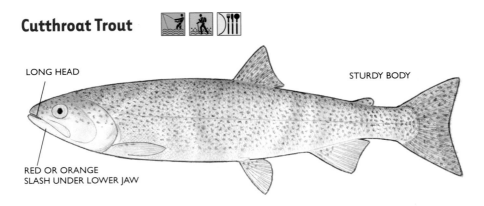

LONG HEAD

STURDY BODY

RED OR ORANGE
SLASH UNDER LOWER JAW

SPECIES: *Oncorhynchus clarkii.* Some publications refer to subspecies *Salmo clarki clarki*
OTHER COMMON NAMES: coastal cutthroat trout, coastal cut-throat trout, coast cutthroat trout, red-throated trout, Clark's trout, sea trout, coastal cutthroat
MAXIMUM RECORDED SIZE: 99 cm (38.9 in) and 18.6 kg (40.9 lb)
DISTRIBUTION: Northern California to Gulf of Alaska. (A subspecies of this fish, *Oncorhynchus clarki lewisi,* inhabits adjacent interior freshwater haunts not connected with the sea.)
HABITAT: During low-water summer months, look closely around sunken logs or along shaded estuarine banks for the lurking Cutthroat Trout.
COMMENTS: The Cutthroat Trout moves, with the changing tides, between salt and freshwater. This active, battling lightweight game fish ascends small streams in late winter or early spring to spawn. River-dwelling (resident) individuals also breed at this time too.

Lurking along shallow, gravelly marine and estuarine beaches, the Cutthroat Trout readily strikes at artificial lures cast from shore or towed from a boat; the proximity of a small stream often further enhances angling chances. Fly-fishing enthusiasts who cast in early, mist-shrouded mornings may actually stalk this quarry, frequently seeing it swirl the calm surface water. The best flies simulate the Cutthroat Trout's primary spring prey: migrating Chum Salmon fry, Pink Salmon fry, or Three-spine Stickleback.

The pinkish flesh of the Cutthroat Trout is particularly moist and tender—an excellent breakfast in the outdoors. Indoors too!

B. Juvenile.

Dolly Varden

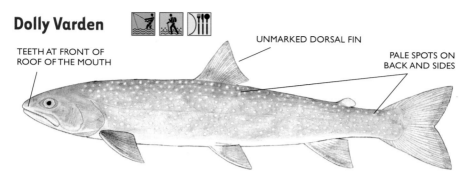

TEETH AT FRONT OF
ROOF OF THE MOUTH

UNMARKED DORSAL FIN

PALE SPOTS ON
BACK AND SIDES

SPECIES: *Salvelinus malma*

OTHER COMMON NAMES: Dolly Varden char, Dolly Varden charr, red spotted char, Pacific brook char, western brook char, sea char, Dolly, *malma* (in Russia). Incorrect: bull trout, red spotted trout, Dolly Varden trout, Rocky Mountain red spotted trout, sea trout, salmon trout, brook trout

MAXIMUM RECORDED SIZE: 101 cm (40 in)

DISTRIBUTION: Northern Washington to the Bering Sea coast of Alaska and throughout the Aleutian Island chain; along the Asian Pacific coast from Siberia to northern Japan and Korea

HABITAT: If the water is clear enough, the shore-strolling naturalist might see the sluggish Dolly Varden in gravelly estuaries or along oceanside beaches. This scenario is most likely in late summer when the various Pacific salmon are migrating to spawn. At this time, the anadromous Dolly Varden follows along to feed on the salmon eggs as they are deposited in the gravel.

COMMENTS: As it possesses a set of teeth on the vomer bone in the roof of its mouth, the Dolly Varden is technically a char.

Historically scorned as a scourge upon trout and salmon, the Dolly Varden—honouring a Charles Dickens' character that wore colourful clothes—once was the subject of bounties. While this underrated gamefish does feed upon salmon and trout, it also preys upon smelts, sticklebacks, sculpins, shrimps, insects, clams and worms.

In addition to those natural baits, the estuarine Dolly Varden takes brightly coloured spoons, spinners and flies, if cast and then retrieved at moderate speeds. Although not renowned as a mighty scrapper, this char will sometimes surprise with its tenacity.

Similar to trout, the Dolly Varden is delicious, particularly when pan-fried and fresh. Try poaching in white wine.

A

B

B. Juvenile.

Atlantic Salmon

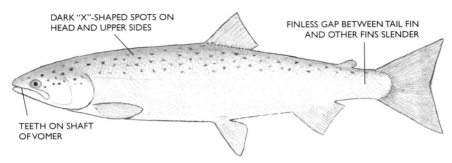

DARK "X"-SHAPED SPOTS ON
HEAD AND UPPER SIDES

FINLESS GAP BETWEEN TAIL FIN
AND OTHER FINS SLENDER

TEETH ON SHAFT
OF VOMER

SPECIES: *Salmo salar*

MAXIMUM RECORDED SIZE: 1.5 m (5 ft) and 35.9 kg (79 lb)

DISTRIBUTION: Naturally occurring in the North Atlantic Ocean from northern Spain through Norway, Iceland, Greenland, Canadian Arctic to Connecticut; "introduced" to the Pacific Northwest

HABITAT: Adult Atlantic Salmon, escapees from salmon farms, have been observed in a number of rivers in British Columbia and Alaska. When Atlantic Salmon escape from salmon farms, specimens are often caught incidentally by both sport and commercial net fishermen, should they be working nearby.

COMMENTS: In 1905 and several subsequent years, eyed eggs of Atlantic Salmon from Canada's east coast were introduced by the Canadian Department of Fisheries to the Cowichan Lake Hatchery on Vancouver Island. Resulting fingerlings and yearlings were liberated into the Cowichan and other rivers with the intention of establishing a recreational fishery. Only a few Cowichan River anglers reported catches during this period and shortly thereafter.

In 1933–34 more eyed eggs were obtained from Scotland but this effort proved even less successful. No subsequent reports of Atlantic Salmon from the Pacific Northwest occurred until the 1980s when Canada's Department of Fisheries and Oceans allowed the importation of Atlantic Salmon eggs for the salmon-farming industry. Farming of Atlantic Salmon via open ocean net pen culture rapidly expanded in both Washington State and British Columbia. Atlantic Salmon now dominate the salmon farming industry.

Inevitable escapes from aquaculture sites soon followed and resulted in large numbers of adult Atlantic Salmon swimming in Pacific Northwest waters as far north as Alaska. Closed containment options would appear to offer the best solution to mitigate any environmental impacts associated with salmon farming.

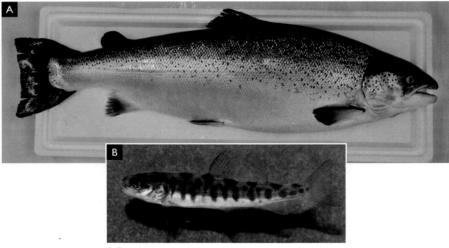

B. Fry.

THE **CODS** (Family Gadidae)

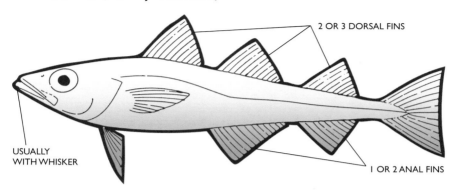

2 OR 3 DORSAL FINS

USUALLY WITH WHISKER

I OR 2 ANAL FINS

Along with the true cods, tomcods, pollacks, true hakes, cusks, lings, rocklings, haddocks, whitings and the Burbot comprise the family of fishes scientifically termed Gadidae. Of the 30 recognized living species, all but the lake- or river-dwelling Burbot live in salt water.

Most cods inhabit the temperate and boreal waters throughout the northern hemisphere. A few species inhabit similar southern hemisphere haunts. Gregarious by nature, most gadids will form schools, often of considerable size. They spend most of their time at or near the sea floor, feeding on a wide variety of prey.

The renowned cods rank economically among the most important fishes in the world. All manner of fishing techniques—from traditional handline and longlining aboard open dories to seining and trawling—annually take vast quantities of gadids for processing into numerous products such as fresh or frozen fillets, the ever-popular salt cod and finnan haddie.

Relatively recent increases in the harvest of the world's cods, associated with improving technologies, have resulted in catastrophic stock declines.

Pacific Cod

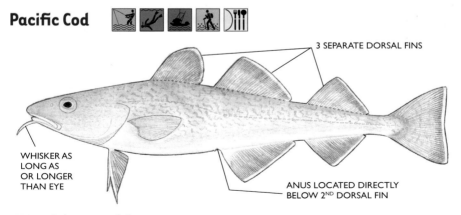

3 SEPARATE DORSAL FINS

WHISKER AS LONG AS OR LONGER THAN EYE

ANUS LOCATED DIRECTLY BELOW 2ND DORSAL FIN

SPECIES: *Gadus macrocephalus*
OTHER COMMON NAMES: grey cod, gray cod, true cod, Alaska cod, whisker cod, greyfish
MAXIMUM RECORDED SIZE: 122 cm (48 in) and 22.7 kg (50 lb)
DISTRIBUTION: Southern California to Bering Strait and Bering Sea coast of Alaska, and south to Korea, Manchuria and Japan

HABITAT: While swimming over soft bottoms, scuba divers sometimes encounter adult Pacific Cod cruising alone or as part of a school. This grey, whiskered fish usually swims along just off the bottom in search of prey such as young Walleye Pollock, pricklebacks, eelpouts, octopus, brittle stars, snails and crabs. However, the juvenile Pacific Cod is most commonly seen by divers. The Pacific Cod may be seen from the surface swimming in clear water, particularly near or even trapped within bait-herring ponds.

COMMENTS: During the winter spawning season, a large female Pacific Cod may swell with as many as 6,400,000 tiny eggs, which she will release for fertilization before she abandons them and lets them float on ocean currents.

Sport fishermen catch Pacific Cod from wharves, jetties or boats over sandy and mixed bottoms. Baits such as herring, marine worms, clams and shrimp as well as lures and jigs are effective.

Though North Americans harvest the Pacific Cod in significant quantities, Asians prize it even more. Historically, hook and line fishing dominated the North American commercial fishery, but more recently modern net-hauling vessels with processing plants aboard fillet the catch or render it into fish sticks. Unfortunately, reduced Pacific Cod abundance makes such products currently less available.

When gutted then chilled quickly, the Pacific Cod is very appetizing. Try it deep-fried for fish and chips. Chowder fans: save the head!

B. Juvenile. Bernard P. Hanby photograph

Pacific Tomcod

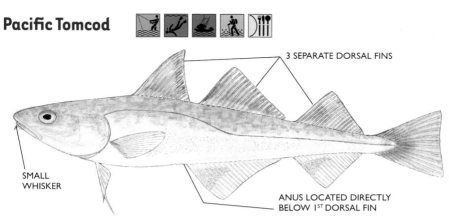

3 SEPARATE DORSAL FINS

SMALL
WHISKER

ANUS LOCATED DIRECTLY
BELOW 1ST DORSAL FIN

SPECIES: *Microgadus proximus*
OTHER COMMON NAMES: tomcod, wachna
MAXIMUM RECORDED SIZE: 37 cm (15 in)
DISTRIBUTION: Central California coast to Unalaska Island and the Bering Sea
HABITAT: Dockside naturalists and scuba divers have the best chance to see Pacific Tomcod with the aid of lights after dark during summer and autumn while juveniles are schooling in shallow bays or inlets. These young specimens frequently mix with juveniles of the larger-eyed Walleye Pollock to feed on shrimp-like planktonic creatures. Distinguishing between the two is difficult. Only rarely does the aquanaut find the deeper-dwelling adult Pacific Tomcod.
COMMENTS: The dusky-coloured Pacific Tomcod spawns in late winter or spring and by June the newly hatched transparent larvae begin a search for tiny planktonic prey at or near the surface.

Sport fishermen catch Pacific Tomcod from wharves, jetties or boats over sandy and muddy bottoms. Baits such as shrimp, small crabs, marine worms, clams or pieces of fish on smallish hooks are effective.

This fish is often a major part of the bycatch for shrimp trawlers and is frequently selected out as a tasty personal seafood item rather than being discarded.

The Pacific Tomcod's sweet, delicate flavour and fine texture make it excellent eating. No need to fillet this small fish—cook it whole because the flesh will fall easily from the backbone.

A

B

B. Juvenile.
Gregory C. Jensen photograph

Walleye Pollock

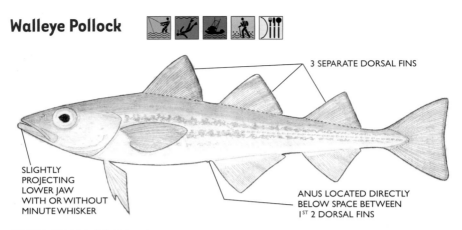

3 SEPARATE DORSAL FINS

SLIGHTLY PROJECTING LOWER JAW WITH OR WITHOUT MINUTE WHISKER

ANUS LOCATED DIRECTLY BELOW SPACE BETWEEN 1ST 2 DORSAL FINS

SPECIES: *Theragra chalcogramma*

OTHER COMMON NAMES: wall-eye pollock, Pacific pollock, Alaska pollack, bigeye, whiting, bugeye, scrapcod. Incorrect: walleye

MAXIMUM RECORDED SIZE: 91 cm (36 in)

DISTRIBUTION: Central California coast to the Chukchi Sea, throughout the Bering Sea and the Aleutian Island chain, Alaska; along the Asian coast from Siberia to southern Japan and Korea

HABITAT: Divers do not find the deeper-dwelling adult Walleye Pollock. While night diving in summer and autumn, the active juvenile may frequently be noticed as it mixes with the smaller-eyed Pacific Tomcod just off sandy or muddy bottoms. A specimen can be easily transfixed for close-up study with the beam of an underwater flashlight. On a calm summer or autumn evening, the pier-side naturalist may often see young Walleye Pollock darting amid beams of light shining into the water

COMMENTS: While the Walleye Pollock often pursues lures and jigs, it most readily bites at baits such as marine worms, shrimp or herring. Seek it at moderate depths and generally over a sandy or muddy bottom.

Increasingly important North American trawl fisheries for Walleye Pollock still lag far behind those of Asia, where even the roe—*tarako*—is highly prized. While historically underutilized—mostly used for mink feed—the Walleye Pollock has most recently become very important as food for people in the Pacific Northwest. By tonnage, its Bering Sea fishery has become the largest in the world, with factory ships reducing the flesh to *surimi* for imitation crab and lobster.

As more traditional fare, avoid its numerous bones and fillet fresh Walleye Pollock before chilling the firm sweet flesh. Braise fillets in white wine.

A

B. Juvenile.
C. Tiny cods (gadids) sheltering amid the
tentacles of the Lion's Mane jelly.
Sharon Jeffery photograph

Saffron Cod

Eleginus gracilis

Primarily an Arctic denizen, the Saffron Cod strays as far south as southeastern Alaska. It inhabits depths of less than 200 m (660 ft) and sometimes moves into the brackish waters of river estuaries. Distinctively, the lateral line (on each side) continues only to the beginning of the second dorsal fin. The Saffron Cod grows to a maximum recorded length of 55 cm (21.5 in). Sport divers are most likely to encounter the Saffron Cod in the most northerly Pacific Northwest locales.

Scott Johnson photograph

THE **MERLUCCID HAKES** (Family Merlucciidae)

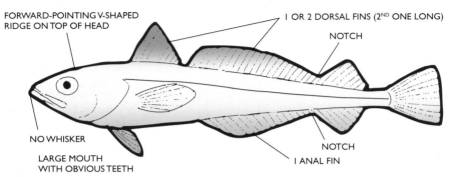

FORWARD-POINTING V-SHAPED RIDGE ON TOP OF HEAD

I OR 2 DORSAL FINS (2ND ONE LONG)

NOTCH

NO WHISKER

LARGE MOUTH WITH OBVIOUS TEETH

NOTCH

I ANAL FIN

A small family only recently separated from the similar cods, the Merlucciidae contains 13 species primarily found in temperate seas. Unlike most cods, which have three small separate dorsal fins and two similar anal fins, the merluccid hakes almost always possess two dorsal fins (the second being much longer) and a single elongate anal fin.

These elongate silvery fish roam the marine waters of the Atlantic and Pacific oceans, where they live along the continental shelves and upper slopes. Voracious predators, adults feed on various smaller fish while juveniles prefer planktonic invertebrates.

The schooling merluccid hakes are subject to huge trawl fisheries and are economically very important throughout the world.

Pacific Hake

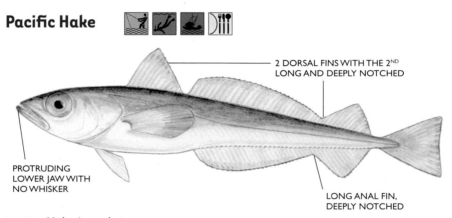

2 DORSAL FINS WITH THE 2ND LONG AND DEEPLY NOTCHED

PROTRUDING LOWER JAW WITH NO WHISKER

LONG ANAL FIN, DEEPLY NOTCHED

SPECIES: *Merluccius productus*
OTHER COMMON NAMES: Pacific whiting, California hake, hake
MAXIMUM RECORDED SIZE: 91 cm (36 in)
DISTRIBUTION: An isolated population in the Gulf of California; and from southern Baja California, Mexico, to Attu Island, in the Aleutian Island chain, Alaska
HABITAT: By day, Pacific Hake collect in long narrow schools at depths as great as 980 m (3,280 ft). After dark, they rise to the surface and disperse to feed on shrimp-like plankton and young salmon. By daybreak, these active fish have again congregated in deep dark waters. Because Pacific Hake only rise near the surface nocturnally, a night dive offers the best viewing opportunity for scuba divers.
COMMENTS: Still-fishing salmon anglers or moochers who use herring as bait periodically catch the schooling Pacific Hake as an unwanted incidental. This usually occurs in summer when darkness falls and this sharp-toothed fish rises to feed near the surface. Some less-selective wharf-bound enthusiasts avidly fish for it.

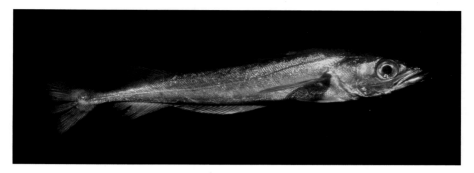

Historically viewed as a nuisance that clogged salmon gillnets and groundfish trawls, the Pacific Hake is now an extremely valuable commercial species. Its increased worth coincides with advances in modern freezing technology and a growing worldwide demand for seafood products. Originally in this fishery, domestic trawlers delivered fish to large foreign processing ships, and together they serviced the huge offshore market. More recently, Canadian and US shore-based operators are processing the catch themselves, increasing domestic employment.

Promptly filleted and chilled, Pacific Hake is fine eating *au gratin*; do not be discouraged by some brownish colour on the long, slender fillets.

THE **VIVIPAROUS BROTULAS** (Family Bythitidae)

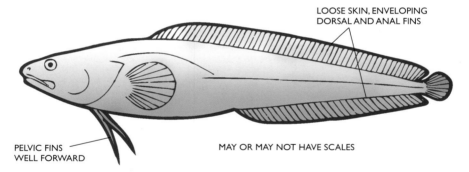

LOOSE SKIN, ENVELOPING DORSAL AND ANAL FINS

PELVIC FINS WELL FORWARD

MAY OR MAY NOT HAVE SCALES

Nearly 100 known living species of viviparous (livebearing) brotulas form the large family scientifically called the Bythitidae. Most species colonize tropical marine haunts where they hide within deep caves and crevices among the shallow coral reefs, particularly in the vast Indo-Pacific. Unusual and diverse habitats, such as caverns very deep on the ocean floor or on lake bottoms, harbour a few specialized bythitids. One of the viviparous brotulas inhabits the 6 km (4 mi) deep Sunda trench in the South Pacific and is thought to be the world's deepest-dwelling fish.

The total darkness of deep marine or freshwater habitats apparently stimulated evolution of certain features in abyssal viviparous brotulas. Many of the secretive bythitids no longer possess functional eyes, while others may have only very tiny rudimentary ones. Compensating for this partial or total loss of sight, these fish have special sensors, similar to taste buds, located on their long, tapering and paired pelvic fins. These sensors allow these slow swimmers to grope for their food before actually devouring it.

Relatively few bythitids inhabit cooler temperate seas. One of those is the Pacific Northwest's Red Brotula.

Red Brotula

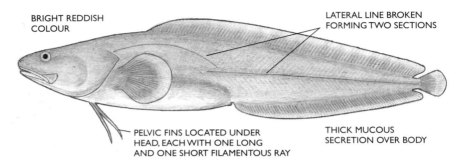

BRIGHT REDDISH COLOUR

LATERAL LINE BROKEN FORMING TWO SECTIONS

PELVIC FINS LOCATED UNDER HEAD, EACH WITH ONE LONG AND ONE SHORT FILAMENTOUS RAY

THICK MUCOUS SECRETION OVER BODY

SPECIES: *Brosmophycis marginata*

OTHER COMMON NAMES: red brotulid

MAXIMUM RECORDED SIZE: 46 cm (18 in)

DISTRIBUTION: Northern Baja California, Mexico, to southeastern Alaska

HABITAT: Diligent searching by divers along rocky reefs and cliff faces at depths below 20 m (66 ft) occasionally reveals a Red Brotula looking out from a deep and rocky cavern. Sometimes, though, a surprised aquanaut may even detect a mated pair hovering at the entrance to a cave, or backing into it when confronted. A colourful find, it is particularly appealing to the underwater photographer. However, the Red Brotula is a very challenging subject, as it often quickly retreats from view.

COMMENTS: The Red Brotula produces live young and is the subject of captive rearing efforts at the Vancouver Aquarium. When ultimately successful, this program could supply other public aquaria with specimens of this colourful and difficult to obtain species.

B. Daniel Hershman photograph

THE **CUSK-EELS** (Family Ophidiidae)

Spotted Cusk-eel

Chilara taylori

The Spotted Cusk-eel is occasionally noticed as far north as northern Washington. It resides in burrows much of the time, thus reducing sighting opportunities for scuba divers. This distinctive species reaches a maximum recorded length of 36 cm (14.3 in).

Daniel W. Gotshall photograph

THE **EELPOUTS** (Family Zoarcidae)

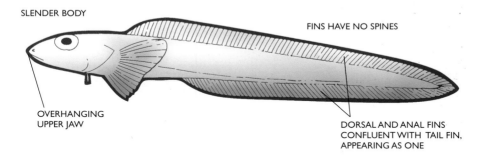

SLENDER BODY

FINS HAVE NO SPINES

OVERHANGING UPPER JAW

DORSAL AND ANAL FINS CONFLUENT WITH TAIL FIN, APPEARING AS ONE

The Zoarcidae is a large group containing nearly 200 recognized living species of eelpouts, soft pouts and ocean pouts. All are marine denizens that live in shallow inshore waters, abyssal regions of oceanic trenches and at all depths in between. Although a few slim zoarcids hover in mid-water well off the bottom, most settle right on soft, gently sloping substrates of the sea floor.

Eelpouts comprise a major portion of the bottom-dwelling biomass and as such, are prey for larger predatory fish. Preying primarily upon small invertebrate creatures, eelpouts represent an important link with many of the commercially harvested species of fish. The importance of eelpouts to fisheries and the marine food web defies calculation.

A large number of Pacific Northwest zoarcids inhabit regions that are very deep and inaccessible to most people.

Blackbelly Eelpout

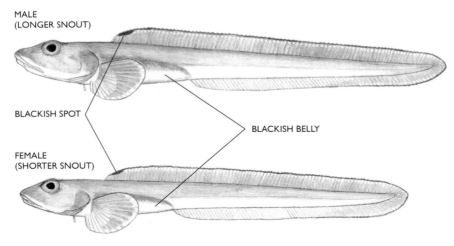

MALE
(LONGER SNOUT)

BLACKISH SPOT

BLACKISH BELLY

FEMALE
(SHORTER SNOUT)

SPECIES: *Lycodes pacificus.* Formerly *Lycodopsis pacifica*
OTHER COMMON NAMES: black-bellied eelpout
MAXIMUM RECORDED SIZE: 46 cm (18 in)
DISTRIBUTION: Northern Baja California, Mexico, to the Aleutian Island chain, Alaska
HABITAT: At night, the very common Blackbelly Eelpout moves into shallow, diveable depths. Search at depths below 15 m (50 ft) and over sandy or muddy substrate. A mature female may lay as many as 52 eggs during the August to January breeding season. At the time of writing, the authors are unaware of anyone who has photo-documented this event.
COMMENTS: Often entwining themselves in the webbing, vast quantities of these economically insignificant creatures fill fine-meshed commercial shrimp trawls dragged over soft, level bottoms at depths to 400 m (1,320 ft). Because of its abundance, the Blackbelly Eelpout is no doubt an important forage fish for many commercial species.

A. Male.
B. Female.
C. Male.

Black Eelpout

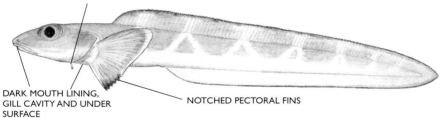

PELVIC FIN ABOUT 1/2 DIAMETER OF EYE

DARK MOUTH LINING, GILL CAVITY AND UNDER SURFACE

NOTCHED PECTORAL FINS

SPECIES: *Lycodes diapterus*
OTHER COMMON NAMES: blackfin eelpout, black-finned eelpout
MAXIMUM RECORDED SIZE: 37.1 cm (14.6 in)
DISTRIBUTION: Southern California to the Bering Sea coast, through the Aleutian Island chain to Siberia and northern Japan
HABITAT: The Black Eelpout lives on soft, level bottoms at depths between 50 and 2,260 m (165 and 7,415 ft)—areas where commercial shrimp trawlers harvest—and is encountered as bycatch.
COMMENTS: Like other fish with a wide distribution, the Black Eelpout, as presently defined, may actually be more than one species.

Molecular biologists who work with genetic coding frequently find differences between populations of fish at the extremes of their distributions. Whether such variations represent separate species is often subject to debate and consultation with traditional taxonomic scientists is important. As the Black Eelpout is not commercially significant, it is not a likely candidate for study anytime soon.

Shortfin Eelpout

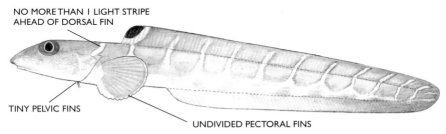

NO MORE THAN 1 LIGHT STRIPE AHEAD OF DORSAL FIN

TINY PELVIC FINS

UNDIVIDED PECTORAL FINS

SPECIES: *Lycodes brevipes*
MAXIMUM RECORDED SIZE: 31.7 cm (12.5 in)
DISTRIBUTION: Northern California to the Bering Sea, the Aleutian Island chain, Alaska and Siberia

HABITAT: The Shortfin Eelpout appearing in the photograph was caught by a trawl net in English Bay, Vancouver, British Columbia, at a depth of less than 15 m (50 ft). This shallow depth record suggests that scuba enthusiasts might spot this species as it rests upon a sandy or muddy substrate.

COMMENTS: The Shortfin Eelpout, like many other small, deeper-dwelling fishes that are of no direct commercial value and are relatively inaccessible for many sampling efforts, receives virtually no research attention. Consequently, details of the Shortfin Eelpout's life history are minimal.

Wattled Eelpout

Lycodes palearis

While documented as far south as Oregon, the Wattled Eelpout's centre of distribution appears to be Alaska. It is distinguished by the first two of its series of light bars being located ahead of the dorsal fin. The species is included here as acknowledgement of its local presence and potential sighting. It grows to a length of 54 cm (21.3 in).

Dr. Catherine Mecklenburg photograph

Unknown Lycodapine Eelpout

The illustrated specimen was captured in 1981 by a trawler off Passage Island, near Vancouver at a depth of less than 30 m (200 ft).

The definitive reference of the day, *Pacific Fishes of Canada* by J.L. Hart, published in 1974, listed three *Lycodapus* species of eelpout. Although the specimen tentatively appeared to be the Blackmouth Eelpout, *Lycodapus fierasfer*, we decided to omit this obscure fish with an uncertain identity from the original volume.

Since then, a new academic authority has appeared. *Fishes of Alaska*, by C.W. Mecklenburg, T.A. Mecklenburg and L.K. Thorsteinson, published in 2002, represents the latest scholarly study of Pacific Northwest fishes. In this reference, the authors list seven similar species of *Lycodapus* living along the British Columbia coast. In a further complication, one of the original three listed in *Pacific Fishes of Canada* is now considered invalid and listed as a possible synonymy for the other two. Confused? So are we. Unfortunately, the specimen has long since disappeared. However, this example illustrates the evolving taxonomy of Pacific Northwest fishes.

THE **SILVERSIDES** (Family Atherinopsidae)

Topsmelt

Atherinops affinis

Recorded as far north as the Queen Charlotte Islands, northern British Columbia, the Topsmelt swims at or very near the surface. It has five to eight scales between the two dorsal fins. California anglers fishing from piers catch this active fish. The Topsmelt grows to a length of 37 cm (14.5 in) and

Daniel W. Gotshall photograph

is most often seen in the Pacific Northwest during warm-water events such as El Niño.

Jacksmelt

Atherinopsis californiensis

The Jacksmelt has an anal fin that begins behind the second dorsal fin (as opposed to the Topsmelt's, which commences directly below) and ten to twelve scales between the dorsal fins. Unless travelling in warm water currents, the Jacksmelt rarely swims as far north as the Queen Charlotte

Daniel W. Gotshall photograph

Islands, northern British Columbia. It attains a maximum length of 44 cm (17.5 in).

THE **LIZARDFISHES** (Family Synodontidae)

California Lizardfish

Synodus lucioceps
The California Lizardfish may be recognized by its cylindrical, elongate body, triangular head and a small adipose fin. It has been recorded on several occasions from Washington and Oregon but is most common in California and northern Mexico. Its appearance in the Pacific Northwest is likely a result of El Niño events. It attains a length of 64 cm (25.2 in).

Kathy deWet-Oleson photograph

THE **BARRACUDAS** (Family Sphyraenidae)

Pacific Barracuda

Sphyraena argentea
Commonly called the California Barracuda, this species has been documented as far north as the Gulf of Alaska. Occurrences north of California correspond well with El Niño events. It reaches a length of 122 cm (4 ft).

Mark Conlin photograph

THE **LANCETFISHES** (Family Alepisauridae)

Longnose Lancetfish

Alepisaurus ferox

Although the Longnose Lancetfish typically lives in the open ocean, live specimens frequently wash ashore on beaches along the exposed shores of the Pacific Northwest. This spectacular species is easily recognized by its large sail-like dorsal fin and prominent, dagger-like teeth. It reaches a length of 2.3 m (7.75 ft).

Alexander Jackson photograph

THE **RIBBONFISHES** (Family Trachipteridae)

King-of-the-Salmon

Trachipterus altivelis

An offshore species that rarely washes ashore, the distinctive King-of-the-Salmon grows to a length of 1.8 m (5.5 ft). It has no anal fin and only a "half-tail." A Makah (Native Americans of Washington State) legend purports that this fish would lead migrating salmon back to their spawning streams and that killing it would halt the process. However, no scientific relationship between King-of-the-Salmon and the better-known Pacific salmon has been established.

Royal British Columbia Museum Archives photograph

THE **STICKLEBACKS** (Family Gasterosteidae)

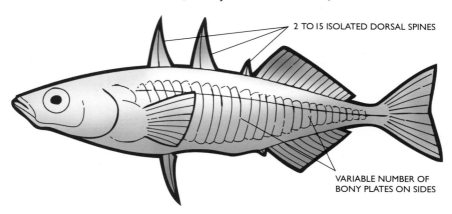

2 TO 15 ISOLATED DORSAL SPINES

VARIABLE NUMBER OF
BONY PLATES ON SIDES

The sticklebacks, or Gasterosteidae, is a small family of fishes containing approximately a dozen valid living species, only one of which inhabits Pacific Northwest shores. All members of the family live only in the temperate and boreal waters of the northern hemisphere, spread fairly evenly around the globe.

Sticklebacks are some of the world's most adaptable fishes. For example, the familiar Threespine Stickleback tolerates, and actually flourishes in, freshwater or salt water and all concentrations of brackish in between.

Sticklebacks are active swimmers that often congregate in large and loosely organized groups. These bony-plated fishes usually frequent very shallow habitats where they can remain at the surface, but yet not too far from the bottom.

The hardy gasterosteids, few of which grow larger than 20 cm (8 in), are very popular animals for experimentation because they are easily and conveniently captured and maintained in aquaria. Innumerable laboratory studies detail the very complex behaviour patterns of these spiny-backed creatures during their courting, mating and territorial interactions. Such laboratory studies compare favourably with ecology field studies.

Threespine Stickleback

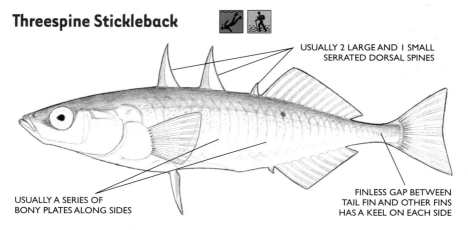

USUALLY 2 LARGE AND 1 SMALL
SERRATED DORSAL SPINES

USUALLY A SERIES OF
BONY PLATES ALONG SIDES

FINLESS GAP BETWEEN
TAIL FIN AND OTHER FINS
HAS A KEEL ON EACH SIDE

SPECIES: *Gasterosteus aculeatus*. This fish is literally evolving before our eyes, with numerous species "developing" in isolated lakes along Pacific Northwest shores.

OTHER COMMON NAMES: three-spine stickleback, three-spined stickleback, two-spine stickleback, saw-finned stickleback, common stickleback, eastern stickleback, New York stickleback, European stickleback, banstickle, spantickle, tiddler. As many as 30 other synonyms exist. Incorrect: pinfish
MAXIMUM RECORDED SIZE: 10 cm (4 in)
DISTRIBUTION: Throughout fresh, brackish and salt waters of the northern hemisphere; in the marine environment of the Pacific coast from northern Baja California, Mexico to the Bering Sea coasts; along the North Alaskan Arctic; also Asian shores from Siberia to southern Japan and Korea
HABITAT: Look for congregations of silvery Threespine Stickleback at the surface while snorkelling to or from a dive site or around pilings and piers; rarely will they be seen, though, below depths of a metre.

Both salt and brackish water tidepools harbour the Threespine Stickleback, particularly while it stakes out territory and breeds. Large numbers of these fish gather around jetties and wharves. Watch a single specimen as it swims jerkily, using its pectoral fin strokes, in a manner very distinct from that of other small, silvery fishes. Boat-bound naturalists, far from shore, may even find the surface-inhabiting Threespine Stickleback hovering beneath bits of flotsam.

COMMENTS: In spite of its formidable spiny protection, the Threespine Stickleback is important prey for many pelagic fishes and seabirds. In turn, it feeds upon a variety of tiny invertebrates, particularly free-living copepods.

C. Bernard P. Hanby photograph

THE **TUBESNOUTS** (Family Aulorhynchidae)

SLENDER CYLINDRICAL BODY

DORSAL FIN WELL BACK ON BODY

ELONGATE SNOUT WITH TINY MOUTH

ABOUT 25 ISOLATED SPINES

Containing only two known living species, the tubesnouts, or Aulorhynchidae, are obviously a minute family. The second tubesnout species, also marine, thrives along the shallow coastal waters of Korea and Japan.

There is a close relationship between present-day tubesnouts and the sticklebacks. Anatomically, a tubesnout is essentially a stretched-out, armourless stickleback.

Although tubesnouts are slow swimmers, they are capable of quick lunges to seize prey.

Tubesnout

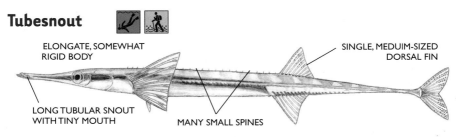

ELONGATE, SOMEWHAT RIGID BODY

SINGLE, MEDIUM-SIZED DORSAL FIN

LONG TUBULAR SNOUT WITH TINY MOUTH

MANY SMALL SPINES

SPECIES: *Aulorhynchus flavidus*
OTHER COMMON NAMES: tube-snout, tubenose. Incorrect: needlefish
MAXIMUM RECORDED SIZE: 18.8 cm (7.5 in)
DISTRIBUTION: Central Baja California, Mexico, to Unalaska Island, Alaska
HABITAT: If diving in shallow, seaweed-choked areas or around docks and pilings, look for Tubesnout schools hovering above the bottom in less than 20 m (65 ft). In late spring, juveniles form distinct schools to search for prey and specimens increase in size throughout the summer. During the spring breeding season, the patient dockside observer may readily see the detailed spawning ritual of the Tubesnout.
COMMENTS: During breeding season, each darkened, mature male, with his fluorescent snout and blue spots, stakes out a territory, often among marine plants hanging from a float or piling. Accompanied by as many as ten mature females, the industrious male binds seaweed together with thread-like strands of his

sticky genital fluid and waits while successive consorts parade into this nest, each to deposit clusters of up to 60 amber-coloured eggs. After he fertilizes each clutch laid in his nest, the amazing male vigorously guards the eggs until, within three weeks, tiny, transparent, 8 mm (0.3 in) Tubesnout larvae hatch and swim off in search of food.

A. Juvenile. B. Courting male.

THE **PIPEFISHES** (Family Syngnathidae)

BODY ENCLOSED IN ARMOUR OF
ENCIRCLING RINGS MAKING IT RIGID

SINGLE DORSAL FIN

LIVE YOUNG INCUBATED IN MALE'S POUCH

The Syngnathidae is a large family of fishes containing approximately 215 recognizable living species of seahorses and pipefishes. The elongate pipefishes grow to a maximum size of 46 cm (18 in). They are essentially stretched-out versions of the familiar seahorses but without the flexible prehensile tails.

Primarily fishes of warm shallow seas, only a few syngnathids, such as the Pacific Northwest's single species, abide cold latitudes.

Within the aquatic world of pipefishes and seahorses, parental care of offspring takes on a novel twist. After the intricate courtship of a mature pair and their subsequent mating, which includes copulation and internal fertilization, the female transfers the viable eggs to a special brood pouch located along the male's lower underside. From this time on, he cares for the tiny developing young while the unburdened female renews regular foraging activities.

Bay Pipefish

MALE

TINY TAIL

TINY MOUTH   NO PELVIC FINS

VERY LONG INFLEXIBLE BODY COVERED WITH ABUTTING BONY PLATES

FEMALE

SPECIES: *Syngnathus leptorhynchus.* Formerly *Syngnathus griseolineatus*
OTHER COMMON NAMES: northern bay pipefish, pipefish, pipe-fish
MAXIMUM RECORDED SIZE: 38.5 cm (15.2 in)
DISTRIBUTION: Southern Baja California, Mexico, to central Gulf of Alaska
HABITAT: Usually lurking among seaweeds, hanging from wharves, or growing along shorelines, or even floating freely in tidelines, the camouflaged Bay Pipefish is a fairly common sight for the observant naturalist.

Watch this creature as it slowly glides in a deliberate search for tiny shrimp-like prey, often carrying its stiff body upright. It moves by vibrating a single transparent dorsal fin.
COMMENTS: Sometime after her eggs have been internally fertilized, the transient female entwines with her mate and transfers viable ova to his long brood pouch. Weeks later his swollen pouch splits, releasing many tiny, black, thread-like baby pipefish into their permanent environment.

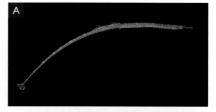

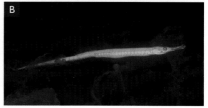

THE **SANDFISHES** (Family Trichodontidae)

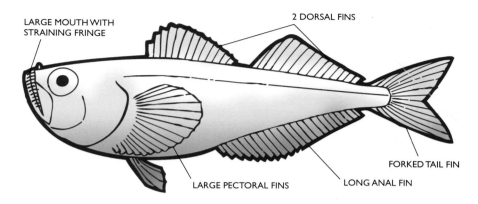

LARGE MOUTH WITH STRAINING FRINGE

2 DORSAL FINS

LARGE PECTORAL FINS

LONG ANAL FIN

FORKED TAIL FIN

The Trichodontidae, popularly known as the sandfishes, is a very tiny family of marine fishes containing only two known living species: one lurks along the North Pacific coast of Asia, while the other frequents the shores of western North America. Neither enters freshwater.

Secretive, sandy-bottom dwellers, the trichodontids—no longer than 33 cm (13 in)—bury themselves in the soft substrate and wait with their upturned, fringed mouths to grasp unsuspecting prey. While there is little commercial interest in the Pacific Northwestern variety, resourceful Asians actively pursue their local species for noteworthy regional fisheries.

Pacific Sandfish

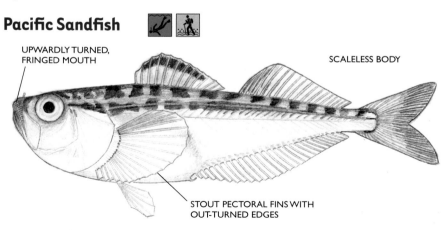

UPWARDLY TURNED, FRINGED MOUTH

SCALELESS BODY

STOUT PECTORAL FINS WITH OUT-TURNED EDGES

SPECIES: *Trichodon trichodon*
OTHER COMMON NAMES: sandfish, sand-fish. Known as *anamlukh* to the Aleut peoples
MAXIMUM RECORDED SIZE: 30 cm (12 in)
DISTRIBUTION: Central California coast to the Bering Sea coast of Alaska, through the Aleutian Island chain and south to the Kuril Islands, Japan
HABITAT: The Pacific Sandfish lives in a very shallow, turbid environment and spends much of its time completely buried in the sand. A scuba diver may encounter juveniles schooling near the surface in shallow, open-coast bays.

On a visit to a sandy, wave-swept beach, the dauntless beachcomber may literally stumble across the Pacific Sandfish because the receding tide may have left it buried in the sand. Try dragging your feet as you walk along the edge of the water; perhaps one might wriggle free.

COMMENTS: The Pacific Sandfish reportedly spawns in late winter, with mature individuals of at least two years of age participating in the courtship and breeding routine. After hatching, each larva swims and forages at the surface until it attains about 2.5 cm (1 in) in length then settles to a sandy bottom.

THE **SURFPERCHES** (Family Embiotocidae)

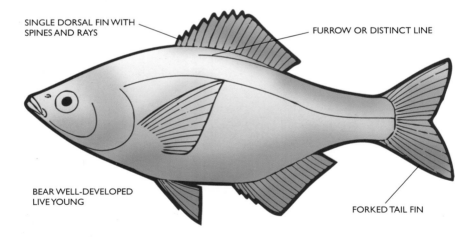

SINGLE DORSAL FIN WITH SPINES AND RAYS

FURROW OR DISTINCT LINE

BEAR WELL-DEVELOPED LIVE YOUNG

FORKED TAIL FIN

Twenty-three known living species of surfperches, seaperches and viviparous perches form a small, noteworthy family of fishes, scientifically called the Embiotocidae. All members inhabit the temperate North Pacific: A few small species thrive along Korean and Japanese shores; the others are North American.

With the exception of the freshwater-dwelling California Tule Perch, embiotocids are all marine creatures and only a few wander into brackish river estuaries. The preferred habitats for most species are shallow and even intertidal locales adjacent to rocky-bottoms. Few live deeper than 30 m (100 ft) and none grow longer than 48 cm (19 in).

Unlike the majority of fishes, the amazing embiotocids are viviparous; they bear large, fully-developed living young. After copulation and fertilization, ripe female surfperches slowly but steadily go through structural and functional changes to accommodate as many as 40 developing and growing young. For nourishing these babies, an elaborate internal system, not entirely unlike that of a female mammal, evolves over the nearly year-long gestation period. When ultimately jettisoned into the sea, the newborn have a special size advantage over other young fish that hatch directly from tiny eggs.

White Seaperch

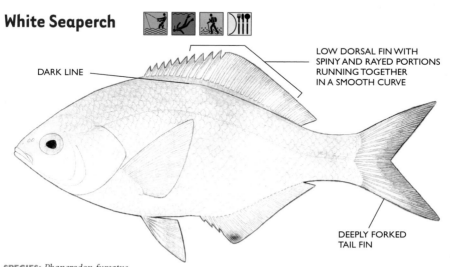

DARK LINE

LOW DORSAL FIN WITH SPINY AND RAYED PORTIONS RUNNING TOGETHER IN A SMOOTH CURVE

DEEPLY FORKED TAIL FIN

SPECIES: *Phanerodon furcatus*
OTHER COMMON NAMES: white surfperch, white perch. Incorrect: silver seaperch
MAXIMUM RECORDED SIZE: 34 cm (13.3 in)
DISTRIBUTION: Northern Baja California, Mexico, to southern Vancouver Island, British Columbia
HABITAT: Divers should search along sandy bottoms of shallow bays when seeking the White Seaperch and pay particular attention to pilings and other shelter.

Although large tidepools might occasionally trap the White Seaperch, it is more often seen around floats or jetties. Specific identification from above water, though, is difficult.
COMMENTS: Wharves and jetties extending over sandy substrates are good angling platforms to bottom-fish for the White Seaperch, especially during summer. For bait, use its natural intertidal prey: clams, snails, piling worms or small shrimp.

Not really abundant in the Pacific Northwest, the small White Seaperch is mainly harvested in California where it is netted in shallow water and sold with other surfperch under the catch-all term, "perch."

Pan-frying the batter-coated, fine-grained flesh of the White Seaperch enhances its delicate flavour. Be wary of small bones, even in fillets.

Pile Perch

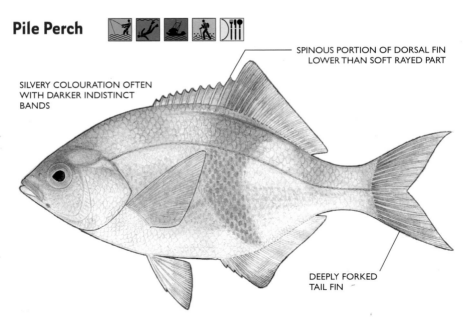

SPINOUS PORTION OF DORSAL FIN
LOWER THAN SOFT RAYED PART

SILVERY COLOURATION OFTEN
WITH DARKER INDISTINCT
BANDS

DEEPLY FORKED
TAIL FIN

SPECIES: *Damalichthys vacca.* Formerly *Rhacochilus vacca*
OTHER COMMON NAMES: pile seaperch, pile surfperch, dusky sea-perch, dusky perch, forktail perch, splittail perch. Incorrect: silver perch, porgy
MAXIMUM RECORDED SIZE: 44.2 cm (17.4 in)
DISTRIBUTION: Central Baja California, Mexico, to central British Columbia
HABITAT: Scuba divers frequently encounter the silvery, schooling Pile Perch near pilings, over shallow reefs, or along shorelines. Notice the ritualistic courtship displays as the aggressive, darker males roll over on their sides and flash in front of the passive, more lightly-hued females.

Readily recognized by beachcombers from above water, the large, silvery, deep-bodied Pile Perch commonly gathers around piers and pilings.

COMMENTS: In summer, a Pile Perch fishing trip is fine family sport. First go to the shore at low tide and gather shore crabs, mussels, snails, piling worms or clams for bait. Later, as the tide comes in, fish for the Pile Perch from a wharf or jetty along a shallow bay or shoreline. A lesson in conservation should occur when someone in the party catches and releases a large pregnant female—obvious with her swollen belly.

Filleted and sold fresh as "perch," the Pile Perch forms a very minor, somewhat incidental catch for Pacific Northwest trawlers.

Many small bones notwithstanding, the fine-grained flesh of the Pile Perch provides fair eating.

A. Juvenile.
B. Bernard P. Hanby photograph

Silver Surfperch

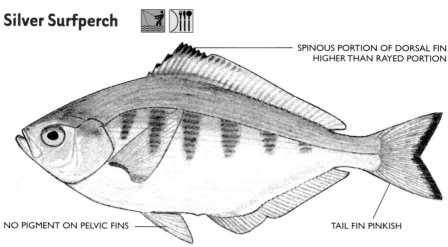

SPINOUS PORTION OF DORSAL FIN
HIGHER THAN RAYED PORTION

NO PIGMENT ON PELVIC FINS

TAIL FIN PINKISH

SPECIES: *Hyperprosopon ellipticum*
OTHER COMMON NAMES: silver perch. Incorrect: porgy
MAXIMUM RECORDED SIZE: 27 cm (10.5 in)
DISTRIBUTION: Northern Baja California, Mexico, to central Vancouver Island, British Columbia
HABITAT: The quick, elusive Silver Surfperch resides along exposed, surf-swept beaches or nearby shallow coves and is potentially, at least, directly in the scuba diver's path. However, turbid summer conditions permit only fleeting glimpses of this schooling fish, no matter how carefully stalked.
COMMENTS: Summer finds large pregnant Silver Surfperch congregating in shallow, calm, seaweed-choked bays and giving birth to as many as 30 tiny, 2 cm (less than 1 in) young. The small Silver Surfperch is occasionally caught incidentally by shorebound anglers fishing surf-swept, open-coast beaches or adjacent bays. By releasing any of these swollen mothers-in-waiting, the angler helps to ensure future supplies of this silvery, schooling fish.

The culinary value of the bone-laden Silver Surfperch is somewhat reduced by its small size: only thin, short fillets slice from even the largest fish.

NOTE: The Spotfin Surfperch, *Hyperprosopon anale*, a similar species to the one featured above, but with a black-splotched, spiny dorsal fin, is documented as far north as central Oregon.

Walleye Surfperch

Hyperprosopon argenteum
Recorded as far north as southern Vancouver Island, British Columbia, the Walleye Surfperch thrives in southern and central California. It is distinguished by black edges on the pelvic fins and grows to a length of 30 cm (12 in).

Daniel W. Gotshall photograph

Redtail Surfperch

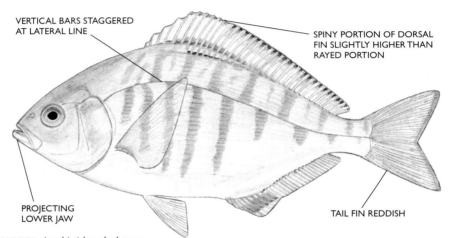

VERTICAL BARS STAGGERED AT LATERAL LINE

SPINY PORTION OF DORSAL FIN SLIGHTLY HIGHER THAN RAYED PORTION

PROJECTING LOWER JAW

TAIL FIN REDDISH

SPECIES: *Amphistichus rhodoterus*
OTHER COMMON NAMES: redtail surf perch, redtail seaperch, redtail perch, redtail. Incorrect: porgy
MAXIMUM RECORDED SIZE: 41 cm (16 in)
DISTRIBUTION: Central California coast to central Vancouver Island, British Columbia
HABITAT: Open, coastal, surf-swept beaches are ideal Redtail Surfperch habitat where it may be seen by a determined diver. By day this schooling species is difficult to approach, but at night with the aid of the beam from an underwater flashlight, a diver may move a little closer.

Occasionally, if the water is clear, the jetty-side naturalist may see the strong-swimming Redtail Surfperch propelling itself along with powerful pectoral fin strokes, but there is usually some difficulty distinguishing this fish from other silvery surfperch.

COMMENTS: Fishermen surf-cast for schooling Redtail Surfperch along sandy beaches directly exposed to the Pacific surge, or from adjacent piers or jetties. For bait, match its normal diet: razor clams, various shrimp, mussels, shore crabs and sand crabs. Or try hooking a piling worm on a small spinner, casting, and slowly retrieving it. When caught on light tackle, the Redtail Surfperch fights tenaciously.

The Redtail Surfperch is a tasty pan fish. Fillet it to remove those many fine, hair-like bones.

Calico Surfperch

Amphistichus koelzi

A common fish in California, the Calico Surfperch is documented from as far north as the northern coast of Washington. This species is very similar to the Redtail Surfperch but has a shallow notch in its dorsal fin profile. It grows to a length of 30 cm (12 in).

Ken Oda photograph

Striped Seaperch

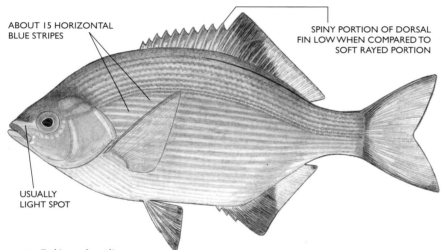

ABOUT 15 HORIZONTAL BLUE STRIPES

SPINY PORTION OF DORSAL FIN LOW WHEN COMPARED TO SOFT RAYED PORTION

USUALLY LIGHT SPOT

SPECIES: *Embiotoca lateralis*
OTHER COMMON NAMES: blue seaperch, blue perch
MAXIMUM RECORDED SIZE: 38 cm (15 in)
DISTRIBUTION: Northern Baja California, Mexico, to southeastern Alaska
HABITAT: Divers often notice schools of Striped Seaperch in shallow areas around seaweed-covered rocks or near pilings and jetties. Even from a wharf, above water, this striped and darker fish is readily distinguishable from other silvery, lighter species.

B. Juvenile.

COMMENTS: During the summer along shallow, rocky shores or around wharves and pilings, the Striped Seaperch is good quarry for the angler bait fishing and using light tackle. At low tide, gather natural bait: piling worms, mussels, shore crabs, snails and clams—fun for the whole family. Later, fish near the bottom with small hooks. Conservation-minded anglers release their large, fat, pregnant Striped Seaperch alive to ensure future catches.

During summer, the female releases her young, conceived the previous year. The newly born, each 4–6 cm (1.6–2.4 in) long, huddle in shallow bays, while every adult female awaits the ritualistic advances of an attentive male.

Striped Seaperch are fair eating but loose hair-like bones as well as the vertebral column require attention.

Kelp Perch

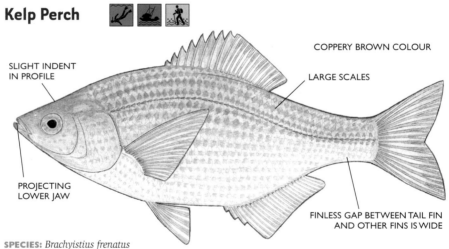

COPPERY BROWN COLOUR

SLIGHT INDENT
IN PROFILE

LARGE SCALES

PROJECTING
LOWER JAW

FINLESS GAP BETWEEN TAIL FIN
AND OTHER FINS IS WIDE

SPECIES: *Brachyistius frenatus*
OTHER COMMON NAMES: kelp sea-perch, kelp surfperch, brown sea-perch, brown perch
MAXIMUM RECORDED SIZE: 22 cm (8.5 in)
DISTRIBUTION: Central Baja California, Mexico, to southeastern Alaska
HABITAT: The Kelp Perch often swims in clear water just below the surface but darts quickly among the kelps where it is difficult to see.

When cruising along shallow shorelines with large, thick growths of kelp, scuba divers should look very closely among the fronds to find the golden brown Kelp Perch at depths less than 30 m (100 ft). Either solitary or as a member of a small group, each one nibbles at the many tiny animals living on and among the lush golden-brown algae.

COMMENTS: Known to be a "cleaner fish," the bold Kelp Perch may fastidiously pick external parasites from the bodies of larger fish; these "clients" even obligingly erect their fins and remain motionless while being relieved of their annoyances.

Kelp-harvesting machines incidentally capture considerable numbers of this commercially unwanted species in California.

Shiner Perch

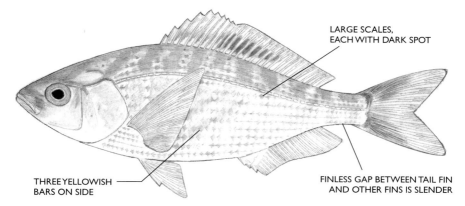

LARGE SCALES, EACH WITH DARK SPOT

THREE YELLOWISH BARS ON SIDE

FINLESS GAP BETWEEN TAIL FIN AND OTHER FINS IS SLENDER

SPECIES: *Cymatogaster aggregata*
OTHER COMMON NAMES: shiner seaperch, shiner surfperch, seven eleven perch, yellow shiner, shiner, seven eleven, pogy
MAXIMUM RECORDED SIZE: 20.3 cm (8 in)
DISTRIBUTION: Northern Baja California, Mexico, to southeastern Alaska
HABITAT: Scuba divers should explore shallow, seaweed-choked bays or around pilings during spring and summer to find the abundant schooling Shiner Perch while it engages in breeding behaviour. The very aggressive, temporarily black males swim rapidly in a bouncing fashion around the females to attract their attention. Ultimately approaching from below and behind, these eager males copulate with the females. At night, look for Shiner Perch in the beam of your underwater flashlight as they huddle against the sandy bottom.

B. Dark adult male.

C. Charlie Gibbs photograph

In summer, schools of Shiner Perch swarm in shallow areas. Beachcombers can look for them around pilings, under floats or even in large tidepools.

COMMENTS: The easily caught Shiner Perch is a very popular summer quarry for children who fish from wharves. At this time it swarms in shallow, sandy-bottomed bays. Attach marine worms, mussels, snails, shrimp, or clams to tiny hooks and look for a school of Shiner Perch swimming just below the surface.

While not actively sought by commercial fishermen, the common Shiner Perch nonetheless shows up abundantly in shrimp trawl nets.

THE **SEA CHUBS** (Family Kyphosidae)

Halfmoon

Medialuna californiensis
A common southern California resident, the Halfmoon has been documented as far north as Vancouver Island, British Columbia, primarily during El Niño years. This fish has a half-moon-shaped tail. It reaches a maximum length of 48 cm (19 in).

Daniel W. Gotshall photograph

THE **TILEFISHES** (Family Malacanthidae)

Ocean Whitefish

Caulolatilus princeps
A single specimen taken off Vancouver Island and documented in 1969 represents the most northerly record for the Ocean Whitefish. Notice the long continuous dorsal fin and "monochrome" colouration. This species' maximum recorded length is currently listed as 102 cm (40 in). It is a warm-water species and therefore its appearance in local waters is usually concurrent with El Niño-like warm-water events.

Daniel W. Gotshall photograph

THE **DRUMS AND CROAKERS** (Family Sciaenidae)

White Croaker

Genyonemus lineatus
Southern Vancouver Island, British Columbia, is the documented northern record for the White Croaker, a species common along the California coast that moves north during warm-water events such as El Niño. This fish has a very deeply notched single dorsal fin and prefers inshore locales with soft bottoms. A maximum length of 41 cm (16.3 in) is recorded.

Daniel W. Gotshall photograph

White Seabass

Astractoscion nobilis
The White Seabass is a rare summertime interloper within coastal Pacific Northwest waters—verified as far north as southeast Alaska. In southern California, this species schools at shallow depths. A long second dorsal fin and projecting lower jaw are distinctive for the White Seabass. It grows to a length of 155 cm (61 in).

Mark Conlin photograph

THE **MEDUSAFISHES** (Family Centrolophidae)

Medusafish

Icichthys lockingtoni
As its name suggests, the name Medusafish relates to the fact that it hides within the tentacles of several species of large jellies (jellyfishes) that drift along with Pacific Northwest currents. A very flaccid fish, it has been recorded as far north as the Aleutian Island chain, Alaska. The Medusafish typically appears in nearshore Pacific Northwest waters during El Niño warm-water events. It grows to as long as 46 cm (18.5 in).

Danny Kent photograph

THE **BUTTERFISHES** (Family Stromateidae)

Pacific Pompano

Peprilus simillimus
Juvenile Pacific Pompano usually huddle with large jellies (jellyfishes) or under flotsam, while adults school closer to the bottom. Although mostly found in Mexico and southern California, this species has been recorded as far north as the Queen Charlotte Islands, northern British Columbia. Its appearance is typically related to El Niño-type events. It grows to a length of 28 cm (11 in).

Chuck Tribolet photograph

THE **RAGFISHES** (Family Icosteidae)

Ragfish

Icosteus aenigmaticus
The only species in this family of fishes, the Ragfish usually lives in deep water and is termed a bathypelagic species. However, this fish is often found shallower as a juvenile. It is only an occasional Pacific Northwest visitor, usually during warm-water events such as El Niño. A very limp, flabby body supported by a cartilaginous skeleton is distinctive. The Ragfish reaches a recorded maximum length of 2.1 m (7 ft).

Danny Kent photograph

THE **POMFRETS** (Family Bramidae)

Pacific Pomfret

Brama japonica
An abundant summer inhabitant of offshore waters, the Pacific Pomfret only infrequently appears inshore. Waters south of the Aleutian Island chain represent the northern known boundary of its distribution. The blunt head with a distinctively arched profile is the helpful aid for identification. It grows to a length of 61 cm (24 in).

Andy Lamb photograph

THE **OPAHS** (Family Lamprididae)

Opah

Lampris guttatus
The distinctive Opah is distributed worldwide in warm and mild seas but wanders as far north as the Gulf of Alaska along North America's Pacific coast. It dwells primarily in the open ocean and reaches a maximum known length of 186 cm (73.2 in).

Michael Maia Mincarone photograph

THE **MOLAS** (Family Molidae)

Ocean Sunfish

Mola mola

A somewhat regular visitor to the Pacific Northwest during summer, the strange looking Ocean Sunfish may even wander into the protected waters of Puget Sound, Washington, and the Strait of Georgia, British Columbia. The Gulf of Alaska (during an El Niño summer) is the northernmost documented record for this species. It grows to a length of 4 m (13.1 ft).

A., B. Marc Chamberlain photographs

THE **ARMORHEADS** (Family Pentacerotidae)

North Pacific Armorhead

Pseudopentaceros wheeleri

Distinguished by its head being encased by exposed bones, this species dwells very far from shore. Specimens were caught by personnel during the years that weather ships were patrolling Ocean Station Papa at approximately 960 km (600 mi) off the British Columbia coast. It attains a maximum recorded length of 54 cm (21.2 in).

Dr. Pierre Dow photograph

THE **GOBIES** (Family Gobiidae)

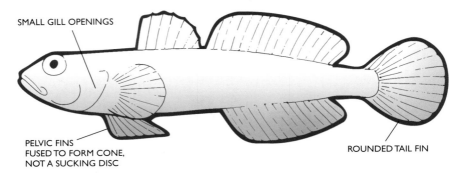

SMALL GILL OPENINGS

PELVIC FINS
FUSED TO FORM CONE,
NOT A SUCKING DISC

ROUNDED TAIL FIN

The largest family of marine fishes, the very successful gobies or Gobiidae contains as many as 2,000 known living species. Most gobies thrive in the warm waters of tropical latitudes, particularly in the Indo-Pacific, the Mediterranean and the Caribbean.

While most live in shallow to moderately deep coastal marine habitats, a few exceptional species live in brackish or even freshwater haunts. Sandy, silty bays and tidal flats are prime territory for most gobiids, but numerous others colonize rocky, more solid substrates.

Active, bottom-dwelling (benthic) creatures, the abundant gobies, few of which attain a length greater than 15 cm (6 in), swim in short bursts punctuated by frequent, often brief, rest stops. They rest on the bottom, their length supported by their pectoral fins and by their distinctive cone-shaped pelvic fins at the front and tail fins at the back. Certain gobiids actively burrow in the sand or mud, creating tunnels to shelter themselves from predators, while other resourceful species seek out the existing burrows of worms, shrimp and crabs, often establishing very special relationships with these invertebrate "tunnel mates."

Generally, people eat only the large species, such as the gargantuan Sleeper Goby of 61 cm (24 in), but the Russians use an unusually small goby—called *bichki*— as a preserve in tomato sauce and Philippine natives make the minute larvae of others into a fish paste.

The world's smallest fish is a tiny gobiid that lives in the Philippines and is no longer than 11 mm (0.4 in).

Blackeye Goby

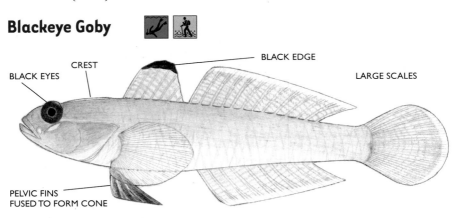

BLACK EYES

CREST

BLACK EDGE

LARGE SCALES

PELVIC FINS
FUSED TO FORM CONE

SPECIES: *Rhinogobiops nicholsii.* Formerly *Coryphopterus nicholsi*
OTHER COMMON NAMES: crested goby, large-scaled goby, bluespot goby
MAXIMUM RECORDED SIZE: 15 cm (6 in)
DISTRIBUTION: Central Baja California, Mexico, to southeastern Alaska
HABITAT: By flaring its gill covers and raising its bright fins, the aggressive Blackeye Goby often boldly challenges the scuba diver.

A very infrequent tidepool hostage, the Blackeye Goby often lives in shallow water where some rock is present. Dockside observers may view this short, robust fish resting on the bottom near natural or man-made cover.

COMMENTS: During the April to October breeding season, the mature and more aggressive than normal male claims a crevice, often removing excess sand or silt. Later he lures any ripe female into this den by erecting all his fins, and repeatedly rising just off the bottom to pause in mid-water briefly before settling back to the sea floor. Once inside the den, the transitory female deposits up to 1,700 minute pink eggs and then the male tenaciously remains to guard them.

C. Nocturnal colouration.
Bernard P. Hanby photograph

Bay Goby

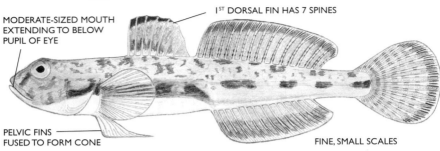

MODERATE-SIZED MOUTH
EXTENDING TO BELOW
PUPIL OF EYE

1ST DORSAL FIN HAS 7 SPINES

PELVIC FINS
FUSED TO FORM CONE

FINE, SMALL SCALES

SPECIES: *Lepidogobius lepidus*

OTHER COMMON NAMES: finescale goby, fine-scale goby

MAXIMUM RECORDED SIZE: 10 cm (4 in)

DISTRIBUTION: Central Baja California, Mexico, to southeastern Alaska

HABITAT: Almost transparent, the light-grey Bay Goby is seldom obvious to even the few divers who explore its typical muddy or silty, level-bottom habitat. Even if noticed, this quick little creature warily swims across the easily stirred-up bottom then often retreats down a tiny hole in the silt, just before the diver gets a good look. The resourceful Bay Goby often shares a burrow with a worm, a geoduck, or a mud shrimp that has excavated the hole.

Observant beach strollers sometimes notice the Bay Goby resting on the sand or among the sea lettuce or eelgrass growing in tidal flats and estuaries. The shallow-dwelling Bay Goby also lives on silty bottoms, under floats or around pilings.

COMMENTS: Found to depths of 201 m (660 ft), the small Bay Goby is undoubtedly prey for many of the commercially important flounders and is consequently of indirect importance to at least some fisheries.

A. Bernard P. Hanby photograph

Arrow Goby

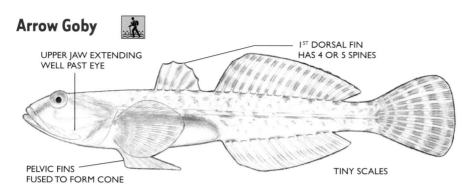

UPPER JAW EXTENDING
WELL PAST EYE

1ST DORSAL FIN
HAS 4 OR 5 SPINES

PELVIC FINS
FUSED TO FORM CONE

TINY SCALES

SPECIES: *Clevelandia ios*

MAXIMUM RECORDED SIZE: 6.4 cm (2.5 in)

DISTRIBUTION: Baja California, Mexico to central British Columbia

HABITAT: The light grey, almost transparent Arrow Goby flourishes along gently sloping muddy tidal flats and adjacent tidepools or lagoons. Beachcombers should look closely along shallow mud flats for the tiny ghost-like Arrow Goby. It usually darts away before disappearing down nearby clam, shrimp or worm burrows.

COMMENTS: An interesting, mutually beneficial relationship, known as symbiosis, exists between this active fish and the creatures that excavate the burrows; for example, the slender Arrow Goby consumes scraps of food left by the feeding shrimp and thereby keeps the shared lodging clean.

In times of danger when kingfishers, terns, Pacific Staghorn Sculpins or Whitespotted Greenlings are on the prowl, the wary Arrow Goby may bury itself using rapid movements of its fins, gill covers and body. Bright summer sun may warm its shallow habitat and heavy winter rains often dilute the surrounding salt water. The stress of such sudden salinity/temperature changes on a frequent basis could be a restrictive factor in its life span. Despite this, this hardy creature can possibly live two or three years.

THE **RONQUILS** (Family Bathymasteridae)

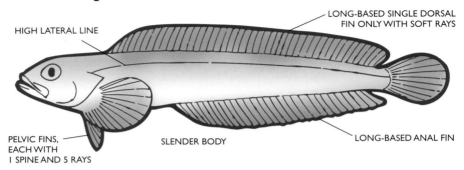

LONG-BASED SINGLE DORSAL FIN ONLY WITH SOFT RAYS

HIGH LATERAL LINE

PELVIC FINS, EACH WITH 1 SPINE AND 5 RAYS

SLENDER BODY

LONG-BASED ANAL FIN

The ronquils and searchers comprise the tiny family known scientifically as the Bathymasteridae. It contains seven living species that reside only within the cool, temperate waters of the North Pacific. All bathymasterids are strictly marine fishes that live at shallow to moderate depths along coastal regions and often establish dens where rocky outcroppings meet sandy or muddy substrates. They never grow longer than 30 cm (12 in).

Collections indicate that the Smallmouth Ronquil, *Bathymaster leurolepis,* is a northern species that has only been documented once south of the Gulf of Alaska and therefore is not included in this guide.

Northern Ronquil

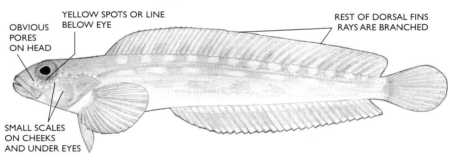

YELLOW SPOTS OR LINE BELOW EYE

OBVIOUS PORES ON HEAD

REST OF DORSAL FINS RAYS ARE BRANCHED

SMALL SCALES ON CHEEKS AND UNDER EYES

SPECIES: *Ronquilus jordani*
OTHER COMMON NAMES: ronquil
MAXIMUM RECORDED SIZE: 20 cm (8 in)
DISTRIBUTION: Southern California coast to the Aleutian Island chain and the Bering Sea, Alaska

A

B. Nocturnal colouration.   *C. Juvenile.*

HABITAT: Divers should search along silty or sandy substrates near adjacent rock formations, flat rocky bottoms, or other shelter, including cans, jars and rubber tires, for the active Northern Ronquil. It is almost never trapped in tidepools.

COMMENTS: During February and March the anal fin of the mature Northern Ronquil male becomes bright blue and yellow and his head develops some dark purple blotches. Enticed by this colouration and his courtship displays, a co-operative gravid female deposits adhesive amber-coloured eggs, usually upon the underside of a flat rock where the male fertilizes them.

Alaskan Ronquil

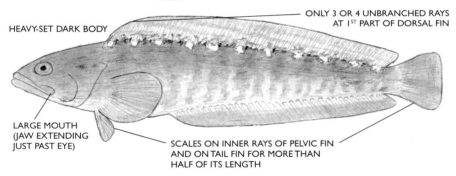

ONLY 3 OR 4 UNBRANCHED RAYS AT 1ST PART OF DORSAL FIN

HEAVY-SET DARK BODY

LARGE MOUTH (JAW EXTENDING JUST PAST EYE)

SCALES ON INNER RAYS OF PELVIC FIN AND ON TAIL FIN FOR MORE THAN HALF OF ITS LENGTH

SPECIES: *Bathymaster caeruleofasciatus*
OTHER COMMON NAMES: bluefin searcher
MAXIMUM RECORDED SIZE: 30 cm (12 in)
DISTRIBUTION: Northern British Columbia to the Commander Islands and Aleutian Island chain, Alaska

A. Bernard P. Hanby photograph

B. Juvenile.
Conor McCracken photograph
C. Female.
Debbie Maas photograph

HABITAT: Subtidal rubble and boulder fields provide prime habitat for this shelter-seeking species. When approached by a diver, the Alaskan Ronquil usually quickly retreats into a crevice or cavern, only to re-emerge and boldly confront the visitor. Such peek-a-boo antics provide an underwater photographer with both opportunity and challenge.

Only very occasionally might an observant beachcomber find an Alaskan Ronquil lurking in a tidepool.

COMMENTS: Like many bottom-dwelling marine species, the Alaskan Ronquil shows colour variation between juvenile and adult, as well as between mature male and female. The accompanying photographs illustrate this phenomenon.

Searcher

Bathymaster signatus

This ronquil is most common in Alaskan waters but has been recorded as far south as Washington State. Divers might see it as shallow as 25 m (80 ft) while an angler could incidentally catch one while bottom-fishing. The Searcher, noteworthy for the black blotch at the front of its dorsal fin, attains a length of 38 cm (15.2 in).

Jan Haaga photograph

THE **KELP BLENNIES** (Family Clinidae)

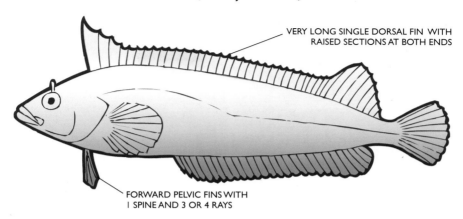

VERY LONG SINGLE DORSAL FIN WITH
RAISED SECTIONS AT BOTH ENDS

FORWARD PELVIC FINS WITH
1 SPINE AND 3 OR 4 RAYS

The Clinidae is a moderate-sized group containing approximately 70 recognized living species of kelpfishes, klipfishes, kelp blennies and scaled blennies. The cool temperate waters of both the northern and southern hemispheres shelter these small, secretive animals. The various and variable clinids live strictly in the marine environment. Most species are shallow, coastal denizens that constantly huddle among rocks encrusted with colourful seaweeds and invertebrate animals.

Masters of camouflage, the attractively marked clinids may alter their colour, both pattern and intensity, in order to obscure their body shapes and to blend in exactly with their underwater surroundings. This ability is advantageous when wandering from one distinctive background to another. Their alterable camouflage not only conceals them from predators, but it also gives an advantage to clinids lurking motionless in wait for their own prey.

Striped Kelpfish

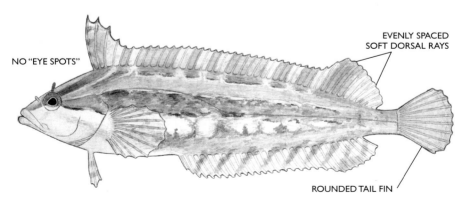

EVENLY SPACED
SOFT DORSAL RAYS

NO "EYE SPOTS"

ROUNDED TAIL FIN

SPECIES: *Gibbonsia metzi*
OTHER COMMON NAMES: striped kelp-fish
MAXIMUM RECORDED SIZE: 24 cm (9.5 in)
DISTRIBUTION: Northern Baja California, Mexico, to Vancouver Island, British Columbia

HABITAT: An adventurous diver daring to explore surf-swept rocky shallows of the exposed Pacific shore might easily drift by the well-camouflaged Striped Kelpfish. Noticing them in the thick seaweed is a challenge. On a calm day, carefully search large tidepools and adjacent waters at depths to 9 m (30 feet).

Beachcombers should search carefully along the algae-choked shallows or in tidepools for the chance to see the secretive, seldom-seen Striped Kelpfish. To catch them, try thrusting a long-handled, fine-meshed dip-net through large kelps and other seaweeds where young specimens most often reside. After your interaction, please be a good environmental steward and release any captives back to their habitat.

COMMENTS: Hatched in spring, tiny, transparent Striped Kelpfish larvae live in surface waters before becoming miniature adults and settling out into their permanent rocky-bottom habitat.

Crevice Kelpfish

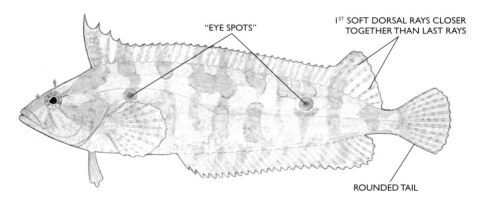

"EYE SPOTS"

1ST SOFT DORSAL RAYS CLOSER TOGETHER THAN LAST RAYS

ROUNDED TAIL

SPECIES: *Gibbonsia montereyensis*
OTHER COMMON NAMES: Incorrect: spotted kelpfish
MAXIMUM RECORDED SIZE: 11 cm (4.5 in)
DISTRIBUTION: Northern Baja California, Mexico, to Vancouver Island, southern British Columbia
HABITAT: Theoretically, divers could encounter the shallow-dwelling Crevice Kelpfish from the intertidal zone to a depth of 37 m (120 ft). Sightings are very rare though, because this often stationary creature changes its colour to blend with any background it rests upon.

The secretive Crevice Kelpfish lurks along seaweed-choked, rocky shores directly exposed to oceanic waves and is difficult for beachcombers to observe (see below).

COMMENTS: To find the Crevice Kelpfish, special techniques are necessary. If a number of keen, active beachcombers are available, plan ahead and try a "tidepool bail." A number of sturdy buckets and waders for participants are required. Using a chain gang approach, a reasonable sized tidepool can be emptied before the tide comes back in. A crevice kelpfish or two may be exposed. After watching and studying the various creatures, return them carefully so others might enjoy them too; the returning water will fill the empty tidepool and rejuvenate all temporarily exposed animals.

Giant Kelpfish

Heterostichus rostratus

Many references list British Columbia as the northern range limit for the Giant Kelpfish—a species most common along the Californian coast. While this unspecific citation may be correct, it could also be the result of confusion with the other two Pacific Northwest kelpfishes featured previously. The Giant Kelpfish is distinguished by a forked tail and large, slightly upturned mouth.

The potential warming of Pacific Northwest shores via climate change may result in new sightings of the Giant Kelpfish. Perhaps a camera-toting diver will be fortunate enough to verify such an event with an image. It reaches a maximum length of 61 cm (24 in).

THE **PRICKLEBACKS** (Family Stichaeidae)

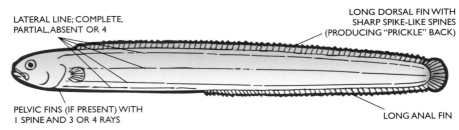

LATERAL LINE; COMPLETE, PARTIAL, ABSENT OR 4

LONG DORSAL FIN WITH SHARP SPIKE-LIKE SPINES (PRODUCING "PRICKLE" BACK)

PELVIC FINS (IF PRESENT) WITH 1 SPINE AND 3 OR 4 RAYS

LONG ANAL FIN

The pricklebacks, cockscombs, warbonnets, shannies and eelblennies total 54 recognizable living species and form the moderate-sized family scientifically termed the Stichaeidae. The vast North Pacific Ocean is where most of these live, but a few species flourish in the Arctic and North Atlantic.

All are purely marine creatures that live on the bottom. However, some pricklebacks reside in shallow, intertidal habitats, and still others colonize rocky, weedy cliff faces or gently sloping muddy sea floors. Some others prefer deep, silty locales.

The Y-prickleback, *Lumpenopsis hypochromis*, a small species with "Y"-shaped marks on its sides and spots along its dorsal fin, dwells in reasonably shallow waters but is, for inexplicable reasons, hardly ever seen.

Longsnout Prickleback

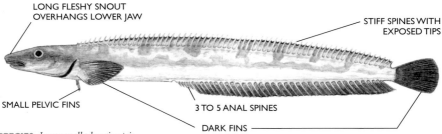

LONG FLESHY SNOUT OVERHANGS LOWER JAW

STIFF SPINES WITH EXPOSED TIPS

SMALL PELVIC FINS

3 TO 5 ANAL SPINES

DARK FINS

SPECIES: *Lumpenella longirostris*
MAXIMUM RECORDED SIZE: 41.7 cm (16.4 in)
DISTRIBUTION: Southern British Columbia to the Bering Sea and the Aleutian Island chain, Alaska
HABITAT: A depth of 92 m (300 ft) is the shallowest record for the Longsnout Prickleback. Consequently, members of the technical diving community, with their deep searching capacity, represent the best source of observations for this poorly known fish.

COMMENTS: This rarely collected prickleback primarily lives as an adult at depths of over 140 m (462 ft)—greater than any other member of its family. It infrequently appears as a bycatch from shrimp-trawling activities. Scientific samplings of surface plankton show that tiny, transparent Longsnout Prickleback larvae swim for the first few weeks of life at the surface where they feed upon tiny shrimp-like animals.

Whitebarred Prickleback

SERIES OF WHITE VERTICAL BARS

LARGE BLUNTLY
ROUNDED TAIL FIN

SPECIES: *Poroclinus rothrocki*
OTHER COMMON NAMES: white-barred blenny
MAXIMUM RECORDED SIZE: 25 cm (10 in)
DISTRIBUTION: Southern California to the Aleutian Island chain and the Bering Sea coast of Alaska
HABITAT: While making dives deeper than 46 m (150 ft), the observant diver might spot the pinkish Whitebarred Prickleback stretched out and resting upon flat, sandy bottoms. Technical divers probably have a better opportunity to observe this slender, easily overlooked creature.
COMMENTS: The light-coloured Whitebarred Prickleback is sometimes swept up in fine-meshed shrimp trawl nets towed over soft substrates at depths down to 128 m (422 ft). Of no economic value, like many other small marine fishes this bottom-dweller has an indirect, indeterminable value as forage for large, economically significant groundfishes.

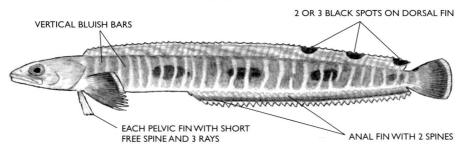

Bluebarred Prickleback

VERTICAL BLUISH BARS

2 OR 3 BLACK SPOTS ON DORSAL FIN

EACH PELVIC FIN WITH SHORT
FREE SPINE AND 3 RAYS

ANAL FIN WITH 2 SPINES

SPECIES: *Plectobranchus evides*
OTHER COMMON NAMES: black-and-white prickleback
MAXIMUM RECORDED SIZE: 13.5 cm (5.5 in)
DISTRIBUTION: Southern California to central British Columbia
HABITAT: The bluebarred prickleback lives upon sandy or muddy bottoms to 274 m (900 ft) where it feeds upon a variety of small invertebrate animals.

A. Rhoda Green photograph

COMMENTS: Inclusion of the seldom recorded Bluebarred Prickleback as a featured species highlights the great value of amateur participation in fish-watching activities. Fortunately in this instance, the skilled observers were able to successfully document the sighting with the photographs that appear in this section.

While on an evening dive at Potlatch Park, Hood Canal, Washington, Rhoda Green noticed the pictured (A)

B. Ryan Silbernagel photograph

Bluebarred Prickleback resting on the bottom, at a depth between 8 and 12 m (25 and 40 ft). An experienced observer from Renton, Washington, she recognized immediately that this specimen was a significant find and took a few photographs.

Later, after some research, Rhoda was able to identify the species. As a veteran participant of Project REEF (Reef Environmental Education Foundation), she has been able to share this experience with many other fish-watching enthusiasts. Fellow REEF diver Ryan Silbernagel has also found and photographed more Bluebarred Pricklebacks in the same general area. One of his images also appears above (B).

Snake Prickleback

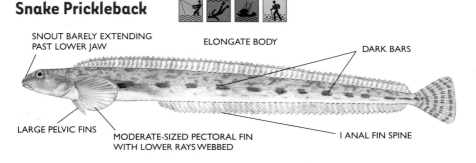

SNOUT BARELY EXTENDING PAST LOWER JAW

ELONGATE BODY

DARK BARS

LARGE PELVIC FINS

MODERATE-SIZED PECTORAL FIN WITH LOWER RAYS WEBBED

I ANAL FIN SPINE

SPECIES: *Lumpenus sagitta*

OTHER COMMON NAMES: Pacific snake prickleback, Pacific snakeblenny, eel-blenny

MAXIMUM RECORDED SIZE: 51 cm (20 in)

DISTRIBUTION: Northern California to the Aleutian Island chain, the Bering Sea coast of Alaska and the Sea of Japan

HABITAT: A sandy or muddy bottom inhabitant, the seasonally abundant Snake Prickleback migrates into shallow coves and inlets during summer and early autumn. By day it is wary and quickly darts off at even a

cautious diver's approach, but at night the beam of an underwater flashlight seems to mesmerize or "freeze" the creature and facilitates a close look. Unlike many other pricklebacks and gunnels that coil their bodies, this light-grey species stretches out, often straight as an arrow.

If the water is clear enough, pier-side naturalists may notice the ghostly and motionless Snake Prickleback on sandy or muddy bottoms.

COMMENTS: During summer, bottom-fishermen—particularly those seeking the various flounders over sandy or silty substrates and those fishing from jetties and piers constructed over flat-bottomed, shallow bays—often unintentionally hook the Snake Prickleback.

Shrimp trawlers commonly catch the unwanted Snake Prickleback as an incidental in shallow summer tows. It is recorded as deep as 425 m (1,394 ft).

Daubed Shanny

Leptoclinus maculatus

Primarily a species found in Arctic and Alaskan seas, the Daubed Shanny has been documented from as far south as northern Washington. It is very similar to the Snake Prickleback, but has the lower five or six rays of each pectoral fin exerted (extended beyond the fin membrane). This fish grows to a length of 20 cm (8 in).

Marc Chamberlain photograph

Slender Eelblenny

Lumpenus fabricii

Another species found in Arctic seas that circle the world, the Slender Eelblenny is similar to the Snake Prickleback, but with its irregular brown markings located well onto its lower sides. This prickleback is recorded as far south as southeastern Alaska, within depths that provide for interaction with recreational fishermen and sport divers. A maximum length of 36.5 cm (14.4 in) is documented for the Slender Eelblenny.

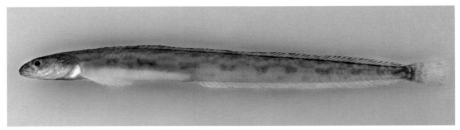

Dr. Catherine Mecklenburg photograph

Stout Eelblenny

Anisarchus medius

The Stout Eelblenny is classified as a circumpolar species, meaning it dwells in Arctic seas around the globe. In the Pacific Northwest, this elongate fish, with its anal and dorsal fins connected to the tail, has been documented only as far south as southeastern Alaska. The Stout Eelblenny often lives at depths shallow enough for recreational divers, anglers and commercial net fishermen to encounter it. It grows to a length of 18 cm (7.2 in).

Dr. Catherine Mecklenburg photograph

Arctic Shanny

Stichaeus punctatus

Although the Arctic Shanny is recorded as far south as northern British Columbia, its centre of abundance is Alaska and farther north. An active species with four to seven dark spots along its dorsal fin, it dwells upon both rocky and sandy substrates in shallow accessible depths. Recreational divers in southeastern Alaska routinely observe the Arctic Shanny, a prickleback that reaches a maximum recorded length of 22 cm (8.8 in).

Nate Chambers photograph/Alaska Sealife Center

Ribbon Prickleback

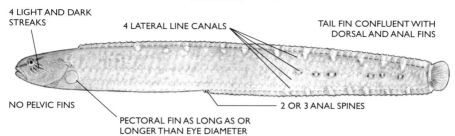

4 LIGHT AND DARK STREAKS

4 LATERAL LINE CANALS

TAIL FIN CONFLUENT WITH DORSAL AND ANAL FINS

NO PELVIC FINS

2 OR 3 ANAL SPINES

PECTORAL FIN AS LONG AS OR LONGER THAN EYE DIAMETER

SPECIES: *Phytichthys chirus*

OTHER COMMON NAMES: belted blenny

MAXIMUM RECORDED SIZE: 21.1 cm (8.4 in)

DISTRIBUTION: Southern California to the Aleutian Island chain and the Bering Sea coast of Alaska

HABITAT: Along the open and surf-swept shores, divers should search very closely in large, seaweed-choked tidepools or in rocky crevices at depths less than 13 m (43 ft) to discover this elusive species. Pay particular attention to the bases of large kelps where their wide, gnarled holdfasts attach to rock; the Ribbon Prickleback often entwines itself around those holdfasts and its colour may match any of its surroundings.

While strolling along cobble or rubble-strewn beaches during an extreme low tide, try carefully overturning some manageable rocks. The elusive Ribbon Prickleback may be found beneath, squirming for shelter. After your interaction please gently replace the rocks as found.

COMMENTS: Surrounding seaweeds such as red and green algae, in addition to numerous shrimp-like creatures, make up most of the primarily herbivorous Ribbon Prickleback's diet.

B. Bernard P. Hanby photograph

Rock Prickleback

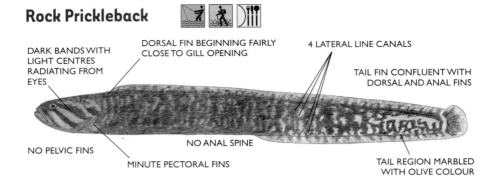

DARK BANDS WITH LIGHT CENTRES RADIATING FROM EYES

DORSAL FIN BEGINNING FAIRLY CLOSE TO GILL OPENING

4 LATERAL LINE CANALS

TAIL FIN CONFLUENT WITH DORSAL AND ANAL FINS

NO PELVIC FINS

MINUTE PECTORAL FINS

NO ANAL SPINE

TAIL REGION MARBLED WITH OLIVE COLOUR

SPECIES: *Xiphister mucosus*

OTHER COMMON NAMES: rock blenny, rock-eel. Incorrect: black eel

MAXIMUM RECORDED SIZE: 58 cm (23 in)

DISTRIBUTION: Southern California to the Gulf of Alaska

HABITAT: The mottled yellow-and-black Rock Prickleback hides under rocks located in weedy shallows, primarily those along open coast areas. Also look very carefully in large tidepools; it may often just poke its head out from beneath shelter. At a moderate to very low tide, turn over seaweed-covered rocks when looking for the abundant Rock Prickleback, a species that can live up to at least 11 years.

COMMENTS: In California, where actual bag limits exist, recreational harvesters surprisingly take the robust Rock Prickleback.

The Rock Prickleback breeds during winter, when gravid females deposit eggs in spherical clusters beneath rocks.

Skeletal remains of the Rock Prickleback found within ancient middens verify that coastal First Nations people have eaten it for centuries.

Black Prickleback

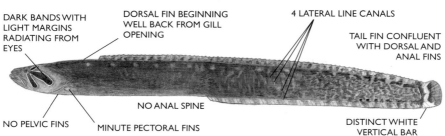

DARK BANDS WITH
LIGHT MARGINS
RADIATING FROM
EYES

DORSAL FIN BEGINNING
WELL BACK FROM GILL
OPENING

4 LATERAL LINE CANALS

TAIL FIN CONFLUENT
WITH DORSAL AND
ANAL FINS

NO ANAL SPINE

NO PELVIC FINS

MINUTE PECTORAL FINS

DISTINCT WHITE
VERTICAL BAR

SPECIES: *Xiphister atropurpureus*

OTHER COMMON NAMES: black blenny

MAXIMUM RECORDED SIZE: 32.7 cm (12.9 in)

DISTRIBUTION: Northern Baja California, Mexico, to the Gulf of Alaska

HABITAT: Sharp-eyed divers exploring shallow rocky shorelines at depths less than 9 m (30 ft) may notice the Black Prickleback lurking beneath loose stones, often with just its head exposed. Upon overturning a sheltering rock for a closer look, you may notice only a blur as it speeds off to hide beneath other nearby stones. Always replace overturned habitat.

Curious beachcombers, particularly those who brave harsh, exposed Pacific shores, may readily discover the Black Prickleback by turning over rocks in the low intertidal zone.

COMMENTS: A very tolerant species, this adaptable fish can survive low salinities created by heavy rainfalls. During the late winter and spring period, mated pairs of Black Pricklebacks breed under boulders on rocky or shell substrates. After spawning, the male parent remains for up to three weeks and guards the spherical egg mass. The tiny larvae hatch and initially swim at the surface of the water.

The herbivorous Black Prickleback feeds upon seaweeds but may also incidentally take in tiny shrimp-like creatures too. It, in turn, is food for creatures such as the Wandering Garter Snake, mink and raccoon.

High Cockscomb

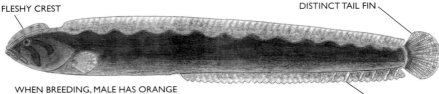

FLESHY CREST

DISTINCT TAIL FIN

WHEN BREEDING, MALE HAS ORANGE
PECTORAL AND ANAL FINS

36 TO 40 ANAL SPINES

FEMALE OFTEN HAS WHITE SPECKLES ON HEAD

SPECIES: *Anoplarchus purpurescens*

OTHER COMMON NAMES: cockscomb prickleback, crested blenny, cockscomb

MAXIMUM RECORDED SIZE: 20 cm (7.8 in)

DISTRIBUTION: Southern California to the Aleutian Island chain and Pribilof Islands, Alaska

HABITAT: A very common inhabitant of water less than 3 m (10 ft), along rocky shorelines or in tidepools, the shy High Cockscomb usually huddles under rocks, and rarely is exposed completely. Most often, only the head of this fish is visible, peering from beneath a boulder or from inside a bottle. If this shelter is overturned, the variably coloured High Cockscomb rapidly scurries away and wriggles underneath another object. This secretive fish often spends some time in the open at night; be particularly vigilant on a nocturnal dive.

Shore-strolling naturalists overturning rocks intertidally nearly always find the writhing High Cockscomb in great abundance. Always replace rocks and specimens as found.

COMMENTS: Many predators, including the Wandering Garter Snake, forage for the plentiful High Cockscomb at low tide. During late winter, a female High Cockscomb may coil around her cluster of whitish eggs and fan them with her caudal and pectoral fins until they hatch.

Bernard P. Hanby photograph

Slender Cockscomb

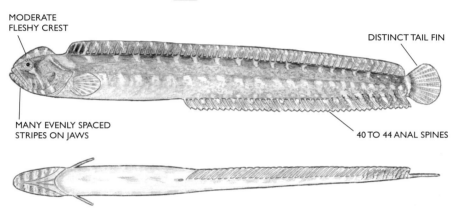

MODERATE
FLESHY CREST

DISTINCT TAIL FIN

MANY EVENLY SPACED
STRIPES ON JAWS

40 TO 44 ANAL SPINES

SPECIES: *Anoplarchus insignis*
OTHER COMMON NAMES: cockscomb
MAXIMUM RECORDED SIZE: 12 cm (4.8 in)
DISTRIBUTION: Northern California to the Aleutian Island chain and Bering Sea, Alaska
HABITAT: While the secretive Slender Cockscomb's rocky habitat is from the surface to a diveable 30 m
(100 ft), even an observant aquanaut seldom knowingly confronts this species because it rarely leaves the
security of its rocky crevice. Even if diligently looking under movable rocks, the diver may have only a
fleeting glimpse of this elusive creature because it quickly scoots away and hides under adjacent cover. Areas
with strong currents seem to suit the shelter-seeking Slender Cockscomb best, but little is known about
many of its other tendencies.

South of Alaska, the difficult-to-distinguish Slender Cockscomb lives at depths inaccessible to intertidal
explorers or dockside naturalists.
COMMENTS: Researchers at the Vancouver Aquarium have bred the Slender Cockscomb in captivity.

Mosshead Warbonnet

DENSE CLUSTER OF EVENLY SIZED THREAD-LIKE
PROJECTIONS (CIRRI) ON TOP OF HEAD ONTO
1ST DORSAL SPINE

12 OR 13 EVENLY SPACED "EYE SPOTS" OR
BARS (MOST NOTICEABLE ON ADULTS)

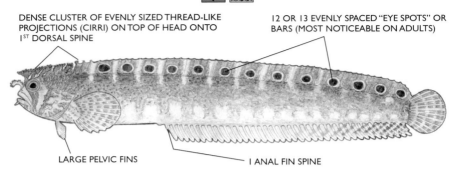

LARGE PELVIC FINS

1 ANAL FIN SPINE

SPECIES: *Chirolophis nugator*

OTHER COMMON NAMES: mosshead prickleback, ornamented blenny

MAXIMUM RECORDED SIZE: 15 cm (6 in)

DISTRIBUTION: Southern California to the Aleutian Island chain, Alaska

HABITAT: A popular species with underwater photographers, the attractive Mosshead Warbonnet lives in various shallow-water locales. It often hides inside empty shells or holes along rocky shores at depths of less than 20 m (66 ft). If diving around pilings, piers or jetties, pay particular attention to the interiors of discarded bottles, cans or pipes, for often only the fluffy-topped head of this creature pokes out. Once disturbed, the skittish Mosshead Warbonnet frequently streaks off to more secure surroundings nearby.

At the very lowest of tides, the curious beachcomber may occasionally find dark Mosshead Warbonnets living among crevices in rocky tidepools. Because this fish is secretive and difficult to see, the best way to study it is by first bailing out the water, exposing the trapped specimens and then placing them in a bucket of that same seawater. After enjoying a close encounter, return any captives to their refilling tidepool.

COMMENTS: Beach cleanups stimulate well-intentioned folks to remove discarded man-made debris from the marine environment. However, such material, particularly if "well-aged," is often home to many creatures, including the Mosshead Warbonnet.

NOTE: The Pearly Prickleback, *Bryozoichthys marjorius,* is a northern species that, because of its "headdress," resembles the two warbonnets featured in this guide. It is a pearly white fish with a pair of long bushy cirri joined at their bases and protruding between the eyes. It lives in deep water as far south as southern British Columbia and is not included in this guide.

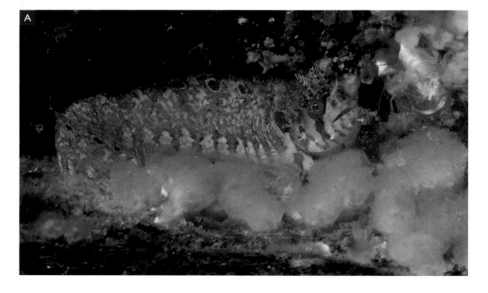

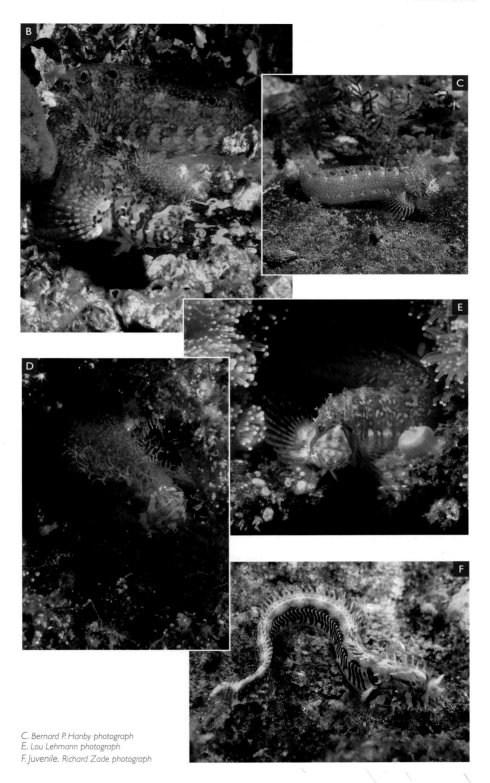

C. *Bernard P. Hanby photograph*
E. *Lou Lehmann photograph*
F. *Juvenile. Richard Zade photograph*

Decorated Warbonnet

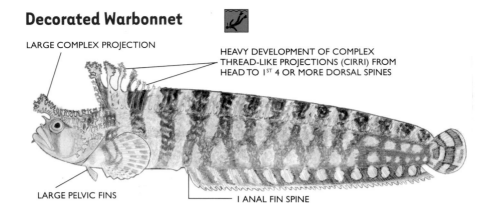

LARGE COMPLEX PROJECTION

HEAVY DEVELOPMENT OF COMPLEX THREAD-LIKE PROJECTIONS (CIRRI) FROM HEAD TO 1ST 4 OR MORE DORSAL SPINES

LARGE PELVIC FINS

I ANAL FIN SPINE

SPECIES: *Chirolophis decoratus*

OTHER COMMON NAMES: decorated prickleback

MAXIMUM RECORDED SIZE: 42 cm (16.5 in)

DISTRIBUTION: Northern California to the Aleutian Island chain and the Bering Sea coast of Alaska

HABITAT: An often-photographed species living at depths between 15 and 91 m (50 and 300 ft), the wary Decorated Warbonnet usually looks out at the diver from among rocky crevices, or the openings of large, hollow sponges. Many photographers enjoy framing its distinctively bushy head against the dark, hollow recesses of its lair. Stalk it carefully though, for once startled the camera-shy Decorated Warbonnet will often retreat deeper inside its shelter or bolt away to another site; do not try to follow this reluctant subject but rather wander along and hope to find another undisturbed model.

COMMENTS: Shrimp and their kin, with which the lurking Decorated Warbonnet frequently shares its cave or sponge, comprise the bulk of the diet for this brownish fish.

NOTE: The Matcheek Warbonnet, *Chirolophis tarsodes*, has dense, bushy cirri on the sides and top of its head as well as extending onto the first few dorsal fin spines. A close look-alike to the Decorated Warbonnet, this species has been recorded as far south as northern British Columbia. It is not included here due to its rare status in the Pacific Northwest.

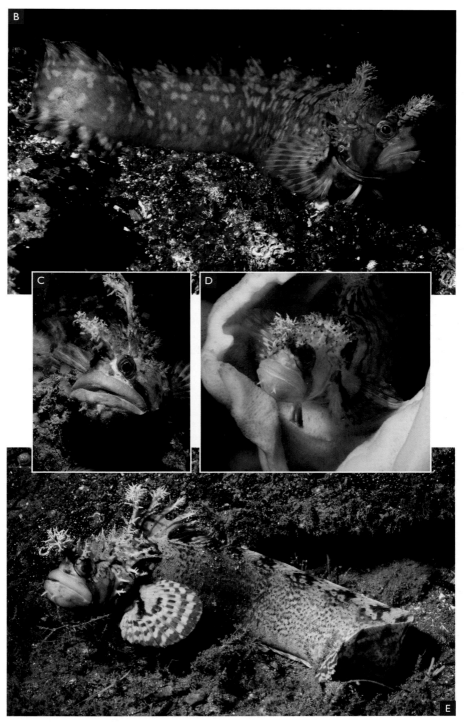

B. Neil McDaniel photograph
D. Juvenile.

THE **GUNNELS** (Family Pholidae)

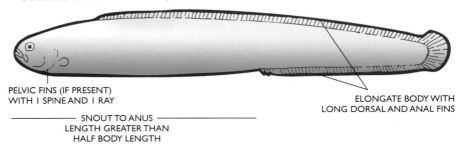

LATERAL LINE: PARTIAL OR ABSENT, BUT NOT MORE THAN ONE

PELVIC FINS (IF PRESENT)
WITH I SPINE AND I RAY

ELONGATE BODY WITH
LONG DORSAL AND ANAL FINS

SNOUT TO ANUS
LENGTH GREATER THAN
HALF BODY LENGTH

A small family of fishes, the gunnels, or Pholidae, contains about 15 recognizable species, most of which live in temperate North Pacific waters while the others inhabit the cool or cold waters of the Arctic or North Atlantic oceans. The pholids are strictly shallow marine and even intertidal denizens. The elongate, usually colourful gunnels frequent various bottom habitats such as marine algae, rocky crevices, pilings and sunken logs where they find secure shelter.

Close contemporary relatives include the very similar pricklebacks and wrymouths—elongate fishes with very lengthy dorsal and anal fins at least partially supported by spines. No gunnels grow to more than a modest 46 cm (18 in). The various species attract no commercial exploitation and only a few photographers, professional aquarists and scientists actively pursue them.

Rockweed Gunnel

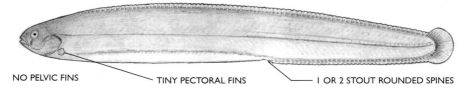

BRIGHT UNIFORM COLOUR

NO PELVIC FINS

TINY PECTORAL FINS

I OR 2 STOUT ROUNDED SPINES

SPECIES: *Apodichthys fucorum.* Formerly *Xererpes fucorum*
OTHER COMMON NAMES: rockweed blenny, fucus blenny
MAXIMUM RECORDED SIZE: 23 cm (9 in)
DISTRIBUTION: Central Baja California, Mexico, to northern British Columbia
HABITAT: The intertidal habitat of the brightly coloured Rockweed Gunnel allows snorkelers the opportunity to find it in the often murky shallows at high tide or in large, weedy tidepools at low tide. Carefully and deliberately search among

A

seaweeds, particularly through the dense, finger-like rockweed (*Fucus*) growing on craggy rock.

At low tide, inspect closely any exposed algae growing on solid rock or overturn weed-covered stones to spot the elusive Rockweed Gunnel. Once located, though, it quickly slithers away. Please return all creatures and habitat as originally found.

COMMENTS: Like other gunnels, the Rockweed Gunnel is a prime target for shorebirds, such as the Great Blue Heron, that carefully stalk prey.

Penpoint Gunnel

ROW OF DARK SPOTS
(SOMETIMES)

NO PELVIC
FINS

DARK BAR
BELOW EYE

MODERATE-SIZED PECTORAL FINS

LARGE PEN NIB-SHAPED SPINE

SPECIES: *Apodichthys flavidus*

OTHER COMMON NAMES: pen-point blenny

MAXIMUM RECORDED SIZE: 46 cm (18 in)

DISTRIBUTION: Southern California to the Gulf of Alaska

HABITAT: Search through seaweeds at low tide in summer for the Penpoint Gunnel. Locating it is easy, but capturing one is exasperatingly difficult. In late winter, overturn rocks exposed by low tide and perhaps find a Penpoint Gunnel coiled about a mass of whitish-coloured eggs. Think conservation: carefully replace their shelter.

COMMENTS: During summer, the Penpoint Gunnel lives among the seaweed and associated rocks. Watch for a green specimen among sea lettuce or eelgrass; the wine-red individual huddling in red algae, and the golden brown one amid the various kelps. Each colour is directly related to diet. When the transparent larval Penpoint Gunnel settles to the bottom to feed, its individual colour gradually begins to appear, although it may alter with a change in diet. In winter, most of these sheltering seaweeds die and this gunnel retreats under the rocks or finds other shelter.

D. Bernard P. Hanby photograph
E. Richard Zade photograph
F. Newly settled juvenile. Richard Zade photograph

Crescent Gunnel

SERIES OF CRESCENT-SHAPED MARKINGS

MINUTE PELVIC FINS EACH WITH I SPINE AND I RAY

SPECIES: *Pholis laeta*
OTHER COMMON NAMES: bracketed blenny
MAXIMUM RECORDED SIZE: 25 cm (10 in)
DISTRIBUTION: Northern California to the Aleutian Island chain, Alaska
HABITAT: Shallow subtidal and intertidal locales with various marine algae and eelgrass are prime territory for the distinctively marked Crescent Gunnel. It often hides under small boulders or in crevices along massive underwater rock formations. This wary creature also often lives around old breakwaters and wharves where it may colonize bottles, jars, cans, tires, or pots and stare curiously back at you. Particularly at night, a slow-moving and careful diver who does not stir up the bottom may find, in the open, an undisturbed, easily photographed Crescent Gunnel.

Especially in summer, the variously coloured Crescent Gunnel inhabits seaweed-filled tidepools or lives under encrusted rocks left exposed in the low intertidal zone. A fine-meshed dip-net is a most helpful tool for capturing this squirming, difficult-to-handle gunnel; scoop steadily along the bottom and among the seaweeds. Dockside naturalists may find the common Crescent Gunnel entwined among the seaweeds or around the marine animals that encrust pilings and the undersides of floats.

COMMENTS: Many bottom-dwelling marine fishes, like the Crescent Gunnel, feature several colour phases that match their surroundings. This phenomenon is known as "cryptic colouration."

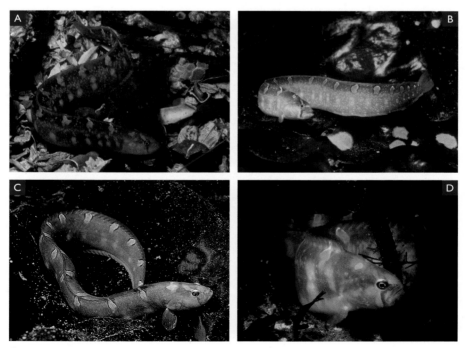

C. Bernard P. Hanby photograph

Saddleback Gunnel

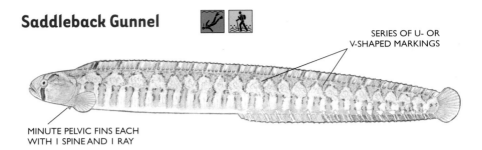

SERIES OF U- OR
V-SHAPED MARKINGS

MINUTE PELVIC FINS EACH
WITH 1 SPINE AND 1 RAY

SPECIES: *Pholis ornata*
OTHER COMMON NAMES: saddled blenny
MAXIMUM RECORDED SIZE: 30 cm (12 in)
DISTRIBUTION: Central California to southern British Columbia; Korea
HABITAT: Shallow muddy substrates densely covered with eelgrass beds are prime locales for divers in search of the secretive Saddleback Gunnel. Although this colourful fish exists at depths down to 37 m (120 ft), aquanauts looking for it are most successful when investigating depths much less than half that figure. The often olive and orange Saddleback Gunnel entwines itself and hides among various seaweeds or beneath scattered rocks or sunken logs.

During summer, beachcombers may find the slippery Saddleback Gunnel under intertidal rocks or lurking in muddy-bottomed, eelgrass-filled tidepools. Seaweeds hanging from wharves and pilings also shelter this cover-seeking animal, but the dockside naturalist must be a patient observer to notice it.

COMMENTS: In late winter and early spring, a mature female Saddleback Gunnel deposits her eggs in a small, round cluster, while a male fertilizes them, and then both parents remain as guards. In this era of genetic research, Korean specimens of the Saddleback Gunnel represent a possible species verification study.

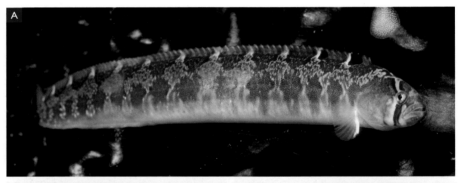

C. Bernard P. Hanby photograph
E. Wendy Carey photograph

Red Gunnel

Pholis schultzi

Inclusion of this species is definitely a work in progress. The Red Gunnel, *Pholis schultzi*, was officially described in 1933. It has been documented from Diablo Cove, on the central California coast, to Rivers Inlet, on the central coast of British Columbia. Specimens are recorded from the intertidal zone to a depth of about 18 m (60 ft).

Aside from 44 specimens taken near Rivers Inlet in 1976, very few Red Gunnels have been collected, definitively identified and documented. Indeed, the authors and their various contacts have yet to find one.

While preparing this edition, we literally stumbled upon the accompanying photograph while enjoying Richard Zade's website *www.underthesound.com*. He encountered the featured specimen at Hudson Point, near Port Townsend, Washington, in July 2008.

The fish pictured did not look like any of the other gunnels commonly found in the Pacific Northwest and immediately we wondered if it was a Red Gunnel. After consulting several ichthyologists, this possibility appears the most viable.

Without a specimen to examine, though, a definitive identification is impossible. We present this notation and hope eventually to see this work in progress completed.

Richard Zade photograph

Longfin Gunnel

SERIES OF LIGHT MARKS WITH
SMALL DARK SPOTS INCLUDED

87 TO 90 DORSAL FIN SPINES

SMALL PELVIC FINS

SPECIES: *Pholis clemensi*

MAXIMUM RECORDED SIZE: 13 cm (5 in)

DISTRIBUTION: Northern California to southeastern Alaska and very likely the Gulf of Alaska

HABITAT: The slender (compared to the others) Longfin Gunnel may stare back intently from among branched leafy red algae or adjacent rocks. In shallow to moderately deep reef locales, divers should concentrate on depths below 8 m (27 ft) and watch closely for undisturbed specimens that may be resting on exposed rock formations before they quickly retreat to sheltering crevices.

The delicate-looking Longfin Gunnel may live in intertidal zones and perhaps knowledgeable beachcombers will verify this.

COMMENTS: Most Pacific Northwest fish species were described in the 19th century; amazingly, the common Longfin Gunnel was only discovered in 1964. Much of its biology, ecology and distribution remain unknown. Personal observations by co-author Phil Edgell suggest that after witnessing a Longfin Gunnel resting inside the mouth of a lingcod, this gunnel is a "cleaner" species.

D. Longfin Gunnel with Lingcod.

E. Female with eggs. Bernard P. Hanby photograph

THE **WOLFFISHES** (Family Anarhichadidae)

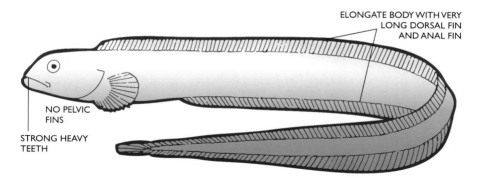

ELONGATE BODY WITH VERY LONG DORSAL FIN AND ANAL FIN

NO PELVIC FINS

STRONG HEAVY TEETH

This small family of robust fishes, scientifically called the Anarhichadidae, is actually made up of two distinguishable subgroups. Most of the family is collectively called "wolffishes" and this subgroup contains five known living species of the North Atlantic and Arctic oceans. All members of this subgroup are only moderately elongate, stubby creatures with distinct, large tail fins. Living in the Pacific Northwest, the Wolf-eel, with its very long, slender body that tapers into a pointed, barely discernible tail fin, is, by itself, the other subgroup of the wolffish family.

The northern Bering Wolffish, *Anarhichas orientalis,* has been recorded only as far south as the Gulf of Alaska and therefore is not featured in this guide.

Wolf-eel

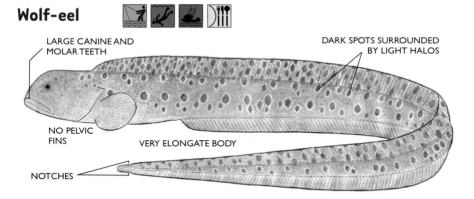

LARGE CANINE AND MOLAR TEETH

DARK SPOTS SURROUNDED BY LIGHT HALOS

NO PELVIC FINS

VERY ELONGATE BODY

NOTCHES

SPECIES: *Anarrhichthys ocellatus*
MAXIMUM RECORDED SIZE: 2.4 m (8 ft) and 18.4 kg (40.6 lb)
DISTRIBUTION: Northern Baja California, Mexico, to the Aleutian Island chain, Alaska
HABITAT: A common inhabitant of the rocky reef and shoreline, the grey Wolf-eel most often lurks within a cave or crevice. A lucky aquanaut may notice a cavern-dwelling mated pair, the whitish, puffy-headed male being easily distinguished from the darker female. Underwater photographers have delighted in locating this tameable species and often, by gentle hand feeding, coax it from its lair. Eventually such "buddies" readily swoop out, slowly and gracefully, to greet all approaching divers. Over-zealous divers sometimes deplete invertebrates, such as Red Sea Urchins, during such activities and as a consequence, this "taming process" is considered very poor form. Much antagonism occurs between the few spear-fishermen who take Wolf-eels and the majority of recreational divers and underwater photographers who simply enjoy peaceful interactions.

COMMENTS: A large Wolf-eel sometimes becomes an unwanted catch for a surprised angler. Exercise extreme caution because its heavy, teeth-laden jaws could inflict a severe and dangerous wound!

Various commercial operations occasionally capture Wolf-eels from depths to 226 m (740 ft). However, since 2001, the fishery has been closed and any bycatch must be released.

Historically, some coastal First Nations people prized the Wolf-eel as the "doctorfish" or *mukah*. Only the medicine man ate the flesh; it was thought to enhance his healing powers.

A. Left to right: Male, female, egg mass.
C. Juvenile.
E., F. Sub-adults.

THE **WRYMOUTHS** (Family Cryptacanthodidae)

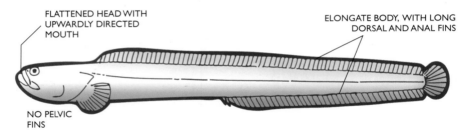

FLATTENED HEAD WITH
UPWARDLY DIRECTED
MOUTH

ELONGATE BODY, WITH LONG
DORSAL AND ANAL FINS

NO PELVIC
FINS

A very small family of fishes, the Cryptacanthodidae contains only four recognizable living species. Some of them grow up to 123 cm (49 in). They are exclusive residents of sandy, muddy or silty bottoms in intertidal, shallow and moderately deep habitats in the North Atlantic and North Pacific oceans.

These elongate, homely-looking and little-known fishes spend nearly all their time buried in the sea floor, often within extensive subterranean tunnels. Here they await prey or mates and avoid predators. The inactive cryptacanthodids only occasionally venture out to prowl slowly over the seascape.

Giant Wrymouth

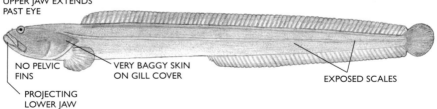

UPPER JAW EXTENDS
PAST EYE

NO PELVIC
FINS

VERY BAGGY SKIN
ON GILL COVER

EXPOSED SCALES

PROJECTING
LOWER JAW

SPECIES: *Cryptacanthodes giganteus.* Formerly *Delolepis gigantea*
OTHER COMMON NAMES: potatohead. Incorrect: congo eel, buckskin eel
MAXIMUM RECORDED SIZE: 123 cm (49 in)
DISTRIBUTION: Northern California to Unalaska Island in the Aleutian Island chain and southeastern Bering Sea, Alaska

A

HABITAT: Not only does the homely Giant Wrymouth usually prefer soft, level bottoms below 20 m (66 ft)—a zone seldom explored by most sport divers—this sandy-coloured creature also spends much of its time buried, with only its large gnarled head sometimes exposed to the diver.

Occasionally the unusual Giant Wrymouth ventures into shallow silty bays where it may even become trapped in a tidepool. Attracted by surface lights, this distinctive species is sometimes observed at night by dock strollers or boat passengers.

B. Neil McDaniel photograph

COMMENTS: Commercial trawlers and longliners infrequently catch the unmarketable Giant Wrymouth. Surprised crab trappers or prawn potters periodically find it writhing awkwardly in their gear.

Dwarf Wrymouth

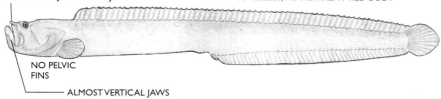

UPPER JAW NOT EXTENDING PAST EYE

NOSTRIL PROJECTS OVER JAW

SCALELESS, TRANSPARENT RED BODY

NO PELVIC FINS

ALMOST VERTICAL JAWS

SPECIES: *Cryptacanthodes aleutensis.* Formerly *Lyconectes aleutensis*
OTHER COMMON NAMES: red devil
MAXIMUM RECORDED SIZE: 31 cm (12.4 in)
DISTRIBUTION: Northern California to Unalaska Island in the Aleutian Island chain and the southeastern Bering Sea, Alaska
HABITAT: Unfortunately unidentifiable by all but a few experts, transparent Dwarf Wrymouth larvae, which are less than 2.5 cm (1 in) long, attracted by dock lights, may swarm at the surface during late spring or early summer. The adults are much easier to identify.
COMMENTS: Like other wrymouths, this species creates a system of tunnels with numerous exits. In the northern parts of its geographic range, the beady-eyed Dwarf Wrymouth tends to live in shallower water than it does in the south—a phenomenon common for many bottom-fish species of North America's Pacific shores.

THE **QUILLFISHES** (Family Ptilichthyidae)

One of the tiniest families of fishes on this planet, the quillfish family contains but a single known species, which lives in the Pacific Northwest. A highly modified creature of which very little is known, the quillfish is most closely related to the various gunnels, pricklebacks and wolffishes.

Quillfish

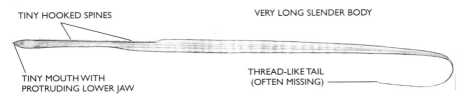

TINY HOOKED SPINES   VERY LONG SLENDER BODY

TINY MOUTH WITH PROTRUDING LOWER JAW

THREAD-LIKE TAIL (OFTEN MISSING)

SPECIES: *Ptilichthys goodei*
OTHER COMMON NAMES: quill-fish
MAXIMUM RECORDED SIZE: 39 cm (15.6 in)
DISTRIBUTION: Oregon to the Bering Sea coast of Alaska, through the Aleutian Island chain to the Okhotsk Sea and the Kuril Islands, Japan
HABITAT: Adults typically rest with their bodies in sinuous curves on soft, shallow substrates. Once disturbed, they slowly "snake away" at a speed easily maintained by divers.

Float-bound observers sometimes notice the thin, mirage-like Quillfish meandering slowly and gracefully at the surface. These sightings are of juveniles and occur at night, particularly in late spring or early summer. Such juveniles appear to be attracted to light beams shining into the sea.

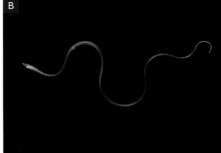

B. Juvenile.   *C. Bernard P. Hanby photograph*

THE **GRAVELDIVERS** (Family Scytalinidae)

Containing only a single known living species, the graveldivers, scientifically termed Scytalinidae, is therefore one of the tiniest families of fishes in the world. In spite of consisting of only one species, the unusual graveldivers are a very distinct group with numerous special anatomical and behavioural features, dictating that they rank as a family. Such single-species families are termed "monotypic."

Graveldiver

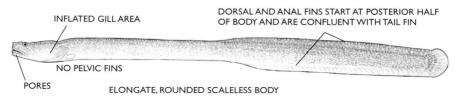

INFLATED GILL AREA

DORSAL AND ANAL FINS START AT POSTERIOR HALF OF BODY AND ARE CONFLUENT WITH TAIL FIN

NO PELVIC FINS

PORES

ELONGATE, ROUNDED SCALELESS BODY

SPECIES: *Scytalina cerdale*
OTHER COMMON NAMES: burrowing blenny
MAXIMUM RECORDED SIZE: 15 cm (6 in)
DISTRIBUTION: Central California coast to the Aleutian Island chain, Alaska
HABITAT: Beachcombers who stroll along pebbly, open coast beaches are the most likely to locate the secretive Graveldiver. Look for it at low tide along loose gravel beaches. Carefully dig into the small stones, either with a shovel or your hands, and watch very closely for these well-camouflaged creatures squirming deeper into the remaining gravel. Once specimens are located, work as a team: one person shovelling scoops of gravel into plastic basins or buckets while others sort through the partially filled containers for trapped Graveldivers. Please return these creatures to their home afterwards.
COMMENTS: Graveldivers are one of the most fascinating fish living in the Pacific Northwest—and one of the least studied.

THE **PROWFISHES** (Family Zaproridae)

There is only one known living species in this tiny family and it is found in the Pacific Northwest. But why does this family contain only one species? Ichthyologists (fish scientists) can only speculate about reasons. Perhaps others remain to be found in the world's oceans. For some reason, perhaps this family design is not a template for species success or "radiation." Other theories can be offered but a definitive answer is most elusive.

Prowfish

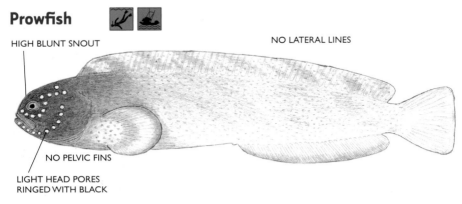

HIGH BLUNT SNOUT

NO LATERAL LINES

NO PELVIC FINS

LIGHT HEAD PORES
RINGED WITH BLACK

SPECIES: *Zaprora silenus*
MAXIMUM RECORDED SIZE: to 1 m (39 in) at least
DISTRIBUTION: Southern California to the Aleutian Island chain, Bering Sea and northern Japan
HABITAT: Recently, sport divers are accessing more remote, northern locales and noticing Prowfish during their explorations. In 2003, a group of research divers noticed numerous specimens while exploring the isolated Bowie Seamount off northern British Columbia. These Prowfish showed little fear and readily approached these lucky divers.
COMMENTS: Prowfish occasionally become an incidental catch for commercial line fishermen. Several of these specimens have been donated to public aquaria where they have adapted well to captivity, feeding on jellies (jellyfish) stuffed with shrimp. The secretive Prowfish apparently hides in caves and crevices, making its sighting unusual.

A. Terry Whalen photograph
B., C. Neil McDaniel photographs
D. Juvenile. Clinton Bauder photograph

THE **JACKS** (Family Carangidae)

Jack Mackerel

Trachurus symmetricus

Although caught as far north as the Gulf of Alaska, the Jack Mackerel is an infrequent summer visitor to the Pacific Northwest—mostly concurrent with El Niño-type warm-water events. This schooling species grows to a length of 81 cm (32 in) and is distinguished by a series of enlarged bony shields or scutes along each median lateral line.

Daniel W. Gotshall photograph

Yellowtail Jack

Seriola lalandi

The Yellowtail Jack is a very popular warm-water game fish that ventures north during El Niño years. Although reported as far north as the Gulf of Alaska, its occurrence is only verified as far north as northern British Columbia. This species attains a maximum length of 152 cm (5 ft). The Yellowtail Jack is distinguished by a dusky stripe that extends from its snout though each eye—a stripe that becomes more yellow as it extends to the tail.

Marc Chamberlain photograph

THE **MACKERELS** (Family Scombridae)

Pacific Chub Mackerel

Scomber japonicus

The Pacific Chub Mackerel sporadically invades the Pacific Northwest during El Niño years when it poses a considerable threat to herring and juvenile salmon—even pursuing them until they actually leave the water. This fish is distinguished by approximately 30 short, narrow dark bars that often slant slightly backward along each upper side. It usually forms large schools. The Gulf of Alaska is the current documented northern limit of its range. A length of 64 cm (25 in) is this species' recorded maximum.

Albacore

Thunnus alalunga

The Albacore is often taken offshore by recreational and commercial fishermen in summer, when it ventures in schools into Pacific Northwest waters. It seldom swims near shore but is recorded as far north as the Gulf of Alaska. Its maximum recorded length is 139 cm (54.8 in). A pair of very long, sabre-shaped pectoral fins distinguish the Albacore.

Pacific Bonito

Sarda chiliensis

A sporadic summer visitor to the Pacific Northwest, the Pacific Bonito is documented as far north as the Gulf of Alaska. Notice the distinct, slightly oblique dark striping along each upper side. A schooling fish that may move inshore, this species' maximum recorded length is 102 cm (40 in).

Daniel W. Gotshall photograph

Skipjack Tuna

Katsuwonus pelamis

The schooling Skipjack Tuna has been documented as far north as southeast Alaska but must be considered an unlikely summer sighting in the Pacific Northwest. The wavy bands of colour appearing along each lower side are distinctive for this species. Its maximum recorded length is 110 cm (44 in).

Ed Roberts, California Fish and Game photograph

THE **DOLPHINFISHES** (Family Coryphaenidae)

Dolphinfish

Coryphaena hippurus
A reported but rare visitor as far north as Washington, the Dolphinfish is distinctive and easily recognized by its very long dorsal fin. Sport or commercial fishermen harvesting offshore during El Niño years are the folks most likely to encounter this beautiful fish. The maximum recorded length is 2.1 m (83 in).

Dolphinfish with lure. David Fleetham photograph

THE **TRIGGERFISHES** (Family Balistidae)

Finescale Triggerfish

Balistes polylepis
Not only is the Finescale Triggerfish a very rare sighting in the Pacific Northwest, it seldom occurs even in California. The centre of abundance for this species is the warm water between Mexico and Chile, though it is known to venture north as far as Southeastern Alaska during El Niño years. A maximum length of 76 cm (30 in) is documented. A very small gill slit on each side of a distinctively shaped body renders this fish readily identifiable in the Pacific Northwest.

THE **TEMPERATE BASSES**[*] (Family Percichthyidae)

Striped Bass

Morone saxitilis
Originally introduced in 1879 to San Francisco Bay, California, from the Atlantic coast of North America, the Striped Bass has successfully established itself as a west coast game fish. Southern Vancouver Island, British Columbia, rates as the documented northern extent of its Pacific distribution. Distinguished by six to nine longitudinal stripes along each side, this species grows to a length of 120 cm (4 ft).

Daniel W. Gotshall photograph

THE **SEA BASSES AND GROUPERS** (Family Serranidae)

Kelp Bass

Paralabrax clathratus
The popular Kelp Bass primarily inhabits the inshore reefs of southern California. Very occasionally it invades Pacific Northwest waters as far north as southern Washington. White splotches on each upper side characterize this fish. This species attains a maximum recorded length of 72 cm (28.5 in).

Daniel W. Gotshall photograph

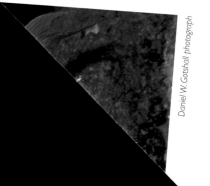

Daniel W. Gotshall photograph

ies of fishes and modified by a different adjective (including
operly modified by a different word (including Striped Bass
incorrectly used for numerous other fish, such as the Black

ROCKFISHES AND OTHER SCORPIONFISHES
(Family Scorpaenidae)

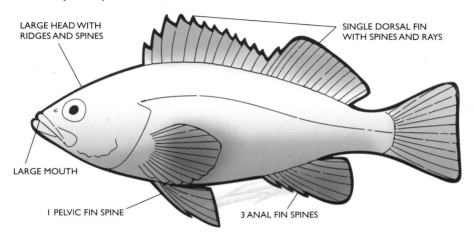

LARGE HEAD WITH
RIDGES AND SPINES

SINGLE DORSAL FIN
WITH SPINES AND RAYS

LARGE MOUTH

I PELVIC FIN SPINE

3 ANAL FIN SPINES

Historically, the family of 420 or so species composing the large worldwide family called Scorpaenidae (referred to as the scorpionfishes) contained the tropical stonefishes, scorpionfishes and lionfishes, as well as the North Pacific rockfishes and thornyheads. More recently, some scientists suggest rockfishes and thornyheads should be assigned their own family, the Sebastidae. Not wishing to become embroiled in this debate, the authors mention both options here and retain the more traditional one at this time.

"Scorpionfishes" is an excellent name because the spines of these creatures carry sacks of venom. The sharp, strong pelvic and anal fin spines of rockfishes and thornyheads may inject a mildly toxic fluid. Exercise caution when handling these fishes, for a jab from their fin spines may cause a throbbing and burning pain, swelling, and even a fever.

The strictly marine scorpaenids prefer shallow to moderately deep habitats and flourish particularly in tropical latitudes such as the Indo-Pacific. However, many of the Pacific Northwest rockfishes live in very deep water and are unlikely to be seen by most people. A number of the warm-water scorpionfishes are primarily motionless, huddling in crevices and crannies of coral reefs, whereas many rockfish species of the cold northern waters swim actively in rocky regions of the continental shelves or school well above the uneven bottom. The largest Northwest rockfishes rank as the giants of the scorpionfish family.

ENDANGERED ROCKFISH

Many rockfishes are very long lived (often attaining 80 years and more) and are quite slow to mature. Many species require at least 15 years to become reproductively active. Incredibly, the oldest, largest females produce the healthiest, most viable young. In addition, rockfish possess an air-filled swim bladder that expands and disables the fish as it is pulled to the surface after capture. This makes successful release back into the wild difficult.

Many rockfish species have now been exploited to dangerous levels. And because of the unique biology and ecology of rockfishes, rebuilding stocks is going to take a very long time.

While measures have been enacted, including closures of both commercial and sport fisheries, ineffective management on a species-by-species basis has been a case of "too little, too late." It is imperative that vital, holistic conservation action begin immediately. The many excuses for inaction offered by various levels of government, with the recent exception of California, are simply not acceptable. With each passing year, our living rockfish resource is being critically depleted. Even if efforts begin now, populations will require many decades to rebuild.

To achieve this goal, there is an overwhelming need to establish a coast-wide network of No-Take Marine Protected Areas. Essentially, these special places would correspond to terrestrial national park systems where all living things are protected from consumptive use. Please refer to the introduction for a more detailed discussion of this elegantly simple concept.

For a spectacular and detailed story about the magnificent rockfishes, *The Rockfishes of the Northeast Pacific,* by Milton S. Love, Mary Yoklavich and Lyman Thorsteinson, is a must read, cover to cover!

Copper Rockfish

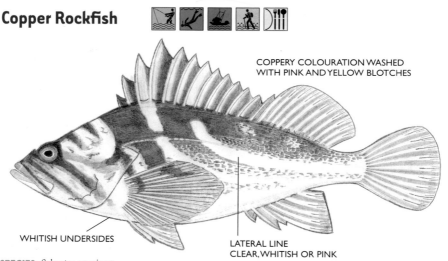

COPPERY COLOURATION WASHED
WITH PINK AND YELLOW BLOTCHES

WHITISH UNDERSIDES

LATERAL LINE
CLEAR, WHITISH OR PINK

SPECIES: *Sebastes caurinus*
OTHER COMMON NAMES: yellow-backed rockfish. Incorrect: white rock cod, rock cod
MAXIMUM RECORDED SIZE: 66 cm (26 in)

DISTRIBUTION: Central Baja California to the northern Gulf of Alaska
HABITAT: Look for juvenile Copper Rockfish loosely aggregated in shallow, weedy bays huddled among rocks or kelp beds, around wharves or even among the floating drift associated with summer tidelines. The non-schooling adult Copper Rockfish often rests propped by its fins on the bottom. While

A

primarily foraging near the bottom, this colourful fish will periodically rise into mid-water for such prey as herring, sand lance, anchovy and Shiner Seaperch. Scuba divers may see adult Copper Rockfish lurking around pilings and jetties or under floats. Tidepools often temporarily trap young specimens.

COMMENTS: Since the 1980s, Copper Rockfish have been heavily exploited by all consumptive users in the Pacific Northwest, particularly for the live rockfish market. Declining populations are now subject to much-needed catch restrictions and other conservation efforts.

Typical of most rockfish, when available, Copper Rockfish flesh is tasty, firm and flaky: excellent for fish and chips or for pan-frying as fillets. It also makes great sushi.

C. Juvenile.
Kent Forsen photograph
D. Intra-specific aggression between Copper Rockfish and Quillback Rockfish.
Tom Sheldon photograph

Quillback Rockfish

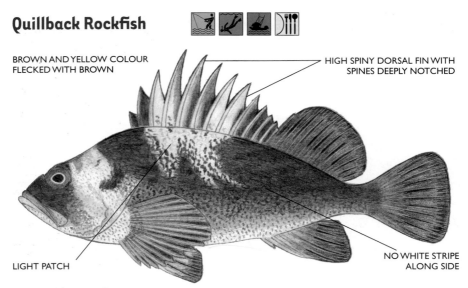

BROWN AND YELLOW COLOUR
FLECKED WITH BROWN

HIGH SPINY DORSAL FIN WITH
SPINES DEEPLY NOTCHED

LIGHT PATCH

NO WHITE STRIPE
ALONG SIDE

SPECIES: *Sebastes maliger*

OTHER COMMON NAMES: speckled rockfish, orange-spotted rockfish, yellow-backed rockfish. Incorrect: brown rockfish, gopher rock cod, rock cod

MAXIMUM RECORDED SIZE: 61 cm (24 in)

DISTRIBUTION: Southern California to the western Gulf of Alaska

HABITAT: The non-schooling Quillback Rockfish rests on the rocky bottom or hovers just above it, but never far from cover. Although barely recognizable, finely spotted juvenile Quillback Rockfish less than 2 cm (0.8 in) long frequently hide among the floating debris of summer tidelines. Scuba divers may find this species at all diveable depths—particularly below 15 m (50 ft). This photogenic species often poses artistically within large cloud sponges, chimney sponges or rocky caverns.

COMMENTS: The female Quillback Rockfish usually grows larger than the male. This species has been severely over-exploited and government agencies throughout the Pacific Northwest have introduced lower bag limits and designated areas closed to rockfish harvest. More drastic measures are still required to successfully rebuild stocks of this lethargic species. However, where available, Quillback Rockfish is good when deep-fried and delicious in nearly any recipe! Try it raw for sushi.

A

D. Juvenile.
Bernard P. Hanby
photograph
E. Juvenile.

Brown Rockfish

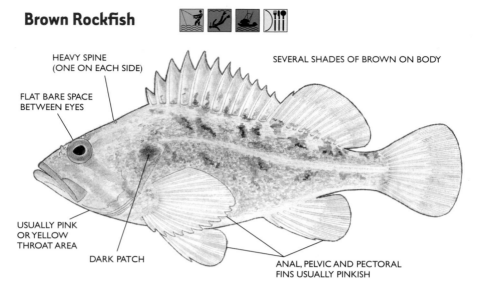

HEAVY SPINE
(ONE ON EACH SIDE)

SEVERAL SHADES OF BROWN ON BODY

FLAT BARE SPACE
BETWEEN EYES

USUALLY PINK
OR YELLOW
THROAT AREA

DARK PATCH

ANAL, PELVIC AND PECTORAL
FINS USUALLY PINKISH

SPECIES: *Sebastes auriculatus*

OTHER COMMON NAMES: bolina. Incorrect: brown rock cod, rock cod, chocolate bass

MAXIMUM RECORDED SIZE: 57 cm (22.4 in)

DISTRIBUTION: Central Baja California, Mexico, to northern Gulf of Alaska

HABITAT: One of the more sedentary rockfishes, this often curious fish lurks among sheltering rocks or around pilings, both easily visited by the scuba diver. A readily approachable creature, the Brown Rockfish is particularly noticeable in lower Puget Sound, Washington, and Stuart Channel in British Columbia's Gulf Islands. The underwater photographer finds this species, with its several beautiful brown tones, a worthy and approachable subject, particularly if the water is clear.

COMMENTS: Like many other rockfish, this species' numbers are much reduced from historical levels by consumptive users.

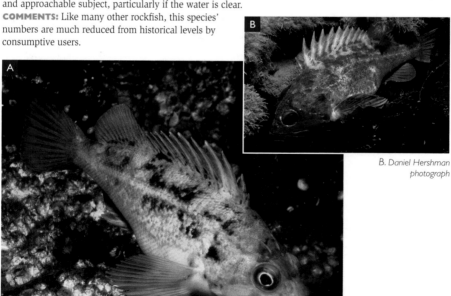

B. Daniel Hershman
photograph

Grass Rockfish

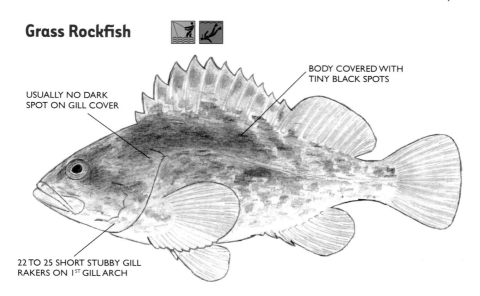

USUALLY NO DARK
SPOT ON GILL COVER

BODY COVERED WITH
TINY BLACK SPOTS

22 TO 25 SHORT STUBBY GILL
RAKERS ON 1ST GILL ARCH

SPECIES: *Sebastes rastrelliger*

MAXIMUM RECORDED SIZE: 57 cm (22.4 in)

DISTRIBUTION: Central Baja California to Vancouver Island in southern British Columbia

HABITAT: In the southern part of its range, the Grass Rockfish prefers rugged rocky reefs with an abundance of caves and crevices.

COMMENTS: The distribution of the Grass Rockfish was formerly thought to reach its northern extreme at central Oregon but two specimens were taken in recent years near Ucluelet on the west coast of Vancouver Island, British Columbia. A large specimen was beach-seined by collecting staff of the Vancouver Aquarium in 1970 and put on display in one of the large exhibits where it survived for some years. Unfortunately, upon

A. *Chris Grossman photograph*

its demise, the carcass was not preserved. This specimen was identified as a probable Grass Rockfish by the co-author, who was on aquarium staff at the time. In the spring of 2006, a tiny juvenile specimen, less than 2.5 cm (1 in) long, was taken on the same beach by aquarium staff. This individual has grown to a stage where it could be confirmed to be a Grass Rockfish by author and rockfish authority Dr. Milton Love. A photograph of it appears below (B).

In November, 2008, diver/photographer Darice Susan Dixon took the photo shown here (C) of a juvenile rockfish at Loman Beach Park, Seattle. Once again, Dr. Love was able to verify its identity as a Grass Rockfish, further confirming this species' presence north of its previously documented range.

B. Juvenile. *Danny Kent photograph*
C. Small juvenile. *Darice Susan Dixon photograph*

China Rockfish

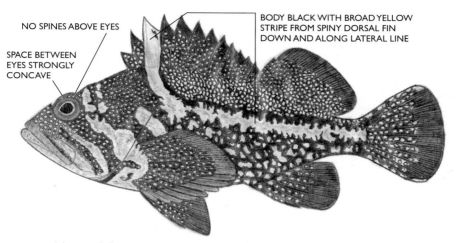

NO SPINES ABOVE EYES

SPACE BETWEEN
EYES STRONGLY
CONCAVE

BODY BLACK WITH BROAD YELLOW
STRIPE FROM SPINY DORSAL FIN
DOWN AND ALONG LATERAL LINE

SPECIES: *Sebastes nebulosus*
OTHER COMMON NAMES: yellowstriped rockfish, yellowstripe rockfish, yellow spotted rockfish, Chinese rockfish, yellow rockfish. Incorrect: black and yellow rockfish, gopher, China rockcod, rockcod, bass
MAXIMUM RECORDED SIZE: 45 cm (18 in)
DISTRIBUTION: Southern California to western Gulf of Alaska
HABITAT: While patrolling shallow, rocky shores or reefs directly exposed to Pacific surge, an aquanaut often finds the territorial and solitary China Rockfish. Curious and unafraid, this beautiful fish often boldly confronts and stares back at the diver, making a popular target for underwater photographers. Take advantage of its head-on pose for nicely framed photos, but bracket exposures to avoid disappointment.
COMMENTS: Formerly a common inhabitant of the outer coast, the distinctively coloured China Rockfish is most accessible to bottom-fishermen angling from boats. Baits such as squid, shrimp and small live fish, or even silvery jigs, at depths less than 25 m (80 ft), attract this fish. If one is hooked, be alert and hoist the fish toward the surface before this shelter-seeker rushes for cover and makes a line-snapping escape. Handle with

care and avoid its sharp and mildly venomous spines. When caught at shallow depths—less than 10 m (33 ft) —a specimen can often be released alive and successfully returned to its environment.

China Rockfish live no deeper than 130 m (427 ft) and are targeted by the live rockfish commercial hook and line fishery. Most of this catch was originally exported to the Orient where this attractive species is particularly prized. More recently, though, almost all of the Canadian catch is sold in domestic markets. Sadly, over-exploitation has resulted in many locales.

If it cannot be successfully released alive, the small China Rockfish's short fillets are worth pan-frying or deep-frying.

B. *Unusual colour variation. Danny Kent photograph*
C. *Unusual colour variation. Bernard P. Hanby photograph*
D. *Juvenile.*

Yellowtail Rockfish

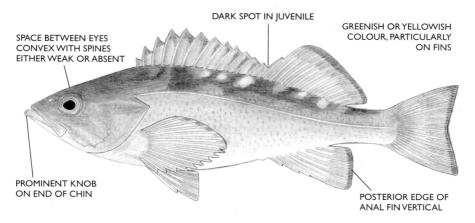

SPACE BETWEEN EYES
CONVEX WITH SPINES
EITHER WEAK OR ABSENT

DARK SPOT IN JUVENILE

GREENISH OR YELLOWISH
COLOUR, PARTICULARLY
ON FINS

PROMINENT KNOB
ON END OF CHIN

POSTERIOR EDGE OF
ANAL FIN VERTICAL

SPECIES: *Sebastes flavidus*

OTHER COMMON NAMES: yellow-tail rockfish, yellow-tail rock-fish. Incorrect: yellowtail rock cod, yellowtail rockcod, green snapper

MAXIMUM RECORDED SIZE: 66 cm (26 in)

DISTRIBUTION: Southern California to the Aleutian Island chain, Alaska

HABITAT: Often associating with other schooling rockfish species, the active Yellowtail Rockfish congregates in open water along steeply sloping shores or above rocky reefs. At other times it holes up amid the cracks and crevices of the sea floor. Excellent underwater photos of Yellowtail Rockfish against a dark background are possible if the water is clear.

Beachcombers should look for Yellowtail Rockfish either as juveniles swarming around floats and pilings or as adults splashing after prey at the surface.

COMMENTS: When congregating near the surface in large, loosely formed schools, scrappy Yellowtail Rockfish provide excellent sport for the light tackle angler who casts lures or still-fishes with bait. Trawling and longlining, at depths down to 549 m (1,801 ft), account for a significant commercial Yellowtail Rockfish catch, which is filleted, either fresh or frozen and sold with other rockfishes. It is facing ever increasing pressure from both commercial and recreational fishing sectors.

Like all rockfish, the Yellowtail is best when filleted and quickly chilled.

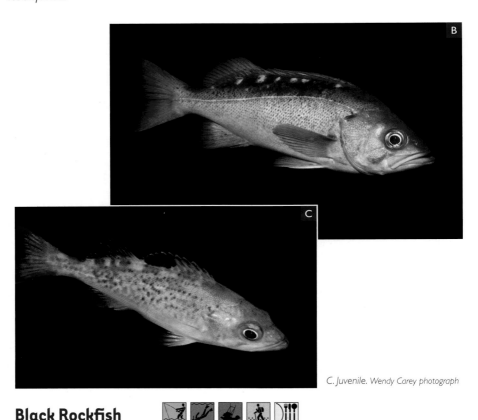

C. Juvenile. *Wendy Carey photograph*

Black Rockfish

GRAY-BLACK COLOUR

SPACE BETWEEN EYES
CONVEX WITH SPINES
EITHER WEAK OR ABSENT

DARK SPOT IN JUVENILE

LARGER
MOUTH

FINLESS GAP BETWEEN TAIL
FIN AND OTHER FINS DEEP

WEAK KNOB
ON END OF
CHIN

UPPER JAW EXTENDS
TO REAR OF EYE

POSTERIOR EDGE
OF ANAL FIN SLANTED
FORWARD

SPECIES: *Sebastes melanops*
OTHER COMMON NAMES: black rock-fish, bass rockfish. Incorrect: black bass, black seabass, black rock cod, black snapper, sea bass, bluefish
MAXIMUM RECORDED SIZE: 69 cm (27 in) and 5 kg (11 lb)
DISTRIBUTION: Southern California to the Aleutian Island chain, Alaska

HABITAT: The diver may see large Black Rockfish, often schooling together with other rockfish species, hovering in the green water above rocky substrate. However, solitary specimens may also huddle among nearby boulders and crevices. Underwater photographers may have trouble determining optimal exposures for this dark fish when "shooting" it against a dark, open-water background.

Easily viewed in summer by the shorebound naturalist, each young streamlined Black Rockfish (about 5 cm/2 in long), has a noticeable black spot on the dorsal fin. Watch for them swarming around wharves and pilings or becoming trapped in tidepools. Adults commonly "break water" when after prey.

B. Juveniles. *Sharon Jeffery photograph*

COMMENTS: One of the gamest of the rockfishes, the schooling Black Rockfish eagerly pursues artificial lures such as jigs, spoons, and even large flies, but may also take bait. Fish near the surface, over kelp-covered reefs, or along rocky shores to catch the largest specimens. Even at night under indirect artificial lighting, anglers may find small ravenous individuals difficult to avoid. Whether trolling or mooching, salmon seekers may take them incidentally as well.

The Black Rockfish comprises a variable part of the yearly commercial rockfish harvest, with quantities being handlined, longlined, or trawled at depths to 360 m (1,200 ft). Vital conservation must occur if future anglers are going to have access to a healthy Black Rockfish population. This species is excellent table fare.

Blue Rockfish

SPACE BETWEEN EYES
CONVEX WITH SPINES
EITHER WEAK OR ABSENT

SMALLISH
MOUTH

WEAK KNOB ON
END OF CHIN

DARK BANDS
ACROSS FOREHEAD

BLUISH-BLACK COLOUR

DARK SPOT IN JUVENILE

POSTERIOR EDGE OF
ANAL FIN SLANTED BACKWARD

SPECIES: *Sebastes mystinus.* Note that current scientific investigations suggest that this species may actually include more than one. See below.

OTHER COMMON NAMES: priestfish, priest-fish. Incorrect: black rockfish, black rockcod, black bass, blueperch, blue perch, bluefish

MAXIMUM RECORDED SIZE: 53 cm (21 in)

DISTRIBUTION: Northern Baja California, Mexico, to northern British Columbia

HABITAT: At first visible only as dark shapes shrouded in the greenish water overhead, the wary Blue Rockfish may eventually cruise nearer and nearer to the diver. Because it only occasionally cowers among boulders or cliff-face crevices, eager underwater photographers usually find it an "open water" challenge. Be patient and look for a school to swim with. Look among and just below lush kelp growths in less than 15 m (50 ft) to find the juvenile Blue Rockfish, often recognizable by its light blue body spotted with brick-red.

Along surf-swept outer coasts, receding tides very occasionally trap juvenile Blue Rockfish in seaweed-choked rocky pools accessible to adventurous beachcombers. Boaters may occasionally notice adults of this species leaping clear of the water while pursuing small fish.

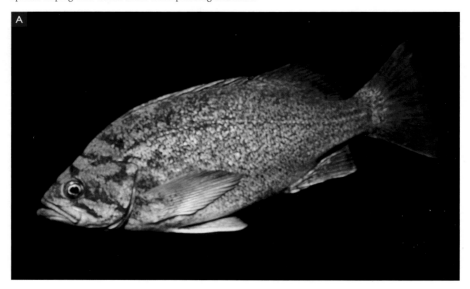

A

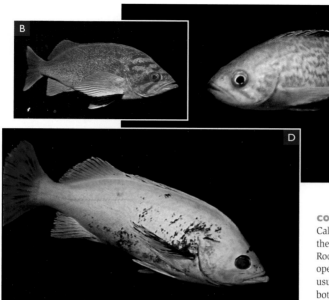

C. Juvenile.

COMMENTS: Particularly for Californian party-boat anglers, the active, schooling Blue Rockfish is a very important open coast gamefish that usually swims well off the bottom near kelp growth or over reefs. While spincasting near the surface is an enjoyable way to catch the Blue Rockfish,

B. Bernard P. Hanby photograph
D. Keith Clements photograph

still-fishing with small silvery fish or squid as bait may also be rewarding.

Californian hook-and-line fishermen extensively harvest Blue Rockfish, fillet it then generally sell it fresh, but trawlers in the north take it only in modest amounts and market it with other rockfishes.

Broiled, baked, pan-fried, deep-fried, boiled, barbecued, or even raw with soy sauce as sashimi, the firm Blue Rockfish tastes delicious.

Undetermined Rockfish

Sebastes sp.

In 2008, diver Keith Clements photographed this rockfish off Mushroom Rock, near Neah Bay, Washington, at a depth of about 15 m (50 ft). Keith suspected that this specimen was different from other Pacific Northwest rockfish he had seen during his dive. Upon viewing the image, we concurred.

While attempting to identify this mysterious rockfish, the trail led to Tom Laidig, a biologist with NOAA's (National Oceanic and Atmospheric Administration) Southwest Fisheries Center, California. Tom and his colleagues are currently studying the Blue Rockfish, *Sebastes mystinus*, and the possibility that it actually includes two species: the Blue-blotched Rockfish (the established one mentioned in publications) has a smaller mouth, blue blotches on the flanks and blue bars on the head, while the Blue-sided Rockfish has a larger mouth, appears more elongate, and does not have blue-blotched flanks but rather a more uniform colour and a more noticeable lateral line.

A. Keith Clements photograph

B. Janna Nichols photograph

Unfortunately, Tom's study has not produced a definitive result at the time this guide went to press. However, he tentatively identified the specimen illustrated by Keith's image as the "blue-sided" form.

Dark Dusky Rockfish

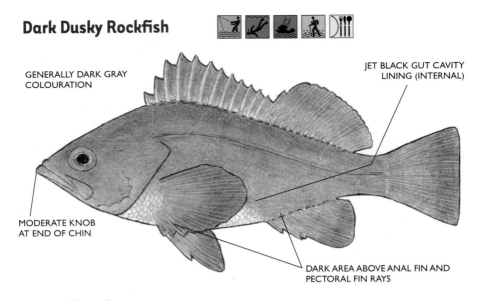

GENERALLY DARK GRAY
COLOURATION

JET BLACK GUT CAVITY
LINING (INTERNAL)

MODERATE KNOB
AT END OF CHIN

DARK AREA ABOVE ANAL FIN AND
PECTORAL FIN RAYS

SPECIES: *Sebastes ciliatus*

OTHER COMMON NAMES: dark rockfish. Incorrect: rock cod

MAXIMUM RECORDED SIZE: 47 cm (18.8 in)

DISTRIBUTION: Central coast of British Columbia to the Bering Sea, Alaska

HABITAT: The active Dark Dusky Rockfish usually hovers in loosely organized groups just above rocky reefs and along shorelines or may rest singly upon the rocky substrate. Resembling several other species found in the Pacific Northwest, it can be sought as far south as the Port McNeill area of British Columbia. Because its gray body "soaks up" the light from a strobe or flash, a dark specimen requires that underwater photographers adjust their F-stops.

A boat passenger sometimes sees dark forms splashing at the surface in pursuit of small schooling silvery shapes that frantically attempt to escape. Although these hungry dark predators may actually be any of several schooling rockfishes—which from such a vantage point are indistinguishable—some may be the Dark Dusky Rockfish.

A

Dr. James Orr photograph

COMMENTS: Try spincasting with buzz bombs, sting sildas or jigs near rocky reefs for the often-schooling Dark Dusky Rockfish. Light-tackle anglers may also enjoy catching it.

Hook and line harvesting, primarily with jigs, targets the Dark Dusky Rockfish in Alaska. It is a nearshore fishery in waters shallower than 160 m (530 ft). This species forms only a small part of the annual coast-wide rockfish take; filleted it sells either fresh or frozen.

Mix Dark Dusky Rockfish flesh with mashed potatoes, egg, salt and pepper, and then form into patties to make fish cakes for frying.

B. Bernard P. Hanby photograph

Light Dusky Rockfish

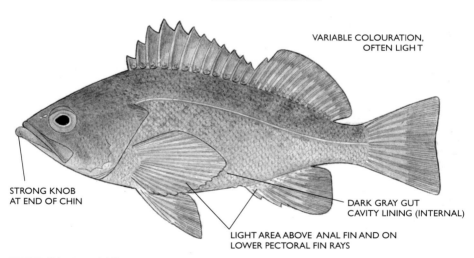

VARIABLE COLOURATION, OFTEN LIGHT

STRONG KNOB AT END OF CHIN

DARK GRAY GUT CAVITY LINING (INTERNAL)

LIGHT AREA ABOVE ANAL FIN AND ON LOWER PECTORAL FIN RAYS

SPECIES: *Sebastes variabilis*
OTHER COMMON NAMES: Incorrect: rock cod
MAXIMUM RECORDED SIZE: 59 cm (23.6 in)
DISTRIBUTION: Central Oregon through Bering Sea, Aleutian Island chain to northern Japan
HABITAT: While the Light Dusky Rockfish usually swims at depths below those of the average scuba enthusiast, it may be encountered in shallower locales. Look for it swimming just off the bottom and perhaps associating with other rockfish.
COMMENTS: Alaskan anglers are most likely to catch the Light Dusky Rockfish when fishing along deep, outer coast shores. Baits or jigs are optimal enticements.

The Light Dusky Rockfish often forms large aggregations offshore along Alaska's outer coastal shelf at depths as great as 679 m (2,228 ft). Consequently, it is targeted by the offshore trawl fleet. Most of the catch reaches market as fillets.

Light Dusky Rockfish fillets are an excellent starting point for most recipes requiring white fish.

B. Bernard P. Hanby photograph

Bocaccio

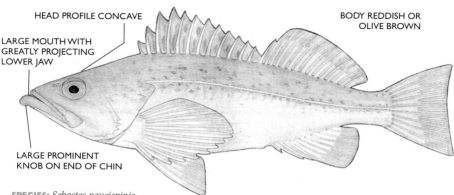

HEAD PROFILE CONCAVE

LARGE MOUTH WITH
GREATLY PROJECTING
LOWER JAW

BODY REDDISH OR
OLIVE BROWN

LARGE PROMINENT
KNOB ON END OF CHIN

SPECIES: *Sebastes paucispinis*
OTHER COMMON NAMES: salmon rockfish. Incorrect: brown bomber, rock salmon, salmon grouper, grouper, rock cod, tomcod
MAXIMUM RECORDED SIZE: 91 cm (36 in) and 6.8 kg (15 lb)
DISTRIBUTION: Central Baja California, Mexico, to Gulf of Alaska
HABITAT: For a Pacific Northwest aquanaut to see an adult Bocaccio is now truly a noteworthy event, given the severely depleted populations in the region due to many years of over-harvesting. Those who wish to accept such a challenge should search particularly near deep offshore reefs. Look among lush kelp growths along the outer coast to find the spotted, orange-tinged juveniles hovering there.

Groups of small juvenile Bocaccio occasionally lurk near jetties or pilings in some locales.

B. Juvenile.

COMMENTS: Formerly a very popular gamefish in California, the Bocaccio, Italian for "large mouth," is now primarily relegated to tales of past glory. Historically, it could be tempted by cast or slowly trolled lures such as herring strip, herring skin or even bucktail flies. While adults dwell primarily in deep water—down to 484 m (1,600 ft)—young Bocaccio sometimes hover under floats and formerly provided enjoyment, particularly for youthful anglers.

Pacific Northwest trawlers historically took some Bocaccio and then sold them along with various other rockfishes. Depletion of stocks by all consumptive user groups has greatly reduced such activities.

If kept chilled to avoid spoilage, the Bocaccio's low-fat flesh is excellent.

Chilipepper

Sebastes goodei

Juvenile Chilipepper inhabit shallow water in California, where they may be noticed by divers. Adults, though, live much deeper. The Pacific Northwest (Southern BC) represents the northern edge of this species' range. It looks somewhat like the Bocaccio but has a much smaller mouth. Mazimum recorded length is 56 cm (22 in).

Daniel W. Gotshall photograph

Silvergray Rockfish

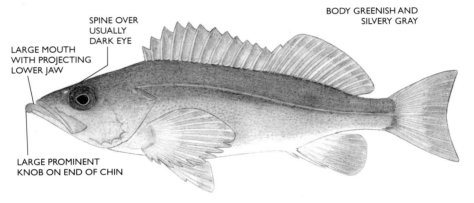

SPINE OVER USUALLY DARK EYE

LARGE MOUTH WITH PROJECTING LOWER JAW

BODY GREENISH AND SILVERY GRAY

LARGE PROMINENT KNOB ON END OF CHIN

SPECIES: *Sebastes brevispinis*

OTHER COMMON NAMES: silvergrey rockfish, shortspine rockfish, short-spined rockfish, short-spined rockfish. Incorrect: rock cod

MAXIMUM RECORDED SIZE: 74 cm (29.2 in)

DISTRIBUTION: Central Baja California, Mexico, to the Bering Sea coast of Alaska

HABITAT: Although present from the surface to 580 m (1,902 ft) in many locales, the drab Silvergray Rockfish usually glides along slowly just above the sea floor. Occasionally it may retreat into the rocky

A

caverns and crevices of solid formations. Smaller specimens live in shallower depths and the average diver is not likely to swim deep enough to observe the largest ones. Divers of today are less likely to observe this species due to overharvesting, primarily by commercial interests.

COMMENTS: Filleted and sold indiscriminately with other rockfish flesh, the Silvergray Rockfish forms a significant part of the trawl catch taken offshore. What once seemed to be an unlimited supply of this species (and many other offshore groundfish) is now in decline.

Subtle differences in flavour and texture occur between the various rockfishes, with the Silvergray's flesh being particularly good. Open your favourite seafood cookbook, turn to the section on white fish, and try this species in any recipe.

Widow Rockfish

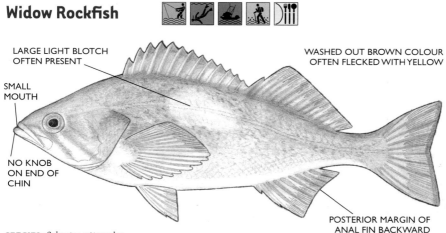

LARGE LIGHT BLOTCH OFTEN PRESENT

WASHED OUT BROWN COLOUR OFTEN FLECKED WITH YELLOW

SMALL MOUTH

NO KNOB ON END OF CHIN

POSTERIOR MARGIN OF ANAL FIN BACKWARD

SPECIES: *Sebastes entomelas*
OTHER COMMON NAMES: Incorrect: soft brown, brown bomber, widow rockcod, rock cod, bass
MAXIMUM RECORDED SIZE: 60 cm (23.6 in)
DISTRIBUTION: Northern Baja California, Mexico, to Kodiak Island, Gulf of Alaska
HABITAT: Scan the greenish mid-water above a rocky reef or steep shoreline dive site and perhaps spot the adult Widow Rockfish slowly cruising in small separate schools or mixed with other species. Only occasionally does it huddle motionless among caves or crevices. However, the more silvery juveniles sometimes school in massive numbers where tidal currents flow strongly. Young of the year occasionally find temporary residence in tidepools.

A boating naturalist, after noticing splashing and commotion at the surface then cruising quickly to the immediate area, may sometimes actually witness the light brown Widow Rockfish chasing herring or other schooling fishes.

COMMENTS: A fine light-tackle gamefish, the sporty Widow Rockfish may often seize buzz bombs or other lures at the surface then battle admirably to escape. At other times, perhaps while angling for salmon, a fisherman may catch one in deeper water.

Before 1980, trawl nets towed along hard and essentially flat bottoms at depths down to 370 m (1,220 ft) harvested limited quantities of the Widow Rockfish to be filleted for market. Subsequently, it was discovered that large numbers could be taken by mid-water trawl. Soon boom turned to bust and the Widow Rockfish is now considered overfished south of British Columbia. How long northern populations will remain harvestable is the question.

Although reputed to be tougher and coarser than that of other rockfishes, the slender Widow Rockfish's flesh provides a worthy meal.

B. Juvenile. *Keith Clements photograph*

Puget Sound Rockfish

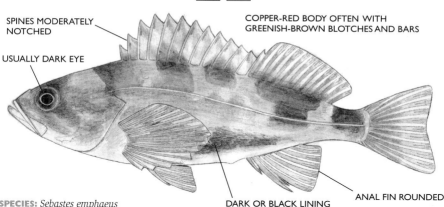

SPINES MODERATELY NOTCHED

COPPER-RED BODY OFTEN WITH GREENISH-BROWN BLOTCHES AND BARS

USUALLY DARK EYE

ANAL FIN ROUNDED

DARK OR BLACK LINING INSIDE GUT CAVITY

SPECIES: *Sebastes emphaeus*
OTHER COMMON NAMES: Incorrect: rock cod
MAXIMUM RECORDED SIZE: 18.3 cm (7.2 in)
DISTRIBUTION: Central California to the Kenai Peninsula, Gulf of Alaska
HABITAT: During exploration of reefs or rocky shorelines, divers frequently encounter loose congregations of the usually orange/tan Puget Sound Rockfish hovering in open water just slightly above the bottom. At other times, this fish nestles warily among crevices and caves, out of strong currents. Swelled with as many as 58,000 minute developing young, mature female Puget Sound Rockfish are easily distinguished from the slimmer males during August and September.

The common Puget Sound Rockfish may venture into shallows accessible to beachcombers and wharf-bound naturalists and is sometimes visible to boat passengers.

COMMENTS: Before the advent of scuba, the Puget Sound Rockfish remained largely unknown, and still much of its biology and ecology awaits investigation. More recently, divers often report an abundance of this species. Is it because larger predatory species are less numerous due to exploitation or because the Puget Sound Rockfish is small and has not been readily harvested? Or, more likely, is it a combination of factors, including a more knowledgeable diving community? With the population declines of larger, desirable species, enterprising anglers in some locales have recently begun using mini-tackle to catch the previously ignored Puget Sound Rockfish.

B. Bernard P. Hanby photograph

Canary Rockfish

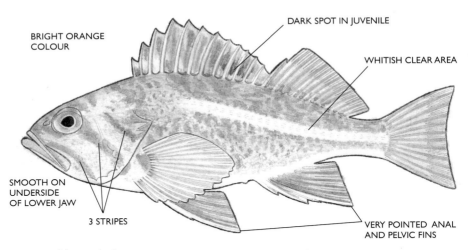

BRIGHT ORANGE COLOUR

DARK SPOT IN JUVENILE

WHITISH CLEAR AREA

SMOOTH ON UNDERSIDE OF LOWER JAW

3 STRIPES

VERY POINTED ANAL AND PELVIC FINS

SPECIES: *Sebastes pinniger*

OTHER COMMON NAMES: orange rockfish, orange rock-fish, fantail rockfish. Incorrect: fantail, yellow snapper, red snapper, red rock cod

MAXIMUM RECORDED SIZE: 76 cm (30 in)

DISTRIBUTION: Northern Baja California, Mexico, to the western Gulf of Alaska

HABITAT: Watch for the bright-orange Canary Rockfish hovering in loosely organized groups above the rocky bottom. A large specimen is usually in deep water while a sub-adult, with a distinct black blotch on the middle of its dorsal fin, swims at shallow, more accessible depths, often where a rocky bottom meets sand. The smaller specimen frequently huddles upon white shell-hash sand near boulders. At any stage, the Canary Rockfish is worthy prey for the underwater photographer.

Tiny, barely recognizable young Canary Rockfish, with their black dorsal spots, only rarely hide within tidepools or huddle under floats.

COMMENTS: A beautiful and worthy prize, the large, active Canary Rockfish readily strikes at slow-moving artificial lures or jigs, as well as baits, particularly small live fish. While a deepwater specimen provides little sport because its gas-filled swim bladder expands and disables the fish as it is hauled up, a shallow-water individual often provides fine light-tackle action.

By dragging their large nets over hard, uneven substrates at depths to 838 m (2,749 ft), offshore trawlers have actively harvested the once plentiful Canary Rockfish for many years. It has now been declared overfished.

Filleted before marketing, it annually ranks in numbers among the top three rockfish species caught. Longliners and salmon trollers may encounter the Canary Rockfish too.

The large Canary Rockfish delivers a good quantity of delicious, firm flesh.

B. Sub-adult.
C. Juvenile.
D. Tiny juvenile.
Keith Clements photograph

Vermilion Rockfish

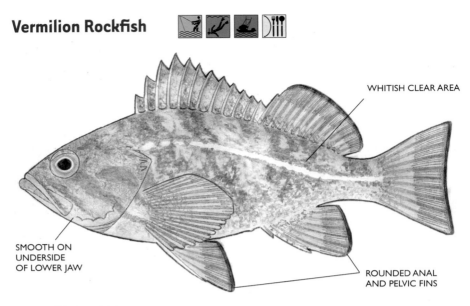

WHITISH CLEAR AREA

SMOOTH ON
UNDERSIDE
OF LOWER JAW

ROUNDED ANAL
AND PELVIC FINS

SPECIES: *Sebastes miniatus*

OTHER COMMON NAMES: vermilion rock-fish, rasher, genuine red. Incorrect: red rock cod, red snapper

MAXIMUM RECORDED SIZE: 76 cm (30 in) and 6.8 kg (15 lb)

DISTRIBUTION: Central Baja California, Mexico, to central the Gulf of Alaska

HABITAT: Cruising in small schools, pairs or singly below 6 m (20 ft), bright-red adult Vermilion Rockfish are an outstanding sight for the sport diver. Underwater photographers particularly enjoy this elusive and shy species that requires patient stalking for that "special shot." A knowledgeable dive buddy can be an effective herder. Look for the usually drab, brownish juvenile Vermilion Rockfish in shallower waters where it may retreat among kelp beds or hole up in rocky crevices.

COMMENTS: Most popular with anglers in the southern part of its range, the Vermilion Rockfish takes baits such as octopus, squid, herring, anchovy and other small silvery fish. Use these baits over rocky reefs, along steep-sloping shorelines, or even from wharves to catch this species, which may put up a good battle.

A large adult female may be particularly prolific and capable of releasing as many as 2,600,000 tiny young, usually in winter.

A

While only occasionally found in Pacific Northwest trawl catches, the impressive Vermilion Rockfish has ranked third among rockfish species netted in California. There, catches occur in water less than 436 m (1,430 ft) and the filleted product reaches the market with other rockfish. Its bright-red colour often incorrectly relegates this rockfish to the false label "red snapper" section of the fish market. However, this species is a member of the rockfish family, not the snapper family. This same attractive hue makes it a potential favourite product in the Asian live market.

To make fish cakes, dice mushrooms into Vermilion Rockfish fillets, rub through a sieve then add bread crumbs and milk preheated in a double boiler. Pour together with beaten eggs into custard cups and bake.

NOTE: In 2008, Dr. John Hyde and his colleagues "split" the Sunset Rockfish, *Sebastes crocotulus*, as a sister species from the Vermilion Rockfish. "Splitting" occurs when one established species, through various research techniques, is determined by taxonomists to be two (or more) distinct entities. The Sunset Rockfish is very similar in appearance, but to date, its range is described as from central California to northern Mexico and at depths below 100 m (330 ft). Therefore it is not featured in this guide.

B. Bernard P. Hanby photograph
D. Juvenile. Clinton Bauder photograph

Rosy Rockfish

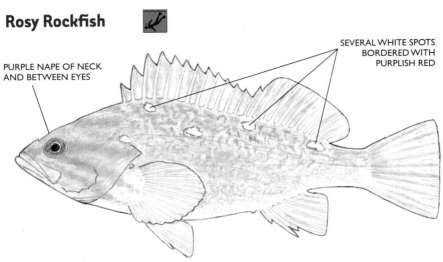

PURPLE NAPE OF NECK
AND BETWEEN EYES

SEVERAL WHITE SPOTS
BORDERED WITH
PURPLISH RED

SPECIES: *Sebastes rosaceus*

MAXIMUM RECORDED SIZE: 36 cm (14 in) and 1.8 kg (4 lb)

DISTRIBUTION: Northern Mexico to northern Washington

HABITAT: The Rosy Rockfish lives amid boulder fields, high-relief reefs or mixed bottoms. It is either solitary or forms small groups, huddling near or directly on the substrate.

COMMENTS: While preparing the second edition of this guide, we were most fortunate to encounter underwater photographer and naturalist diver Keith Clements. Although Keith's initial sighting in 2002 was *sans* photograph, he immediately knew this was an unusual fish. He discussed his finding with staff at the Seattle Aquarium and was convinced that he'd found a Rosy Rockfish.

The following summer, Keith returned to Neah Bay, Washington, and revisited the site of record. There were two specimens under the same ledge where the original visit occurred. This time, Keith verified his sighting with the photograph appearing below.

Each year since, Keith has returned and always found at least one of the specimens. We salute Keith and many others like him for their curiosity, concern and contributions to ichthyology (the study of fish).

Keith Clements photograph

Tiger Rockfish

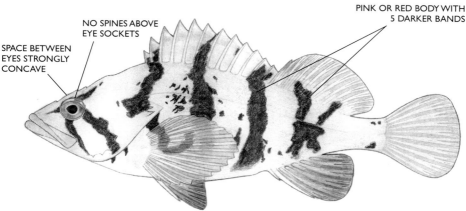

SPACE BETWEEN EYES STRONGLY CONCAVE

NO SPINES ABOVE EYE SOCKETS

PINK OR RED BODY WITH 5 DARKER BANDS

SPECIES: *Sebastes nigrocinctus*

OTHER COMMON NAMES: blackbanded rockfish, banded rockfish. Incorrect: red rock cod, rockcod

MAXIMUM RECORDED SIZE: 61 cm (24 in)

DISTRIBUTION: Southern California to the eastern islands in the Aleutian chain, Alaska

HABITAT: Never straying far from its secure crevice or cavern, the territorial Tiger Rockfish often erects its large spiny fins and boldly confronts all intruders—including divers. Search for this colourful rockfish on deeper sorties because it lives mainly at depths between 10 and 275 m (33 to 900 ft). It is perhaps the most popular rockfish for the underwater photographer due to it colouring, widespread distribution, very accessible depths and its often aggressive behaviour (which lead to good photo ops). The Tiger Rockfish is usually easy to find but sometimes frustrating to coax from its lair.

Surface-bound naturalists seldom encounter the adult Tiger Rockfish, but may easily find juveniles. In spring and summer, look for the distinctive striped and kelp-coloured young among the detached seaweeds that accumulate in long tidelines. As tiny tenants in this temporary and drifting habitat, these nomadic juveniles eventually float to rocky areas and descend to adult territory.

A

A. Pregnant adult female.

COMMENTS: Hook-and-line fishermen, both recreational and commercial, most often catch the darkly banded, pink or red Tiger Rockfish at depths greater than 10 m (33 ft). Small live fish or silvery jigs seem attractive to this solitary animal. The Tiger Rockfish puts up only minimal resistance.

Historically, commercial line fishermen took the Tiger Rockfish incidentally and marketed it as generic "rockfish." Since the 1970s and the rise of the live rockfish hook-and-line fishery, this species is now very eagerly targeted for its attractive appearance.

Firm and flavourful, it is ideal for any recipe requiring fillets of white-fleshed fish.

Yelloweye Rockfish

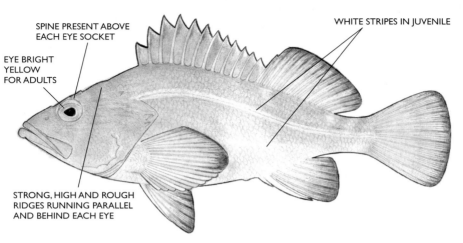

SPINE PRESENT ABOVE
EACH EYE SOCKET

EYE BRIGHT
YELLOW
FOR ADULTS

WHITE STRIPES IN JUVENILE

STRONG, HIGH AND ROUGH
RIDGES RUNNING PARALLEL
AND BEHIND EACH EYE

SPECIES: *Sebastes ruberrimus*
OTHER COMMON NAMES: rasphead rockfish, red rockfish, turkey red rockfish, goldeneye rockfish.
Incorrect: pot belly, red snapper, red rock cod, red cod, drum
MAXIMUM RECORDED SIZE: 91 cm (36 in) and 11.3 kg (25 lb)
DISTRIBUTION: Northern Baja California, Mexico, to the Aleutian Island chain, Alaska
HABITAT: Showing two narrow, bold white stripes along each side, the juvenile Yelloweye Rockfish is more
observable for divers than the large, yellowish-orange adult because the young inhabit shallower regions of a
rocky reef or cliff face. While the casual underwater camera buff stalks and films the photogenic juvenile,
which often peers out of a deep crevice, only those with more technical gear and training are likely to
descend deep enough to "shoot" the large, slow-swimming and yellow-eyed adult. Look for the popular
Yelloweye Rockfish—adult or juvenile—below 15 m (50 ft).

A

A. Very pregnant large female.

COMMENTS: Even though it provides poor sport—its gas-filled swim bladder expands rapidly, often forcing its gut out of its mouth and bulging its eyes as the fish moves toward the surface—seafood-eating anglers have historically pursued the large Yelloweye Rockfish zealously. Overzealously in many areas! Now, sadly, large adult specimens are seldom encountered in much of the Pacific Northwest.

Longlining halibut fishermen once discarded the now-valued Yelloweye Rockfish. Today, this species' flesh is very popular and fetches a high price. Historic wastage and poor fishery management have reduced supply and combined with increased demand to drive up consumer cost.

With lower oil content than other rockfishes, the Yelloweye Rockfish is particularly delicious deep-fried as fish and chips.

B. Sub-adult.
C. Large juvenile.
D. Tiny juvenile.
E. Juvenile.

Splitnose Rockfish

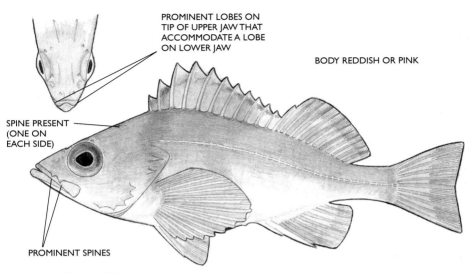

PROMINENT LOBES ON TIP OF UPPER JAW THAT ACCOMMODATE A LOBE ON LOWER JAW

BODY REDDISH OR PINK

SPINE PRESENT (ONE ON EACH SIDE)

PROMINENT SPINES

SPECIES: *Sebastes diploproa*

OTHER COMMON NAMES: lobe-jawed rockfish. Incorrect: small red rock cod, red snapper

MAXIMUM RECORDED SIZE: 46 cm (18 in)

DISTRIBUTION: Central Baja California, Mexico, to the western Gulf of Alaska

HABITAT: Although abundant and thriving much deeper than most divers dare venture, the bright-red adult Splitnose Rockfish only very rarely moves into depths shallower than 36 m (120 ft). The technical diver, particularly of the camera-toting variety, may find this a worthy challenge.

Summer boat passengers may find tiny juvenile Splitnose Rockfish nestling among floating debris dotting long tide lines, or accumulating under floats. Look especially in detached marine seaweeds for this tiny kelp-coloured juvenile that is distinguishable by its large eyes. The most common juvenile "stowing away" among the British Columbia's Strait of Georgia tideline's kelp, the young Splitnose Rockfish, at a size of less than 5 cm (2 in), descends to deep, dark adult habitat by autumn.

COMMENTS: Swept indiscriminately into trawl nets along with other larger and more valuable fish, the moderate-sized Splitnose Rockfish forms a minor part of the total rockfish catch taken between 91 and 800 m (300 and 2,640 ft). A few of the biggest specimens reach the market as generic "rockfish" fillets.

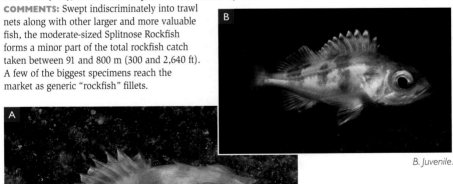

B. Juvenile.

Redstripe Rockfish

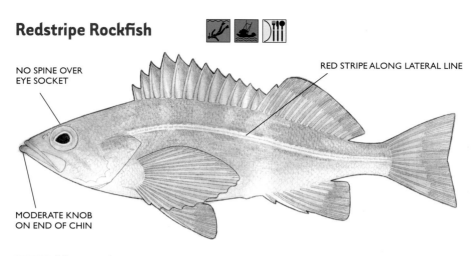

NO SPINE OVER
EYE SOCKET

RED STRIPE ALONG LATERAL LINE

MODERATE KNOB
ON END OF CHIN

SPECIES: *Sebastes proriger*

OTHER COMMON NAMES: red-striped rock-fish. Incorrect: rock cod

MAXIMUM RECORDED SIZE: 61 cm (24 in)

DISTRIBUTION: Southern Baja California, Mexico, to the Bering Sea coast of Alaska

HABITAT: Divers should look for an adult Redstripe Rockfish, with a lateral light-red band on each side, at depths in excess of 25 m (85 ft) where rocky reefs and steep silt-covered cliff faces meet gently sloping sandy or muddy bottoms. The juvenile Redstripe Rockfish may be encountered as shallow as 5 m (17 ft), where it often hides amid seaweed on gently sloping substrate.

COMMENTS: Trawlers dragging their nets along the coast from Oregon to Alaska at depths to 425 m (1,403 ft) frequently take large numbers of Redstripe Rockfish. After filleting it, commercial processors sell it either fresh or frozen along with other rockfish species.

Of delicate flavour and flaky texture, Redstripe Rockfish flesh is ideal for poaching in white wine then garnishing with butter, lemon and parsley. Or why not just slice the fresh raw fillets into long narrow strips and dip into soya sauce, Japanese-style, before eating?

B. Juvenile. Bernard P. Hanby photograph

Greenstriped Rockfish

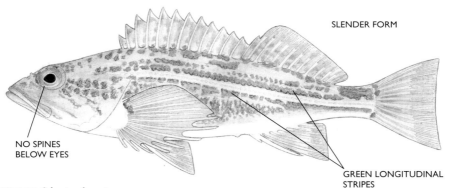

SLENDER FORM

NO SPINES
BELOW EYES

GREEN LONGITUDINAL
STRIPES

SPECIES: *Sebastes elongatus*
OTHER COMMON NAMES: greenstripe rockfish, striped rockfish, strawberry rockfish. Incorrect: poinsettia, strawberry rockcod
MAXIMUM RECORDED SIZE: 47 cm (18.5 in)
DISTRIBUTION: Central Baja California, Mexico, to western Gulf of Alaska
HABITAT: Rarely invading water less than 30 m (100 ft) deep, the reddish-tinged Greenstriped Rockfish encounters only the most determined sport diver.

One of the few rockfish species that consistently lives upon sandy or silty sea floors, it may also cruise near and seek out loose boulders and rocky outcroppings for shelter. It is frequently found in long, deep inlets.

COMMENTS: Commercial trawlers take significant quantities of Greenstriped Rockfish as part of the total groundfish catch harvested over level, rock-sprinkled bottoms at depths to 1,145 m (3,756 ft). Only the largest specimens, though, are suitable for processing into fillets. Unfortunately, small ones are unwanted and discarded—a wasteful byproduct of the trawling process.

While the Greenstriped Rockfish is somewhat small, its flesh has a distinct delicious flavour and an appealing texture. After filleting, coat the tiny but worthwhile results with bread crumbs and then fry briefly.

B

A

Stripetail Rockfish

Sebastes saxicola

If encountered at all in the Pacific Northwest, the Stripetail Rockfish will most likely be noticed as a juvenile. Once it has matured, this species becomes mostly bright red and lives at depths inaccessible to recreational anglers or divers. This rockfish attains a maximum recorded length of 39 cm (15.3 in).

A. Juvenile.
Daniel W. Gotshall photograph
B. *John Butler photograph*

Undetermined Juvenile Rockfish

Sebastes sp.

In 1997, while photographing invertebrates for the book *Marine Life of the Pacific Northwest*, Bernard P. Hanby captured this image off Mulkiteo, Washington, at approximately 10 m (36 ft). Juvenile rockfish are often problematic to identify and this 5 cm (2 in) individual proved particularly vexing. Without an actual specimen to examine, several rockfish taxonomists were uncertain as to its pedigree. Perhaps over time, the mystery can be solved.

Bernard P. Hanby photograph

Shortspine Thornyhead

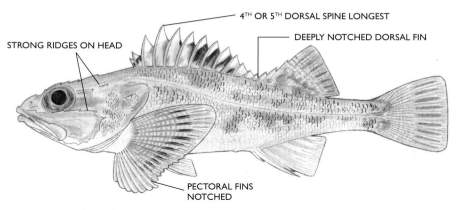

4TH OR 5TH DORSAL SPINE LONGEST

DEEPLY NOTCHED DORSAL FIN

STRONG RIDGES ON HEAD

PECTORAL FINS
NOTCHED

SPECIES: *Sebastolobus alascanus*

OTHER COMMON NAMES: spinycheek rockfish, spiny-cheek rockfish, shortspine channel rockfish, spinyheaded rockfish, lobe-finned rockfish. Incorrect: thornyhead, idiotfish, scorpion, bonehead, idiot, hooligan, red rock cod, channel rockcod, channel cod, gurnard, gurrnet

MAXIMUM RECORDED SIZE: 82 cm (32.3 in)

DISTRIBUTION: Northern Baja California, Mexico, to the Bering Sea, the Okhotsk Sea and Japan

HABITAT: Because the bright-red Shortspine Thornyhead lives primarily at depths greater than recreational divers explore, a scuba sighting at diveable depths would be noteworthy.

Although the deepwater Shortspine Thornyhead is obviously inaccessible to surface-bound naturalists, its drifting and fertilized egg masses are not. Always found at night and floating at the surface, variously shaped hollow gelatinous egg balloons, up to 60 cm (24 in) long, each encase a single layer of many tiny eggs.

COMMENTS: The colourful Shortspine Thornyhead thrives at depths between 150 and 1,524 m (495 and 5,000 ft) where it's taken by groundfish and shrimp trawlers. In more recent times, this previously ignored species has become the focus of a major fishery. However, like other long-lived species, the Shortspine Thornyhead likely will not support sustainable landings long term. Hopefully, it will be managed wisely for future generations.

The Shortspine Thornyhead's white flesh is somewhat sweeter than that of most other rockfish.

NOTE: The Longspine Thornyhead, *Sebastolobus altivelis*, also lives throughout the Pacific Northwest—but generally at greater, less accessible depths. A long third dorsal fin spine distinguishes this smaller species from its short-spined relative featured here.

THE **SABLEFISHES** (Family Anoplopomatidae)

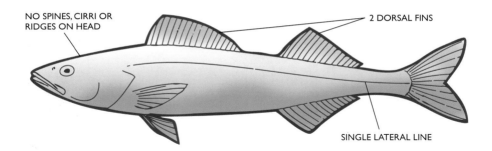

NO SPINES, CIRRI OR RIDGES ON HEAD

2 DORSAL FINS

SINGLE LATERAL LINE

The family Anoplopomatidae is tiny. Only two living species are known and both are found in shallow water as juveniles but migrate to considerable depths as adults. One is the popular and common Sablefish; the other is the large Skilfish, an offshore Pacific Northwest creature rarely seen by naturalists.

The sablefishes have existed for more than 12 million years and are related to the rockfishes, sculpins, greenlings, poachers and snailfishes in that they all have a suborbital stay—a small, heavy bone beneath each eye—a feature not recognizable by the casual observer.

Sablefish

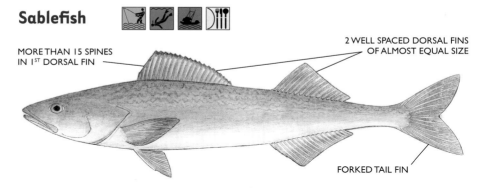

MORE THAN 15 SPINES IN 1ST DORSAL FIN

2 WELL SPACED DORSAL FINS OF ALMOST EQUAL SIZE

FORKED TAIL FIN

SPECIES: *Anoplopoma fimbria*

OTHER COMMON NAMES: Alaska blackcod, blackcod, coalfish, coalcod, black cod. Incorrect: blue cod, bluefish, candlefish, skil-fish, skil

MAXIMUM RECORDED SIZE: 114 cm (45 in) and 25 kg (55 lb)

DISTRIBUTION: Central Baja California, Mexico, to the Bering Sea coasts of Alaska, Kamchatka, Russia and Japan

HABITAT: Divers exploring the sandy, silty bottoms of shallow bays might possibly see the sleek grey shapes of young Sablefish cruising near the bottom.

COMMENTS: In some locales, young Sablefish are a nuisance catch for salmon anglers who troll or mooch with herring. Pier-bound bait-fishermen may

A

occasionally enjoy light-tackle sport provided by active juvenile Sablefish found near jetties and wharves during summer.

First Nations people traditionally dried the oily Sablefish. Commercial handliners, longliners, trawlers and trap fishermen have all historically harvested Sablefish from the surface to depths of 2,740 m (9,040 ft). Today, trap fishermen (primarily) and commercial longliners harvest this valuable species, which is typically smoked and sold as smoked Alaska blackcod. This fishery is thought to be one of the most well-managed commercial enterprises in the Pacific Northwest, with harvester associations working closely with government agencies setting sustainable catch limits.

Using either a homemade or an inexpensive retail smoker, anyone may create delicious smoked Alaska blackcod. Do a little reading and some experimenting. Smoke only large, adult Sablefish, though, because their high oil content ensures success. The orange or yellow colour of the commercially available product is an additive and unnecessary.

Skilfish

Erilepis zonifer

John Lozanski is one person fortunate enough not only to have seen several live Skilfish, but also to have captured and transported them live to a public aquarium for other people to enjoy. While fishing for salmon during a mid-summer 1971 cruise of the now-defunct Canadian weather ship *Vancouver*, the meteorological technician was surprised to spot six stout juvenile Skilfish, each about 30 cm (12 in) long. The dark-blue bodies, boldly blotched with large white patches, had pursued his tackle to the surface. Instead of quickly fleeing, they inquisitively milled about beside the large ship. John had time to run to the stern of the ship, grab a long-handled dip-net and then deftly capture these curious creatures. Within an hour of being placed in an aquarium tank in the ship's laboratory, the friendly captives were feeding from his hand, a behaviour most unusual for wild and just-captured fish. Growing half again their initial capture size during the remainder of

the cruise, the exceedingly tame Skilfish, now the ship's pets, were eventually transported to larger permanent quarters at the Vancouver Aquarium.

For nearly 15 years, these amazing specimens delighted visitors and staff alike, growing very large but well short of their potential dimensions of 91 kg (200 lb) and 178 cm (70 in).

Skilfish are seldom encountered by commercial fishermen.

Dr. Murray Newman photograph

THE **GREENLINGS** (Family Hexagrammidae)

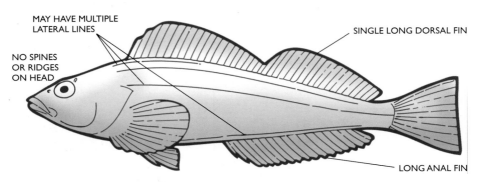

MAY HAVE MULTIPLE LATERAL LINES

SINGLE LONG DORSAL FIN

NO SPINES OR RIDGES ON HEAD

LONG ANAL FIN

Greenlings and combfishes, along with the Lingcod and Atka Mackerel, make up the Hexagrammidae. This is a small family of fishes containing perhaps 11 known living species—all of which live in the North Pacific Ocean.

Except for the voracious Lingcod, the largest of the clan at 152 cm (5 ft), most greenlings prefer shallow, even intertidal, rocky or weedy bottoms. Here, these colourful aggressive fish stake out small but definite territories and staunchly defend them, particularly during mating season.

With the notable exception of the large and valuable Lingcod, the greenlings are not as severely harvested as many other traditionally targeted Pacific Northwest species because modern trawl techniques do not function well over uneven, shallow substrates.

Rock Greenling

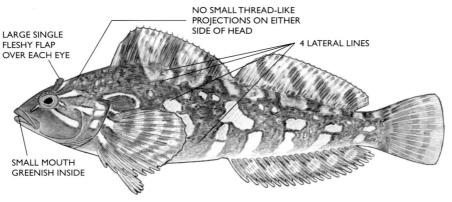

NO SMALL THREAD-LIKE PROJECTIONS ON EITHER SIDE OF HEAD

4 LATERAL LINES

LARGE SINGLE FLESHY FLAP OVER EACH EYE

SMALL MOUTH GREENISH INSIDE

SPECIES: *Hexagrammos lagocephalus.* Formerly *Hexagrammos superciliosus*
OTHER COMMON NAMES: fringed greenling. Incorrect: red rock trout
MAXIMUM RECORDED SIZE: 61 cm (24 in)
DISTRIBUTION: Central California coast to the Bering Sea, Alaska, and through to Japan
HABITAT: Adventurous underwater camera buffs will find the adult Rock Greenling a challenging quarry as it lives in the heavy surge present along outer rocky shores. Variously a turquoise, red and white species, this colouration is particularly garish and obvious in the male. However, it is well camouflaged among surrounding seaweeds. In summer, tiny silvery Rock Greenling, distinguished by their bright-red eyes, most often live in more sheltered nearby bays.

Very difficult to see among the colourful seaweeds growing luxuriantly along the outer rocky coast, the gaudy Rock Greenling may actually rest within arm's length of even the most diligent beachcomber.
COMMENTS: If adventurous enough to fish along rugged, surf-pounded, rocky shorelines at depths less than 16 m (55 ft), the angler may catch this worthy but somewhat elusive species. Baits include clams, small crabs and marine worms. After seizing a hook, this active greenling usually retreats into crevices—try to make this fish head shoreward immediately.

Simmer flour, cooked onion, pepper, tomato, brown sugar, vinegar and mustard; then add Rock Greenling strips with kidney beans and simmer again.

A. Adult male.
Bernard P. Hanby photograph
B. Adult female.
C. Juvenile.
D. Juvenile.

Kelp Greenling

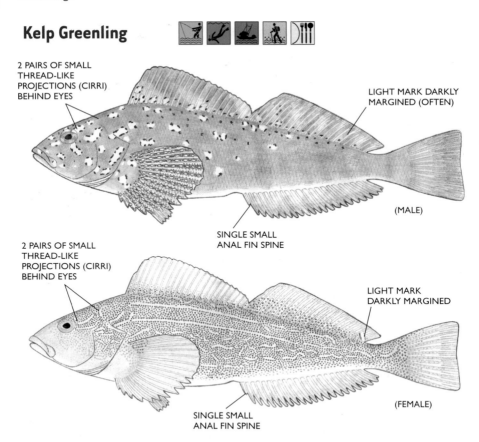

2 PAIRS OF SMALL THREAD-LIKE PROJECTIONS (CIRRI) BEHIND EYES

LIGHT MARK DARKLY MARGINED (OFTEN)

(MALE)

SINGLE SMALL ANAL FIN SPINE

2 PAIRS OF SMALL THREAD-LIKE PROJECTIONS (CIRRI) BEHIND EYES

LIGHT MARK DARKLY MARGINED

(FEMALE)

SINGLE SMALL ANAL FIN SPINE

SPECIES: *Hexagrammos decagrammus*
OTHER COMMON NAMES: Incorrect: greenling sea trout, speckled sea trout, rock trout, bluefish, tommy cod
MAXIMUM RECORDED SIZE: 61 cm (24 in) and 2.1 kg (4.6 lb)
DISTRIBUTION: Southern California to the Aleutian Island chain, Alaska

A

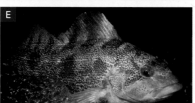

HABITAT: A very common companion of divers in the Pacific Northwest, the inquisitive Kelp Greenling often follows the aquanaut—a valuable factor to the underwater photographer. Once believed to be two different species, the adult male and adult female both flourish at depths less than 15 m (50 ft), where they lurk among seaweed or boulders. During autumn and winter, adult male Kelp Greenling—usually very pale—actively guard clusters of mauve or pale-blue-coloured eggs deposited earlier by one or more females. Look in empty Giant Barnacle casings to find egg clusters, some of which may even "twinkle" as the tiny young twist inside the eggs.

Silvery young, less than 5 cm (2 in) long, are sometimes trapped in tidepools but are not usually recognized as Kelp Greenlings.

COMMENTS: The common Kelp Greenling bites at nearly any temptation and therefore it is very popular with bait-fishermen who cast into shallow water from the shore or from a jetty or boat. Jerk a silvery jig to catch this aggressive fish. Use light tackle and enjoy the scrappy, active Kelp Greenling.

Historically overlooked, the Kelp Greenling is being increasingly exploited by commercial fishermen for the live market trade.

The Aleut Native Americans prize this species and call it *idyajuk*. Try filleting the tasty Kelp Greenling then cooking it with yogurt and some favourite spices for a low-calorie seafood meal.

A. Adult male.
B. Adult female.
C. Adult male.
D. Courting adult male.
E. Adult female.
F. Juvenile. Bernard B. Hanby photograph
G. Sub-adult male.

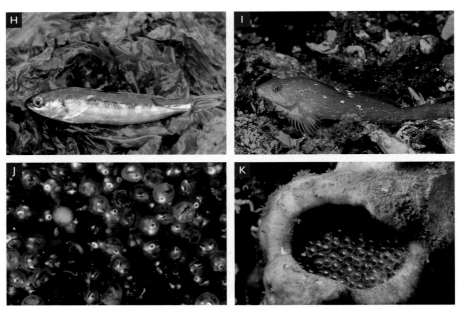

H. Juvenile.
I. Juvenile male. *Bernard P. Hanby photograph*
J. Soon to hatch young. *Charlie Gibbs photograph*
K. Fertilized eggs. *Charlie Gibbs photograph*

Masked Greenling

Hexagrammos octogrammus

Very common in the shallow waters of the Bering Sea, the Masked Greenling is recorded as far south as northern British Columbia. It is similar to the Whitespotted Greenling but has a stouter caudal peduncle (space between dorsal fin and tail fin) and fewer than 20 spines on first dorsal fin. Its maximum recorded length is 42 cm (16.5 in).

Nate Chambers/Alaska SeaLife Center photograph

Whitespotted Greenling

SHORT 1ST AND 4TH LATERAL LINES
(4TH EXTENDING ONLY AS FAR AS
PELVIC FINS)

WHITE SPOTS ON BODY

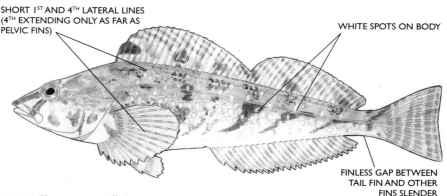

FINLESS GAP BETWEEN
TAIL FIN AND OTHER
FINS SLENDER

SPECIES: *Hexagrammos stelleri*
OTHER COMMON NAMES: Incorrect: rock trout, tommy cod, kelp cod
MAXIMUM RECORDED SIZE: 48 cm (l9 in) and 1.6 kg (3.6 lb)
DISTRIBUTION: Northern Washington to the Bering and Beaufort Seas, Alaska, through to Japan
HABITAT: The active Whitespotted Greenling lives on shallow sandy bottoms, mainly among eelgrass or other marine seaweeds growing on nearby rocky outcroppings at depths less than 15 m (50 ft). In winter, the beautiful golden males with their temporarily darkened fins fearlessly guard the egg masses deposited by females in cracks of rocky outcroppings and may even boldly swim circles around divers.

While not usually trapped in tidepools, the common Whitespotted Greenling usually lives in shallows, and it may be visible to an observant wharf-bound naturalist.

COMMENTS: After hatching from small bright blue, mauve or green eggs, the tiny larvae feed upon minute young crabs, barnacles and floating fish eggs. By mid-spring, though, young Whitespotted Greenlings have grown to about 5 cm (2 in) and have passed through a silvery, surface-dwelling stage before settling to a bottom residence.

A

Anglers find the easily caught Whitespotted Greenling an enjoyable summertime quarry. This olive-hued fish snaps at natural baits such as marine worms, small crabs and fish when bottom-fished from jetties and wharves. It is small and not too scrappy.

Toast some bread; place boiled Whitespotted Greenling face-up with cheese and catsup and then broil for tasty canapés.

B. Breeding male.
C. Male guarding nest.
 Richard Zade photograph
D. Breeding male.
Maris Kazmers photograph
E. Juvenile.
F. Nest with several clutches of
eggs. *Maris Kazmers photograph*

Lingcod

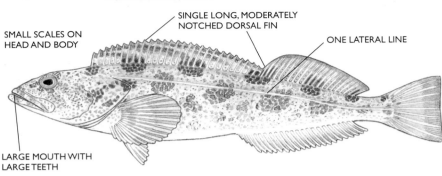

SMALL SCALES ON
HEAD AND BODY

SINGLE LONG, MODERATELY
NOTCHED DORSAL FIN

ONE LATERAL LINE

LARGE MOUTH WITH
LARGE TEETH

SPECIES: *Ophiodon elongatus*

OTHER COMMON NAMES: Pacific cultus. Incorrect: ling, buffalo cod, blue cod, cultus cod

MAXIMUM RECORDED SIZE: 152 cm (60 in) and 45 kg (100 lb)

DISTRIBUTION: Northern Baja California, Mexico, to the Alaskan Peninsula, Alaska

HABITAT: The aggressive Lingcod lives primarily over rocky bottoms at depths to 450 m (1,485 ft) though it is common in shallow water accessible to scuba divers. Clear water occasionally permits the shorebound naturalist to see an adult Lingcod. Eelgrass often hides juveniles during their first year. While chasing herring near the surface, small specimens may even leap clear of the water.

COMMENTS: Once the prize target for Pacific Northwest spear-fishermen, Lingcod populations have become severely depleted throughout this region. Harvest restrictions, growing interest in underwater photography and an increasing conservation ethic have drastically reduced participation in this once popular activity. In many regions, thoughtful divers have joined with organizations such as the Vancouver Aquarium to participate in annual Lingcod egg mass surveys. At a minimum, conservation-minded enthusiasts should not disturb any male that guards a large white egg mass—even if no restrictions exist.

Lingcod is an important sport-fishing species in the Pacific Northwest and fishing pressure has aided the depletion of populations in many areas. Be sure to observe local catch limits, minimum-size restrictions and other published conservation measures.

Where legal, fish for this ravenous species along shores and over reefs, particularly where strong currents flow, and use heavy silvery jigs or small live fish as bait. A powerful predator that may seize other small just-hooked fish, the scrappy Lingcod usually fights hardest at the surface. Use a sturdy rod and strong line for this leviathan.

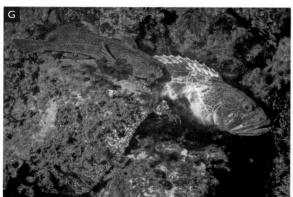

An important economic commodity, the popular Lingcod is caught by longliners, handliners and trawlers. Much of the now greatly depleted catch enters the fish and chip trade.

Lingcod is delicious. The occasional blue-green fleshed specimen becomes white after cooking.

E. Adult male guarding nest.
F. Seizing a Buffalo Sculpin.
G. Spawning pair (light female).
Tom Sheldon photograph

Painted Greenling

ELONGATE POINTED HEAD
WITH 2 PAIRS OF BUSHY
PROJECTIONS

ONE LATERAL LINE

DARK BARS

NOTCHED ANAL FIN

SPECIES: *Oxylebius pictus*
OTHER COMMON NAMES: convictfish
MAXIMUM RECORDED SIZE: 25 cm (10 in)
DISTRIBUTION: Central Baja California,
Mexico, to central Alaska
HABITAT: Active in shallow rocky habitats,
the distinctive Painted Greenling—generally
with red stripes on a whitish background—
lurks singly or in pairs. Seemingly unafraid
as it moves from one perch to another, it
often confronts the diver. When seeking the
most colourful specimens, the aquanaut
should patrol areas profusely encrusted with
a variety of brightly hued invertebrate
animals. On rare occasions, really lucky
divers may meet the young Painted Greenling
nestling among the large tentacles of sea
anemones, apparently immune to the
tentacular stinging cells. In some locales, the
Painted Greenling actively skulks around
pilings and under wharves.

B

A

COMMENTS: Throughout a winter spawning season the mature male Painted Greenling is often almost totally black compared to the typically striped female. As a female deposits a cluster of eggs in a rocky crevice, the pugnacious male fertilizes them and then guards the nest.

Due to its small size, there is little interest in the Painted Greenling by either sport or commercial fishermen.

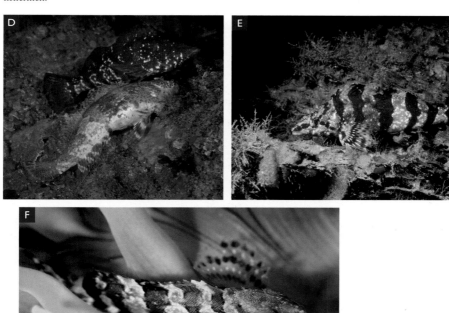

D. Mating pair. Clinton Bauder photograph
E. Male guarding nest.
F. Juvenile nestling amid anemone tentacles. Wes Kozak photograph

Longspine Combfish

1ST 3 DORSAL SPINES LONG
(2ND LONGEST SOMETIMES BROKEN)

LONG TAPERING SLENDER BODY

FINLESS GAP BETWEEN TAIL FIN
AND OTHER FINS NARROW

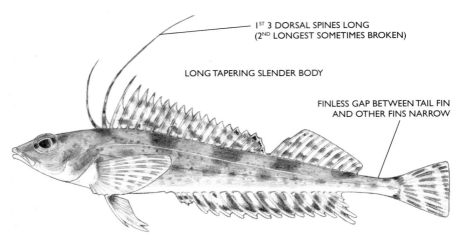

SPECIES: *Zaniolepis latipinnis*

OTHER COMMON NAMES: longspined greenling

MAXIMUM RECORDED SIZE: 30 cm (12 in)

DISTRIBUTION: Central Baja California, Mexico, to southern British Columbia

HABITAT: The Longspine Combfish has a spotty distribution. It lives on sand or silt substrates. Aquanauts wishing to observe this seldom-seen fish should night dive and explore depths below 18 m (60 ft). It most often rests still upon the bottom, with its distinctive dorsal fin folded down. Photographing one with this fin extended is difficult as such a pose usually indicates that the specimen will soon move away.

COMMENTS: Trawlers dragging their nets to depths of 180 m (600 ft) occasionally find a Longspine Combfish as an unwanted part of the catch. When taken from the gear, this fish frequently assumes a stiff, C-shaped pose—an interesting behaviour shared with many of the elongate poachers. Perhaps it is an attempt to dissuade predation by feigning death or to make it more difficult for a predator to swallow.

A

B. Adult courting male.

Atka Mackerel

Pleurogrammus monopterygius

Not at all related to the true mackerels but rather a member of the greenling family, this wide-ranging species is documented as far south as California. The Atka Mackerel is primarliy a northern denizen with a centre of abundance in the Bering Sea and the Gulf of Alaska. It is very distinctive and easily recognized. Its maximum recorded length is 56.5 cm (22.2 in).

THE **SCULPINS** (Superfamily Cottoidea)

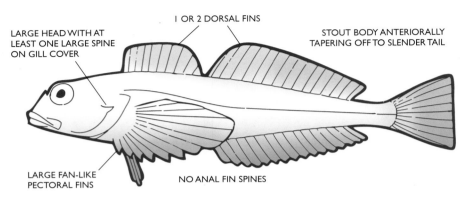

I OR 2 DORSAL FINS

LARGE HEAD WITH AT
LEAST ONE LARGE SPINE
ON GILL COVER

STOUT BODY ANTERIORALLY
TAPERING OFF TO SLENDER TAIL

LARGE FAN-LIKE
PECTORAL FINS

NO ANAL FIN SPINES

The Cottoidea, an enormous superfamily, contains approximately 350 described living species including sculpins, Irish lords and sea ravens, as well as the Cabezon. Recently though, the traditional sculpin family (Cottidae) was divided into four newly established families. Taxonomists determined that there are enough anatomical differences between the sculpins (Cottidae), the sailfin sculpins (Hemitripteridae), the fathead sculpins (Psychrolutidae) and the grunt sculpins (Rhamphocottidae) to make this separation. However, in an effort to simplify matters, the superfamily designation Cottoidea is used here to introduce the sculpin groupings.

An adaptable group, the cottoids lurk in both freshwater and marine habitats, while a few also tolerate intermediate brackish environments. Virtually all depths of water and types of substrate provide habitat for these mostly sluggish bottom-dwellers.

in), most cottoids grow only
rimp trawl nets, they are not

species of sculpin. There are
e correctly named bullheads.
bulosus, which lives in fresh-

Padded Sculpin

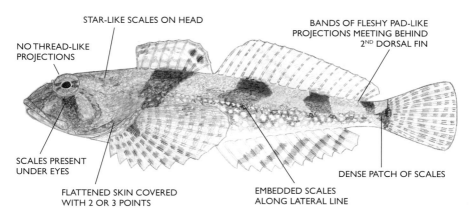

NO THREAD-LIKE
PROJECTIONS

STAR-LIKE SCALES ON HEAD

BANDS OF FLESHY PAD-LIKE
PROJECTIONS MEETING BEHIND
2ND DORSAL FIN

SCALES PRESENT
UNDER EYES

FLATTENED SKIN COVERED
WITH 2 OR 3 POINTS

EMBEDDED SCALES
ALONG LATERAL LINE

DENSE PATCH OF SCALES

SPECIES: *Artedius fenestralis*
OTHER COMMON NAMES: Incorrect: bullhead
MAXIMUM RECORDED SIZE: 14 cm (5.5 in)
DISTRIBUTION: Southern California to the Aleutian Island chain, Alaska
HABITAT: Most often spotted by divers exploring jetty and piling habitat, the cryptically coloured Padded Sculpin also lurks among eelgrass growing intertidally or slightly deeper. However, this species does live at depths to 60 m (200 ft). Look very carefully to find it, for this usually motionless sculpin is very difficult to spot, and once disturbed darts headlong for nearby shelter.

Peering into the water, the dockside observer may notice the gray Padded Sculpin resting among the barnacles and mussels growing upon the pilings, but this often stationary and irregularly marked creature blends beautifully with any background it has chosen. Seaside strollers should look for the Padded Sculpin along the rocky shore, either in tidepools or beneath adjacent rocks.

COMMENTS: During winter, the gravid female Padded Sculpin deposits small clusters of purple or gray eggs on the bottom, under rocks.

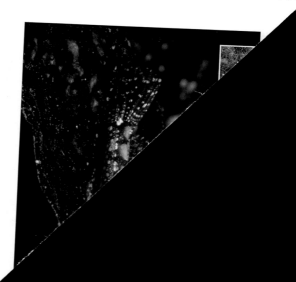

Smoothhead Sculpin

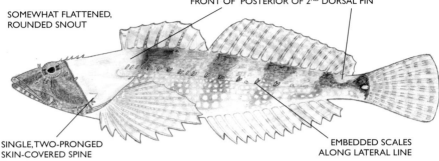

SINGLE BAND OF SCALES ALONG UPPER SIDE
FROM JUST BEHIND 1ST DORSAL FIN TO JUST IN
FRONT OF POSTERIOR OF 2ND DORSAL FIN

SOMEWHAT FLATTENED,
ROUNDED SNOUT

SINGLE, TWO-PRONGED
SKIN-COVERED SPINE

EMBEDDED SCALES
ALONG LATERAL LINE

SPECIES: *Artedius lateralis*
OTHER COMMON NAMES: flathead sculpin. Incorrect: bullhead
MAXIMUM RECORDED SIZE: 14 cm (5.5 in)
DISTRIBUTION: Northern Baja California, Mexico, to the Aleutian Island chain, Alaska
HABITAT: One of many small sculpins a diver may encounter, the well-camouflaged Smoothhead Sculpin lurks at less than 14 m (46 ft). At the start or finish of a shore dive, look for this species in the shallows. Look closely, though, because it is difficult to locate among seaweed-covered rocks or upon encrusted vertical pilings.

In tidepools or under moist rocks left exposed by the receding tide, the variably hued Smoothhead Sculpin is difficult to see because its irregular banded colouration blends too well with its background.
COMMENTS: In winter each gravid female Smoothhead Sculpin lays small clusters of adhesive, cherry-red, yellow, or orange eggs under rocks.

Generally dismissed as a tiny, bait-stealing nuisance by the pier-fishing crowd, the unpopular Smoothhead Sculpin often grabs any hooked offering and charges off into the pilings.

NOTE: Most abundant in California, the Bonehead Sculpin, *Artedius notospilotus* (sometimes called the Bonyhead Sculpin), might be encountered by readers as far north as Oregon. It is very similar to the Smoothhead Sculpin.

B. Male guarding nest. Bernard P. Hanby photograph

B

A

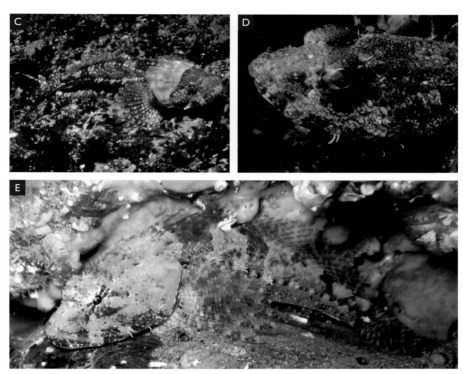

D. *Charlie Gibbs photograph*
E. *Rhoda Green photograph*

Coralline Sculpin

Artedius corallinus

Reported as far north as Orcas Island, Washington, the Coralline Sculpin is most common in central California. It is very similar to the Smoothhead Sculpin included in this guide and the two can only be separated by the relative number of scales that appear in a row along their sides. Consequently, the possibility of confusion exists, particularly for divers underwater. The Corallin Sculpin reaches a maximum recorded length of 14 cm (5.5 in).

Daniel W. Gotshall photograph

Scalyhead Sculpin

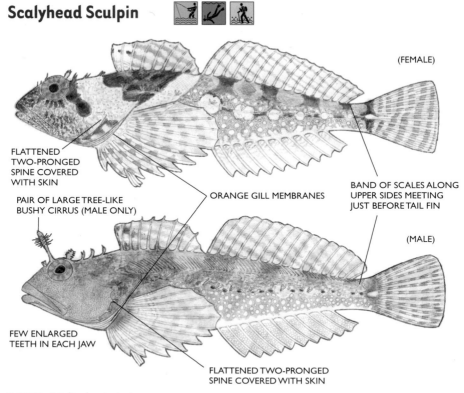

(FEMALE)

FLATTENED TWO-PRONGED SPINE COVERED WITH SKIN

PAIR OF LARGE TREE-LIKE BUSHY CIRRUS (MALE ONLY)

ORANGE GILL MEMBRANES

BAND OF SCALES ALONG UPPER SIDES MEETING JUST BEFORE TAIL FIN

(MALE)

FEW ENLARGED TEETH IN EACH JAW

FLATTENED TWO-PRONGED SPINE COVERED WITH SKIN

SPECIES: *Artedius harringtoni*

OTHER COMMON NAMES: plumose sculpin, white-spotted sculpin. Incorrect: bullhead

MAXIMUM RECORDED SIZE: 10 cm (4 in)

DISTRIBUTION: Southern California to the Aleutian Island chain, Alaska

HABITAT: A very abundant inhabitant of shallow reefs or rocky shores, the intricately patterned Scalyhead Sculpin actively darts about amid the colourful attached seaweeds and animals. Divers should also look among the growth that encrusts pilings to find this bold sculpin. Underwater photographers find this common little fish a subject that tests their skills with a macro lens. When guarding a nest, an adult male, with its exaggerated cirri and spotted mouth, is an inviting photography subject.

A

Tidepools formed at the very lowest tides often strand the common Scalyhead Sculpin until the returning sea frees it again. However, even a studious beachcomber may have difficulty in spotting one. A fine-mesh dip-net scooped through seaweeds may produce a specimen. Dockside observers more readily notice this creature perched upon pilings and their supports.

COMMENTS: Although yellow gill membranes distinguish an adult Scalyhead from other sculpins, juvenile specimens may be more difficult to separate from those of the previous few species in particular.

An incidental, unwanted but common catch for bait-fishermen who angle from docks or floats, the pesky Scalyhead Sculpin is too small to be of much interest.

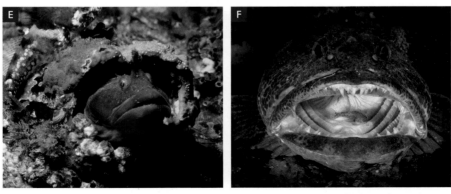

C. Adult male guarding nest.
D. Male aggressive behaviour. Dale Sanders photograph
E. Adult male.
F. Exhibiting cleaning behaviour with Lingcod. Jan Kocian photograph

Puget Sound Sculpin

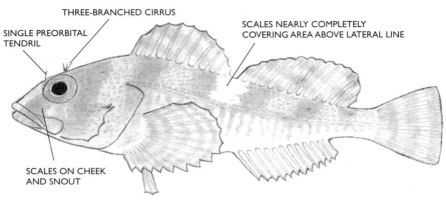

THREE-BRANCHED CIRRUS

SINGLE PREORBITAL
TENDRIL

SCALES NEARLY COMPLETELY
COVERING AREA ABOVE LATERAL LINE

SCALES ON CHEEK
AND SNOUT

SPECIES: *Ruscarius meanyi*. Formerly *Artedius meanyi*

MAXIMUM RECORDED SIZE: 5.9 cm (2.4 in)

DISTRIBUTION: Northern California to southeastern Alaska

HABITAT: The Puget Sound Sculpin is most likely to be found at recreational diving depths. Reportedly it prefers lurking upon large boulders or vertical rock outcrops, sites often visited by curious divers. Look closely though, for this drably coloured sculpin usually rests motionlessly on the bottom and therefore represents a difficult quarry.

Fortunately the Puget Sound Sculpin sometimes dwells in intertidal haunts. It is one of many tiny sculpins, most of which look very similar and might be found during a low-tide stroll along a rocky shore.

COMMENTS: The Puget Sound Sculpin is a tiny, inconspicuous species that lives at depths down to 82 m (270 ft). It is very poorly known and verifiable diver observations are rare.

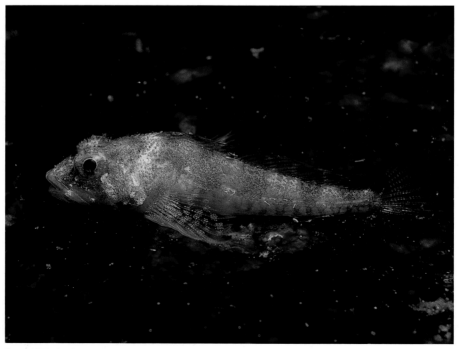

Bernard P. Hanby photograph

Tidepool Sculpin

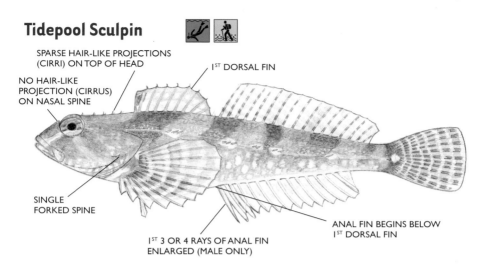

SPARSE HAIR-LIKE PROJECTIONS (CIRRI) ON TOP OF HEAD

1ST DORSAL FIN

NO HAIR-LIKE PROJECTION (CIRRUS) ON NASAL SPINE

SINGLE FORKED SPINE

1ST 3 OR 4 RAYS OF ANAL FIN ENLARGED (MALE ONLY)

ANAL FIN BEGINS BELOW 1ST DORSAL FIN

SPECIES: *Oligocottus maculosus*

OTHER COMMON NAMES: tide-pool sculpin. Incorrect: tidepool johnny, bullhead

MAXIMUM RECORDED SIZE: 9 cm (3.6 in)

DISTRIBUTION: Southern California to the Bering Sea and the Aleutian Island chain, Alaska

HABITAT: A very common intertidal sighting by beachcombers and divers entering or leaving the water, the mobile Tidepool Sculpin often darts along the shore as the tide ebbs and flows. It is frequently trapped in even the smallest tidepool or under a rock. Tolerant of high temperatures and low salinities in the intertidal realm, this variably coloured sculpin may easily return to its "home" territory when dislocated by man, animal, wave or tide.

COMMENTS: Mating season for this fish occurs from November to May when, after copulation, a female deposits small clusters of emerald-green or maroon adhesive eggs among mussels or barnacles.

Fluffy Sculpin

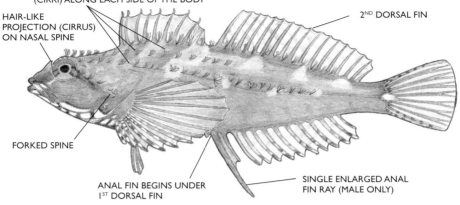

3 ROWS OF CLUSTERED, BUSHY PROJECTIONS
(CIRRI) ALONG EACH SIDE OF THE BODY

HAIR-LIKE
PROJECTION (CIRRUS)
ON NASAL SPINE

2ND DORSAL FIN

FORKED SPINE

ANAL FIN BEGINS UNDER
1ST DORSAL FIN

SINGLE ENLARGED ANAL
FIN RAY (MALE ONLY)

SPECIES: *Oligocottus snyderi*

OTHER COMMON NAMES: cirriated sculpin. Incorrect: bullhead

MAXIMUM RECORDED SIZE: 9 cm (3.6 in)

DISTRIBUTION: Northern Baja California, Mexico, to the Gulf of Alaska

HABITAT: Intolerant of higher temperatures and lower salinities characteristic of upper intertidal areas, the adult Fluffy Sculpin lurks in tidepools situated amid lower exposed zones. This sculpin is best seen by shallow-water divers using snorkelling gear. Look along exposed rocky-bottomed shallows or in nearby tidepools. Be patient though, as startled Fluffy Sculpins may require time before re-emerging into view.

COMMENTS: Capturing Fluffy Sculpins with a fine-meshed dip-net is often the best way for a close look. The thoughtful observer always returns such a catch from whence it came.

C. Bernard P. Hanby photograph

Saddleback Sculpin

SCALES IN THE FORM OF
PRICKLES OVER ENTIRE BODY

1ST DORSAL FIN

BLUNT SNOUT PROFILE

BLUNT, UPCURVED
UNFORKED SPINE

ANAL FIN BEGINS UNDER
1ST DORSAL FIN

SPECIES: *Oligocottus rimensis*
OTHER COMMON NAMES: Incorrect: prickly sculpin, bullhead
MAXIMUM RECORDED SIZE: 6.5 cm (2.6 in)
DISTRIBUTION: Northern Baja California, Mexico, to southeastern Alaska
HABITAT: Only "blue ribbon" fish-watching divers spot the tiny Saddleback Sculpin because it usually frequents murky shallows along silty or sandy shorelines. This seldom-noticed sculpin stakes out its territory amid dense growths of luxuriant eelgrass and other seaweed growing along the seashore or in tidepools. This active fish may also hide among the growth dangling from floats or pilings. Its colour pattern often blends so well with the surroundings that the little creature must move before even the most observant naturalist sees it.

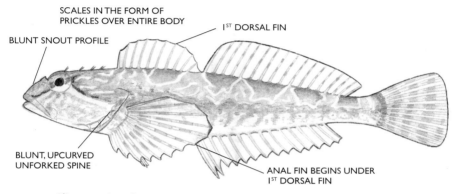

Sharpnose Sculpin

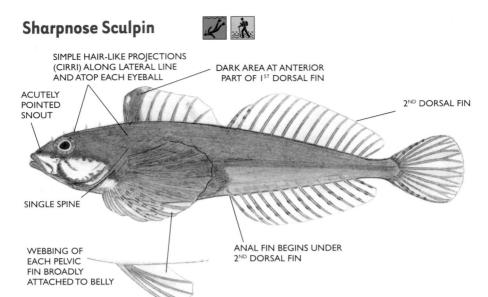

SIMPLE HAIR-LIKE PROJECTIONS (CIRRI) ALONG LATERAL LINE AND ATOP EACH EYEBALL

DARK AREA AT ANTERIOR PART OF 1ST DORSAL FIN

ACUTELY POINTED SNOUT

2ND DORSAL FIN

SINGLE SPINE

WEBBING OF EACH PELVIC FIN BROADLY ATTACHED TO BELLY

ANAL FIN BEGINS UNDER 2ND DORSAL FIN

SPECIES: *Clinocottus acuticeps*
OTHER COMMON NAMES: Incorrect name: bullhead
MAXIMUM RECORDED SIZE: 6.3 cm (2.5 in)
DISTRIBUTION: Central California coast to the Aleutian Island chain, Alaska
HABITAT: Only observant snorkelers or divers who search diligently along shorelines precisely where the water's surface meets the rocks might spy the active but elusive Sharpnose Sculpin.

While strolling along the seashore, look for this colourful sculpin on seaweed-covered seawalls or rocks. It follows the ebb and flow of the tide, generally remaining within centimeters of the surface.

COMMENTS: Primarily when young, this species is able to tolerate the lower salinities brought about by heavy rains. Consequently, it may venture into the brackish water of river estuaries.

Female swollen with eggs.

Calico Sculpin

FLESHY TUBERACLE AT
CENTRE OF UPPER LIP

NARROW
SNOUT

BUSHY HAIR-LIKE PROJECTIONS (CIRRI)
ALONG LATERAL LINE AND ON HEAD

2ND DORSAL FIN

SINGLE
BLUNT SPINE

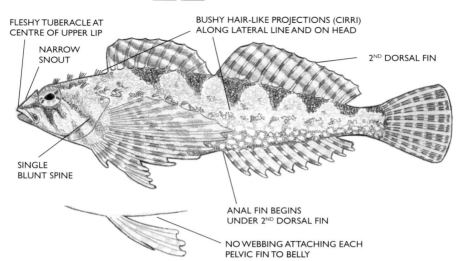

ANAL FIN BEGINS
UNDER 2ND DORSAL FIN

NO WEBBING ATTACHING EACH
PELVIC FIN TO BELLY

SPECIES: *Clinocottus embryum*
OTHER COMMON NAMES: mossy sculpin. Incorrect: bullhead
MAXIMUM RECORDED SIZE: 7 cm (2.8 in)
DISTRIBUTION: Northern Baja California, Mexico, to the Aleutian Island chain, Alaska
HABITAT: The constant surging and crashing of waves and associated poor visibility in its shallow or intertidal habitat discourages most divers from searching for the tiny Calico Sculpin. A snorkeler might have some luck searching carefully in a large, rocky tidepool.

Shoreside naturalists commonly find this species in rocky, weed-choked tidepools of nearly any size along shorelines directly swept by the Pacific. This secretive sculpin usually lurks amid the branches of pink coralline algae. Beachcombers should wait patiently for a hungry specimen to betray its whereabouts when darting after a tiny shrimp or other creature.

Mosshead Sculpin

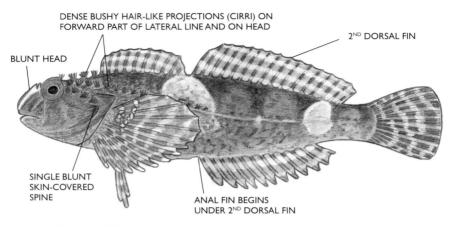

DENSE BUSHY HAIR-LIKE PROJECTIONS (CIRRI) ON FORWARD PART OF LATERAL LINE AND ON HEAD

2ND DORSAL FIN

BLUNT HEAD

SINGLE BLUNT SKIN-COVERED SPINE

ANAL FIN BEGINS UNDER 2ND DORSAL FIN

SPECIES: *Clinocottus globiceps*

OTHER COMMON NAMES: globe-headed sculpin, round-headed sculpin. Incorrect: bullhead

MAXIMUM RECORDED SIZE: 19 cm (7.5 in)

DISTRIBUTION: Southern California to the Gulf of Alaska

HABITAT: An intertidal creature nestling in the crevices of large rock formations, the boldly marked Mosshead Sculpin sits very still much of the time and therefore may be difficult for divers to observe. Aquanauts snorkelling in large tidepools sheltered from direct crashing surf have the best opportunity to study this creature.

Beachcombers should look for this distinctive sculpin in the middle to lower intertidal zone, but only along shores exposed directly to Pacific waves.

COMMENTS: The Mosshead Sculpin sometimes displays amphibious tendencies by wriggling from the water and perching on adjacent rocks. Once disturbed, though, they quickly retreat, splashing back into the water.

NOTE: A primary resident of California, the Bald Sculpin, *Clinocottus recalvus,* might be noticed along shallow Oregon shores. It is very similar to the Mosshead Sculpin.

Rosylip Sculpin

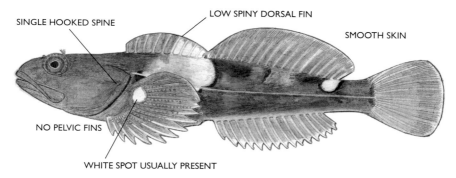

SINGLE HOOKED SPINE

LOW SPINY DORSAL FIN

SMOOTH SKIN

NO PELVIC FINS

WHITE SPOT USUALLY PRESENT

SPECIES: *Ascelichthys rhodorus*
OTHER COMMON NAMES: rosy-lipped sculpin. Incorrect: bullhead
MAXIMUM RECORDED SIZE: 15 cm (6 in)
DISTRIBUTION: Central California coast to the Gulf of Alaska
HABITAT: The smooth-skinned Rosylip Sculpin inhabits gravel beaches, rocky shorelines or seaweed-choked bays at depths of less than 15 m (50 ft). In such generally murky locales, its dark colouration and habit of huddling motionless amid surrounding shelter combine to conceal it from even the most observant diver.

Rocky tidepools, even very tiny ones or those located high in the intertidal zone, may contain this species. In late spring, young specimens less than 2.5 cm (1 in) are common along gravel beaches or among adjacent seaweeds.

Prickly Sculpin

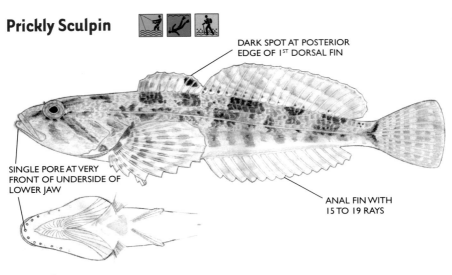

DARK SPOT AT POSTERIOR
EDGE OF 1ST DORSAL FIN

SINGLE PORE AT VERY
FRONT OF UNDERSIDE OF
LOWER JAW

ANAL FIN WITH
15 TO 19 RAYS

SPECIES: *Cottus asper*

OTHER COMMON NAMES: Incorrect: prickly bullhead, bullhead

MAXIMUM RECORDED SIZE: 15 cm (6 in)

DISTRIBUTION: Southern California to Seward, on the Kenai Peninsula, Alaska

HABITAT: Only an occasional intruder into the marine environment, the pugnacious Prickly Sculpin usually stays reasonably close to stream mouths, living at depths less than 10 m (33 ft). Search for it in and around river estuaries, the waters of which are often murky.

This grayish-brown sculpin can also be found along the banks of stream or river estuaries, lurking upon gravelly and sandy bottoms. This common species moves periodically to search for prey such as migrating salmon fry that pass through its territory, while avoiding its own numerous predators.

COMMENTS: There are several races of Prickly Sculpin but the one without prickles on its skin lives along the coast and may invade salt water.

Anglers who still-fish with bait along the sandbars of coastal river estuaries often catch the sluggish Prickly Sculpin. However, virtually all fishermen consider it a time-wasting and bait-thieving nuisance.

NOTE: Two related and very similar-looking sculpins that live in the Pacific Northwest freshwaters, the Coastrange Sculpin, *Cottus aleuticus,* and the Slimy Sculpin, *Cottus cognatus,* might conceivably stray into estuarine or marine environments.

Manacled Sculpin

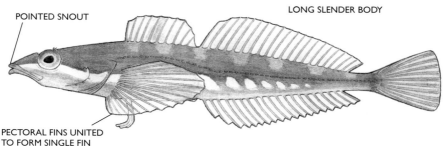

POINTED SNOUT

LONG SLENDER BODY

PECTORAL FINS UNITED
TO FORM SINGLE FIN

SPECIES: *Synchirus gilli*
MAXIMUM RECORDED SIZE: 7.5 cm (3 in)
DISTRIBUTION: Southern California to the Aleutian Island chain, Alaska
HABITAT: In shallows, divers should search through the other seaweeds growing in kelp forests or attached to floats to see the greenish, golden-brown or mauve Manacled Sculpin.

The slender Manacled Sculpin swims among the sea lettuce, kelp and other algae that hang from current-swept floats, piers and pilings making easy viewing for the beachcomber. Seldom is it trapped in tidepools.
COMMENTS: Between short bursts of activity, this little sculpin rests upon fronds of kelp or other vegetation. The male Manacled Sculpin has a very prominent silvery lateral stripe on each side, large pelvic fins, a long jaw with a definite knob on its chin and a genital papilla. This species preys upon tiny shrimp and their kin.

A. Female swollen with eggs. Mary P. O'Malley photograph
B. Adult male.

Longfin Sculpin

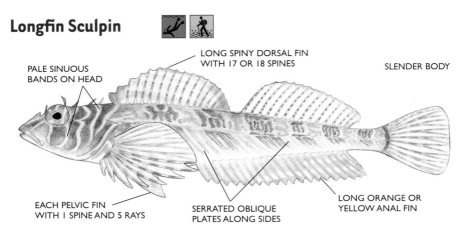

PALE SINUOUS
BANDS ON HEAD

LONG SPINY DORSAL FIN
WITH 17 OR 18 SPINES

SLENDER BODY

EACH PELVIC FIN
WITH 1 SPINE AND 5 RAYS

SERRATED OBLIQUE
PLATES ALONG SIDES

LONG ORANGE OR
YELLOW ANAL FIN

SPECIES: *Jordania zonope*

OTHER COMMON NAMES: bandeye sculpin

MAXIMUM RECORDED SIZE: 15 cm (6 in)

DISTRIBUTION: Central California coast to the Gulf of Alaska

HABITAT: Before the advent of scuba gear, scientists seldom observed the Longfin Sculpin. Today, the shallow rocky reef habitat of this brightly hued creature makes it a common find for divers cruising depths less than 30 m (100 ft). Look among the caves and crevices for this sculpin, which constantly moves in fits and starts. When momentarily stationary, it rests propped upon its fanlike pectoral fins. On other occasions it might linger on vertical cliffs or even "hang" upside down and horizontally along a cavern roof.

At very extreme low tides, beachcombers can explore rocky-bottom tidepools for a glimpse of the Longfin Sculpin. Persevere, though, for sightings are uncommon.

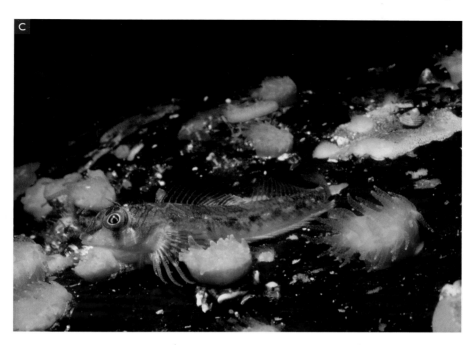

COMMENTS: Following an elaborate series of courtship manoeuvres, a gravid female Longfin Sculpin lays several small clusters of amber-coloured eggs, which the darkened male doggedly guards until they hatch. The Vancouver Aquarium has successfully reared offspring numerous times.

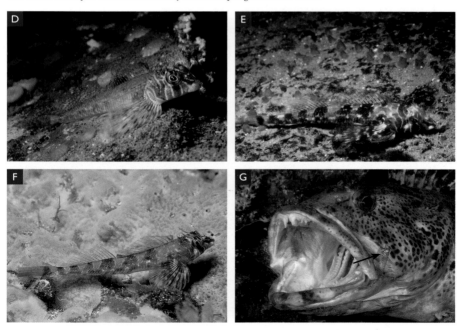

C. Juvenile.
E. Nocturnal colouration.
F. Bernard P. Hanby photograph
G. Cleaning Lingcod. Jan Kocian photograph

Spinynose Sculpin

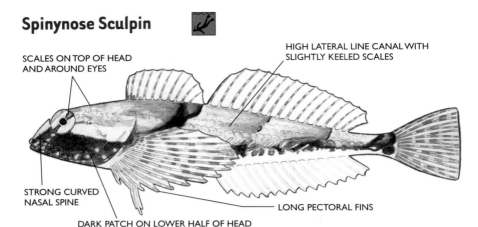

SCALES ON TOP OF HEAD
AND AROUND EYES

HIGH LATERAL LINE CANAL WITH
SLIGHTLY KEELED SCALES

STRONG CURVED
NASAL SPINE

DARK PATCH ON LOWER HALF OF HEAD

LONG PECTORAL FINS

SPECIES: *Radulinus taylori.* Formerly *Asemichthys taylori*
OTHER COMMON NAMES: Taylor's sculpin
MAXIMUM RECORDED SIZE: 7.5 cm (3 in)
DISTRIBUTION: Northern Washington to the British Columbia/Alaska border
HABITAT: Easily overlooked by most divers, the slender elongate Spinynose Sculpin usually rests on or buries itself partially in the shell hash that gathers in level terraces of reefs and around the bases of rocky outcroppings below 10 m (33 ft). It is very difficult to see unless it moves. Reddish-pink specimens prefer to lurk near pink, coralline algae-coated rock, adjacent to the favoured shell-hash substrate.

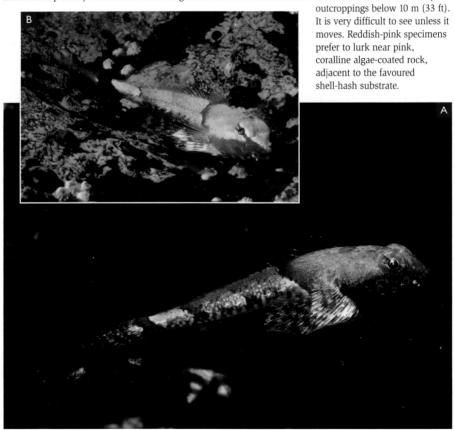

Snubnose Sculpin

PROMINENT SCALES ON
TOP OF HEAD

PROMINENT, CONTINUOUS ROW
OF SCALES FROM THE BEGINNING
OF 1ST DORSAL FIN TO END OF 2ND

SHORT
BLUNT
SNOUT

ANUS LOCATED ON BELLY MUCH CLOSER TO
BASE OF PECTORAL FINS THAN TO THE ANAL FIN

SPECIES: *Orthonopias triacis*

MAXIMUM RECORDED SIZE: 10 cm (4 in)

DISTRIBUTION: Baja California, northern Mexico, to central California (see below)

HABITAT: In June of 2009, co-author Andy Lamb located a population of Snubnose Sculpin living along the northwest coast of Vancouver Island—a discovery that extends the "officially documented" northern range from central California by over 1,400 km (875 mi). The specimens were found at remote Solander Island, a seldom (if ever) dived site. The bottom on which the Snubnose Sculpins were found was a gentle slope, consisting of small boulders on shell-hash sand. The depth was about 16 m (50 ft).

COMMENTS: Photographer Keith Clements captured the accompanying images while Andy collected three live specimens that were subsequently deposited at the Vancouver Aquarium. At the time of this writing, two were still alive.

A., B. Keith Clements photographs

Northern Sculpin

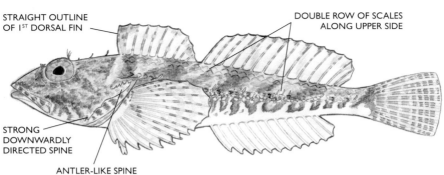

STRAIGHT OUTLINE
OF 1ST DORSAL FIN

DOUBLE ROW OF SCALES
ALONG UPPER SIDE

STRONG
DOWNWARDLY
DIRECTED SPINE

ANTLER-LIKE SPINE

SPECIES: *Icelinus borealis*

OTHER COMMON NAMES: comb sculpin. Incorrect: bullhead

MAXIMUM RECORDED SIZE: 10.2 cm (4 in)

DISTRIBUTION: Northern Washington to the Aleutian Island chain and Bristol Bay, Alaska

HABITAT: The drab Northern Sculpin lives on the bottom at depths below 10 m (33 ft) and prefers to sit upon large, smooth rocky outcroppings or barren reefs that are covered by silt but little else. Its tiny brownish-grey form usually remains unnoticed unless it stirs up silt as it moves. Night dives offer aquanauts the best chance of observing the Northern Sculpin.

COMMENTS: Enticed by captive prawns and smaller shrimps, hungry Northern Sculpins often find their way into prawn traps or are dragged up from the bottom as bycatch by shrimp trawlers at depths to 248 m (815 ft).

Dusky Sculpin

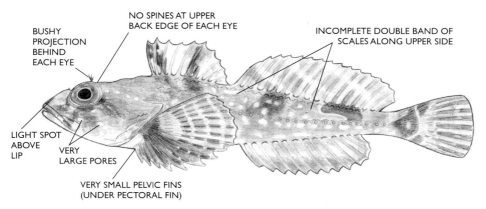

BUSHY PROJECTION BEHIND EACH EYE

NO SPINES AT UPPER BACK EDGE OF EACH EYE

INCOMPLETE DOUBLE BAND OF SCALES ALONG UPPER SIDE

LIGHT SPOT ABOVE LIP

VERY LARGE PORES

VERY SMALL PELVIC FINS (UNDER PECTORAL FIN)

SPECIES: *Icelinus burchami*

OTHER COMMON NAMES: Incorrect: bullhead

MAXIMUM RECORDED SIZE: 13 cm (5 in)

DISTRIBUTION: Southern California to southeastern Alaska

HABITAT: The greyish Dusky Sculpin's minimum depth is thought to be 61 m (200 ft), relegating it to very doubtful status on any casual diver's list of viewable fishes. However, as technical divers descend into virgin dive locales, some intrepid explorer may yet find and verify a population of Dusky Sculpins living upon silty or sandy bottoms.

COMMENTS: The Dusky Sculpin has been caught incidentally by shrimp trawlers towing their gear over level bottoms as deep as 570 m (1,880 ft).

Spotfin Sculpin

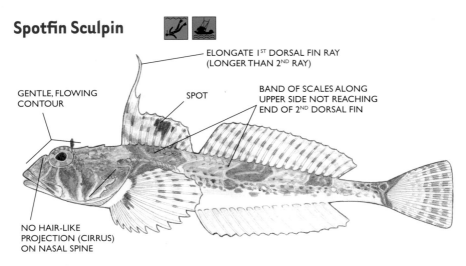

ELONGATE 1ST DORSAL FIN RAY
(LONGER THAN 2ND RAY)

GENTLE, FLOWING
CONTOUR

SPOT

BAND OF SCALES ALONG
UPPER SIDE NOT REACHING
END OF 2ND DORSAL FIN

NO HAIR-LIKE
PROJECTION (CIRRUS)
ON NASAL SPINE

SPECIES: *Icelinus tenuis*
OTHER COMMON NAMES: lesser filamented sculpin. Incorrect: bullhead
MAXIMUM RECORDED SIZE: 15.9 cm (6.3 in)
DISTRIBUTION: Central Baja California, Mexico, to southeastern Alaska
HABITAT: Often, while searching along sandy bottoms at depths below 12 m (40 ft), night divers spy the slender Spotfin Sculpin illuminated in the beams of their underwater flashlights. Either huddled belly down on the sand or propped up on its pectoral fins, this nocturnal fish waits motionless for small shrimps or other prey. In the southern portions of its range, more colourful Spotfin Sculpins often favour rocky habitat.
COMMENTS: Shrimp trawlers who drag their fine-mesh nets over flat, soft bottoms at depths to 370 m (1,220 ft) sometimes capture the commercially valueless Spotfin Sculpin. Attracted by a possible meal, this opportunistic fish occasionally enters prawn traps set upon its level-bottomed habitat.

B., C. Marc Chamberlain photographs

Threadfin Sculpin

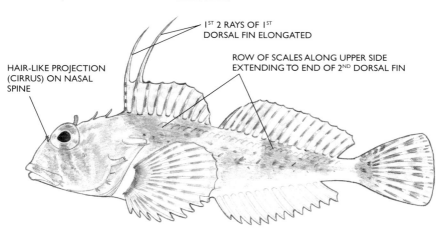

1ST 2 RAYS OF 1ST DORSAL FIN ELONGATED

ROW OF SCALES ALONG UPPER SIDE EXTENDING TO END OF 2ND DORSAL FIN

HAIR-LIKE PROJECTION (CIRRUS) ON NASAL SPINE

SPECIES: *Icelinus filamentosus*

OTHER COMMON NAMES: filamented sculpin, long-rayed sculpin. Incorrect: bullhead

MAXIMUM RECORDED SIZE: 27 cm (10.7 in)

DISTRIBUTION: Southern California to the Gulf of Alaska

HABITAT: As yet, the bulbous-headed Threadfin Sculpin has only been found in water as shallow as 37 m (122 ft), just below depths explored by most sport divers. However, it is conceivable that this deepwater creature may invade shallower depths. More likely though, the Threadfin Sculpin might be found by technical divers.

COMMENTS: The moderate-sized Threadfin Sculpin is sometimes captured incidentally by commercial shrimp trawlers dragging their nets over nearly level bottoms at depths to 373 m (1,224 ft). After finding this opportunistic creature trapped in their gear, resourceful prawn trappers could put it in a bucket of saltwater and contact a local public aquarium about donating it for display.

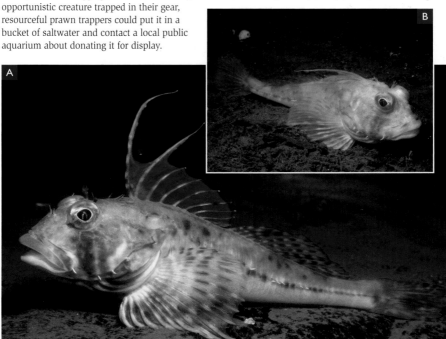

Fringed Sculpin

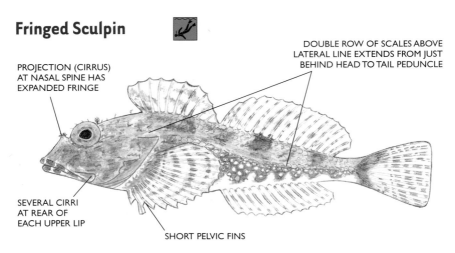

PROJECTION (CIRRUS) AT NASAL SPINE HAS EXPANDED FRINGE

DOUBLE ROW OF SCALES ABOVE LATERAL LINE EXTENDS FROM JUST BEHIND HEAD TO TAIL PEDUNCLE

SEVERAL CIRRI AT REAR OF EACH UPPER LIP

SHORT PELVIC FINS

SPECIES: *Icelinus fimbriatus*

MAXIMUM RECORDED SIZE: 19 cm (7.5 in)

DISTRIBUTION: Southern California to southern British Columbia

HABITAT: During the years since the first version of this guide appeared, co-author Andy Lamb and others have encountered several Fringed Sculpins in Porpoise Bay, British Columbia. These individuals were found on or adjacent to steep walls of outcrop rock. Recognizing these specimens as different and likely of a species undocumented this far north, two were collected and photographed by Bernard P. Hanby and co-author Phil Edgell. Two of the resulting images appear here. Since then, additional specimens have been observed and all have been spotted in Porpoise Bay.

B. Bernard P. Hanby photograph

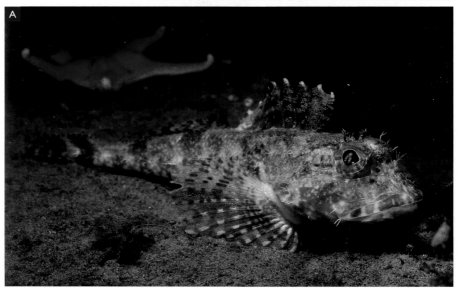

Unidentified Sculpin

Co-author Phil Edgell took this photograph in Howe Sound, British Columbia, before the first edition of this guide was published in 1986. At the time, we were uncertain as to the identity of this sculpin and elected not to include it in the publication. We have since decided to include the photograph in this edition with the hope that it will stimulate discussion about the specimen's identity. Our best guess is the Thorny Sculpin, *Icelus spiniger*.

Ribbed Sculpin

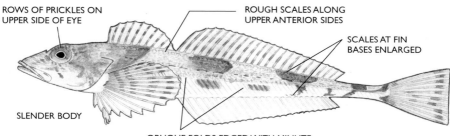

ROWS OF PRICKLES ON UPPER SIDE OF EYE

ROUGH SCALES ALONG UPPER ANTERIOR SIDES

SCALES AT FIN BASES ENLARGED

SLENDER BODY

OBLIQUE FOLDS EDGED WITH MINUTE SCALES BELOW LATERAL LINE

SPECIES: *Triglops pingelii.* Formerly *Triglops pingeli*
MAXIMUM RECORDED SIZE: 20 cm (8 in)
DISTRIBUTION: Northern Washington to the Bering Sea then west through the Aleutian chain to Hokkaido, northern Japan, as well as east through the Arctic to Hudson Bay, Cape Cod and Denmark

B. Courting pair, with male to the right. Richard Zade photograph

HABITAT: Unless exploring flat, uninteresting mud and gravel bottoms, the casual diver will not likely encounter, let alone recognize, the elusive Ribbed Sculpin. This active little fish usually cruises along slowly, punctuated by brief stops. As a diver catches up, the little beast invariably moves off again. This performance is both tantalizing and frustrating to the aquanaut attempting to identify and/ or photograph it.

Young colourful Ribbed Sculpin often live in and around the eelgrass beds at depths as shallow as 3 m (10 ft.). Consequently, the species is a sighting possibility for the beach stroller.

COMMENTS: Shrimp trawlers sometimes incidentally catch the unmarketable Ribbed Sculpin from soft level substrates at depths between 5 and 482 m (17 and 1,581 ft).

Roughspine Sculpin

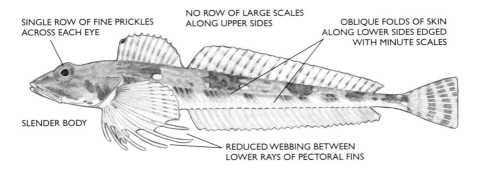

SINGLE ROW OF FINE PRICKLES
ACROSS EACH EYE

NO ROW OF LARGE SCALES
ALONG UPPER SIDES

OBLIQUE FOLDS OF SKIN
ALONG LOWER SIDES EDGED
WITH MINUTE SCALES

SLENDER BODY

REDUCED WEBBING BETWEEN
LOWER RAYS OF PECTORAL FINS

SPECIES: *Triglops macellus*

OTHER COMMON NAMES: rough-spine sculpin

MAXIMUM RECORDED SIZE: 26.4 cm (10.6 in)

DISTRIBUTION: Washington to the Bering Sea and Aleutian Island chain, Alaska

HABITAT: Night divers should watch for the nocturnally active Roughspine Sculpin. This slender and tapered fish forages actively for small invertebrate prey and often rests on the bottom perched upon its pectoral and tail fins. The underwater photographer may then take a good picture of the creature highlighted by a lack of background instead of it being obscured by the nondescript bottom. On other occasions the brownish-grey Roughspine Sculpin may fold its pectoral fins, huddle belly-down on the sand and remain quite inconspicuous. A diver moving cautiously can easily approach any such stationed specimen without it fleeing into the dark. Look for Roughspine Sculpin, particularly upon sandy bottoms, well clear of any rocky outcroppings, at depths below 15 m (50 ft).

COMMENTS: NOTE: Three other very similar *Triglops* sculpins are recorded from the Pacific Northwest. Most abundant in the Gulf of Alaska, the Scissortail Sculpin, *Triglops forficatus*, the Spectacled Sculpin, *Triglops scepticus,* and the Highbrow Sculpin, *Triglops metopias*, perhaps might be encountered by readers based in southeastern Alaska and north.

Slim Sculpin

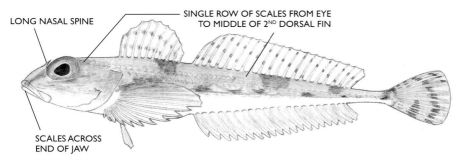

LONG NASAL SPINE

SINGLE ROW OF SCALES FROM EYE
TO MIDDLE OF 2ND DORSAL FIN

SCALES ACROSS
END OF JAW

SPECIES: *Radulinus asprellus*

OTHER COMMON NAMES: Incorrect: darter sculpin

MAXIMUM RECORDED SIZE: 15 cm (6 in)

DISTRIBUTION: Northern Baja California, Mexico, to the Aleutian Island chain, Alaska

HABITAT: While patrolling sandy or muddy bottoms, particularly at night, an observant diver might find the slender Slim Sculpin huddling. An underwater photographer who finds one should approach it from down current, so that particulate matter does not drift over and obscure the specimen, thus spoiling a noteworthy image.

COMMENTS: The Slim Sculpin illustrates an interesting geographic-depth relationship also exhibited by other marine fishes of North America's western shore. Within the boundaries of its known range, the farther south the Slim Sculpin is found, the more likely it will have come from deep water. In California, for example, scientists have captured this sculpin at depths as great as 284 m (930 ft), while specimens in British Columbia have been gathered at a maximum of 180 m (594 ft). Consequently, scientists believe that the slender Slim Sculpin has a preferential temperature range, and these temperatures occur deeper in more southerly latitudes.

Darter Sculpin

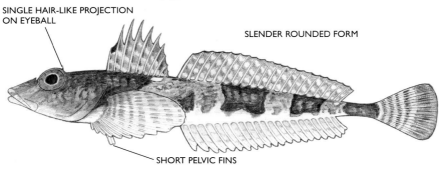

SINGLE HAIR-LIKE PROJECTION
ON EYEBALL

SLENDER ROUNDED FORM

SHORT PELVIC FINS

SPECIES: *Radulinus boleoides*
MAXIMUM RECORDED SIZE: 14 cm (5.5 in)
DISTRIBUTION: Southern California to the Gulf of Alaska
HABITAT: Unfortunately, the Darter Sculpin is like some of the other small and rarely-seen sculpin species—there simply is not any typical habitat information available in the literature. However, during a memorable September 1981 night dive in Howe Sound, British Columbia, Bernard P. Hanby and co-author Andy Lamb happened upon what was obviously an unusual fish resting upon the steeply sloping, muddy and debris-littered bottom at about 21 m (70 ft). It was photographed, captured and transported back to the laboratory where it was identified as a Darter Sculpin. Sketched later by Andy and re-photographed by co-author Phil Edgell, this was the fifth such catch recorded in British Columbia, and the first ever by divers. However, in the many years since, the Darter Sculpin has not been observed by us or anyone within our circle of contact.

Thornback Sculpin

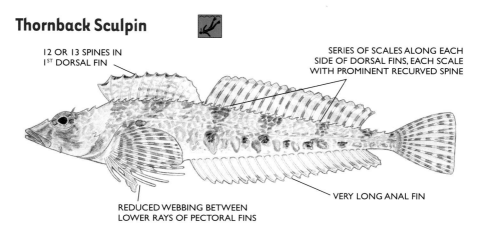

12 OR 13 SPINES IN
1ˢᵀ DORSAL FIN

SERIES OF SCALES ALONG EACH
SIDE OF DORSAL FINS, EACH SCALE
WITH PROMINENT RECURVED SPINE

REDUCED WEBBING BETWEEN
LOWER RAYS OF PECTORAL FINS

VERY LONG ANAL FIN

SPECIES: *Paricelinus hopliticus*
MAXIMUM RECORDED SIZE: 20 cm (7.8 in)
DISTRIBUTION: Southern California to northern British Columbia
HABITAT: Infrequently observed by divers, the distinctive Thornback Sculpin offers a worthy challenge for the neoprene-suited divers. Look for this elusive fish on silt-covered barren, rocky reefs or cliff faces, and along their sandy bases at depths below 20 m (66 ft). Propped by its pectoral and tail fins, it will probably be resting upon the bottom, scanning its environment for predator or prey.

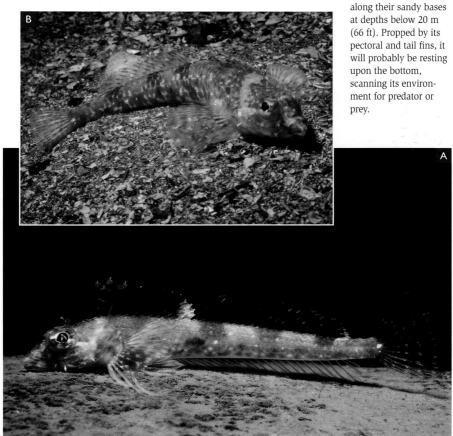

Roughback Sculpin

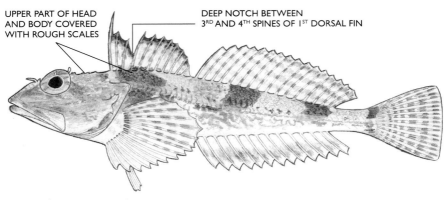

UPPER PART OF HEAD AND BODY COVERED WITH ROUGH SCALES

DEEP NOTCH BETWEEN 3RD AND 4TH SPINES OF 1ST DORSAL FIN

SPECIES: *Chitonotus pugetensis*

OTHER COMMON NAMES: Incorrect: bullhead

MAXIMUM RECORDED SIZE: 23 cm (9 in)

DISTRIBUTION: Southern Baja California, Mexico, to northern British Columbia

HABITAT: While depths to 143 m (470 ft) provide the typical habitat for this inconspicuous fish, the nocturnally active Roughback Sculpin is also a very common sight for night divers cruising over sandy bottoms at depths below 9 m (30 ft). By wriggling its greyish body to and fro and scooping with its fan-like pectoral fins, this creature often buries itself in the mud or sand, leaving only its back and large eyes exposed. The Roughback Sculpin may also be seen by dockside observers when drawn to lights that shine into the water from a float or pier.

COMMENTS: As its long breeding season approaches, a mature male often darkens the irregular red bands on his sides, intensifies his colour and likely develops a bright red, orange or white flash on top of each eye. After being courted by such a "dashing" suitor, the gravid female deposits clusters of fertilized, bright, salmon-coloured eggs on small twigs or worm tubes protruding from the sea floor.

Spinyhead Sculpin

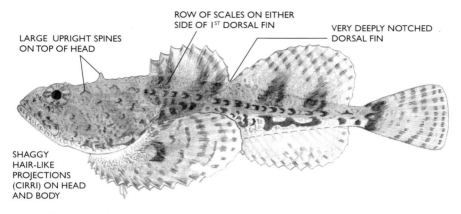

ROW OF SCALES ON EITHER SIDE OF 1ST DORSAL FIN

VERY DEEPLY NOTCHED DORSAL FIN

LARGE UPRIGHT SPINES ON TOP OF HEAD

SHAGGY HAIR-LIKE PROJECTIONS (CIRRI) ON HEAD AND BODY

SPECIES: *Dasycottus setiger*

OTHER COMMON NAMES: Incorrect: wooly sculpin bullhead

MAXIMUM RECORDED SIZE: 45 cm (18 in)

DISTRIBUTION: Northern Washington to the Aleutian Island chain and the Bering Sea of Alaska, and west to the Sea of Japan

HABITAT: The bright beam of a night diver's flashlight sometimes illuminates the warty-headed Spinyhead Sculpin as it nestles upon sandy or silty bottoms at depths below 15 m (50 ft). A dull pink-to-grey colour provides camouflage while it hides amid drab surroundings. A Spinyhead Sculpin usually remains very still and may even submit to gentle prodding for a posed photograph. The specimen shown here (A) opened its mouth in response to photographer Phil Edgell's touch.

COMMENTS: Shrimp trawlers and, to a lesser extent, prawn trappers, who fish their gear on sandy or silty substrates to depths up to 855 m (2,806 ft), incidentally catch the unprofitable Spinyhead Sculpin.

Blackfin Sculpin

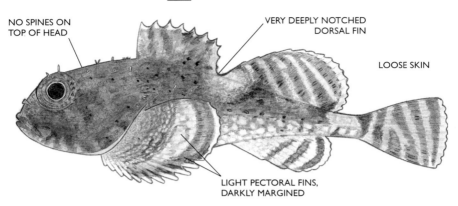

NO SPINES ON
TOP OF HEAD

VERY DEEPLY NOTCHED
DORSAL FIN

LOOSE SKIN

LIGHT PECTORAL FINS,
DARKLY MARGINED

SPECIES: *Malacocottus kincaidi*
OTHER COMMON NAMES: Incorrect: bullhead
MAXIMUM RECORDED SIZE: 10.6 cm (4.2 in)
DISTRIBUTION: Northern Washington to northern British Columbia
HABITAT: Sometimes while night diving over silty bottoms where boulders lie scattered about, an observant aquanaut may encounter a stationary Blackfin Sculpin. Expect to find it at depths below 18 m (60 ft), but search patiently because the globular head and brownish colouration of this creature make it fairly difficult to spot. Technical divers able to use mixed gases and go deeper are much more likely to observe the Blackfin Sculpin.

COMMENTS: NOTE: The very similar Darkfin Sculpin, *Malacocottus zonurus*, has been recorded as far south as Washington. With a minimum recorded depth of 93 m (304 ft), it is unlikely to be encountered by this readership.

Tadpole Sculpin

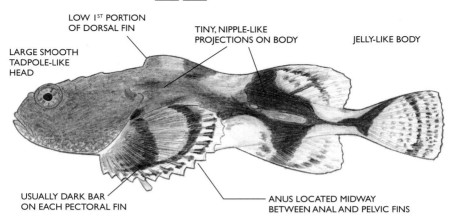

LOW 1ST PORTION
OF DORSAL FIN

TINY, NIPPLE-LIKE
PROJECTIONS ON BODY

JELLY-LIKE BODY

LARGE SMOOTH
TADPOLE-LIKE
HEAD

USUALLY DARK BAR
ON EACH PECTORAL FIN

ANUS LOCATED MIDWAY
BETWEEN ANAL AND PELVIC FINS

SPECIES: *Psychrolutes paradoxus*
MAXIMUM RECORDED SIZE: 6.5 cm (2.6 in)
DISTRIBUTION: Northern Washington to the Bering Sea, Aleutian Island chain, Alaska, and through to the Sea of Japan
HABITAT: Resting upon silty bottoms, occasionally at depths down to 220 m (720 ft), the brownish Tadpole Sculpin, with its black-edged and often orange-centred pectoral fins, is abundant in certain shallow areas. During the summer, this slow swimmer huddles among the eelgrass or rests upon the surrounding mud.

The Tadpole Sculpin commonly swarms into muddy, shallow bays where a keen-eyed naturalist may see it from piers or jetties in spring and summer. At night, though, an observer may see them more easily because they readily swim off the bottom toward dock lights. Dip-net a specimen, lift it from the water, and notice that its flaccid body appears to be an inert glob of jelly. Be a good environmental steward and release it unharmed.

Soft Sculpin

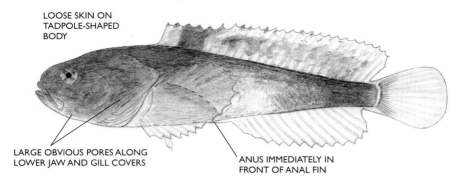

LOOSE SKIN ON
TADPOLE-SHAPED
BODY

LARGE OBVIOUS PORES ALONG
LOWER JAW AND GILL COVERS

ANUS IMMEDIATELY IN
FRONT OF ANAL FIN

SPECIES: *Psychrolutes sigalutes.* Formerly *Gilbertidia sigalutes*

MAXIMUM RECORDED SIZE: 8.3 cm (3.3 in)

DISTRIBUTION: Northern Washington to the Aleutian Island chain, Alaska

HABITAT: In certain areas, a night diver might notice the slow-swimming Soft Sculpin in shallow waters around floats. Look for the greyish form over silty bottoms adjacent to eelgrass beds, where it often rises off the bottom and swims toward artificial light.

COMMENTS: The late Dr. Charles Moffett, a psychiatrist from Friday Harbor, Washington, annually greeted the springtime arrival of the Soft Sculpin. On still, windless evenings, he watched for this abundant, slow-swimming fish to approach his "night light," which hung from a neighbour's float. Occasionally forming distinct schools, a behaviour very unusual for sculpins, they swam about, just beneath the surface.

NOTE: The giant Blob Sculpin, *Psychrolutes phrictus,* resembles the above species but lives at depths below 480 m (1,584 ft) and grows to 70 cm (28 in). With a maximum recorded size of 70 cm (28 in) and 9.5 kg (21 lb), it would be a magnificent creature to behold!

Silverspotted Sculpin

LONG, PROMINENT HAIR-LIKE PROJECTIONS (CIRRI) ON SNOUT AND LOWER JAW

DEEPLY NOTCHED 1ˢᵀ DORSAL FIN

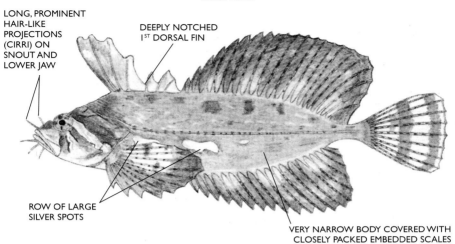

ROW OF LARGE SILVER SPOTS

VERY NARROW BODY COVERED WITH CLOSELY PACKED EMBEDDED SCALES

SPECIES: *Blepsias cirrhosus*

OTHER COMMON NAMES: silverspot sculpin. Incorrect: silver spot

MAXIMUM RECORDED SIZE: 20 cm (8 in)

DISTRIBUTION: Northern California to the Aleutian Island chain and Bering Sea coast of Alaska, through to the Sea of Japan

HABITAT: Although the beautiful Silverspotted Sculpin resides commonly at shallow, diveable depths, only dedicated aquanauts who persevere through very thick growths of seaweeds will likely find it. Its golden or dark-green colour, lacy appearance and sinuous swimming behaviour often give this large-finned fish the appearance of a ragged piece of kelp "wagging" in the current.

So well is the golden brown or green Silverspotted Sculpin camouflaged that the surface-bound naturalist will seldom see it without first using the indispensible dip-net. To find one, try scooping through the thick carpets of seaweed growing along rocky shores or in tidepools, or hanging from pilings and floats. In spring, lacy-looking young flourish in eelgrass meadows and along shallow kelp-choked shores.

B. Bernard P. Hanby photograph

Crested Sculpin

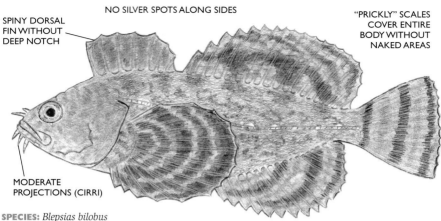

NO SILVER SPOTS ALONG SIDES

SPINY DORSAL
FIN WITHOUT
DEEP NOTCH

"PRICKLY" SCALES
COVER ENTIRE
BODY WITHOUT
NAKED AREAS

MODERATE
PROJECTIONS (CIRRI)

SPECIES: *Blepsias bilobus*

MAXIMUM RECORDED SIZE: 27 cm (11 in)

DISTRIBUTION: Northern British Columbia to the Aleutian Island chain and Bering Sea coast of Alaska, through to the Sea of Japan

HABITAT: Although the Crested Sculpin is a truly magnificent sight for the scuba diver, unfortunately its primarily northern distribution eliminates many folks from an opportunity for interaction. However, when seen in northern waters, this sculpin frequents shallow depths conducive to casual divers. It also swims slowly, frequently spreading its spectacular fins when stopping. In particular, this variably coloured and patterned fish will occasionally twirl its pectoral fins like a fan dancer. Once hidden amid surrounding seaweeds, though, the Crested Sculpin's camouflage challenges the observational skills of even the most seasoned diver.

B. Jan Haaga photograph

B

A

A. Bernard P. Hanby photograph

Sailfin Sculpin

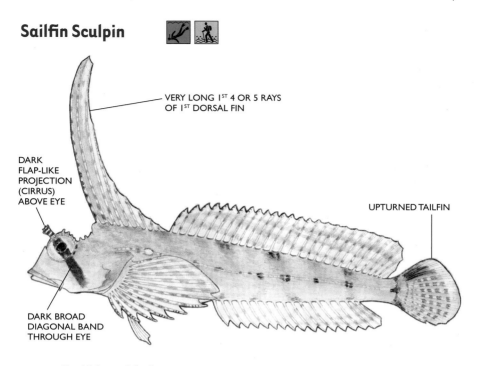

VERY LONG 1ST 4 OR 5 RAYS
OF 1ST DORSAL FIN

DARK
FLAP-LIKE
PROJECTION
(CIRRUS)
ABOVE EYE

UPTURNED TAILFIN

DARK BROAD
DIAGONAL BAND
THROUGH EYE

SPECIES: *Nautichthys oculofasciatus*
OTHER COMMON NAMES: sailorfish, sailor fish
MAXIMUM RECORDED SIZE: 20 cm (8 in)
DISTRIBUTION: Southern California to the Gulf of Alaska
HABITAT: This sinuous swimmer is most abundant in shallow waters where it cruises along rocky outcroppings, cliff faces or upon adjacent sandy areas. It may also live around jetties and pilings. A common sight for the night diver, the graceful Sailfin Sculpin swims over the bottom by holding its body stiff while

A

B. Bernard P. Hanby photograph

C. Young juvenile.

moving its dorsal and anal fin rays independently, one after another in a continuous series of waves. Patiently watch a specimen lower its long first dorsal fin rays over its head, then move them back and forth—a distinctive behaviour often occurring just before this sculpin gulps a tiny shrimp or other prey.

Watch for the slow-swimming Sailfin Sculpin at night from well-lighted docks or jetties. Receding tides occasionally trap it in cool northern tidepools.

When frequenting depths as great as 110 m (363 ft), the resourceful Sailfin Sculpin may show pinkish or orange colouring.

By day, the nocturnally active Sailfin Sculpin hides motionless inside caves or crevices and is an uncommon sighting.

COMMENTS: In spring, female Sailfin Sculpins lay small clusters of orange eggs among mussels in the intertidal zone, and the tiny larvae that hatch from these eggs, sporting exaggerated, enlarged fins (C), spend their first few weeks at the surface.

NOTE: Lacking the long first portion of the first dorsal fin that is distinctive for the above species, the Eyeshade Sculpin, *Nautichthys pribilovius,* and the Shortmast Sculpin, *Nautichthys robustus,* otherwise are very similar. Both are northern species, rarely encountered and very unlikely to be seen south of Alaska.

Grunt Sculpin

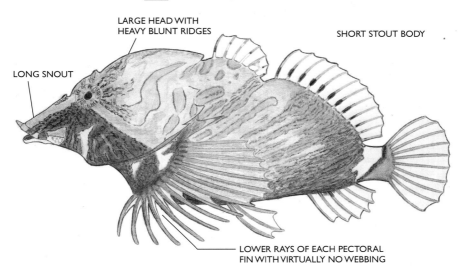

LARGE HEAD WITH
HEAVY BLUNT RIDGES

SHORT STOUT BODY

LONG SNOUT

LOWER RAYS OF EACH PECTORAL
FIN WITH VIRTUALLY NO WEBBING

SPECIES: *Rhamphocottus richardsonii*. Formerly *Rhamphocottus richardsoni*
OTHER COMMON NAMES: Richardson's sculpin. Incorrect: gruntfish, pigfish, northern sea horse
MAXIMUM RECORDED SIZE: 8.9 cm (3.5 in)
DISTRIBUTION: Southern California to the Gulf of Alaska, Japan

B. Bernard P. Hanby photograph

B

A

HABITAT: Finding a Grunt Sculpin, with its big head, pig-like snout and orange tail fin, is a highlight of any dive. Search for it along rocky shores or reefs, among encrusting invertebrate animals growing there.

Very rarely trapped in tidepools, the amusing Grunt Sculpin does seek shelter under floats or piers where it may be observed by shorebound naturalists.

COMMENTS: Often the Grunt Sculpin's snout protrudes from an empty Giant Barnacle casing and makes this casing appear to contain a live but closed barnacle within. This tiny fish may turn around within the casing, stick its tail fin out and wave it back and forth and appear to be a feeding barnacle actively waving its cirri to capture microscopic planktonic prey. If such natural shelter is unavailable, the determined Grunt Sculpin often colonizes debris, such as discarded bottles or cans. A sexually mature Grunt Sculpin will often claim this artificial habitat (or the more natural barnacle casing) and seek to entice a potential mate within.

When moving along the sea floor this creature rarely swims but instead "walks" along on its finger-like lower pectoral fin rays. A careful diver can catch a specimen by hand and actually feel it producing quiet vibrations that, perhaps, suggest its name.

The Grunt Sculpin has been recorded in shrimp trawls at depths of 165 m (545 ft).

E. Juvenile.

Cabezon

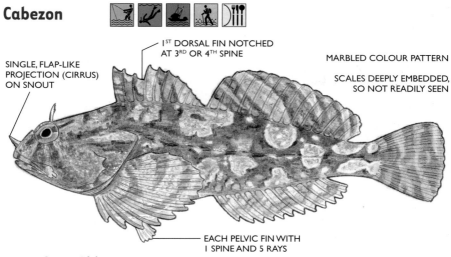

SINGLE, FLAP-LIKE
PROJECTION (CIRRUS)
ON SNOUT

1ST DORSAL FIN NOTCHED
AT 3RD OR 4TH SPINE

MARBLED COLOUR PATTERN

SCALES DEEPLY EMBEDDED,
SO NOT READILY SEEN

EACH PELVIC FIN WITH
1 SPINE AND 5 RAYS

SPECIES: *Scorpaenichthys marmoratus*
OTHER COMMON NAMES: giant marbled sculpin, giant sculpin. Incorrect: blue garnet, bull cod, bullhead
MAXIMUM RECORDED SIZE: 99 cm (39 in) and 14 kg (30 lb)
DISTRIBUTION: Central Baja California, Mexico, to southeastern Alaska

HABITAT: Often a diver is startled by a large Cabezon as it bolts powerfully for nearby kelp or other cover. However, in late winter an adult male Cabezon usually does not bolt, but rather may charge and "bump" a diver while steadfastly guarding a nest of large adhesive wine-red or purple eggs.

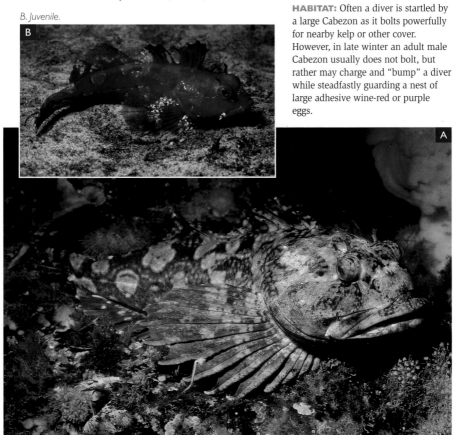

B. Juvenile.

B

A

After just a month of life, the silvery, almost square-looking young Cabezon, very different from its parents, may hide among the floating seaweeds associated with summer tidelines. Tidepools frequently trap slightly larger, more adult-like specimens.

COMMENTS: A dominant male may mate with a number of females sequentially, producing various clutches of eggs and resulting in the ova being different shades of red, purple and green.

Popular among sport fishermen in California, the bottom-dwelling Cabezon ravenously seizes most baits. Cast for this large sculpin from jetties, boats or shorelines, especially near kelp beds, but expect only one strong short burst of action before landing it.

Californian longliners enthusiastically harvest the popular Cabezon along with other species, but Pacific Northwest commercial fishermen seldom catch it.

The Cabezon is an excellent-tasting fish. Try it barbecued. Occasional specimens with green-tinged flesh will lose this colour once cooked. Do not eat the roe: it is highly toxic.

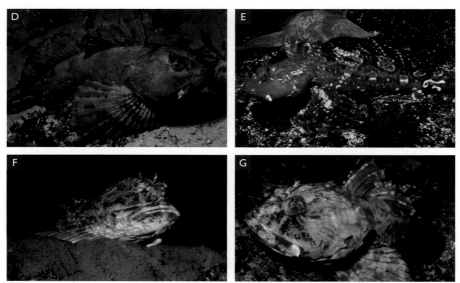

F. Male guarding nest.

Great Sculpin

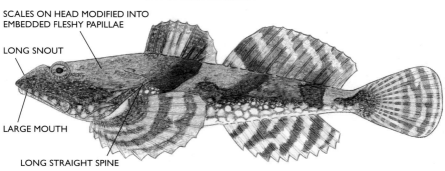

SCALES ON HEAD MODIFIED INTO EMBEDDED FLESHY PAPILLAE

LONG SNOUT

LARGE MOUTH

LONG STRAIGHT SPINE

SPECIES: *Myoxocephalus polyacanthocephalus*

OTHER COMMON NAMES: Incorrect: bullhead

MAXIMUM RECORDED SIZE: 76 cm (30 in)

DISTRIBUTION: Northern Washington to the Bering Sea coast of Alaska, the Aleutian Island chain, through northern Japan

HABITAT: Divers sometimes encounter the large-headed Great Sculpin resting upon silt-covered rocky outcroppings or adjacent sandy substrates at depths less than 20 m (66 ft). Wharves, pilings and their associated underwater debris often shelter this large sculpin. Although its usually drab colouration matches well with its preferred dull surroundings, more attractively hued specimens lurk among more colourful backgrounds.

In spring, barely recognizable juvenile Great Sculpins hide in very shallow water, often amid eelgrass.

COMMENTS: The sluggish Great Sculpin greedily gulps down sport-fishing baits of nearly any size or kind lowered onto the shallow bottom. Jetty or wharf-bound anglers most often take it.

Try cooking the Great Sculpin into an unusual "fish loaf." Melt butter, stir in flour and some milk and then cook. Cool the mixture before adding the Great Sculpin, celery, bread crumbs, parsley, onion, salt and tomato sauce. Finally, mold into a pan and bake.

NOTE: The Frog Sculpin, *Myoxocephalus stelleri*, and the Plain Sculpin, *Myoxocephalus jaok*, are very similar to the Great Sculpin. However, because they are primarily northern Alaska species, there is little chance of confusing them with their more southerly relative in the Pacific Northwest.

Shorthorn Sculpin

Myoxocephalus scorpius

The Shorthorn Sculpin commonly occurs in shallow water. It has been recorded as far south as northern British Columbia and grows to a maximum recorded length of 60 cm (24 in). These factors combine to make the species a possible sighting for Pacific Northwest fish watchers. Hopefully, camera-toting divers will find this a compelling situation, document it in the southern portion of its range and add to our knowledge about this species.

Danny Kent photograph

Bigmouth Sculpin

Hemitripterus bolini

Over the years since the first edition of this guide appeared, we have conferred with several divers claiming to have seen the Bigmouth Sculpin near the northern end of Vancouver Island—well within the established geographic limits for the species. This fish is very distinctive and the observers have been knowledgeable fish watchers. It is usually encountered by trawlers working below 60 m (200 ft).

Consequently, we include the often deeper-dwelling Bigmouth Sculpin to alert readers and hopefully stimulate further reporting. The aptly-named Bigmouth Sculpin is large, attaining a maximum recorded length of 74 cm (29.2 in).

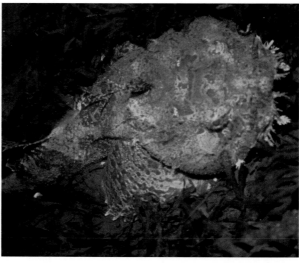

Jerry Vandergriff photograph

Buffalo Sculpin

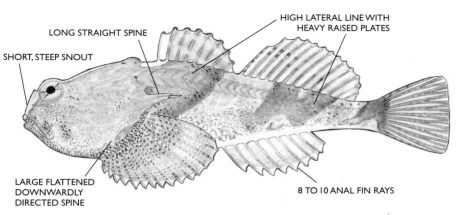

HIGH LATERAL LINE WITH
HEAVY RAISED PLATES

LONG STRAIGHT SPINE

SHORT, STEEP SNOUT

LARGE FLATTENED
DOWNWARDLY
DIRECTED SPINE

8 TO 10 ANAL FIN RAYS

SPECIES: *Enophrys bison*

OTHER COMMON NAMES: buffalo fish. Incorrect: bullhead

MAXIMUM RECORDED SIZE: 37 cm (14.6 in)

DISTRIBUTION: Central California to the Gulf of Alaska

HABITAT: Motionless and concealed amid seaweed or animal-encrusted rocks at depths less than 20 m (66 ft), the variably coloured Buffalo Sculpin is well camouflaged. It usually remains very still and a careful, deliberate diver can sometimes actually pick one up.

During February or March, mature Buffalo Sculpins guard large clumps of variously coloured eggs and thus provide the underwater photographer with an especially good opportunity. Spawning occurs at shallow depths and even intertidally in some locales. In late spring, the barely recognizable young populate shallow eelgrass-choked beaches.

Only occasionally found in tidepools, the shallow-water Buffalo Sculpin may, however, be visible from a float or pier.

A

COMMENTS: While trying to catch more popular quarry, shorebound anglers often take the lethargic Buffalo Sculpin. It ravenously gulps virtually any bait lowered onto seaweed-coated rocky shores, or under floats and piers. Handle this fish carefully; avoid its large, sharp preopercular spines but notice the hum that emanates from the vibrating and annoyed specimen.

B. Male guarding nest.

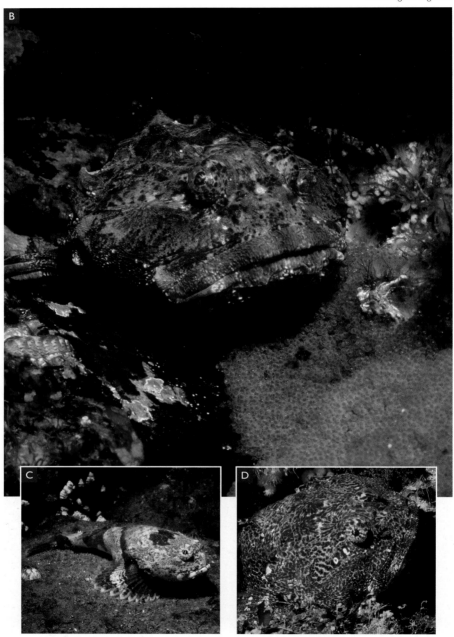

Leister Sculpin

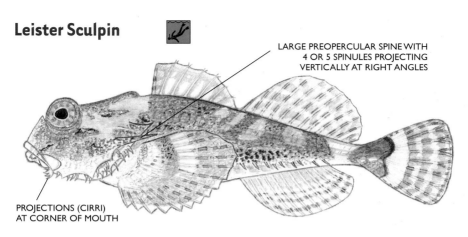

LARGE PREOPERCULAR SPINE WITH
4 OR 5 SPINULES PROJECTING
VERTICALLY AT RIGHT ANGLES

PROJECTIONS (CIRRI)
AT CORNER OF MOUTH

SPECIES: *Enophrys lucasi*

OTHER COMMON NAMES: Incorrect: bullhead

MAXIMUM RECORDED SIZE: 25 cm (10 in)

DISTRIBUTION: Northern British Columbia to the Aleutian Island chain and the Bering Sea, Alaska

HABITAT: Just after completing the first edition of this book, co-author Phil Edgell and several other divers collected and photographed a Leister Sculpin (A). This resulted in the official range of the species being extended south from Alaska. Numerous additional encounters, such as the one shown here, photographed by Bernard P. Hanby in 1989 (B), have followed.

COMMENTS: NOTE: The Antlered Sculpin, *Enophrys dicerus,* is very similar to the species featured here. However, its first preopercular spines are much longer and usually have more spinules on each. Currently southeastern Alaska is the documented southern distribution limit of the Antlered Sculpin.

B. Bernard P. Hanby photograph

Red Irish Lord

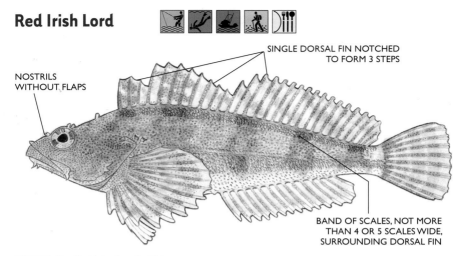

NOSTRILS
WITHOUT FLAPS

SINGLE DORSAL FIN NOTCHED
TO FORM 3 STEPS

BAND OF SCALES, NOT MORE
THAN 4 OR 5 SCALES WIDE,
SURROUNDING DORSAL FIN

SPECIES: *Hemilepidotus hemilepidotus*

OTHER COMMON NAMES: red Irish lord sculpin, spotted Irish lord, red sculpin. Incorrect: bullhead

MAXIMUM RECORDED SIZE: 51 cm (20 in)

DISTRIBUTION: Central California to the Aleutian Island chain, the Bering Sea, Alaska, and Siberia

HABITAT: Popular with underwater photographers because of its variable, often brilliant colouration and sedentary behaviour, the Red Irish Lord flourishes in shallow habitats. So well does this common creature blend with its usual background of colourful encrusting seaweed and animal life, the image-taker may have trouble highlighting it in order to make it "stand out" in the picture. With a little careful prodding or even gentle handling, though, a determined photographer may relocate a co-operative specimen to a more suitable background.

Spawning occurs in winter when ripe females deposit large masses of pink, yellow, purple or blue eggs, which the easily approached and attentive male tenaciously guards.

Juvenile Red Irish Lords frequently lurk in tidepools.

COMMENTS: A gluttonous feeder, the Red Irish Lord usually swallows the bait (almost anything) completely. An easily landed catch for bottom fishermen, it rates low with most sport anglers.

When harvesting valuable groundfish, longliners and trawlers capture and discard the unwanted Red Irish Lord.

Cook, then flake some Red Irish Lord fillets; mix with onion, green pepper, chopped celery, salt, cracker crumbs and mayonnaise. Chill the mixture, stuff it in hollowed tomatoes and then serve on lettuce.

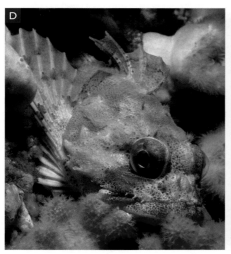

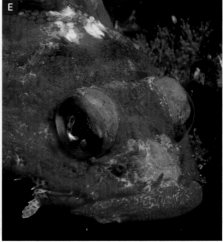

E. Lou Lehmann photograph

Brown Irish Lord

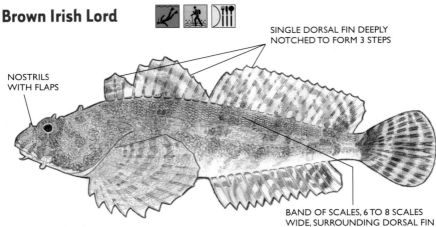

SINGLE DORSAL FIN DEEPLY NOTCHED TO FORM 3 STEPS

NOSTRILS WITH FLAPS

BAND OF SCALES, 6 TO 8 SCALES WIDE, SURROUNDING DORSAL FIN

SPECIES: *Hemilepidotus spinosus*

OTHER COMMON NAMES: Incorrect: bullhead

MAXIMUM RECORDED SIZE: 29 cm (11.4 in)

DISTRIBUTION: Southern California to the Gulf of Alaska

HABITAT: The sluggish Brown Irish Lord can be found in depths to 97 m (318 ft); it can also be observed in shallow waters, along rocky shores exposed to direct Pacific surges. Divers who brave these conditions might happen upon the usually motionless Brown Irish Lord. However, nestling among the caverns and crevices of solid outcroppings—particularly where pink, branching coralline algae coats the bottom—this well-camouflaged creature is most difficult to find.

Shorebound naturalists may find the Brown Irish Lord in tidepools.

COMMENTS: Why not try a meal of Brown Irish Lord Taipei? Gently fry onion until tender and add cooked rice and soy sauce. Pour in beaten eggs. Cook while stirring gently before finally adding water chestnuts and the cooked, flaked fillets.

NOTE: A northern species, the Yellow Irish Lord, *Hemilepidotus jordani*, has been recorded as far south as southeastern Alaska. It is distinguished by yellow *branchiostegals* (ventral gill membrane supports below the gill coverings) and a deep notch in its first dorsal fin.

C. Bernard P. Hanby photograph

Pacific Staghorn Sculpin

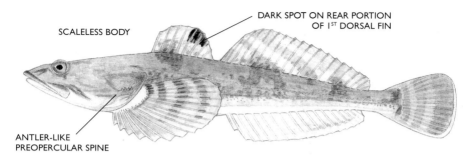

SCALELESS BODY

DARK SPOT ON REAR PORTION
OF 1ˢᵀ DORSAL FIN

ANTLER-LIKE
PREOPERCULAR SPINE

SPECIES: *Leptocottus armatus*
OTHER COMMON NAMES: staghorn sculpin. Incorrect: cabezon, bullhead
MAXIMUM RECORDED SIZE: 48 cm (19 in)
DISTRIBUTION: Northern Baja California, Mexico, to the Bering Sea coast of Alaska
HABITAT: Because the Pacific Staghorn Sculpin often buries itself in silty, muddy bottoms, a diver must look closely to see its greyish, olive-green form.

Docks or jetties built over bays and river estuaries provide excellent viewing platforms from which to watch the slow-swimming sculpin. Summer bathers shuffling through tidal flats often startle juveniles that dart away in all directions.

COMMENTS: A very common catch for anglers, the Pacific Staghorn Sculpin flourishes in bays and inlets with gently sloping silt or mud bottoms. It greedily devours virtually any bait (even raw bacon), but after giving one or two meek tugs, even a large one easily comes ashore. Use caution when removing the hook from a squirming specimen because its sharp, ragged preopercular spines can inflict a painful wound.

Commercial trawlers straying over shallow muddy substrates inadvertently take this unmarketable sculpin from depths less than 91 m (300 ft).

B. Bernard P. Hanby photograph

THE **TOADFISHES** (Family Batrachoididae)

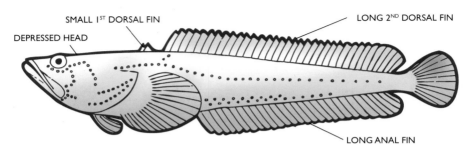

SMALL 1ˢᵀ DORSAL FIN

LONG 2ᴺᴰ DORSAL FIN

DEPRESSED HEAD

LONG ANAL FIN

The moderate-sized Batrachoididae translates from the Greek to mean "frog-like family." This is because many have bulging eyes, wide mouths and slippery skin similar to frogs. The family possesses about 69 recognized living species of midshipmen and toadfishes and has been around for more than 12 million years. They inhabit a variety of coastal environments from dark, cold, deep water to shallow bays and are mostly found on soft muddy and sandy bottoms. Only one batrachoidid, the Plainfin Midshipman, resides in the Pacific Northwest. Nearly all of the sluggish, bottom-dwelling toadfishes flourish in tropic latitudes and the species are spread fairly evenly around the globe. Only a very few members of this primarily marine family invade brackish or freshwater realms. Much of the time the batrachoidid fishes, including the local Plainfin Midshipman, burrow in the silt while awaiting prey or hiding from predators. Only periodically do they rise off the bottom to move about.

It is popularly believed that the underwater world is silent, but such is not the case. Shrimps and various other aquatic animals are noisy. The toadfishes are among the noisiest. Nearly all produce a variety of sounds by vibrating certain inner-ear bones against connecting gas-filled swim bladders to achieve a resonating effect. An audible repertoire of grunts, squeaks, whistles, hums and croaks allows these fish to communicate territorial and breeding information to each other. Most toadfishes grow to a modest maximum size of 51 cm (20 in).

Plainfin Midshipman

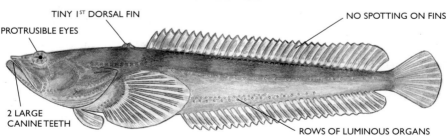

TINY 1ˢᵀ DORSAL FIN

NO SPOTTING ON FINS

PROTRUSIBLE EYES

2 LARGE
CANINE TEETH

ROWS OF LUMINOUS ORGANS

SPECIES: *Porichthys notatus*
OTHER COMMON NAMES: northern midshipman, midshipman. Incorrect: singing fish, bullhead, cabezon
MAXIMUM RECORDED SIZE: 38 cm (15 in)
DISTRIBUTION: Southern Baja California, Mexico, to central British Columbia

HABITAT: During daylight hours, the abundant Plainfin Midshipman usually remains buried. At night, this darkly coloured fish commonly emerges from the mud and often hovers nearly motionless just off the bottom. Divers should look closely at its undersides for the characteristic rows of bioluminescent photophores. These silvery little dots form a pattern like the buttons that decorate the jacket of a naval or merchant marine midshipman.

During a late spring or summer low tide, the beachcomber might try turning over rocks to see the Plainfin Midshipman guarding a nest. On the underside of the overturned stone, notice the yellow or orange, kernel-shaped eggs or even the tiny attached young. If possible, return on a tide sequence two weeks later and notice the developmental changes. Carefully replace the rock to hide the nest and its guardian.

COMMENTS: Some folks refer to this fish as the "roaring bullhead." The humming noise it may generate during its breeding cycle is so loud that it can penetrate boat hulls from a distance and cause concern to owners who might mistake the noise for an electrical malfunction.

Of no direct commercial value, the unwanted Midshipman, with its sharp needle-like teeth, catches on and often fills fine-meshed shrimp trawls dragged from depths to 366 m (1,200 ft).

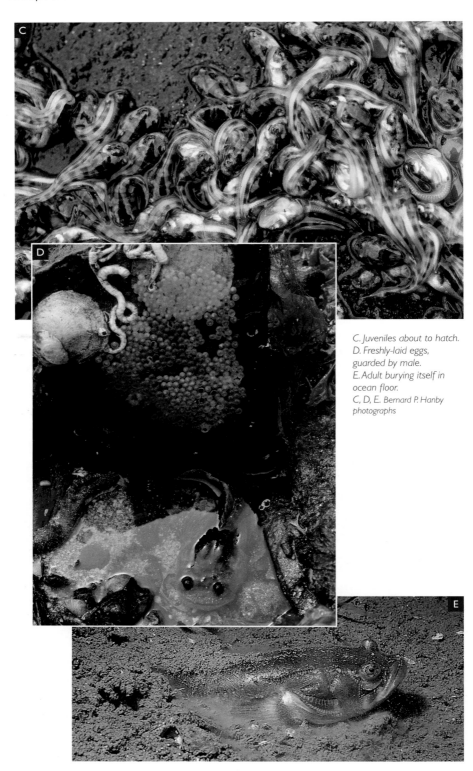

C. Juveniles *about to hatch.*
D. Freshly-laid eggs,
guarded by male.
E. Adult burying itself in
ocean floor.
C, D, E. Bernard P. Hanby
photographs

THE **POACHERS** (Family Agonidae)

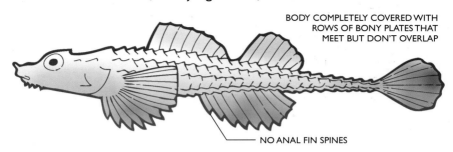

BODY COMPLETELY COVERED WITH ROWS OF BONY PLATES THAT MEET BUT DON'T OVERLAP

NO ANAL FIN SPINES

The Agonidae, a moderately large group of fishes, includes the starsnouts, alligator-fishes and the Rockhead, as well as the poachers. Of the approximately 50 known varieties, most live in the northern Pacific Ocean.

These fishes occupy a wide variety of habitats ranging from shallow rocky and inter-tidal shores to sandy or muddy substrates at considerable depths.

Primarily because of their rigid or relatively inflexible bodies, the small and bone-plated agonids swim with a sculling motion of their pectoral fins while dragging their bodies like rudders. However, during times of extreme danger or stress, they adopt a frenzied wriggling as an escape mechanism—especially the numerous elongate species. The few short and stubby poachers crawl along, using their pectoral, anal and caudal fins. Poachers were thought to have lived in shallow marine seas at least 40 million years ago.

For some reason, several Pacific Northwest poachers are not commonly encountered and include the Pricklebreast Poacher, *Stellerina xyosterna*, the Warty Poacher, *Chesnonia verrucosa*, and the Sawback Poacher, *Leptagonus frenatus*.

Spinycheek Starsnout

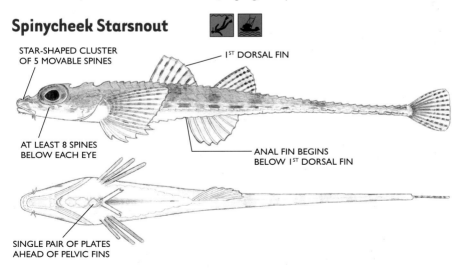

STAR-SHAPED CLUSTER OF 5 MOVABLE SPINES

1ST DORSAL FIN

AT LEAST 8 SPINES BELOW EACH EYE

ANAL FIN BEGINS BELOW 1ST DORSAL FIN

SINGLE PAIR OF PLATES AHEAD OF PELVIC FINS

SPECIES: *Bathyagonus infraspinatus.* Formerly *Bathyagonus infraspinata* and *Asterotheca infraspinata*
OTHER COMMON NAMES: spinycheek starnose, spiny-cheeked star-snout
MAXIMUM RECORDED SIZE: 14.3 cm (5.7 in)
DISTRIBUTION: Northern California to the Bering Sea coast of Alaska

HABITAT: Although not rare, and an inhabitant of depths accessible to scuba enthusiasts, few divers actually see the inconspicuous Spinycheek Starsnout. It lives upon level sandy or muddy substrates and only when this slender greyish fish moves does it become noticeable. Upon actually finding one, an aquanaut usually gets a good look because a specimen seldom moves very far or very fast.

COMMENTS: While not specifically seeking the tiny and unmarketable Spinycheek Starsnout, commercial shrimp harvesters nevertheless take it in their fine-meshed nets towed over flat, soft bottoms at depths between 20 and 200 m (66 and 660 ft) and then discard it.

Gray Starsnout

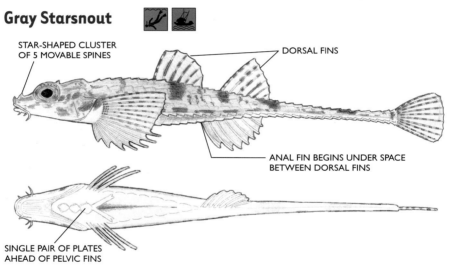

STAR-SHAPED CLUSTER OF 5 MOVABLE SPINES

DORSAL FINS

ANAL FIN BEGINS UNDER SPACE BETWEEN DORSAL FINS

SINGLE PAIR OF PLATES AHEAD OF PELVIC FINS

SPECIES: *Bathyagonus alascanus.* Formerly *Bathyagonus alascana* and *Asterotheca alascana*
OTHER COMMON NAMES: gray star-snout, gray starnose
MAXIMUM RECORDED SIZE: 14.1 cm (5.6 in)
DISTRIBUTION: Northern California to the Bering Sea coast of Alaska

HABITAT: Only very observant divers who make forays along sandy or muddy bottoms at depths greater than 20 m (66 ft) might find the inconspicuous Gray Starsnout. Usually, it is either belly down on the substrate or swimming in a number of short bursts by sculling with its large pectoral fins and dragging its slender, stiff body behind. When photographing a specimen, the thoughtful underwater camera buff approaches the wary Gray Starsnout from down current so that any stirred-up silt or debris does not drift over the specimen and spoil a good "shot."

COMMENTS: Though unmarketable, the insignificant Gray Starsnout nevertheless enters the catch of commercial shrimp trawlers who tow fine-meshed nets over flat, soft bottoms at depths between 20 and 250 m (66 and 825 ft).

Bigeye Poacher

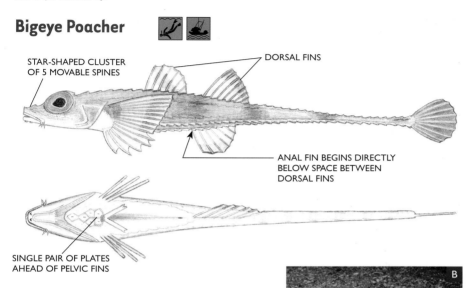

STAR-SHAPED CLUSTER OF 5 MOVABLE SPINES

DORSAL FINS

ANAL FIN BEGINS DIRECTLY BELOW SPACE BETWEEN DORSAL FINS

SINGLE PAIR OF PLATES AHEAD OF PELVIC FINS

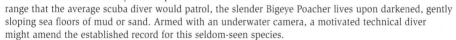

SPECIES: *Bathyagonus pentacanthus.* Formerly *Asterotheca pentacanthus*
OTHER COMMON NAMES: bigeye starsnout, bigeye starnose
MAXIMUM RECORDED SIZE: 26.2 cm (10.5 in)
DISTRIBUTION: Southern California to the Gulf of Alaska
HABITAT: Documented only from depths well below the range that the average scuba diver would patrol, the slender Bigeye Poacher lives upon darkened, gently sloping sea floors of mud or sand. Armed with an underwater camera, a motivated technical diver might amend the established record for this seldom-seen species.

COMMENTS: Joe Bauer of Steveston, British Columbia, documented the first specimen of this pale poacher ever taken in British Columbia. Joe, a commercial shrimp trawler and knowledgeable naturalist, noticed it while sorting through a large shrimp catch hauled from a sandy bottom at 125 m (413 ft) off Galiano Island. He reported it to Dr. Wilbert Clemens, who was updating *Fishes of the Pacific Coast of Canada* in 1961.

Blackfin Poacher

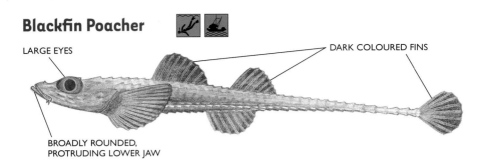

LARGE EYES

DARK COLOURED FINS

BROADLY ROUNDED,
PROTRUDING LOWER JAW

SPECIES: *Bathyagonus nigripinnis*

OTHER COMMON NAMES: black-finned sea-poacher, blackfin starsnout, blackfin starnose

MAXIMUM RECORDED SIZE: 24.2 cm (9.6 in)

DISTRIBUTION: Northern California to the Bering Sea coast of Alaska, through the Aleutian Island chain to Siberia

HABITAT: The Blackfin Poacher thrives at depths well below those explored by scuba aficionados. However, in the northern portion of its range, this species has been recorded as shallow as 18 m (60 ft), within safe recreational diving limits.

COMMENTS: While the small Blackfin Poacher is of no direct monetary value, shrimp trawlers frequently net specimens as bycatch. Flourishing on fine sand or mud bottoms as far down as 1,250 m (4,125 ft), this large-eyed creature ranks as one of the deepest-dwelling poachers.

Blacktip Poacher

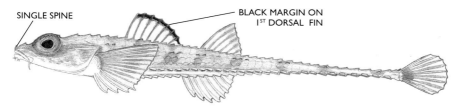

SINGLE SPINE

BLACK MARGIN ON
1ST DORSAL FIN

SPECIES: *Xeneretmus latifrons*
OTHER COMMON NAMES: blackedge poacher, black-tipped sea-poacher
MAXIMUM RECORDED SIZE: 19 cm (7.5 in)
DISTRIBUTION: Baja California, northern Mexico, to northern British Columbia
HABITAT: While enjoying a dive on a dull overcast day or even at night, the aquanaut may notice a pale gray Blacktip Poacher resting upon its pectoral fins at depths of 20 m (66 ft) or more. The northern section of the Blacktip Poacher's distribution affords the diver the best locales for viewing this species. In southern regions, it lives in much deeper water—over 400 m (1,300 ft). Search over level or gently sloping bottoms where log-booming activities litter the sand or silt with wood chips.
COMMENTS: Although unsought, the common Blacktip Poacher frequently wriggles among the valuable shrimp harvested by trawlers from nets towed over soft substrates.

NOTE: The Bluespotted Poacher, *Xeneretmus triacanthus,* and the Smootheye Poacher, *Xeneretmus leiops,* are generally found in deep water with their centres of distribution being California. Both have been recorded in the Pacific Northwest and are very similar to the Blacktip Poacher.

Pygmy Poacher

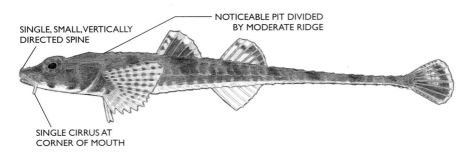

SINGLE, SMALL, VERTICALLY
DIRECTED SPINE

NOTICEABLE PIT DIVIDED
BY MODERATE RIDGE

SINGLE CIRRUS AT
CORNER OF MOUTH

SPECIES: *Odontopyxis trispinosa*

OTHER COMMON NAMES: pygmy sea-poacher

MAXIMUM RECORDED SIZE: 9.5 cm (3.8 in)

DISTRIBUTION: Central Baja California, Mexico, to the Gulf of Alaska

HABITAT: Observant divers frequently encounter the Pygmy Poacher resting upon a sandy or muddy bottom. Sightings are possible by day or night, but unless this well-camouflaged creature moves, it is nearly impossible to see at any time. Divers exploring waters within the northern part of the Pygmy Poacher's range are more likely to see this fish, because in the southern areas it lives at much greater depths: 373 m (1,230 ft) or more.

On a very low tide, an observant beach stroller may find a Pygmy Poacher at the water's edge upon a sandy or muddy substrate.

COMMENTS: Although the shrimp fisherman may incidentally take the Pygmy Poacher in fine-meshed trawls, it is of no commercial value.

Tubenose Poacher

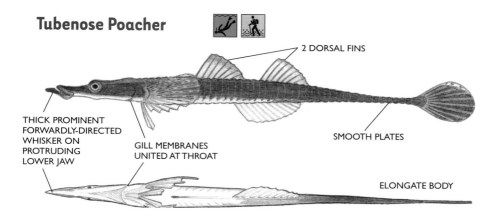

2 DORSAL FINS

THICK PROMINENT
FORWARDLY-DIRECTED
WHISKER ON
PROTRUDING
LOWER JAW

GILL MEMBRANES
UNITED AT THROAT

SMOOTH PLATES

ELONGATE BODY

SPECIES: *Pallasina barbata.* Formerly *Pallasina barbata aix*

OTHER COMMON NAMES: tubesnout poacher

MAXIMUM RECORDED SIZE: 21 cm (8.3 in)

DISTRIBUTION: Northern California to the Bering Sea, the Aleutian Island chain and through to Siberia, Japan and Korea

HABITAT: Divers venturing into shallows might observe the dark Tubenose Poacher. It often lives either among eelgrass growing in sheltered sandy coves or amid surf grass clinging tightly to rocky depressions along surge-swept shorelines. The fronds and floats of the dense kelp also provide shelter for this poacher. The Tubenose Poacher is one of the few family members that consistently and actively swim well off the bottom.

COMMENTS: Large tidepools or rocky shorelines are prime locales for the elongate Tubenose Poacher. Often obscured among the dense algae, this thin creature may swim near pilings or floats from where naturalists may identify it in part by the jerky sculling movement produced by its pectoral fins.

Smooth Alligatorfish

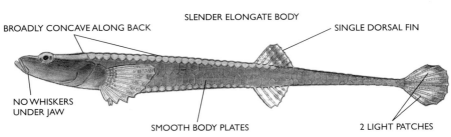

BROADLY CONCAVE ALONG BACK

SLENDER ELONGATE BODY

SINGLE DORSAL FIN

NO WHISKERS UNDER JAW

SMOOTH BODY PLATES

2 LIGHT PATCHES

SPECIES: *Anoplagonus inermis*

OTHER COMMON NAMES: smooth poacher, smooth sea-poacher

MAXIMUM RECORDED SIZE: 15 cm (6 in)

DISTRIBUTION: Central California to the Aleutian Island chain, Alaska

HABITAT: An observant diver may very easily swim past a Smooth Alligatorfish without seeing it at all, or may mistake it for a tiny, submerged stick lying on the sea floor. Usually this dark-brown creature rests motionless upon sandy bottoms near large, rocky outcroppings. Also look for it on bottoms littered with wood chips from log booms. Living as shallow as 5 m (16 ft), the slender Smooth Alligatorfish may occasionally rest upon steep cliff faces.

COMMENTS: When sorting through their catches, shrimp trawlers sometimes find a Smooth Alligatorfish in nets hauled up from a flat, boulder-strewn bottom.

B. Bernard P. Hanby photograph

Northern Spearnose Poacher

POINTED SNOUT WITH 2 BLUNT,
SKIN-COVERED SPINES

MOUTH ON
UNDERSIDE

LIGHT SPOT IN CENTRE
SURROUNDED BY DARK AREA

SPECIES: *Agonopsis vulsa.* Formerly *Agonopsis emmulane*
OTHER COMMON NAMES: windowtail poacher, window-tailed sea-poacher. Incorrect: dark alligatorfish, northern spearnose
MAXIMUM RECORDED SIZE: 20 cm (8 in)
DISTRIBUTION: Southern California to the Gulf of Alaska
HABITAT: Nocturnal divers searching along sandy bottoms adjacent to rocky outcroppings and cliff faces frequently come across the Northern Spearnose Poacher. When it moves, this greyish-brown creature propels itself with its large pectoral fins and drags its stiff body rudder-like behind it. However, it usually rests motionless on the bottom and its colour makes it difficult to see. If disturbed, this poacher will stiffen its body in a crescent shape and remain motionless—even if subsequently handled (D).

During spring and summer nights, the juvenile Northern Spearnose Poacher may swim toward lights shining on the water from piers or jetties. With a proportionately large dark tail and the huge spine beginning between its eyes, the young specimen bears little resemblance to an adult. Occasionally an adult may be noticed intertidally.

COMMENTS: Fine-meshed shrimp trawls towed along soft level bottoms sometimes take the Northern Spearnose Poacher as bycatch at depths between 10 and 180 m (33 and 594 ft).

A

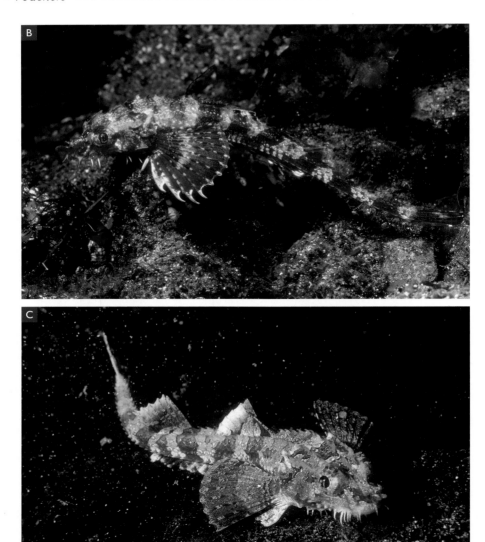

C. Courting adult male. *Charlie Gibbs photograph*

E. Juvenile. *Bernard P. Hanby photograph*

Sturgeon Poacher

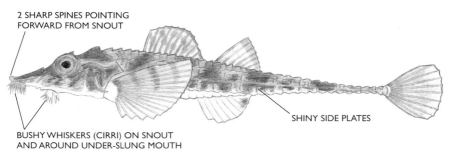

2 SHARP SPINES POINTING
FORWARD FROM SNOUT

SHINY SIDE PLATES

BUSHY WHISKERS (CIRRI) ON SNOUT
AND AROUND UNDER-SLUNG MOUTH

SPECIES: *Podothecus accipenserinus*. Formerly *Agonus acipenserinus*
OTHER COMMON NAMES: sturgeon-like sea-poacher
MAXIMUM RECORDED SIZE: 30 cm (12 in)
DISTRIBUTION: Northern California to the Bering Sea and the Aleutian Island chain, Alaska, and through to Siberia
HABITAT: Look for the yellowish Sturgeon Poacher while diving along shallow, soft substrate. Beachcombers can wade out into the shallows of a muddy-bottomed bay and look for the yellowish-brown juvenile Sturgeon Poacher as it huddles among eelgrass or flees, startled by threatening steps.
COMMENTS: Before consuming bottom-dwelling prey such as shrimp and other shrimp-like creatures, this slow-moving fish must first locate them by grovelling through the sand or silt with its bushy, tastebud-bearing cirri, prominently located beneath its mouth.

While seeking shrimp, inshore trawlers incidentally scoop up the unsaleable Sturgeon Poacher from flat bottoms at depths to 300 m (1,000 ft).

*A. Bernard P. Hanby photograph
B. Juvenile.*

Fourhorn Poacher

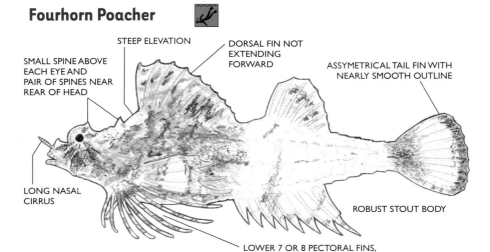

STEEP ELEVATION

DORSAL FIN NOT EXTENDING FORWARD

SMALL SPINE ABOVE EACH EYE AND PAIR OF SPINES NEAR REAR OF HEAD

ASSYMETRICAL TAIL FIN WITH NEARLY SMOOTH OUTLINE

LONG NASAL CIRRUS

ROBUST STOUT BODY

LOWER 7 OR 8 PECTORAL FINS, RAYS HAVE NO MEMBRANE

SPECIES: *Hypsagonus quadricornis*

OTHER COMMON NAMES: four-horned sea-poacher

MAXIMUM RECORDED SIZE: 10.5 cm (4.1 in)

DISTRIBUTION: Northern Washington to the Bering Sea, the Aleutian Island chain, Alaska, and through to the Sea of Japan

HABITAT: The Fourhorn Poacher is a species that a diver would be most fortunate to find. It is small, very well camouflaged, moves very slowly and spends much of its time motionless. In addition, this elusive fish sometimes has hydroids and seaweeds growing upon its skin. The Fourhorn Poacher dwells on both rocky and soft bottoms as shallow as 15 m (50 ft), well within safe scuba limits. However, this poacher has been found as deep as 452 m (1,482 ft).

Kelp Poacher

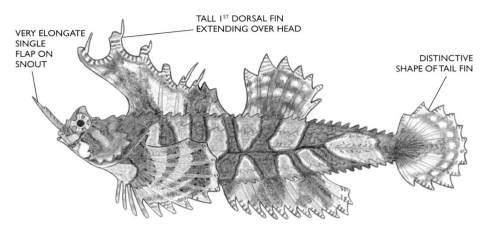

VERY ELONGATE SINGLE FLAP ON SNOUT

TALL 1ST DORSAL FIN EXTENDING OVER HEAD

DISTINCTIVE SHAPE OF TAIL FIN

SPECIES: *Hypsagonus mozinoi*. Formerly *Agonomalus mozinoi*

MAXIMUM RECORDED SIZE: 8.9 cm (3.5 in)

DISTRIBUTION: Central California to northern British Columbia

HABITAT: This dragon-like creature is surely the most difficult of all Pacific Northwest fishes to see amid its surf-swept, surging, open-coast habitat and among the dense growths of colourful surrounding seaweeds. Divers in California find this beautifully ornate fish to be most active at night.

Keen-eyed beachcombers may find the strange-looking but well-camouflaged Kelp Poacher in open-coast tidepools.

COMMENTS: Amazingly, researchers collected the elusive Kelp Poacher for the first time in the 1970s, illustrating that significant natural history discoveries still await mankind—particularly divers and shore-bound naturalists. Beachcombers found the first few specimens in tidepools and transported them to the Vancouver Aquarium where researchers watched closely as a pair courted and spawned, producing small clusters of between 6 and 25 adhesive, spherical, bright-red fertilized eggs.

B., C. Bernard P. Hanby photographs

Rockhead

VERY DEEP PIT IN HEAD WITH
RIDGE DOWN CENTRE OF PIT

2 DORSAL FINS

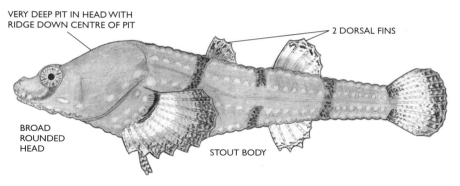

BROAD
ROUNDED
HEAD

STOUT BODY

SPECIES: *Bothragonus swanii.* Formerly *Bothragonus swani*
OTHER COMMON NAMES: deep-pitted poacher, deep-pitted sea-poacher, pitted poacher, pithead poacher
MAXIMUM RECORDED SIZE: 8.9 cm (3.5 in)
DISTRIBUTION: Central California to the Gulf of Alaska
HABITAT: Adventurous, keen-eyed divers exploring along rocky shores directly exposed to Pacific surge may catch a glimpse of the Rockhead. Look carefully, though—it nestles among the cracks and crevices at depths less than 20 m (66 ft), but it is well camouflaged in the colourful seaweed and animal life of its surroundings.

Rocky or pebble-bottomed tidepools of the exposed coast provide an intertidal habitat for this poacher. Slow-moving and often stationary, when once observed, it is easily captured with a dip-net. Listen closely as the specimen may produce low-pitched vibrations or humming sounds. Be certain to return it to the tidepool.

A. Bernard P. Hanby photograph

THE **SNAILFISHES** (Family Liparidae)

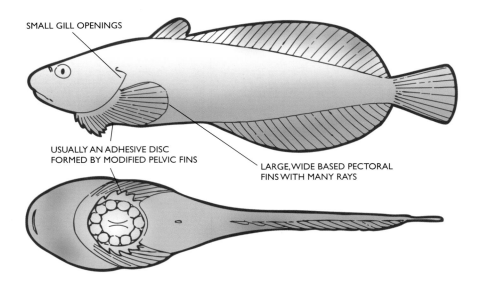

SMALL GILL OPENINGS

USUALLY AN ADHESIVE DISC
FORMED BY MODIFIED PELVIC FINS

LARGE, WIDE BASED PECTORAL
FINS WITH MANY RAYS

Nearly 200 known living fishes comprise the Liparidae, popularly termed the snailfishes or sea snails, perhaps because of their resemblance to slugs when curled up and stuck on something. The temperate and frigid seas of the North Pacific provide shelter for nearly three-quarters of the world's snailfishes. The remainder live in the North Atlantic, Arctic and Antarctic oceans, as well as in very deep and cold tropical waters. At least 25 species flourish in the Pacific Northwest. The Liparidae are entirely marine fishes found in a wide range of habitats from tidepools of the splash zone to the abyssal haunts in the great oceanic trenches.

Most are characterized by a "sucking" disc on their bellies, which is formed by a radical modification of their paired pelvic fins. These adhering structures allow the snailfishes to hold position on the substrate and are especially valuable in currents. While a few species without sucking discs swim in mid-water, well above the sea floor, bottom habitats are home for most liparids.

Lobefin Snailfish

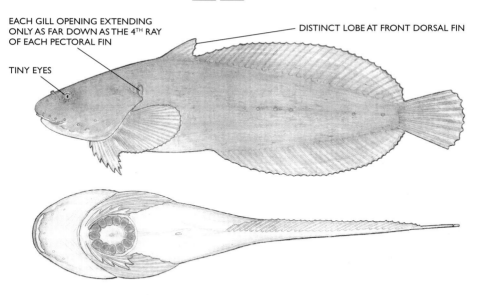

EACH GILL OPENING EXTENDING ONLY AS FAR DOWN AS THE 4ᵀᴴ RAY OF EACH PECTORAL FIN

DISTINCT LOBE AT FRONT DORSAL FIN

TINY EYES

SPECIES: *Liparis greeni.* Formerly *Polypera greeni*
OTHER COMMON NAMES: Green's liparid
MAXIMUM RECORDED SIZE: 30 cm (12 in)
DISTRIBUTION: Gulf of Alaska and the Aleutian Island chain to Washington
HABITAT: Snorkelers as well as scuba enthusiasts might find the Lobefin Snailfish because it commonly cowers among the dense summer growth of kelp trailing from floats and pilings. Even a sharp-eyed diver must look for it intently, however, as its golden colour matches identically that of the algae to which it adheres. Move kelp fronds carefully; if startled this shy snailfish will dart away.

Even though present amid the kelp that hangs from floats, the Lobefin Snailfish is almost impossible to notice without first scooping it (and the kelp) with a dip-net. Be considerate and gently return specimens after an interaction.

Spotted Snailfish

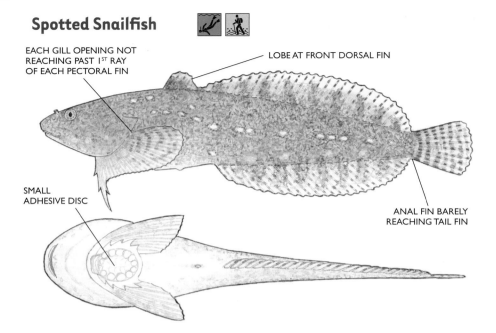

EACH GILL OPENING NOT
REACHING PAST 1ST RAY
OF EACH PECTORAL FIN

LOBE AT FRONT DORSAL FIN

SMALL
ADHESIVE DISC

ANAL FIN BARELY
REACHING TAIL FIN

SPECIES: *Liparis callyodon*
OTHER COMMON NAMES: Pallas's liparid
MAXIMUM RECORDED SIZE: 12.7 cm (5 in)
DISTRIBUTION: Oregon to the Aleutian Island chain and Bering Sea, Alaska
HABITAT: Alert night divers cruising along shallow, sandy-bottomed beaches with profuse eelgrass or
scattered rock might catch a brief glimpse of the small Spotted Snailfish. By day, however, the wary creature
usually hides beneath any available shelter.

Strolling along boulder-strewn beaches at low tide, a
curious beachcomber might locate the greenish-grey or
brown Spotted Snailfish by overturning rocks, shells or
other shelter.

Tidepool Snailfish

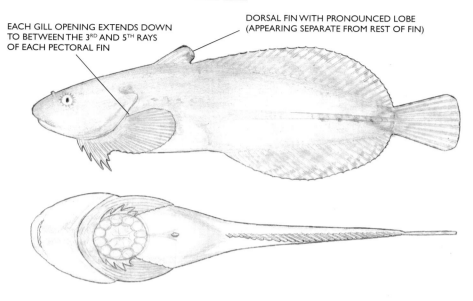

EACH GILL OPENING EXTENDS DOWN TO BETWEEN THE 3RD AND 5TH RAYS OF EACH PECTORAL FIN

DORSAL FIN WITH PRONOUNCED LOBE (APPEARING SEPARATE FROM REST OF FIN)

SPECIES: *Liparis florae*
OTHER COMMON NAMES: shore liparid
MAXIMUM RECORDED SIZE: 18.3 cm (7.3 in)
DISTRIBUTION: Southern California to the Gulf of Alaska
HABITAT: Snorkelers may find the often olive-green Tidepool Snailfish because it lives in very shallow water, usually nestling among colourful seaweeds. However, because this small, shy fish hides extremely well, the diver must search most diligently for it.

For shoreside naturalists, very careful observation among kelps and other seaweeds in tidepools or along the sea's edge may produce a glimpse of this inconspicuous snailfish. The best way to view and study a specimen closely, however, is either by dip-netting it from among seaweed or by overturning rocks and exposing one, as it clings to the underside of a stone. Always return the specimen and its habitat as originally found.

B., C. Juveniles. Charlie Gibbs photographs

Slipskin Snailfish

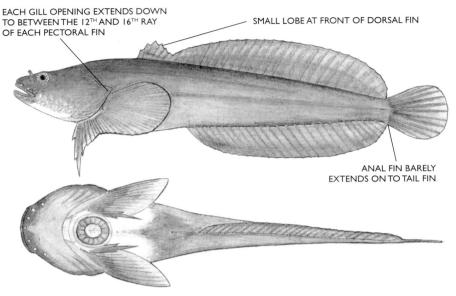

EACH GILL OPENING EXTENDS DOWN TO BETWEEN THE 12TH AND 16TH RAY OF EACH PECTORAL FIN

SMALL LOBE AT FRONT OF DORSAL FIN

ANAL FIN BARELY EXTENDS ON TO TAIL FIN

SPECIES: *Liparis fucensis*

OTHER COMMON NAMES: Juan de Fuca liparid

MAXIMUM RECORDED SIZE: 18 cm (7 in)

DISTRIBUTION: Central California to the Aleutian Island chain and Bering Sea coast of Alaska

HABITAT: Scuba divers may find the shy, secretive Slipskin Snailfish by turning over rocks and sunken logs or looking inside bottles and shells. Typically, this variably coloured snailfish spends most of its time hiding. When exposed by a curious aquanaut, this fish will invariably rush to other nearby shelter.

COMMENTS: While of no direct economic value, the soft Slipskin Snailfish is known to enter prawn traps at depths from 6 to 388 m (20 to 1,280 ft) while seeking small shrimp-like prey.

NOTE: The seldom-encountered Ringtail Snailfish, *Liparis rutteri*, is very similar to the species featured here. Only minor differences in anus location, gill slit size, pigmentation, disc size and fin ray count separate the two.

Ribbon Snailfish

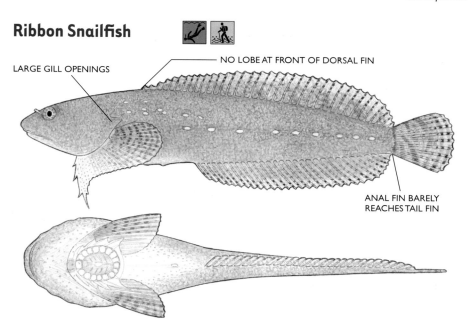

LARGE GILL OPENINGS

NO LOBE AT FRONT OF DORSAL FIN

ANAL FIN BARELY
REACHES TAIL FIN

SPECIES: *Liparis cyclopus*
OTHER COMMON NAMES: Gunther's liparid
MAXIMUM RECORDED SIZE: 11.4 cm (4.5 in)
DISTRIBUTION: Oregon to the Aleutian Island chain and Bering Sea coast of Alaska
HABITAT: The Ribbon Snailfish thrives intertidally and at shallow subtidal depths. Consequently, it is readily available to both the beachcomber and the recreational diver. This well-camouflaged species hides very well and is difficult to find.

COMMENTS: NOTE: Seldom encountered, the Slimy Snailfish, *Liparis mucosus,* is very similar to the species featured here. Only minor differences in fin ray counts and dorsal fin anatomy separate the two.

Marbled Snailfish

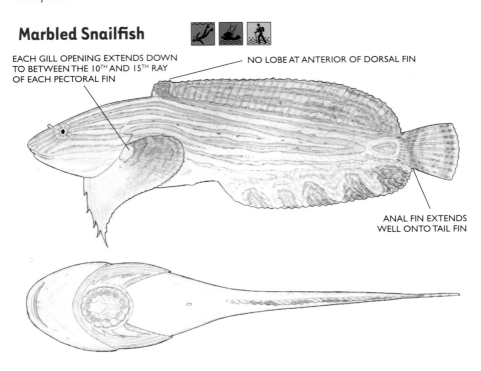

EACH GILL OPENING EXTENDS DOWN
TO BETWEEN THE 10TH AND 15TH RAY
OF EACH PECTORAL FIN

NO LOBE AT ANTERIOR OF DORSAL FIN

ANAL FIN EXTENDS
WELL ONTO TAIL FIN

SPECIES: *Liparis dennyi*
OTHER COMMON NAMES: Denny's liparid
MAXIMUM RECORDED SIZE: 30 cm (12 in)
DISTRIBUTION: Puget Sound, northern Washington to Unimak Island in the Aleutian chain, Alaska
HABITAT: Truly a master of camouflage, the secretive Marbled Snailfish is a worthy quarry for the fish-watching diver. Perhaps the best opportunity for a sighting is during a night dive because one's concentration focuses on what appears in a flashlight's beam. Exercise stealth as this elusive fish may quickly vanish into its surroundings when disturbed.

B. *Gregory C. Jensen photograph*

COMMENTS: Although the Marbled Snailfish is of no direct economic value, it often wriggles about among the marine life brought aboard vessels that trawl or trap shrimp. This large snailfish apparently prefers sandy or silty bottoms at depths between 10 and 225 m (33 and 743 ft) where fine-meshed nets easily dislodge it from scattered rubble onto which it has adhered.

NOTE: Primarily an inhabitant of northern Alaska waters, the Variegated Snailfish, *Liparis gibbus*, is very similar to the species featured here. Only vertebral and fin ray counts can be used to separate the two. Debate remains as to whether the Variegated Snailfish is even a legitimate species or rather just a subspecies of the Marbled Snailfish.

C. *Juvenile. Charlie Gibbs photograph*

Showy Snailfish

STRAIGHT CONTOUR OF DORSAL FIN

BROAD HEAD WITH
WIDELY SPACED EYES

TAIL FIN ALMOST COMPLETELY
INCLUDED WITHIN THE
DORSAL AND ANAL FINS

B. Brent Cook photograph
C. Keith Clements photograph

SPECIES: *Liparis pulchellus*

OTHER COMMON NAMES: shorttail snailfish, continuous-finned liparid

MAXIMUM RECORDED SIZE: 25.4 cm (10.1 in)

DISTRIBUTION: Central California to the Aleutian Island chain and the Bering Sea coast of Alaska

HABITAT: Periodically, a secretive Showy Snailfish will venture out from under solid shelter and cruise slowly over sandy bottoms at depths below 10 m (33 ft). This occurs more often nocturnally and is therefore usually observed by night divers. By day this attractive fish adheres to the undersides of rocks and shells or huddles inside empty bottles, cans and other discarded man-made paraphernalia.

COMMENTS: Fine-meshed nets towed by shrimp trawlers sometimes dislodge and then drag the unwanted Showy Snailfish to the surface from depths as great as 183 m (600 ft).

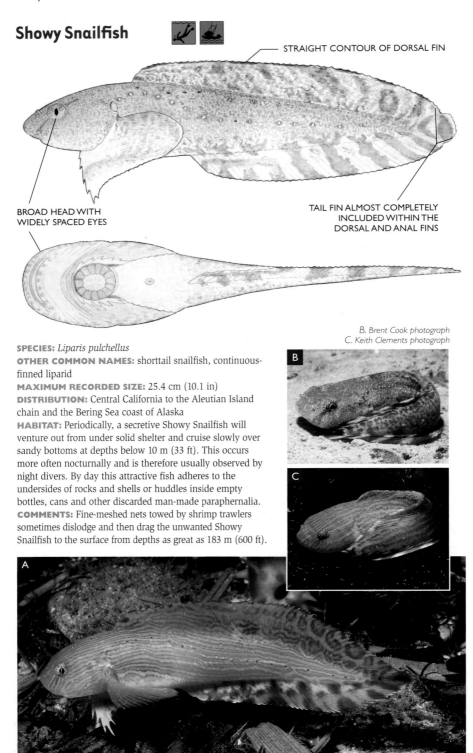

Tadpole Snailfish

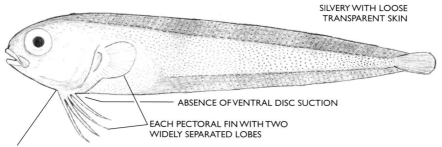

SILVERY WITH LOOSE
TRANSPARENT SKIN

ABSENCE OF VENTRAL DISC SUCTION

EACH PECTORAL FIN WITH TWO
WIDELY SEPARATED LOBES

ANUS OPENING UNDERNEATH
(VERTICALLY BELOW EYES) IN TROUGH

SPECIES: *Nectoliparis pelagicus*
OTHER COMMON NAMES: tadpole liparid
MAXIMUM RECORDED SIZE: 6.5 cm (2.5 in)
DISTRIBUTION: Southern California to the Aleutian Island chain, the Bering Sea, Alaska, and Siberia
HABITAT: Lacking the definitive family suction disc, the Tadpole Snailfish is adapted to a pelagic—
free-swimming, open water—existence. Its documented depth range is from near the surface to 3,400 m
(11,154 ft), but whether specimens entered the sampling trawl at its ultimate depth is uncertain.

Recent closing trawl studies from Monterey Bay show the Tadpole Snailfish is common in the mesope-
lagic zone—200 to 1,000 m (650 to 3,280 ft). It is occasionally seen by divers as witnessed by the accompanying photographs that appeared in the first edition
of this guide. Some specimens trawled from great
depths are believed to have been inhabiting water
low in dissolved oxygen.

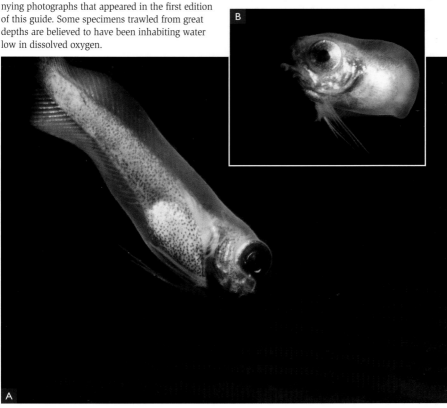

THE **LUMPSUCKERS** (Family Cyclopteridae)

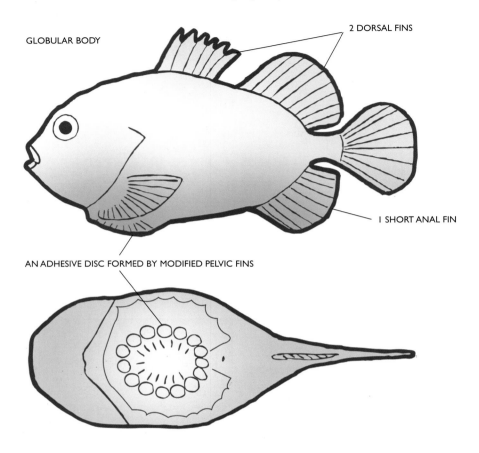

GLOBULAR BODY

2 DORSAL FINS

I SHORT ANAL FIN

AN ADHESIVE DISC FORMED BY MODIFIED PELVIC FINS

Recent taxonomic reviews have acknowledged significant differences within the traditional family Liparidae. Consequently, experts have split the group in two—separating the lumpsuckers and placing the 27 species (all from cold northern hemisphere seas) in the Cyclopteridae.

The famously gourmet Lumpfish, from the Atlantic coast, is the largest species, attaining a length of 62 cm (24.4 in) and a weight of 9.5 kg (21 lb)!

Like the snailfishes, lumpsuckers also possess the distinctive suction structures that have evolved from the paired pelvic fins and are located on their bellies. Unlike the snailfishes, cyclopterids are stubby, usually have two (rarely one) small dorsal fins and their bodies are generally covered with large, cone-shaped protuberances.

The Smooth Lumpsucker, *Aptocyclus ventricosus*, a large flabby species with no cone-shaped tubercles and only one dorsal fin, is found as far south as northern British Columbia. Sometimes accessible and found inshore, surprisingly this less-than-graceful swimmer is recorded from mid-water.

Pacific Spiny Lumpsucker

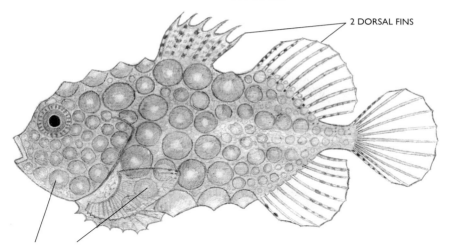

2 DORSAL FINS

STOCKY BODY AND HEAD COVERED WITH
SPINY CONE-SHAPE PROTUBERANCES

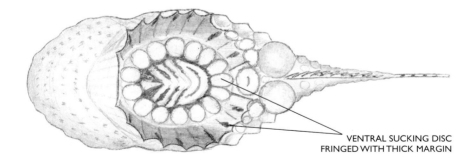

VENTRAL SUCKING DISC
FRINGED WITH THICK MARGIN

SPECIES: *Eumicrotremus orbis*
OTHER COMMON NAMES: spiny lumpsucker
MAXIMUM RECORDED SIZE: 12.7 cm (5 in)
DISTRIBUTION: Northern Washington to the Bering Sea, along the Aleutian Island chain to Siberia and northern Japan

HABITAT: A chance of sighting the lovable Pacific Spiny Lumpsucker makes worthwhile a shallow dive into a bay choked with eelgrass or kelp. Watch for this rotund little creature resting with its sucking disc attached to something solid such as seaweed, a sunken log, or a piece of shell. This fish is amusing because its almost invisible fins propel its globular body like an underwater helicopter or miniature ping-pong ball with fins as it huffs and puffs about in no apparently predictable direction. A slow swimmer, easily tracked by the diver, this stubby creature always appears to be gasping even when at rest.

Seldom seen unless it moves, the Pacific Spiny Lumpsucker commonly swims among seaweeds or rests attached to pilings or rocks—within view of the surface-bound naturalist. It may approach lights at night.

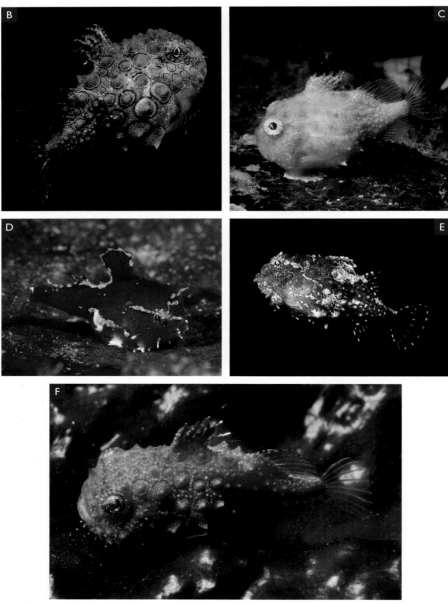

B. Bernard P. Hanby photograph
D. Tiny juvenile. Clinton Bauder photograph
E. Juvenile.

THE **CLINGFISHES** (Family Gobiesocidae)

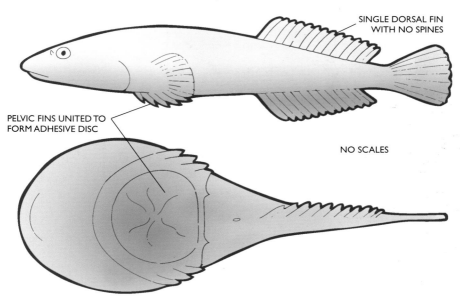

SINGLE DORSAL FIN
WITH NO SPINES

PELVIC FINS UNITED TO
FORM ADHESIVE DISC

NO SCALES

The family of clingfishes, scientifically designated the Gobiesocidae, is a moderately large one of about 110 known living species, most of which live intertidally or in shallow, rocky coastal regions. The cover-seeking gobiesocids inhabit primarily tropical and temperate waters. Only two species are found along Pacific Northwest shores.

The conspicuous sucking disc, formed by the modification of the pelvic fins and located under the belly area of each species, is the most significant gobiesocid trait. By adhering to solid objects with suction organs, these resourceful creatures can maintain their positions in swift currents or against crashing waves. These organs also allow the animals to conserve energy while in active, turbulent habitats inhospitable to many other fishes. Although a superficial comparison of clingfish sucking discs to those of the snailfishes immediately suggests a close relationship between the two groups, closer anatomical study reveals many significant differences and indicates that the two are not closely related. At present, the inconspicuous clingfishes have no truly close relatives.

Kelp Clingfish

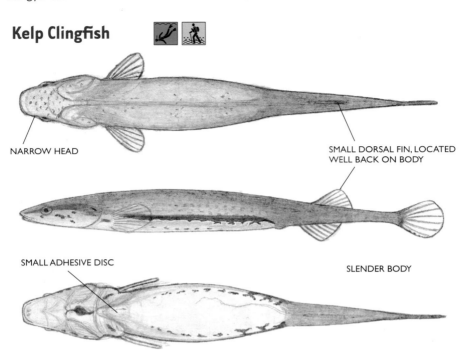

NARROW HEAD

SMALL DORSAL FIN, LOCATED WELL BACK ON BODY

SMALL ADHESIVE DISC

SLENDER BODY

SPECIES: *Rimicola muscarum*

OTHER COMMON NAMES: slender cling-fish

MAXIMUM RECORDED SIZE: 7 cm (2.8 in)

DISTRIBUTION: Southern Baja California, Mexico, to southeastern Alaska

HABITAT: While very common in shallow, weedy bays adjacent to direct Pacific surge, the emerald green and yellow or golden-brown Kelp Clingfish proves to be an elusive quarry for the diver because it adheres to seaweeds that share its colours.

Although rarely frequenting tidepools, the sometimes speckled Kelp Clingfish flourishes in the exposed eelgrass and kelp-choked shallows in which curious beachcombers may wade.

COMMENTS: If a specimen is collected by dip-netting, place the captive in a glass container for a closer look. When the tiny fish attaches itself to the transparent surface, it is easy to see the throb of its minute red heart. In summer, if your captive is a gravid female, her eggs will be readily visible inside her body as tiny green spheres. An adult male will have an elongate genital papilla (penis-like structure) and a groove from his sucking disc to his anal fin. Please return captives to their homes.

Northern Clingfi

BODY FLATTENED
AT FRONT

LARGE BROAD HEAD

DARK NET-LIKE MARKING
OVER DORSAL SURFACE

LARGE ADHESIVE DISC

SPECIES: *Gobiesox maeandricus*
OTHER COMMON NAMES: flathead clingfish, common cling-fish
MAXIMUM RECORDED SIZE: 16.5 cm (6.5 in)
DISTRIBUTION: Northern Baja California, Mexico, to southeastern Alaska

A

Juvenile.

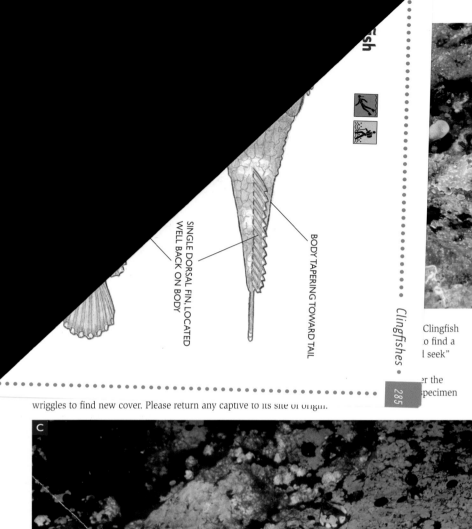

SINGLE DORSAL FIN, LOCATED WELL BACK ON BODY

BODY TAPERING TOWARD TAIL

Clingfish
o find a
l seek"

er the
specimen

wriggles to find new cover. Please return any captive to its site of origin.

C

THE **SAND FLOUNDERS** (Family Paralichthyidae)

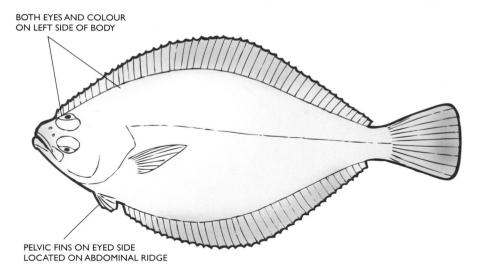

BOTH EYES AND COLOUR
ON LEFT SIDE OF BODY

PELVIC FINS ON EYED SIDE
LOCATED ON ABDOMINAL RIDGE

Containing about 200 recognizable living species of fishes, including the small sanddabs of the Pacific Northwest, the Paralichthyidae is a very large family of bottom-dwelling flat-fishes, popularly known as sand flounders. They were formerly called the left-eyed flounders (Family Bothidae) and this terminology may still be encountered in some literature.

Members of this strictly marine group live in all seas from tropical to boreal latitudes. The species known as the California Halibut is the giant of the family, attaining a maximum length of 152 cm (5 ft), but most sand flounders only grow to half that size.

A newborn paralichthyid begins life near the surface with a symmetrical body and an eye on each side of its head, not unlike that of any other fish. After a definite species-specific period though, two very dramatic changes begin: the migration of the right eye to the left side of the head, beside the other eye; and a corresponding and necessary twisting of the skull. During this dramatic transition, the strange-looking young flounder swims with an every-increasing sideways tilt to compensate for the ongoing anatomical changes. By the time this eye migration process is completed, the body of the young fish has also deepened noticeably and become darkly pigmented, but almost always only on its left or "eyed" side. Now resembling its parents, the young sand flounder takes up permanent residence on the bottom—either lying flat upon its right or "sightless" side or swimming about near the bottom with its pigmented side up—and propelled by undulating body movements.

Other flatfish groups, such as the Pacific Northwest's own righteye flounders, are closely related to the sand flounders, and ichthyologists believe they all originally descended from an ancient, symmetrical perch-like ancestor that began lying on its side.

Pacific Sanddab

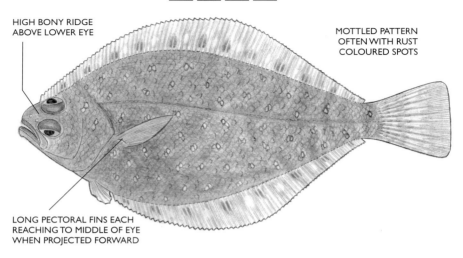

HIGH BONY RIDGE
ABOVE LOWER EYE

MOTTLED PATTERN
OFTEN WITH RUST
COLOURED SPOTS

LONG PECTORAL FINS EACH
REACHING TO MIDDLE OF EYE
WHEN PROJECTED FORWARD

SPECIES: *Citharichthys sordidus*

OTHER COMMON NAMES: mottled sanddab, mottled sand dab, soft flounder. Incorrect: melgrim

MAXIMUM RECORDED SIZE: 41 cm (16 in)

DISTRIBUTION: Southern Baja California, Mexico, to southeastern Alaska

HABITAT: Divers infrequently encounter the Pacific Sanddab because it usually thrives in deeper water. Perhaps because the Pacific Sanddab may come into shallower water to feed nocturnally, night divers have better chances of viewing this thick-bodied fish.

COMMENTS: Anglers who bottom fish from boats most often catch the Pacific Sanddab because it frequents soft bottoms at depths greater than 15 m (50 ft). Try baits such as marine worms, squid, shrimp, clams or pieces of fish.

While trawlers in the Pacific Northwest incidentally take only modest quantities of Pacific Sanddab, which is marketed as "sole," this prized species receives much greater attention in California.

The tasty, flaky flesh of the Pacific Sanddab is excellent either baked or fried. In California, many gourmets consider it a delicacy and some of the finest restaurants there specifically list it on their menus and serve it whole.

Speckled Sanddab

NO RIDGE ABOVE
LOWER EYE

SPECKLED PATTERN

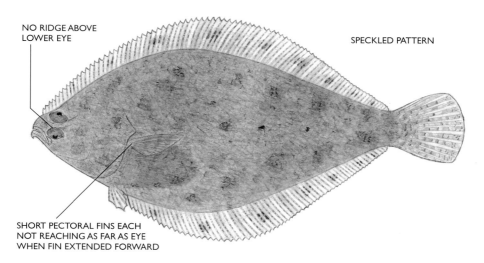

SHORT PECTORAL FINS EACH
NOT REACHING AS FAR AS EYE
WHEN FIN EXTENDED FORWARD

SPECIES: *Citharichthys stigmaeus*

OTHER COMMON NAMES: speckled sand dab, Catalina sand dab

MAXIMUM RECORDED SIZE:
17 cm (6.8 in)

DISTRIBUTION: Southern Baja California, Mexico, to the Gulf of Alaska

HABITAT: The ultimate in camouflage, a resting Speckled Sanddab is very difficult to notice until it moves. Even then, this shallow water denizen may be difficult to relocate once it stops again. Divers should look for the deceptive Speckled Sanddab at depths less than 15 m (50 ft).

COMMENTS: Found at depths to 549 m (1,800 ft), the Speckled Sanddab is primarily an incidental, unmarketable catch for trawlers.

This species is commonly caught by anglers bait fishing from piers or jetties.

Particularly vulnerable to winged predators such as cormorants, gulls or herons, the grey Speckled Sanddab readily flees before beachcombers who wade through shallows on tidal flats.

California Halibut

Paralichthys californicus

Recorded from as far north as Washington, the California Halibut is most common in the waters of its namesake state. There, its maximum size of 117 cm (3.8 ft) and 33 kg (73 lb) makes it a very popular gamefish. The California Halibut has a tail fin that arches backward and a lateral line that sweeps above each pectoral fin.

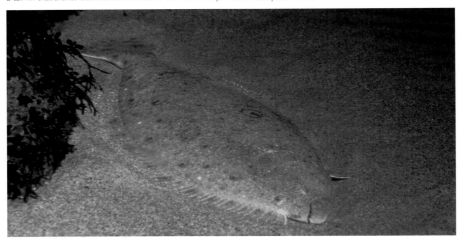

Daniel W. Gotshall photograph

THE **TONGUEFISHES** (Family Cynoglossidae)

California Tonguefish

Symphurus atricaudus

Easily distinguished by its lack of pectoral fins as well as a pointed tail fin united with its anal and dorsal counterparts, the small California Tonguefish attains a length of 21 cm (8.3 in). Northern Washington represents its northern most recorded distribution.

Gregory C. Jensen photograph

THE **RIGHTEYE FLOUNDERS** (Family Pleuronectidae)

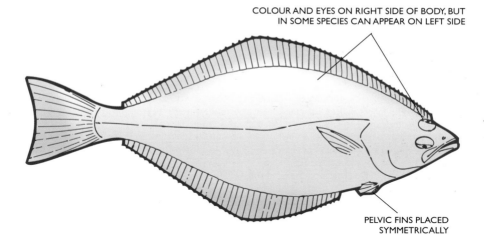

COLOUR AND EYES ON RIGHT SIDE OF BODY, BUT
IN SOME SPECIES CAN APPEAR ON LEFT SIDE

PELVIC FINS PLACED
SYMMETRICALLY

The righteye flounders, known scientifically as the Pleuronectidae, which means "side family," contains approximately 100 known species, nearly all of which live in the marine waters of the northern hemisphere in the Pacific and Atlantic oceans.

A larval righteye flounder begins life like any other fish with an eye on each side of its head. However, an amazing transformation soon occurs. For a righteye flounder, its left eye usually migrates to the right side of the head, accompanied by a requisite twisting of the skull. Additionally, its body broadens, while the dorsal and anal fins lengthen. Finally, the "eyed" side develops its typical dark pigment and the "blind" side becomes white. The resulting young flounder is now beautifully adapted to the sandy-bottom-dwelling existence of an adult.

The Alaska Plaice, *Pleuronectes quadrituberculatus,* lives in shallow water but is very unlikely to be found south of southeastern Alaska.

Pacific Halibut

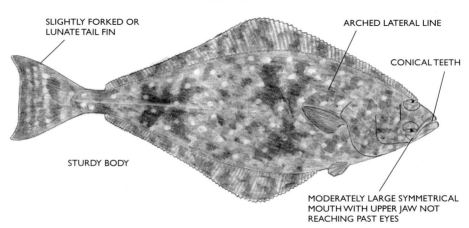

SLIGHTLY FORKED OR
LUNATE TAIL FIN

ARCHED LATERAL LINE

CONICAL TEETH

STURDY BODY

MODERATELY LARGE SYMMETRICAL
MOUTH WITH UPPER JAW NOT
REACHING PAST EYES

SPECIES: *Hippoglossus stenolepis*

OTHER COMMON NAMES: halibut

MAXIMUM RECORDED SIZE: 267 cm (105 in) and 225 kg (495 lb)

DISTRIBUTION: Northern Baja California, Mexico, to the Bering Sea and the Aleutian Island chain, through to Siberia and northern Japan

HABITAT: Few divers see the distinctly shaped Pacific Halibut because it thrives on mixed bottoms below recreational scuba depths. However, those that have seen it attest to how amazing and breathtaking the experience is, especially when a specimen swims along above the sea floor.

COMMENTS: The recreational charter fleet, catering to fishermen seeking the Pacific Halibut, has expanded greatly over the last few decades. It is a sensible option considering a novice angler fishing from his or her own boat is often ill-prepared and may be without the necessary heavy tackle. Regardless of the circumstance, subdue this large fish before hauling it into your boat because the slapping tail of a large Pacific Halibut has maimed and even killed people.

Using longlines, halibut fishermen harvest carefully controlled quantities along North America's shores. Small Pacific Halibut, between 9 and 12 pounds (4.1 and 5.4 kg), sell as "chicks" or "chicken" halibut while very large specimens are sometimes called "whales."

In 1932, Canada and the United States founded the International Pacific Halibut Commission to manage this very important fishery.

The thick-bodied Pacific Halibut remains one of the finest seafoods available from the Pacific Northwest.

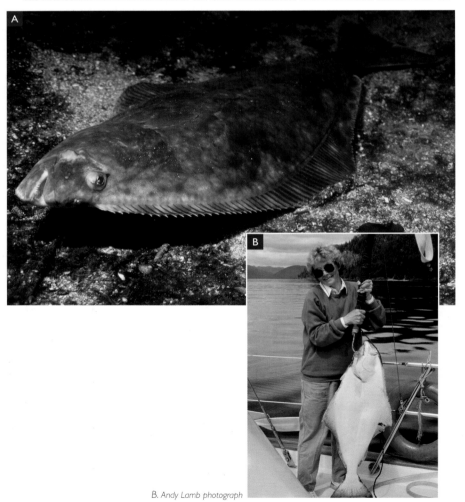

B. *Andy Lamb photograph*

Arrowtooth Flounder

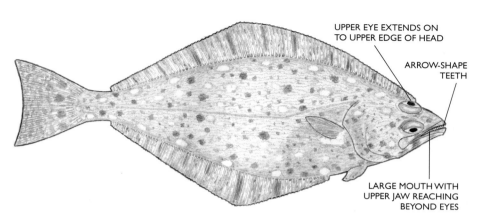

UPPER EYE EXTENDS ON
TO UPPER EDGE OF HEAD

ARROW-SHAPE
TEETH

LARGE MOUTH WITH
UPPER JAW REACHING
BEYOND EYES

SPECIES: *Atheresthes stomias*

OTHER COMMON NAMES: arrowtooth sole, long-jawed flounder, needle-toothed halibut, arrowtooth halibut, American arrowtooth halibut, bastard halibut, French sole. Incorrect: turbot

MAXIMUM RECORDED SIZE: 86 cm (33.9 in) and 7.7 kg (17 lb)

DISTRIBUTION: Central California to the Aleutian Island chain and the Bering Sea coasts of Alaska and Siberia

HABITAT: A species that only rarely invades depths as shallow as 12 m (40 ft), the greyish-brown Arrowtooth Flounder is most likely to cross the diver's path at night.

COMMENTS: The Arrowtooth Flounder is not a targeted game fish or a species that finds significant commercial market, though it does form a considerable portion of the groundfish catch in the northern reaches of its distribution. The Arrowtooth Flounder's flesh becomes mushy when cooked and is therefore not found on seafood menus. However, with ever-increasing pressure on seafood stocks and creative product development, Arrowtooth Flounder may yet become an important economic entity.

Petrale Sole

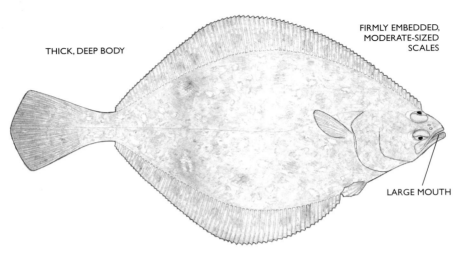

THICK, DEEP BODY

FIRMLY EMBEDDED, MODERATE-SIZED SCALES

LARGE MOUTH

SPECIES: *Eopsetta jordani*

OTHER COMMON NAMES: brill, round-nosed sole, Cape sole, petrale. Incorrect: English sole

MAXIMUM RECORDED SIZE: 70 cm (27.5 in) and 3.6 kg (8 lb)

DISTRIBUTION: Northern Baja California, Mexico, to the Aleutian Island chain, Alaska

HABITAT: The Petrale Sole inhabits shallower, more diver-friendly waters in the northern portion of its distribution. As more recreational aquanauts explore such territory, this large, distinctive fish will likely be observed more often.

COMMENTS: Only those anglers bottom-fishing at considerable depths might catch the desirable Petrale Sole, a large-mouthed flounder. It forages heavily upon small fish such as herring and anchovy.

Next to the renowned Pacific Halibut, the heavy Petrale Sole has always rated as the number-one flounder in the Pacific Northwest. While halibut longliners do incidentally take some Petrale Sole, trawlers harvest the bulk of the catch, hauling it from depths to 457 m (1,500 ft). Because of heavy fishing pressure and overharvesting, the take of this valuable fish has steadily declined.

Just filleting the heavy, thick-bodied Petrale Sole can be a thrill for the chef anticipating a delicious seafood experience. This flounder is one of the finest species in the Pacific Northwest to eat. It has even garnered specific attention from gourmet gurus like Julia Child, who recommended it by name in her famous recipes.

Flathead Sole

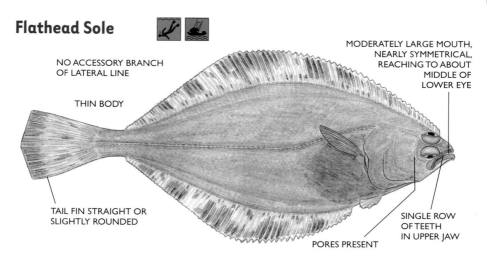

MODERATELY LARGE MOUTH, NEARLY SYMMETRICAL, REACHING TO ABOUT MIDDLE OF LOWER EYE

NO ACCESSORY BRANCH OF LATERAL LINE

THIN BODY

TAIL FIN STRAIGHT OR SLIGHTLY ROUNDED

SINGLE ROW OF TEETH IN UPPER JAW

PORES PRESENT

SPECIES: *Hippoglossoides elassodon*

OTHER COMMON NAMES: paper sole, cigarette paper

MAXIMUM RECORDED SIZE: 56 cm (22 in)

DISTRIBUTION: Central California to the Aleutian Island chain, the Bering Sea through to Siberia and the Sea of Japan

HABITAT: While the brownish Flathead Sole lives upon muddy bottoms at depths as shallow as 5 m (16 ft), it flourishes deeper than most sport divers go. A habit of burying itself, either completely or partially, further hinders observations by aquanauts.

COMMENTS: Although the paper-thin Flathead Sole is often the most abundant flounder hauled up in trawl nets from depths to 1,053 m (3,456 ft), it never sells as human food and only rarely as animal food or for reduction. For some as yet unknown reason (likely pollution), a large percentage of specimens in some locales grow nodular or cauliflower-shaped tumors upon their bodies.

Slender Sole

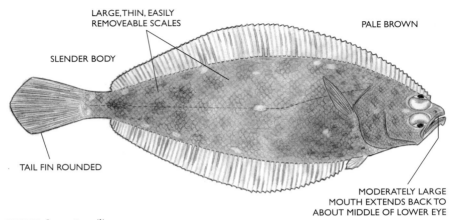

LARGE, THIN, EASILY REMOVEABLE SCALES

PALE BROWN

SLENDER BODY

TAIL FIN ROUNDED

MODERATELY LARGE MOUTH EXTENDS BACK TO ABOUT MIDDLE OF LOWER EYE

SPECIES: *Lyopsetta exilis*

OTHER COMMON NAMES: slender flounder, rough sole

MAXIMUM RECORDED SIZE: 35 cm (13.8 in)

DISTRIBUTION: Southern Baja California, Mexico to the Gulf of Alaska

HABITAT: Under cover of darkness, the light-brown Slender Sole may migrate into shoreline habitats as shallow as 10 m (33 ft), where night divers may encounter it. Unfortunately for the interested diver, this large-scaled species often digs itself into the sea floor by "swimming on the spot" then letting the silt settle back down onto its body—making it difficult to locate.

COMMENTS: Although commercial trawlers, with fine-meshed nets, take large quantities of Slender Sole at depths to 800 m (2,640 ft), its small size eliminates it from the seafood market. Mid-water trawl samples of the abundant Slender Sole indicate that it sometimes swims well above the bottom in search of floating or planktonic shrimp-like prey.

Butter Sole

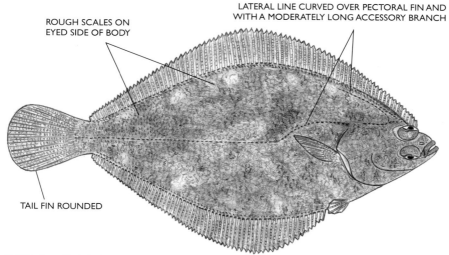

ROUGH SCALES ON
EYED SIDE OF BODY

LATERAL LINE CURVED OVER PECTORAL FIN AND
WITH A MODERATELY LONG ACCESSORY BRANCH

TAIL FIN ROUNDED

SPECIES: *Isopsetta isolepis*

OTHER COMMON NAMES: scalyfin sole, scaly-fin sole, scaly-finned sole flounder, Bellingham sole, Skidegate sole

MAXIMUM RECORDED SIZE: 55 cm (22 in)

DISTRIBUTION: Southern California to the Aleutian Island chain and Bering Sea, Alaska

HABITAT: While patrolling over muddy-bottomed areas, an observant diver may sometimes notice the brownish Butter Sole, but usually only after it has moved. Buried or partially obscured specimens often remain undetected by cruising aquanauts.

COMMENTS: Though trawlers do take the sporadically abundant Butter Sole from all depths to 425 m (1,402 ft), it rates poorly as a marketable commodity and the commercial fisherman often discards it. It occasionally appears in animal food.

Yellowfin Sole

Limanda aspera
Reported as far south as southern British Columbia, the Yellowfin Sole's centre of abundance is Alaska, where it dwells at shallow accessible depths. Its dorsal and anal fins are yellowish with a narrow black line at their bases. A length of 49 cm (19.6 in) is the maximum recorded for this species.

Jeff Mondragon photograph

Rock Sole

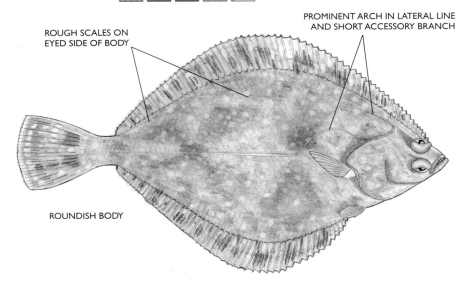

ROUGH SCALES ON
EYED SIDE OF BODY

PROMINENT ARCH IN LATERAL LINE
AND SHORT ACCESSORY BRANCH

ROUNDISH BODY

SPECIES: *Lepidopsetta bilineata*. Formerly *Pleuronectes bilineata*
OTHER COMMON NAMES: roughscale sole, broadfin sole, broad-fin sole, whitebellied sole. Incorrect: two-lined dab
MAXIMUM RECORDED SIZE: 59 cm (23.2 in)
DISTRIBUTION: Baja California, Mexico, to the Aleutian Island chain, Alaska
HABITAT: Present throughout all diveable depths, the active Rock Sole commonly dwells upon sandy or muddy bottoms but may frequently move onto smooth rocky outcroppings. This flounder seldom seems to bury its often rusty-brown body in the sea floor and consequently may be more obvious to the diver.

The young Rock Sole often flourishes around wharves and jetties within easy view of pier-side naturalists.

COMMENTS: Popular with bottom-fishing anglers, the Rock Sole eagerly seizes piling worms, clams and shrimp when fished on sandy, silty or muddy substrates. Artificial lures, including trout flies, spinners, and jigs, attract this aggressive feeder. A large Rock Sole can provide good sport on light tackle.

Highly regarded since the early 1960s, the thick-bodied Rock Sole is a primary target of the groundfish trawl fleet when fishing its nets down to 339 m (1,112 ft). In the Pacific Northwest this species is marketed specifically as "rock sole" because of its fine quality.

A delicious flavour and firm, flaky texture makes this a favourite for the ever-popular "fillet of sole"—a dish with many variations.

NOTE: In 2000, scientists officially "split" the traditional rock sole into two species, the Rock Sole and the Northern Rock Sole. The Northern Rock Sole, *Lepidopsetta polyxystra,* has been recorded as far south as Puget Sound, Washington, but its centre of abundance is Alaska and the Bering Sea. Anatomical differences are distinctive but not obvious to the casual observer. The northern sister species has more gill rakers (visible underneath the gill covers or opercula), more pores (tiny) on the head and a creamier white on the underside.

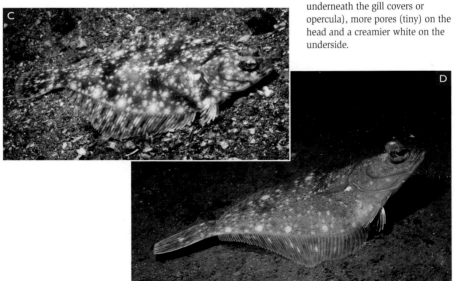

English Sole

LATERAL LINE WITHOUT HIGH ARCH
AND WITH A LONG ACCESSORY BRANCH

UPPER EYE
PARTIALLY VISIBLE
FROM BLIND SIDE

SOMEWHAT SLENDER BODY

SMALL SCALES

POINTED SNOUT
WITH SMALL MOUTH

SPECIES: *Parophrys vetulus.* Formerly *Pleuronectes vetulus* and *Parophrys vetula*

OTHER COMMON NAMES: lemon sole, pointed-nosed sole, common sole, California sole

MAXIMUM RECORDED SIZE: 61.9 cm (24.4 in)

DISTRIBUTION: Central Baja California, Mexico, to the Aleutian Island chain and Bering Sea coast of Alaska

HABITAT: One of the most common flounders within the scuba diver's domain, the variably-patterned English Sole is often difficult to see, especially when completely or partially buried.

Although very difficult to distinguish from the young of several other species, juvenile English Sole flourish in shallow bays and tidal flats where they often flee before wading beach strollers.

COMMENTS: The slippery English Sole is common, popular quarry for bottom-fishermen who lower baits such as marine worms, clams and small crabs onto sandy or silty substrates.

One of the most heavily exploited groundfish, the valuable English Sole is filleted and sold after being hauled from depths as great as 550 m (1,815 ft).

Keep English Sole chilled to ensure the best eating of its tasty but fine-grained flesh.

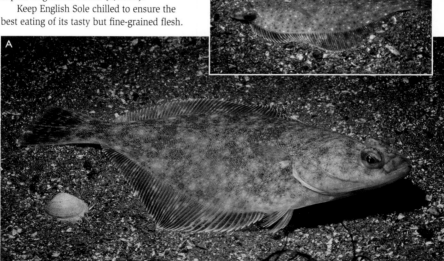

Forkline Sole

Although natural hybridization is considered an unusual phenomenon, the "cross" of the Starry Flounder and the English Sole does periodically occur and survive. Although not a species and therefore not requiring a binomial name, this hybrid has been called the Forkline Sole and *Inopsetta ischyrus*.

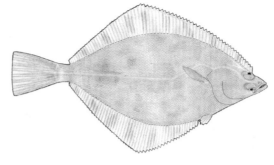

While creating the first edition of this guide, we were lucky enough to capture one of these while trawling near Vancouver, British Columbia. Fortunately, while it was in captivity the accompanying sketch was created. Unfortunately, during a subsequent attempt to obtain an *au naturel* photograph, the specimen escaped *sans* image. It is distinguished by a short forked branch of lateral line on the head that highlights its name, and attains a length of 46 cm (18 in).

Dover Sole

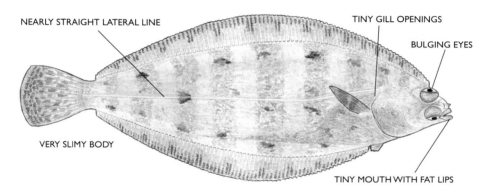

NEARLY STRAIGHT LATERAL LINE

TINY GILL OPENINGS

BULGING EYES

VERY SLIMY BODY

TINY MOUTH WITH FAT LIPS

SPECIES: *Microstomus pacificus*
OTHER COMMON NAMES: slime sole, slippery sole, shortfinned sole, short finned sole, rubber sole, Chinese sole. Incorrect: lemon sole, smear dab, tongue sole
MAXIMUM RECORDED SIZE: 76 cm (30 in) and 4.6 kg (10.1 lb)
DISTRIBUTION: Southern Baja California, Mexico, to the Aleutian Island chain and Bering Sea coast of Alaska

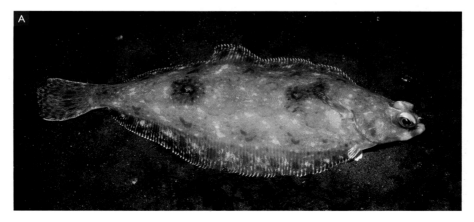

HABITAT: Often burying itself in the sea floor with only its distinctive, bulbous eyes protruding, the slender Dover Sole often lives at depths below those scoured by most recreational divers.

COMMENTS: A favourite with many bottom-fishermen, the large Dover Sole may seize baits such as clams, worms or shrimp. Use small hooks for this tiny-mouthed fish. A large specimen can provide good light-tackle action.

Once scorned because of its habit of exuding great quantities of slime that readily spoiled entire catches, the now highly prized Dover Sole comprises a large, important share of the retained flatfish trawl catch. It is quickly washed, filleted and skinned to eliminate the slime problems.

Place Dover Sole fillets in a single layer in a buttered baking dish; brush with lemon juice and let stand for ten minutes. Then broil fillets on one side before removing from heat and adding a sauce, parmesan cheese, salad dressing and onion.

Rex Sole

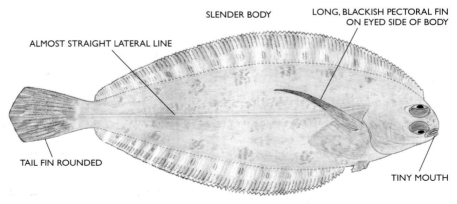

SLENDER BODY

LONG, BLACKISH PECTORAL FIN
ON EYED SIDE OF BODY

ALMOST STRAIGHT LATERAL LINE

TAIL FIN ROUNDED

TINY MOUTH

SPECIES: *Glyptocephalus zachirus.* Formerly *Errex zachirus*

OTHER COMMON NAMES: longfin sole, long-finned sole. Incorrect: witch

MAXIMUM RECORDED SIZE: 61 cm (24 in)

DISTRIBUTION: Central Baja California, Mexico, to the Aleutian Island chain and Bering Sea coasts of Alaska and Asia

HABITAT: Night divers venturing over gently sloping sandy bottoms sometimes find the pale Rex Sole being very still on the substrate. If gently coaxed, rather than rudely startled, this distinctive fish will almost effortlessly coast along the bottom and erect its long, dark, sickle-shaped pectoral fin.

COMMENTS: Hauled up in abundance from soft bottoms at depths as great as 850 m (2,800 ft), the Rex Sole comprises much of the total trawl catch of flatfish. However, its very thin and difficult-to-fillet body is usually discarded in favour of more robust and profitable species. Occasionally, the Rex Sole has been reduced for fertilizer.

Do not fillet the thin Rex Sole—it's too frustrating. Instead, remove its head, fins and viscera, then coat the remainder with flour before frying.

A. Juvenile.

Sand Sole

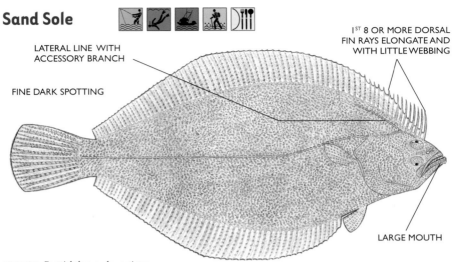

LATERAL LINE WITH ACCESSORY BRANCH

FINE DARK SPOTTING

1ST 8 OR MORE DORSAL FIN RAYS ELONGATE AND WITH LITTLE WEBBING

LARGE MOUTH

SPECIES: *Psettichthys melanostictus*

OTHER COMMON NAMES: fringe sole, sand flounder, spotted flounder

MAXIMUM RECORDED SIZE: 63 cm (24.8 in) and 2.3 kg (5 lb)

DISTRIBUTION: Southern California to the Aleutian Island chain and Bering Sea coast of Alaska, near the Alaskan Peninsula

HABITAT: Even though the Sand Sole thrives at shallow depths, its finely speckled colouration and burying behaviour make it a very difficult sighting for even the most observant diver.

COMMENTS: Try bottom-fishing for this species by using its natural food as bait—marine worms, clams, shrimp, herring or anchovy. The Sand Sole commonly rests upon shallow sandy habitats and is also accessible to beach anglers.

Not specifically targeted, the Sand Sole forms only a minor portion of the flatfish trawl catch. It is marketed with several others as "sole," either fresh or frozen.

Try flounder *à l'orange*. Place fillets skin-side down in a buttered baking pan; add frozen orange juice concentrate, butter and nutmeg; then bake.

B. Juvenile.

Starry Flounder

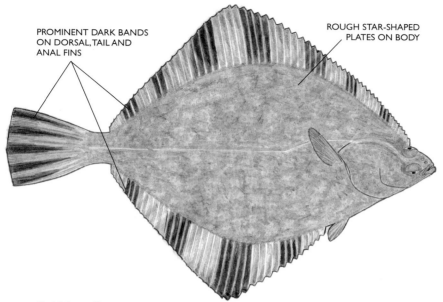

PROMINENT DARK BANDS
ON DORSAL, TAIL AND
ANAL FINS

ROUGH STAR-SHAPED
PLATES ON BODY

SPECIES: *Platichthys stellatus*

OTHER COMMON NAMES: Incorrect: grindstone, leatherjacket

MAXIMUM RECORDED SIZE: 91 cm (36 in) and 9.1 kg (20 lb)

DISTRIBUTION: Southern California to the Bering Sea and along the Arctic coast to the Coronation Gulf, Northwest Territories; from the Bering Strait to Korea and southern Japan

HABITAT: Often resting partially or completely buried in soft substrates at depths as shallow as the intertidal zone, the greyish Starry Flounder may also slowly cruise along the bottom in search of prey. Divers should look for it in areas adjacent to eelgrass beds, under wharves and even in the brackish waters of river mouths.

Starry Flounders often scatter in all directions before the wading beachcomber who wanders through the shallows of gently sloping tidal flats.

A

Bernard P. Hanby photograph

COMMENTS: Popular with anglers fishing from wharves, jetties or shorelines, the aggressive Starry Flounder readily accepts baits. Small spinners slowly retrieved near the sandy bottom also attract this good light-tackle battler. Fly fishermen seeking a novel experience can cast for this species when it rises to the surface at night, attracted by pier lights.

Trawlers secure modest numbers of the Starry Flounder, fillet them and sell them as "sole."

While the rough, leathery skin was once used as emergency sandpaper, it is now discarded and only the tasty flesh retained as an ideal "sole" food.

C-O Sole

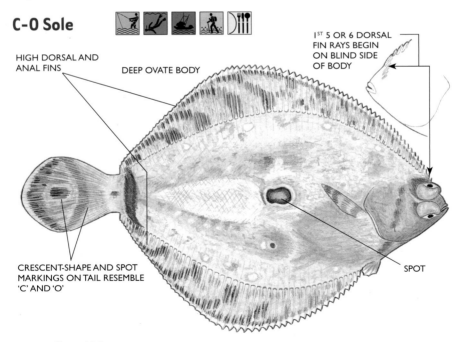

HIGH DORSAL AND ANAL FINS

DEEP OVATE BODY

1ST 5 OR 6 DORSAL FIN RAYS BEGIN ON BLIND SIDE OF BODY

CRESCENT-SHAPE AND SPOT MARKINGS ON TAIL RESEMBLE 'C' AND 'O'

SPOT

SPECIES: *Pleuronichthys coenosus*

OTHER COMMON NAMES: spot flounder, popeye sole, muddy flounder. Incorrect: C-O turbot, mottled turbot, turbot, stinker

MAXIMUM RECORDED SIZE: 36 cm (14 in) and 0.43 kg (0.9 lb)

DISTRIBUTION: Northern Baja California, Mexico, to southeastern Alaska

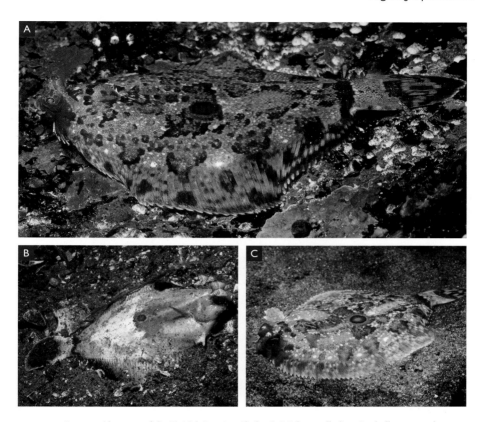

HABITAT: So named because of the "initials" on its tail, the C-O Sole usually lives in shallow water, less than 15 m (50 ft), and often where sandy substrates adjoin rocky shores. It even perches upon rocky outcrops. Divers tend to see it more than they see some other flounders. While the C-O Sole usually has rich tones of brown on its body, specimens living around the pink coralline algae may have beautiful pink splotches. Consequently, it is one of the few flounders attracting the discriminating underwater photographer.

Beachcombers wading through eelgrass beds, or sharp-eyed dockside naturalists peering into the water, might notice the rounded form of the C-O Sole.

COMMENTS: While bait-fishing from jetties, piers or the shore, anglers sometimes catch the popeyed C-O Sole on small hooks baited with marine worms, clams and shrimp.

Trawl fleets of the Pacific Northwest do not often net the C-O Sole but their Californian counterparts consider it to be moderately important.

Minus its head, fins and entrails, or filleted, the small, round and thick body of the C-O Sole is excellent for any recipe calling for sole.

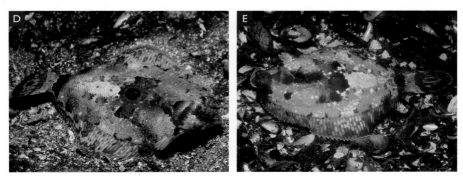

Curlfin Sole

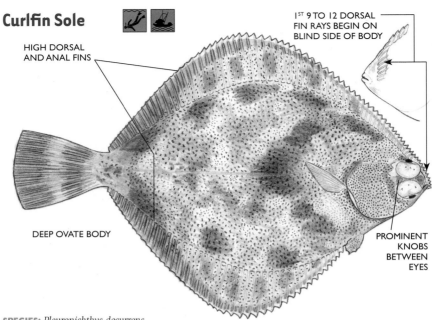

HIGH DORSAL
AND ANAL FINS

1ST 9 TO 12 DORSAL
FIN RAYS BEGIN ON
BLIND SIDE OF BODY

DEEP OVATE BODY

PROMINENT
KNOBS
BETWEEN
EYES

SPECIES: *Pleuronichthys decurrens*

OTHER COMMON NAMES: curl-fin sole. Incorrect: curlfin turbot, California turbot

MAXIMUM RECORDED SIZE: 36 cm (14 in) and 0.77 kg (1.7 lb)

DISTRIBUTION: Southern Baja California, Mexico, to the Aleutian Island chain, Alaska

HABITAT: The almost-round Curlfin Sole does not seem to be abundant anywhere in the Pacific Northwest, and therefore seldom crosses the path of the local sport diver.

B. Bernard P. Hanby photograph

COMMENTS: Seldom harvested by Pacific Northwest trawlers, the thick-bodied Curlfin Sole, along with several other very similar species, is harvested in California. There, it is marketed with other similar species as "turbot."

Acknowledgements

Without the very special efforts of many people, we would have been unable to produce this book. We thank them all most heartily.

Collection and transportation of specimens for photography, image acquisition and artwork was a major, time-consuming requirement. The following folks diligently assisted with these tasks:

Mark Ahern, the late John Allan, the late George Baker, Joe Bauer, Dr. Dick Beamish, Dr. Tillman Benfey, Jim Borrowman, Bud Bowles, Phil Bruecker, Jim Cave, the late Dave Christie, Gord Cox, Ted Davies, Dr. John Davis, Ralph Delisle, Jack Dibold, Lauralee Edgell, John Fisher, John Gawron, Charlie Gibbs, Donna Gibbs, Duane Goertson, John Goertson, Martha Goertson, Martha Goertson Jr., Rita Goertson, Roger Goertson, Mike Gray, Barbara Hale, Bernie Hanby, Gavin Hanke, Bob Harrison, Calvin Hass, Darren Hass, Dr. Ian Hass, Julia Hass, Morgan Hass, Sarah Hass, Coleen Hay, Ian Hay, the late Jack Heading, Kal Helyar, Gil Hewlett, Richard Hocking, Sharon Jeffery, Colin Jerome, Craig Jerome, Ernie Jerome, Mary Jerome, Dick Jones, Lee Keary, Danny Kent, Ken Kollman, Dr. George Kruzinski, Alec Lamb, Susan Lamb, Virginia Lamb, Finn Larsen, Don Lawseth, Mike Lever, Joyce Lockhart, Carmen McConnell, Neil McDaniel, Bill McKay, Dr. Don McPhail, Don McQuarrie, Brian Markert, Jack Markert, Susan Markert, Sandy Matheson, Andrea (Smith) May, Renate (Christie) Mendria, Abby (Bowers) Moffett, the late Dr. Charles Moffett, Jenny (von Veh) Moffett, Mimi (Henninger) Moffett, Sarah (Heaton) Moffett, Takuji Oyama, Catherine Po, Garnett Rawle, John Rawle, Louise Richardson, Kelly Sendall, Ian Shand, Boyd Shirley, Edith Shirley, the late Paul Shirley, Dr. Susan Shirley, Dee Smith, Judy Smith, Dr. John Stockner, Doug Swanston, Jim Thompson, Les Tulloch, Dr. Glen Van Der Kraak, Lynn Webber, Jergen Westrhiem, the late Dr. Norman J. Wilimovsky, Billy Wong.

People who contributed artistic and literary skills include: Ralph Delisle, Helen Dye, Lauralee Edgell, Roy Edgell, Charlie Gibbs, Donna Gibbs, Dr. Larry Giovando, Daniel W. Gotshall, the late Jack Grundle, Bernie Hanby, Sue Hanby, Bob Hodge, Tom Laidig, the late Bess Lamb, Lou Lehmann, Linda Manheim, Dr. James Orr, Dr. Chris Pharo, Gordon Soules, Peter Vassilopoulos, Lon Wood.

The following institutions and businesses generously contributed their facilities: Bamfield Marine Station, *Diver* Magazine, Harrisons's Fishing Lodge, Living Elements, Mainstream Canada, MV *Nautilus Explorer*, Pacific Biological Station, Pacific Bio-Marine Laboratories, Rendezvous Dive Ventures, Seacology, Stubbs Island Charters, University of Washington, Vancouver Aquarium Marine Science Centre, *Western Angling* magazine, West Vancouver Laboratory, Wordtex.

Thanks to Dr. Robert N. Lea, Dr. Milton Love and Dr. Jeff Marliave for their generous scientific editing.

Thanks to the publisher and entire crew at Harbour Publishing, including production assistants Natalia Cornwall, Marysia McGilvray and Rob Rao, production manager Teresa Karbashewski and managing editor Anna Comfort. Thanks as well to editors Peter Robson and Rebecca Hendry, graphic designer Martin Nichols, and proofreaders Lenore Hietkamp and Amelia Gilliland.

Photography Acknowledgements

The most exciting and satisfying new feature in the second edition is the additional images contributed by a group of outstanding photographers. Each and every one greatly enhances the publication. We are most honoured to acknowledge these folks and their fine efforts:

Franco Banfi, Clinton Bauder, John Butler, Wendy Carey, Dr. Marc Chamberlain, Nate Chambers/Alaska Sealife Center, Keith Clements, Mark Conlin, Brent Cook, Darice Susan Dixon, Dr. Pierre Dow, David Fleetham, Kent Forsen, Charlie Gibbs, Chris Gotschalk, Daniel W. Gotshall, Rhoda Green, Jon Gross, Chris Grossman, Jan Haaga, Bernie Hanby, Cindy Hansen, the late Ib Hansen, Daniel Hershman, Jackie Hildering, Alexander Jackson, Sharon Jeffery, Gregory C. Jensen, Scott Johnson, Maris Kazmers, Danny Kent, Jan Kocian, Wes Kozak, Lou Lehmann, Monterey Bay Aquarium Research Institute (MBARI, Kim Fulton-Bennett), Conor McCracken, Neil McDaniel, Mick McMurray, Debbie Maas, Dr. Catherine Mecklenburg, Michael Maia Mincarone, Jeff Mondragon, David Murphy, Kim Musgrove, Dr. Murray Newman, Janna Nichols, Ken Oda, Mary P. O'Malley, Dr. James Orr, Takuji Oyama, Perry Poon, Ed Roberts, Royal British Columbia Museum Archives, Dale Sanders, Tom Sheldon, Ryan Silbernagel, Marty Snyderman, Catherine Statham, Chuck Tribolet, Jerry Vandergriff, Terry Whalen, Richard Zade.

Bernie Hanby.
Sue Hanby photograph

Over the many years since *Coastal Fishes of the Pacific Northwest* was conceived until the arrival of this second edition, we have had the encouragement and assistance of **Bernie Hanby**. Bernie has significantly contributed in numerous and varied ways. We are very pleased to include many of his outstanding images in this guide.

Above all, Bernie is a special advocate for fish. Building upon decades of experience as a recreational angler and scuba diver, he has worked tirelessly to conserve the threatened species of the Pacific Northwest. In particular, his passion for No-Take Marine Protected Areas and their establishment is boundless. We share this passion.

Lou Lehmann's early underwater photography also had a great influence on the photography presented in this book. Lou set the standard of the day with his underwater photographs and was a great diving buddy for many years.

NOTE: All photos not credited were taken by co-author Phil Edgell. Live fish images taken by Phil were shot "on location" or by capturing specimens and temporarily releasing them in appropriate habitats for photography before returning them to their place of origin. Andy Lamb used live specimens as models for creation of shaded, labelled and proportionally accurate sketches. Occasionally, when a specimen was too large or otherwise unavailable, a composite was prepared from numerous images accumulated during photographic activities. The important features that distinguish each species are labelled on the artwork to focus the reader's attention upon the most relevant factors for identification.

APPENDIX
Aquaria: Public Viewing Opportunities for Pacific Northwest Fishes

Public aquaria are valuable resources for people interested in Pacific Northwest fishes, particularly those unable to readily access natural viewing options. Even for divers, fishermen and beachcombers, these institutions offer comfortable viewing and educational opportunities.

Major Aquaria in the Pacific Northwest
The following facilities have significant exhibits featuring many of the species contained in this publication. In addition, they generally have major research, conservation and education programs focusing on Pacific Northwest marine life.

Alaska Sealife Center, 301 Railway Road, Seward, Alaska. 907-224-6300, www. alaskasealife.org

Aquarium of the Pacific, 100 Aquarium Way, Long Beach, California. 562-590-1629, www.aquariumofthepacific.org

Birch Aquarium at Scripts Institute of Oceanography, 2300 Expedition Way, La Jolla, California. 858-534-3474, www.calacademy.org

Cabrillo Marine Aquarium, 372 Stephen M. White Drive, San Pedro, California. 310-548-7572, www.cabrillomarineaquarium.org

Hatfield Marine Science Center, 2030 Marine Science Drive, Newport, Oregon. 541-867-0100, www.hatfieldmarinecenter.org

Monterey Bay Aquarium, 886 Cannery Row, Monterey, California. 831-648-4800, www.montereybayaquarium.org

Oregon Coast Aquarium, 2820 S.E. Ferry Slip Road, Newport, Oregon. 541-867-3474, www.oregoncoastaquarium.org

Point Defiance Aquarium, 5400 N. Pearl Street, Point Defiance Park, Tacoma, Washington. 253-591-5333, www.pdza.org

Seattle Aquarium, 1483 Alaskan Way, Seattle, Washington. 206-386-4300, www.seattleaquarium.org

Shaw Ocean Discovery Centre, 9811 Seaport Place, Sidney, British Columbia. 250-665-7511, www.oceandiscovery.ca

Steinhart Aquarium, 55 Music Concourse Drive, Golden Gate Park, San Francisco, California. 415-379-5451, www.calacademy.org

Vancouver Aquarium Marine Science Centre, 845 Avison Way, Stanley Park, Vancouver, British Columbia. 604-659-3474, www.van.aqua.org

Minor Aquaria in the Pacific Northwest

The following facilities have some exhibits that feature species contained in this publication. In addition, they generally have outreach/education programs focusing on Pacific Northwest marine life.

Bellingham Marine Life Center, 1801 Roeder Avenue, Bellingham, Washington. 360-671-2431, www.marinelifecenter.org

Feiro Marine Life Center, 315 N. Lincoln Street, Port Angeles, Washington. 360-417-6254, www.olypen.com

Ocean World, 304 Highway 101 South, Crescent City, California. 707-464-4900, www.oceanworldonline.com

Poulsbo Marine Science Center, 18743 Front Street, Poulsbo, Washington. 360-598-4460, www.poulsbomsc.org

Port Townsend Marine Science Center, 532 Battery Way, Ford Worden State Park, Port Townsend, Washington. 360-385-5582, www.ptmsc.org

Seaside Aquarium, 200 N. Promenade, Seaside, Oregon. 503-738-6211, www.seasideaquarium.com

Seymour Center at Long Marine Lab, end of Delaware Avenue, Santa Cruz, California. 831-459-4568, www.seymourcenter.ucsc.edu

Ucluelet Aquarium, Whiskey Landing Wharf, Ucluelet, British Columbia. 604-648-8182, www.uclueletaquarium.org

Westport Aquarium & Gift Shop, 321 Harbor, Westport, Washington. 360-268-0471, www.westportwa.com

‌

SELECTED BIBLIOGRAPHY

During preparation of this book, a very large number of references were consulted for the sake of accuracy, completeness and currency. Unfortunately, space is unavailable to cite all of these excellent scientific works. However, the following short list is presented as a selected group of publications that may assist those readers interested in further study.

Childerhose, R.J., and M. Trim. *Pacific Salmon and Steelhead Trout*. Vancouver: Douglas & McIntyre, 1979.

Coad, B.W. *Encyclopedia of Canadian Fishes*. Ottawa: Canadian Museum of Nature, 1995.

Eschmeyer, W.N., E.S. Herald, and H. Hammann. *A Field Guide to the Pacific Coast Fishes of North America*. Boston: Houghton Mifflin, 1983.

Forester, J.E., and A.D. Forester. *Fishing: British Columbia's Commercial Fishing History*. Vancouver: Hancock House, 1976.

Gotshall, D.W. *Pacific Coast Inshore Fishes, 5th Edition Revised*. Gig Harbor: Sea Challengers, Inc., 2009.

Hart, J.L. *Pacific Fishes of Canada*. Ottawa: Fisheries Research Board of Canada, Bulletin 180, 1974.

Haw, F., and R.M. Buckley. *Saltwater Fishing in Washington*. Seattle: Stan Jones Publishing Company, 1973.

Humann, P., and N. DeLoach. *Coastal Fish Identification, Alaska to California, 2nd Edition*. Jacksonville: New World Publications, Inc., 2008.

Jackson, A. *Vancouver Aquarium Seafood Recipes*. Vancouver: Gordon Soules Book Publishers, 1977.

Lamb, A., and B.P. Hanby. *Marine Life of the Pacific Northwest*. Madeira Park: Harbour Publishing, 2005.

Love, M.S., M. Yoklavich, and L. Thorsteinson. *The Rockfishes of the Northeast Pacific*. Berkeley: University of California Press, 2002.

Mecklenburg, C.W., T.A. Mecklenburg, and L.K. Thorsteinson. *Fishes of Alaska*. Bathesda: American Fisheries Society, 2001.

Migadalski, E.C. *How to Make Fish Mounts and Other Fish Trophies*. New York: Ronald Press, 1960.

Nelson, J.S., et al. *Common and Scientific Names of Fishes from the United States, Canada, and Mexico, 6th Edition*. Bathesda: American Fisheries Society, Special Publication 29, 2004."

Peden, A.E. *Collecting and Preserving Fishes*. Victoria: Queen's Printer, British Columbia Provincial Museum, Museum Methods Manual 3, 1976.

Pollard, W.R., et al. *Field Identification of Juvenile Salmonids*. Madeira Park: Harbour Publishing, 1997.

Starchild, A., and J. Holahan. *Starchild's and Houlahan's Seafood Cookbook*. Seattle: Pacific Press, 1978.

Stewart, H. *Indian Fishing: Early Methods on the Northwest Coast*. Seattle: University of Washington Press, 1977.

Wilson, D., and F. Vander Werff. *New Techniques for Catching Bottom Fish*. Mercer Island, Washington: The Writing Works, 1977.

INDEX

Acipenseridae. *See* **STURGEONS**

Acipenser medirostris (Green Sturgeon), 44

Acipenser transmontanus (White Sturgeon), 43

Agonidae. *See* **POACHERS**

Agonomalus mozinoi. See Hypsagonus mozinoi

Agonopsis vulsa (Northern Spearnose Poacher), 263

Agonus acipenserinus. See Podothecus accipenserinus

Alaska blackcod. *See* Sablefish

Alaska cod. *See* Pacific Cod

Alaska Plaice, 291

Alaska pollock. *See* Walleye Pollock

Alaskan Ronquil, 107–108

Alaska Skate, 33

Albacore, 144

Alepisauridae. *See* **LANCETFISHES**

Alepisaurus ferox (Longnose Lancetfish), 84

Aleutian Skate, 33

alewives. *See* **HERRINGS**

Alligatorfish, Smooth, 262

Allosmerus elongatus (Whitebait Smelt), 49

Alopias vulpinus (Common Thresher Shark), 31

Alopiidae. *See* **THRESHER SHARKS**

Alosa sapidissima (American Shad), 47

American arrowtooth halibut. *See* Arrowtooth Flounder

American river lamprey. *See* River Lamprey

American Shad, 47

Ammodytes hexapterus (Pacific Sand Lance), 54

Ammodytidae. *See* **SAND LANCES**

Amphistichus koelzi (Calico Surfperch), 95

Amphistichus rhodoterus (Redtail Surfperch), 94

Anarhichadidae. *See* **WOLFFISHES**

Anarrhichthys ocellatus (Wolf-eel), 133

ANCHOVIES (Engraulidae), 48–49

Northern Anchovy, 48–49

anchovy. *See* Northern Anchovy

anchovy, California. *See* Northern Anchovy

Anchovy, Northern, 48–49

anchovy, plain. *See* Northern Anchovy

ANGEL SHARKS (Squatinidae), 32

Pacific Angel Shark, 32

Anisarchus medius (Stout Eelblenny), 116

Anoplagonus inermis (Smooth Alligatorfish), 262

Anoplarchus insignis (Slender Cockscomb), 121

Anoplarchus purpurescens (High Cockscomb), 120

Anoplopoma fimbria (Sablefish), 184

Anoplopomatidae. *See* **SABLEFISHES**

Antlered Sculpin, 247

Apodichthys flavidus (Penpoint Gunnel), 127–128

Apodichthys fucorum (Rockweed Gunnel), 126–127

Apristurus brunneus (Brown Catshark), 23, 24

Aptocyclus ventricosus (Smooth Lumpsucker), 280

Arctic sandlance. *See* Pacific Sand Lance

Arctic Shanny, 116

Armorhead, North Pacific, 101

ARMORHEADS (Pentacerotidae), 101

North Pacific Armorhead, 101

Arrow Goby, 105

Arrowtooth Flounder, 293

arrowtooth halibut. *See* Arrowtooth Flounder

arrowtooth sole. *See* Arrowtooth Flounder

Artedius corallinus (Coralline Sculpin), 203

Artedius fenestralis (Padded Sculpin), 201

Artedius harringtoni (Scalyhead Sculpin), 204–205

Artedius lateralis (Smoothhead Sculpin), 202–203

Artedius meanyi. See Ruscarius meanyi

Artedius notospilotus (Bonehead Sculpin), 202

Ascelichthys rhodorus (Rosylip Sculpin), 213

Asemichthys taylori. See Radulinus taylori

Asterotheca alascana. See Bathyagonus alascanus

Asterotheca infraspinata. See Bathyagonus infraspinatus

Asterotheca pentacanthus. See Bathyagonus pentacanthus

Astractoscion nobilis (White Seabass), 99

Atheresthes stomias (Arrowtooth Flounder), 293

Atherinops affinis (Topsmelt), 82

Atherinopsidae. *See* **SILVERSIDES**

Atherinopsis californiensis (Jacksmelt), 82

Atka Mackerel, 186, 199

Atlantic Ratfish, 41
Atlantic Salmon, 70
Aulorhynchidae. *See* **TUBESNOUTS**
Aulorhynchus flavidus (Tubesnout), 87

Bald Sculpin, 212
Balistes polylepis (Finescale Triggerfish), 145
Balistidae. *See* **TRIGGERFISHES**
banded rockfish. *See* Tiger Rockfish
bandeye sculpin. *See* Longfin Sculpin
banstickle. *See* Threespine Stickleback
Barracuda, California, 83
Barracuda, Pacific, 83
BARRACUDAS (Sphyraenidae), 83
  California Barracuda, 83
Basking Shark, 28
BASKING SHARKS (Cetorhinidae), 28
  Basking Shark, 28
bass rockfish. *See* Black Rockfish
bastard halibut. *See* Arrowtooth Flounder
Bat Ray, 39
*Bathyagonus alascana. See Bathyagonus
  alascanus*
Bathyagonus alascanus (Gray Starsnout), 256
*Bathyagonus infraspinata. See Bathyagonus
  infraspinatus*
Bathyagonus infraspinatus (Spinycheek
  Starsnout), 255
Bathyagonus nigripinnis (Blackfin Poacher),
  258
Bathyagonus pentacanthus (Bigeye Poacher),
  257
Bathymaster caeruleofasciatus (Alaskan
  Ronquil), 107
Bathymaster signatus (Searcher), 108
Bathymasteridae. *See* **RONQUILS**
Bathyraja aleutica (Aleutian Skate), 33
Bathyraja interrupta (Sandpiper Skate), 36
Bathyraja parmifera (Alaska Skate), 33
Batrachoididae. *See* **TOADFISHES**
Bay Goby, 104
Bay Pipefish, 88
Bellingham sole. *See* Butter Sole
belted blenny. *See* Ribbon Prickleback
Beluga of Northern Asia. *See* **STURGEONS**
bichki, 102
Bigeye Poacher, 257
bigeye. *See* Walleye Pollock
bigeye starnose *See* Bigeye Poacher
bigeye starsnout. *See* Bigeye Poacher
Bigmouth Sculpin, 244
Big Skate, 33, 35–36

black-and-white prickleback. *See* Bluebarred
  Prickleback
blackbanded rockfish. *See* Tiger Rockfish
black-bellied eelpout. *See* Blackbelly Eelpout
Blackbelly Eelpout, 80
black blenny. *See* Black Prickleback
blackcod. *See* Sablefish
blackcod, Alaska. *See* Sablefish
black cod. *See* Sablefish
Black Eelpout, 81
blackedge poacher. *See* Blacktip Poacher
Blackeye Goby, 102–103
blackfin eelpout. *See* Black Eelpout
black-finned eelpout. *See* Black Eelpout
black-finned sea-poacher. *See* Blackfin
  Poacher
Blackfin Poacher, 258Blackfin Sculpin, 232
blackfin starnose. *See* Blackfin Poacher
blackfin starsnout. *See* Blackfin Poacher
Black Hagfish, 17
Blackmouth Eelpout, 82
blackmouth salmon. *See* Chinook Salmon
Black Prickleback, 119
Black Rockfish, 146, 158–159
black skate. *See* Sandpaper Skate
black-tipped sea-poacher. *See* Blacktip
  Poacher
Blacktip Poacher, 259
BLENNIES, KELP (Clinidae), 109–111
blenny, belted. *See* Ribbon Prickleback
blenny, black. *See* Black Prickleback
blenny, bracketed. *See* Crescent Gunnel
blenny, crested. *See* High Cockscomb
blenny, ornamented. *See* Mosshead
  Warbonnet
blenny, pen-point. *See* Penpoint Gunnel
blenny, rock. *See* Rock Prickleback
blenny, rockweed. *See* Rockweed Gunnel
blenny, saddled. *See* Saddleback Gunnel
blenny, white-barred. *See* Whitebarred
  Prickleback
Blepsias bilobus (Crested Sculpin), 236
Blepsias cirrhosus (Silverspotted Sculpin),
  235
Blob Sculpin, 234
blue back. *See* Sockeye Salmon
blueback salmon. *See* Sockeye Salmon
Bluebarred Prickleback, 113–114
blue-blotched rockfish. *See* Blue Rockfish
bluefin searcher. *See* Alaskan Ronquil
blue perch. *See* Striped Seaperch
Blue Rockfish, 160–161

blue seaperch. *See* Striped Seaperch
Blue Shark, 27
blue-sided rockfish. *See* Blue Rockfish
bluespot goby. *See* Blackeye Goby
Bluespotted Poacher, 259
Bluntnose Sixgill Shark, 21–23
Bocaccio, 165
bolina. *See* Brown Rockfish
Bonehead Sculpin, 202
bone shark (Atlantic). *See* Basking Shark
Bonito, Pacific, 144
Bothidae. *See* Sand Flounders.
Brachyistius frenatus (Kelp Perch), 96
bracketed blenny. *See* Crescent Gunnel
Brama japonica (Pacific Pomfret), 100
Bramidae. *See* **POMFRETS**
brill. *See* Petrale Sole
broadfin sole. *See* Rock Sole
Broadnose Sevengill Shark, 21–22
Brosmophycis marginata (Red Brotula), 78
Brotula, Red, 77–78
BROTULAS, VIVIPAROUS (Bythitidae), 77–78
Brown Catshark, 23–24
Brown Irish Lord, 250
brown perch. *See* Kelp Perch
Brown Rockfish, 152
brown sea-perch. *See* Kelp Perch
brown shark. *See* Brown Catshark
Bryozoichthys marjorius (Pearly Prickleback), 122
buffalo fish. *See* Buffalo Sculpin
Buffalo Sculpin, 195, 245–246
bugeye. *See* Walleye Pollock
bullhead. *See* **SCULPINS**
bullhead, roaring. *See* Plainfin Midshipman
Burbot. *See* **CODS**
BUTTERFISHES (Stromateidae), 99
   Pacific Pompano, 99
Butter Sole, 297
Bythitidae. *See* **VIVIPAROUS BROTULAS**

Cabezon, 200, 241–242
calico salmon. *See* Chum Salmon
Calico Sculpin, 211
Calico Surfperch, 95
California anchovy. *See* Northern Anchovy
California Barracuda, 83
California hagfish. *See* Pacific Hagfish
California hake. *See* Pacific Hake
California Halibut, 287, 290
California Lizardfish, 83

California pilchard. *See* Pacific Sardine
California sole. *See* English Sole
California Tonguefish, 290
California Tule Perch. *See* **SURFPERCHES**
Canary Rockfish, 170–171
candlefish. *See* Eulachon
Capelin, 49, 52–53
capelin, Pacific. *See* Capelin
Cape sole. *See* Petrale Sole
Carangidae. *See* **JACKS**
Carcharhinidae. *See* **REQUIEM SHARKS**
Carcharodon carcharias (Great White Shark), 26
Catalina sand dab. *See* Speckled Sanddab
catshark. *See* Brown Catshark
Catshark, Brown, 23–24
CATSHARKS (Scyliorhinidae), 23–24
   Brown Catshark, 23–24
Caulolatilus princeps (Ocean Whitefish), 98
Centrolophidae. *See* **MEDUSAFISHES**
Cetorhinidae. *See* **BASKING SHARKS**
Cetorhinus maximus (Basking Shark), 28
char, Pacific brook. *See* Dolly Varden
char, red spotted. *See* Dolly Varden
char, sea. *See* Dolly Varden
chars. *See* **SALMON AND TROUT**
char, western brook. *See* Dolly Varden
Chesnonia verrucosa (Warty Poacher), 255
Chilara taylori (Spotted Cusk-Eel), 79
Chilipepper, 166
Chimaera monstrosa (Atlantic Ratfish), 41
chimaera. *See* Spotted Ratfish
CHIMAERAS, SHORTNOSE (Chimaeridae), 40–42
Chimaeridae. *See* **SHORTNOSE CHIMAERAS**
China Rockfish, 155–156
chinese rockfish. *See* China Rockfish
Chinese sole. *See* Dover Sole
Chinook Salmon, 55, 62–63, 66
Chirolophis decoratus (Decorated Warbonnet), 124–125
Chirolophis nugator (Mosshead Warbonnet), 122–123
Chirolophis tarsodes (Matcheek Warbonnet), 124
Chitonotus pugetensis (Roughback Sculpin), 230
chub salmon. *See* Chinook Salmon
CHUBS, SEA (Kyphosidae), 98
chucka. *See* Eulachon
Chum Salmon, 56, 58–59, 68
cigarette paper. *See* Flathead Sole

cirriated sculpin. *See* Fluffy Sculpin
Citharichthys sordidus (Pacific Sanddab), 288
Citharichthys stigmaeus (Speckled Sanddab), 289
Clark's trout. *See* Cutthroat Trout
Clevelandia ios (Arrow Goby), 105
cling-fish, common. *See* Northern Clingfish
CLINGFISHES (Gobiesocidae), 283–286
    Kelp Clingfish, 284
    Northern Clingfish, 285–286
clingfish, flathead. *See* Northern Clingfish
Clingfish, Kelp, 284
Clingfish, Northern, 285–286
cling-fish, slender. *See* Kelp Clingfish
Clinidae. *See* **KELP BLENNIES**
Clinocottus acuticeps (Sharpnose Sculpin), 210
Clinocottus embryum (Calico Sculpin), 211
Clinocottus globiceps (Mosshead Sculpin), 212
Clinocottus recalvus (Bald Sculpin), 212
Clupea harengus pallasi. See Clupea pallasii.
Clupea pallasii (Pacific Herring), 45–46
Clupeidae. *See* **HERRINGS**
coalcod. *See* Sablefish
coalfish. *See* Sablefish
coastal cut-throat trout. *See* Cutthroat Trout
coastal cutthroat. *See* Cutthroat Trout
coastal rainbow trout. *See* Steelhead (Rainbow Trout)
coast cutthroat trout. *See* Cutthroat Trout
Coastrange Sculpin, 214
Cockscomb, High, 120–121
cockscomb, prickleback. *See* High Cockscomb
cockscomb. *See* High Cockscomb and Slender Cockscomb
Cockscomb, Slender, 121
cod, Alaska. *See* Pacific Cod
cod, black. *See* Sablefish
cod, gray. *See* Pacific Cod
cod, grey. *See* Pacific Cod
Cod, Pacific, 71–72
CODS (Gadidae), 71–75
    Pacific Cod, 71–72
    Pacific Tomcod, 73, 74
    Saffron Cod, 75
    Walleye Pollock, 72, 73, 74–75
Cod, Saffron, 75
cod, true. *See* Pacific Cod
cod, whisker. *See* Pacific Cod
Coho Salmon, 64–66
Columbia River salmon. *See* Chinook Salmon

Columbia River smelt. *See* Eulachon
Columbia Sturgeon. *See* White Sturgeon
Combfish, Longspine, 198–99
comb sculpin. *See* Northern Sculpin
common cling-fish. *See* Northern Clingfish
common hagfish. *See* Pacific Hagfish
common sole. *See* English Sole
common stickleback. *See* Threespine Stickleback
Common Thresher Shark, 31
continuous-finned liparid. *See* Showy Snailfish
convictfish. *See* Painted Greenling
Copper Rockfish, 148–149
Coralline Sculpin, 203
Coregoninae. *See* **SALMON AND TROUT**
Coryphaena hippurus (Dolphinfish), 145
Coryphaenidae. *See* **DOLPHINFISHES**
Coryphopterus nicholsi. See Rhinogobiops nicholsii
C-O Sole, 306–307
Cottoidea. *See* **SCULPINS**
Cottus aleuticus (Coastrange Sculpin), 214
Cottus asper (Prickly Sculpin), 214
Cottus cognatus (Slimy Sculpin), 214
COW SHARKS (Hexanchidae), 21–23
    Bluntnose Sixgill Shark, 21–23
    Broadnose Sevengill Shark, 21–22
cowshark, six-gill. *See* Bluntnose Sixgill Shark
Crescent Gunnel, 129
crested blenny. *See* High Cockscomb
crested goby. *See* Blackeye Goby
Crested Sculpin, 236
Crevice Kelpfish, 110–111
Croaker, White, 99
Cryptacanthodes aleutensis (Dwarf Wrymouth), 137
Cryptacanthodes giganteus (Giant Wrymouth), 136–137
Cryptacanthodidae. *See* **WRYMOUTHS**
cultus, Pacific. *See* Lingcod
Curlfin Sole, 308
CUSK-EELS (Ophidiidae), 79
    Spotted Cusk-eel, 79
Cusk-eel, Spotted, 79
cusks. *See* **CODS**
Cutthroat Trout, 68
Cyclopteridae. *See* **LUMPSUCKERS**
Cymatogaster aggregata (Shiner Perch), 97–98
Cynoglossidae. *See* **TONGUEFISHES**

Damalichthys vacca (Pile Perch), 92
Dark Dusky Rockfish, 162–163
dark rockfish. *See* Dark Dusky Rockfish
Darter Sculpin, 228
Dasyatidae. *See* **STINGRAYS**
Dasycottus setiger (Spinyhead Sculpin), 231
Daubed Shanny, 115
decorated prickleback. *See* Decorated
    Warbonnet
Decorated Warbonnet, 124
deep-pitted poacher. *See* Rockhead
deep-pitted sea-poacher. *See* Rockhead
Delolepis gigantea. See Cryptacanthodes
    giganteus
Denny's liparid. *See* Marbled Snailfish
DEVIL RAYS (Mobulidae), 39
devil, red. *See* Dwarf Wrymouth
dogfish, Pacific. *See* Pacific Spiny Dogfish
dogfish, piked. *See* Pacific Spiny Dogfish
DOGFISH SHARKS (Squalidae), 29–30
    Pacific Spiny Dogfish, 29–30
dog salmon. *See* Chum Salmon
Dogfish, Spiny, 29–30
Dolly. *See* Dolly Varden
Dolly Varden char. *See* Dolly Varden
Dolly Varden, 69
Dolphinfish, 145
DOLPHINFISHES (Coryphaenidae), 145
    Dolphinfish, 145
Dover Sole, 301–302
DRUMS AND CROAKERS (Sciaenidae), 99
    White Croaker, 99
    White Seabass, 99
dusky perch. *See* Pile Perch
Dusky Sculpin, 221
dusky sea-perch. *See* Pile Perch
Dwarf Wrymouth, 137

EAGLE RAYS (Myliobatidae), 39
    Bat Ray, 39
eastern stickleback. *See* Threespine
    Stickleback
eel-blenny. *See* Snake Prickleback
Eelblenny, Slender, 116
Eelblenny, Stout, 116
Eelpout, Black, 81
eelpout, black-bellied. *See* Blackbelly Eelpout
Eelpout, Blackbelly, 80
eelpout, black-finned. *See* Black Eelpout
eelpout, blackfin. *See* Black Eelpout
Eelpout, Blackmouth, 82
EELPOUTS (Zoarcidae), 79–82

Blackbelly Eelpout, 80
Black Eeelpout, 81
Shortfin Eelpout, 81–82
Unknown Lycodapine Eelpout, 82
Wattled Eelpout, 82
Eelpout, Shortfin, 81–82
Eelpout, Unknown Lycodapine, 82
Eelpout, Wattled, 82
electric ray. *See* Pacific Electric Ray
ELECTRIC RAYS (Torpedinidae), 37–38
    Pacific Electric Ray, 37–38
Eleginus gracilis (Saffron Cod), 75
elephant-fish. *See* Spotted Ratfish
Embiotoca lateralis (Striped Seaperch), 95–96
Embiotocidae. *See* **SURFPERCHES**
English Sole, 300–301
Engraulidae. *See* **ANCHOVIES**
Engraulis mordax (Northern Anchovy),
    48–49
Enophrys bison (Buffalo Sculpin), 245–246
Enophrys dicerus (Antlered Sculpin), 247
Enophrys lucasi (Leister Sculpin), 247
Eopsetta jordani (Petrale Sole), 294
Eptatretus deani (Black Hagfish), 17
Eptatretus stoutii (Pacific Hagfish), 17–18
Erilepis zonifer (Skilfish), 185
Errex zachirus. See Glyptocephalus zachirus
Eulachon, 49–51
Eumicrotremus orbis (Pacific Spiny
    Lumpsucker), 281–282
European stickleback. *See* Threespine
    Stickleback
Eyeshade Sculpin, 238

fall salmon. *See* Chum Salmon
fantail rockfish. *See* Canary Rockfish
fathom fish. *See* Eulachon
filamented scupin. *See* Threadfin Sculpin
finescale goby. *See* Bay Goby
fine-scale goby. *See* Bay Goby
Finescale Triggerfish, 145
flathead clingfish. *See* Northern Clingfish
flathead sculpin. *See* Smoothhead Sculpin
Flathead Sole, 295
Flounder, Arrowtooth, 293
flounder, long-jawed. *See* Arrowtooth
    Flounder
flounder, muddy. *See* C-O Sole
flounder, sand. *See* Sand Sole
flounder, slender. *See* Slender Sole
flounder, soft. *See* Pacific Sanddab
flounder, spot. *See* C-O Sole

flounder, spotted. *See* Sand Sole
Flounder Starry, 305–306
FLOUNDERS, RIGHTEYE (Pleuronectidae), 287, 291–308
FLOUNDERS, SAND (Paralichthyidae), 287–290
Fluffy Sculpin, 208
Forkline Sole, 301
forktail perch. *See* Pile Perch
Fourhorn Poacher, 266
four-horned sea-poacher. *See* Fourhorn Poacher
French sole. *See* Arrowtooth Flounder
fringed greenling. *See* Rock Greenling
Fringed Sculpin, 224
fringe sole. *See* Sand Sole

Gadidae. *See* **CODS**
Gadus macrocephalus (Pacific Cod), 71–72
Galeorhinus galeus (Tope), 30
Gairdner's salmon. *See* Steelhead (Rainbow Trout)
Gasterosteidae. *See* **STICKLEBACKS**
Gasterosteus aculeatus (Threespine Stickleback), 85–86
genuine red. *See* Vermilion Rockfish
Genyonemus lineatus (White Croaker), 99
Giant Kelpfish, 111
Giant Manta, 39
giant marbled sculpin. *See* Cabezon
giant sculpin. *See* Cabezon
Giant Wrymouth, 136–137
Gibbonsia metzi (Striped Kelpfish), 109
Gibbonsia montereyensis (Crevice Kelpfish), 110–111
Gilbertidia sigalutes. See Psychrolutes sigalutes
globe-headed sculpin. *See* Mosshead Sculpin
Glyptocephalus zachirus (Rex Sole), 302
goatfish. *See* Spotted Ratfish
GOBIES (Gobiidae), 102–105
    Arrow Goby, 105
    Bay Goby, 104
    Blackeye Goby, 102–103
Gobiesocidae. *See* **CLINGFISHES**
Gobiesox maeandricus (Northern Clingfish), 285–286
Gobiidae. *See* **GOBIES**
Goby, Arrow, 105
Goby, Bay, 104
Goby, Blackeye, 102–103
goby, bluespot. *See* Blackeye Goby

goby, crested. *See* Blackeye Goby
goby, finescale. *See* Bay Goby
goby, fine-scale. *See* Bay Goby
goby, large-scaled. *See* Blackeye Goby
Goby, Sleeper, 102
goldeneye rockfish. *See* Yelloweye Rockfish
Grass Rockfish, 153–154
Graveldiver, 139
GRAVELDIVERS (Scytalinidae), 139
    Graveldiver, 139
gray cod. *See* Pacific Cod
gray starnose. *See* Gray Starsnout
Gray Starsnout, 256–257
grayfish, Pacific. *See* Pacific Spiny Dogfish
graylings. *See* **SALMON AND TROUT**
Great Sculpin, 243
Great White Shark, 26
Green Sturgeon, 44
Green's liparid. *See* Lobefin Snailfish
greenling, fringed. *See* Rock Greenling
Greenling, Kelp, 188–189
Greenling, Masked, 190
Greenling, Painted, 196–197
Greenling, Rock, 186–187
GREENLINGS (Hexagrammidae), 186–199
    Atka Mackerel, 186, 199
    Kelp Greenling, 188–189
    Lingcod, 132, 186, 194–195, 205, 217
    Longspine Combfish, 198
    Masked Greenling, 190
    Painted Greenling, 196–197
    Rock Greenling, 186–187
    Whitespotted Greenling, 105, 191–193
Greenling, Whitespotted, 105, 191–193
Greenstriped Rockfish, 181
grey cod. *See* Pacific Cod
greyfish. *See* Pacific Cod
Grunt Sculpin, 239–240
Gunnel, Crescent, 129
Gunnel, Longfin, 132
Gunnel, Penpoint, 127–128
Gunnel, Red, 131
Gunnel, Rockweed, 126–127
GUNNELS (Pholidae), 126–132
    Crescent Gunnel, 129
    Longfin Gunnel, 132
    Penpoint Gunnel, 127–128
    Red Gunnel, 131
    Rockweed Gunnel, 126–127
    Saddleback Gunnel, 130
Gunnel, Saddleback, 130–131
Gunther's liparid. *See* Ribbon Snailfish

haddocks. *See* **CODS**
Hagfish, Black, 17
hagfish, California. *See* Pacific Hagfish
hagfish, common. *See* Pacific Hagfish
HAGFISHES (Myxinidae), 17–18. *See also*
  LAMPREYS
  Black Hagfish, 17
  Pacific Hagfish, 17–18
Hagfish, Pacific, 17–18
hagfish. *See* Pacific Hagfish
hake, California. *See* Pacific Hake
Hake, Pacific, 76–77
hake. *See* Pacific Hake
HAKES, MERLUCCID (Merlucciidae), 76–77
Halfmoon, 98
halfpounder. *See* Steelhead (Rainbow Trout)
halibut. *See* Pacific Halibut
halibut, American arrowtooth. *See*
  Arrowtooth Flounder
halibut, arrowtooth. *See* Arrowtooth Flounder
halibut, bastard. *See* Arrowtooth Flounder
Halibut, California, 287, 290
halibut, needle-toothed. *See* Arrowtooth
  Flounder
Halibut, Pacific, 291–292, 294
hardhead. *See* Steelhead (Rainbow Trout)
hare, water. *See* Spotted Ratfish
Hemilepidotus hemilepidotus (Red Irish
  Lord), 248–249
Hemilepidotus jordani (Yellow Irish Lord),
  250
Hemilepidotus spinosus (Brown Irish Lord),
  250
Hemitripterus bolini (Bigmouth Sculpin), 244
herring. *See* Pacific Herring.
Herring, Pacific, 20, 49, 54, 45–46
HERRINGS (Clupeidae), 45–47
  American Shad, 47
  Pacific Herring, 20, 49, 54, 45–46
  Pacific Sardine, 46–47
Heterostichus rostratus (Giant Kelpfish), 111
Hexagrammidae. *See* **GREENLINGS**
Hexagrammos decagrammus (Kelp
  Greenling), 188–189
Hexagrammos lagocephalus (Rock Greenling),
  186–187
Hexagrammos octogrammus (Masked
  Greenling), 190
Hexagrammos stelleri (Whitespotted
  Greenling), 191
Hexagrammos superciliosus. See
  Hexagrammos lagocephalus

Hexanchidae. *See* **COW SHARKS**
Hexanchus griseus (Bluntnose Sixgill Shark),
  22–23
Highbrow Sculpin, 226
High Cockscomb, 120–121
Hippoglossoides elassodon (Flathead Sole), 295
Hippoglossus stenolepis (Pacific Halibut),
  291–192
hookbill. *See* Chinook Salmon
hooknose. *See* Coho Salmon.
HOUND SHARKS (Triakidae), 30–31
  Leopard Shark, 31
  Tope (Soupfin Shark), 30
humpback salmon. *See* Pink Salmon
humpie. *See* Pink salmon
Hydrolagus colliei (Spotted Ratfish), 41–42
Hyperprosopon anale (Spotfin Surfperch), 94
Hyperprosopon argenteum (Walleye
  Surfperch), 94
Hyperprosopon ellipticum (Silver Surfperch),
  93
Hypomesus pretiosus (Surf Smelt), 51
Hypsagonus mozinoi (Kelp Poacher), 267–268
Hypsagonus quadricornis (Fourhorn
  Poacher), 266

Icelinus borealis (Northern Sculpin), 220
Icelinus burchami (Dusky Sculpin), 221
Icelinus filamentosus (Threadfin Sculpin),
  223
Icelinus fimbriatus (Fringed Sculpin), 224
Icelinus tenuis (Spotfin Sculpin), 222
Icelus spiniger (Thorny Sculpin), 225
Icichthys lockingtoni (Medusafish), 99
Icosteidae. *See* **RAGFISHES**
Icosteus aenigmaticus (Ragfish), 100
Irish Lord, Brown, 250
Irish Lord, Red, 248–249
Irish lord, spotted. *See* Red Irish Lord
Irish lord, yellow. *See* Brown Irish Lord.
ironhead. *See* Steelhead (Rainbow Trout)
Isopsetta isolepis (Butter Sole), 297
Isurus oxyrinchus (Shortfin Mako), 26

Jack Mackerel, 142
JACKS (Carangidae), 142
  Jack Mackerel, 142
  Yellowtail Jacks, 142
Jacksmelt, 82
jack spring. *See* Chinook Salmon
jacks (salmon). *See* Chinook Salmon
Jack, Yellowtail, 142

Jordania zonope (Longfin Sculpin), 216–217
Juan de Fuca liparid. *See* Slipskin Snailfish

Katsuwonus pelamis (Skipjack Tuna), 144
KELP BLENNIES (Clinidae), 109–111
    Crevice Kelpfish, 110–111
    Giant Kelpfish, 111
    Striped Kelpfish, 109–110
Kelp Clingfish, 284
Kelpfish, Crevice, 110–111
Kelpfish, Giant, 111
Kelpfish, Striped, 109–110
Kelp Greenling, 188–189
Kelp Perch, 96–97
Kelp Poacher, 267
kelp sea-perch. *See* Kelp Perch
kelp surfperch. *See* Kelp Perch
keta salmon. *See* Chum Salmon
King-of-the-Salmon, 84
king salmon. *See* Chinook Salmon
Kyphosidae. *See* **SEA CHUBS**

Lamna ditropis (Salmon Shark), 25–26
Lamnidae. *See* **MACKEREL SHARKS**
Lampetra richardsoni (Western Brook
    Lamprey), 18
Lampetra tridentata (Pacific Lamprey), 19
*Lampetra tridentatus. See Lampetra
    tridentata*
lamprey, American river. *See* River Lamprey
lamprey, Pacific sea. *See* Pacific Lamprey
Lamprey, Pacific, 18–19
lamprey, parasitic river. *See* River Lamprey
Lamprey, River, 18, 20
LAMPREYS (Petromyzontidae), 18–20. *See
    also* **HAGFISHES**
    Pacific Lamprey, 18–19
    River Lamprey, 18, 20
lamprey, sea. *See* Pacific Lamprey
lamprey, three-toothed. *See* Pacific Lamprey
lamprey, tridentate. *See* Pacific Lamprey
lamprey, western brook. *See* River Lamprey
lamprey, western river. *See* River Lamprey
lamprey, western. *See* River Lamprey
Lamprididae. *See* **OPAHS**
Lampris guttatus (Opah), 100
LANCETFISHES (Alepisauridae), 84
    Longnose Lancetfish, 84
Lancetfish, Longnose, 84
large-scaled goby. *See* Blackeye Goby
left-eyed flounders. *See* **SAND FLOUNDERS**
Leister Sculpin, 247

lemon sole. *See* English Sole
Leopard Shark, 31
Lepidogobius lepidus (Bay Goby), 104
Lepidopsetta bilineata (Rock Sole), 298–299
Leptagonus frenatus (Sawback Poacher), 255
Lepidopsetta polyxystra (Northern Rock Sole),
    299
Leptoclinus maculatus (Daubed Shanny), 115
Leptocottus armatus (Pacific Staghorn
    Sculpin), 251
lesser filamented sculpin. *See* Spotfin Sculpin
Light Dusky Rockfish, 163–164
Limanda aspera (Yellowfin Sole), 298
Lingcod, 132, 186, 194–195, 205, 217
lings. *See* **CODS**
liparid, continuous-finned. *See* Showy
    Snailfish
liparid, Denny's. *See* Marbled Snailfish
liparid, Green's. *See* Lobefin Snailfish
liparid, Gunther's. *See* Ribbon Snailfish
liparid, Juan de Fuca. *See* Slipskin Snailfish
liparid, Pallas's. *See* Spotted Snailfish
liparid, shore. *See* Tidepool Snailfish
liparid, shorttail. *See* Showy Snailfish
liparid, tadpole. *See* Tadpole Snailfish
Liparidae. *See* **SNAILFISHES**
Liparis callyodon (Spotted Snailfish), 272
Liparis cyclopus (Ribbon Snailfish), 275
Liparis dennyi (Marbled Snailfish), 276–277
Liparis florae (Tidepool Snailfish), 273
Liparis fucensis (Slipskin Snailfish), 274
Liparis gibbus (Variegated Snailfish), 277
Liparis greeni (Lobefin Snailfish). 271
Liparis mucosus (Slimy Snailfish), 275
Liparis pulchellus (Showy Snailfish), 278
Liparis rutteri (Ringtail Snailfish), 274
Lizardfish, California, 83
LIZARDFISHES (Synodontidae), 83
    California Lizardfish, 83
lobe-finned rockfish. *See* Shortspine
    Thornyhead
Lobefin Snailfish, 271
lobe-jawed rockfish. *See* Splitnose Rockfish
Longfin Gunnel, 132
long-finned smelt. *See* Longfin Smelt
long-finned sole. *See* Rex Sole
Longfin Sculpin, 216–217
Longfin Smelt, 50
longfin sole. *See* Rex Sole
long-jawed flounder. *See* Arrowtooth
    Flounder
Longnose Lancetfish, 84

Longnose Skate, 34
long-nose skate. *See* Longnose Skate
long-rayed sculpin. *See* Threadfin Sculpin
Longsnout Prickleback, 112
Longspine Combfish, 198–199
longspined greenling. *See* Longspine Combfish
Longspine Thornyhead, 183
Lumpenella longirostris (Longsnout Prickleback), 112
Lumpenus fabricii (Slender Eelblenny), 116
Lumpenus sagitta (Snake Prickleback), 114–115
Lumpsucker, Pacific Spiny, 281–282
LUMPSUCKERS (Cyclopteridae), 280–282
    Pacific Spiny Lumpsucker, 281–282
Lumpsucker, Smooth, 280
Lycodapus fierasfer (Unknown Lycodapine Eelpout), 82
Lycodes brevipes (Shortfin Eelpout), 81
Lycodes diapterus (Black Eelpout), 81
Lycodes pacificus (Blackbelly Eelpout), 80
Lycodes palearis (Wattled Eelpout), 82
Lycodopsis pacifica. See Lycodes pacificus
Lyconectes aleutensis. See Cryptacanthodes aleutensis
Lyopsetta exilis (Slender Sole), 296

Mackerel, Atka, 186, 199
Mackerel, Jack, 142
Mackerel, Pacific Chub, 143
MACKERELS (Scombridae), 143–144
    Albacore, 144
    Pacific Bonito, 144
    Pacific Chub Mackerel, 143
    Skipjack Tuna, 144
mackerel shark. *See* Salmon Shark
MACKEREL SHARKS (Lamnidae), 25–26
    (Great) White Shark, 26
    Salmon Shark, 25-26
    Shortfin Mako, 26
Mako, Shortfin, 26
Malacanthidae. *See* **TILEFISHES**
Malacocottus kincaidi (Blackfin Sculpin), 232
Malacocottus zonurus (Darkfin Sculpin), 232
Mallotus villosus (Capelin), 52
Manacled Sculpin, 215
MANTAS (Mobulidae), 39
    Giant Manta, 39
Manta birostris, 39
Manta, Giant, 39
Marbled Snailfish, 276–277

Masked Greenling, 190
Medialuna californiensis (Halfmoon) 98
MEDUSAFISHES (Centrolophidae), 99
    Medusafish, 99
menhaden. *See* **HERRINGS**
MERLUCCID HAKES (Merlucciidae), 76–77
    Pacific Hake, 76–77
Merlucciidae. *See* **MERLUCCID HAKES**
Merluccius productus (Pacific Hake), 76–77
metalhead. *See* Steelhead (Rainbow Trout)
Microgadus proximus (Pacific Tomcod), 73
Microstomus pacificus (Dover Sole), 301–302
Midshipman, Plainfin, 253–254
midshipman. *See* Plainfin Midshipman
midshipman, northern. *See* Plainfin Midshipman
Mobulidae. *See* **MANTAS** *Mola mola* (Ocean Sunfish), 101
MOLAS (Molidae), 101
    Ocean Sunfish, 101
Molidae. *See* **MOLAS**
mosshead prickleback. *See* Mosshead Warbonnet
Mosshead Sculpin, 212
Mosshead Warbonnet, 122–123
mossy sculpin. *See* Calico Sculpin
mottled sanddab. *See* Pacific Sanddab
muddy flounder. *See* C-O Sole
mud shark. *See* Bluntnose Sixgill Shark and Pacific Spiny Dogfish
Myliobatidae. *See* **EAGLE RAYS**
Myliobatis californica (Bat Ray), 39
Myoxocephalus jaok (Plain Sculpin), 243
Myoxocephalus polyacanthocephalus (Great Sculpin), 243
Myoxocephalus scorpius (Shorthorn Sculpin), 244
Myxocephalus stelleri (Frog Sculpin), 243
Myxinidae. *See* **HAGFISHES**

Nautichthys oculofasciatus (Sailfin Sculpin), 237–238
Nautichthys pribilovius (Eyeshade Sculpin), 238
Nautichthys robustus (Shortmast Sculpin), 238
Nectoliparis pelagicus (Tadpole Snailfish), 279
needlefish. *See* Pacific Sand Lance
needle-toothed halibut. *See* Arrowtooth Flounder
New York stickleback. *See* Threespine Stickleback
Night Smelt, 50

North Pacific Armorhead, 101
Northern Anchovy, 48–49
northern bay pipefish. *See* Bay Pipefish
Northern Clingfish, 285–286
northern midshipman. *See* Plainfin
  Midshipman
Northern Rock Sole, 299
Northern Ronquil, 106–107
Northern Sculpin, 220
Northern Spearnose Poacher, 263–264
*Notorynchus maculatus. See Notorynchus
  cepedianus*
Notorynchus cepedianus (Broadnose Sevengill
  Shark), 21–22
nurse sharks. *See* **CATSHARKS**

Ocean Sunfish, 101
Ocean Whitefish, 98
Odontopyxis trispinosa (Pygmy Poacher), 260
oilfish. *See* Eulachon
Oligocottus maculosus (Tidepool Sculpin), 207
Oligocottus rimensis (Saddleback Sculpin), 209
Oligocottus snyderi (Fluffy Sculpin), 208–209
Oncorhynchus clarkii (Cutthroat Trout), 68
Oncorhynchus gorbuscha (Pink Salmon),
  56–57
Oncorhynchus keta (Chum Salmon), 58–59
Oncorhynchus kisutch (Coho Salmon),
  64–66
Oncorhynchus mykiss (Steelhead [Rainbow
  Trout]) 66–67
Oncorhynchus nerka (Sockeye Salmon),
  60–61
Oncorhynchus tshawytscha (Chinook
  Salmon), 62–63, 66
Opah, 100
OPAHS (Lamprididae), 100
  Opah, 100
Ophidiidae. *See* **CUSK-EELS**
Ophiodon elongatus (Lingcod), 194–195, 132,
  186, 205, 217
orange rockfish. *See* Canary Rockfish
orange-spotted rockfish. *See* Quillback
  Rockfish
Oregon sturgeon. *See* White Sturgeon
ornamented blenny. *See* Mosshead
  Warbonnet
Orthonopias triacis (Snubnose Sculpin), 219
Osmeridae. *See* **SMELTS**
Osmerus mordax (Rainbow Smelt), 53
Oxylebius pictus (Painted Greenling), 196–197
Pacific Angel Shark, 32

Pacific barndoor skate. *See* Big Skate
Pacific Barracuda, 83
Pacific Bonito, 144
Pacific brook char. *See* Dolly Varden
Pacific capelin. *See* Capelin
Pacific Chub Mackerel, 143
Pacific Cod, 71–72
Pacific cultus. *See* Lingcod
Pacific dogfish. *See* Pacific Spiny Dogfish
Pacific Electric Ray, 37–38
Pacific grayfish. *See* Pacific Spiny Dogfish
Pacific great skate. *See* Big Skate
Pacific Hagfish, 17–18
Pacific Hake, 76–77
Pacific Halibut, 291–292, 294
Pacific Herring, 20, 49, 54, 45–46. Pacific
  Lamprey, 18–19
Pacific pollock. *See* Walleye Pollock
Pacific Pomfret, 100
Pacific Pompano, 99
Pacific Sand Lance, 54
Pacific Sanddab, 288
Pacific Sandfish, 89–90
Pacific Sardine, 46–47
Pacific sea-lamprey. *See* Pacific Lamprey
Pacific Sleeper Shark, 27
Pacific Smelt. *See* Longfin Smelt
Pacific snakeblenny. *See* Snake Prickleback
Pacific snake prickleback. *See* Snake
  Prickleback
Pacific Spiny Dogfish, 29–30
Pacific Spiny Lumpsucker, 281–282
Pacific Staghorn Sculpin, 251
Pacific sturgeon. *See* White Sturgeon
Pacific Tomcod, 73, 74
Pacific torpedo ray. *See* Pacific Electric Ray
Pacific whiting. *See* Pacific Hake
Padded Sculpin, 201
Painted Greenling, 196–197
Pallasina barbata (Tubenose Poacher), 261
Pallasina barbata aix. See Pallasina barbata
Pallas's liparid. *See* Spotted Snailfish
paper sole. *See* Flathead Sole
Paralichthyidae. *See* **SAND FLOUNDERS**
Paralichthys californicus (California Halibut),
  290
parasitic river lamprey. *See* River Lamprey
Paricelinus hopliticus (Thornback Sculpin),
  229
Parophrys vetula. See Parophrys vetulus
Parophrys vetulus (English Sole), 300
Pelagic Stingray, 40

pen-point blenny. *See* Penpoint Gunnel
Penpoint Gunnel, 127–128
Pentacerotidae. *See* **ARMORHEADS**
Peprilus simillimus (Pacific Pompano), 99
perch, blue. *See* Striped Seaperch
perch, brown. *See* Kelp Perch
Perch, California Tule. *See* **SURFPERCHES**
perch, dusky. *See* Pile Perch
perch, forktail. *See* Pile Perch
Perch, Kelp, 96–97
Perch, Pile, 92
perch, redtail. *See* Redtail Surfperch
perch, seven eleven. *See* Shiner Perch
Perch, Shiner, 97–98
perch, silver. *See* Silver Surfperch
perch, spiltttail. *See* Pile Perch
perch, white. *See* White Seaperch
Petrale Sole, 294
Petromyzontidae. *See* **LAMPREYS**
Phanerodon furcatus (White Seaperch), 91
Pholidae. *See* **GUNNELS**
Pholis clemensi (Longfin Gunnel), 132
Pholis laeta (Crescent Gunnel), 129
Pholis ornata (Saddleback Gunnel), 130–131
Pholis schultzi (Red Gunnel), 131
Phytichthys chirus (Ribbon Prickleback), 117
piked dogfish. *See* Pacific Spiny Dogfish
pilchard, California. *See* Pacific Sardine
pilchard. *See* Pacific Sardine
Pile Perch, 92
pile seaperch. *See* Pile Perch
pile surfperch. *See* Pile Perch
Pink Salmon, 56–57, 68
pipefish. *See* Bay Pipefish
Pipefish, Bay, 88
PIPEFISHES (Syngnathidae), 88
Bay Pipefish, 88
pipe-fish. *See* Bay Pipefish
pithead poacher. *See* Rockhead
pitted poacher. *See* Rockhead
Plaice, Alaska, 291
plain anchovy. *See* Northern Anchovy
Plainfin Midshipman, 253–254
Platichthys stellatus (Starry Flounder), 305–306
Plectobranchus evides (Bluebarred Prickleback), 113–114
Pleurogrammus monopterygius (Atka Mackerel) 199
Pleuronectes bilineata. See Lepidopsetta bilineata

Pleuronectes quadrituberculatus (Alaska Plaice), 291
Pleuronectes vetulus. See Parophrys vetulus
Pleuronectidae. *See* **RIGHTEYE FLOUNDERS**
Pleuronichthys coenosus (C-O Sole), 306–307
Poacher, Bigeye, 257
poacher, blackedge. *See* Blacktip Poacher
Poacher, Blackfin, 258, 259
Poacher, Blacktip, 259
Poacher, Bluespotted, 259
poacher, deep-pitted. *See* Rockhead
Poacher, Fourhorn, 266
Poacher, Kelp, 267–268
Poacher, Northern Spearnose, 263–264
poacher, pithead. *See* Rockhead
poacher, pitted. *See* Rockhead
Poacher, Pricklbreast, 255
Poacher, Pygmy, 260
POACHERS (Agonidae), 255–269
Bigeye Poacher, 257
Blackfin Poacher, 258, 259
Blacktip Poacher, 259
Fourhorn Poacher, 266
Gray Starsnout, 256–257
Kelp Poacher, 267–268
Northern Spearnose Poacher, 263–264
Pygmy Poacher, 260
Rockhead, 255, 269
Smooth Alligatorfish, 262
Spinycheek Startsnout, 255–256
Sturgeon Poacher, 265
Tubenose Poacher, 261
Poacher, Sawback, 255
poacher, smooth. *See* Smooth Alligatorfish
Poacher, Smootheye, 259
Poacher, Sturgeon, 265
Poacher, Tubenose, 261
poacher, tubesnout. *See* Tubenose Poacher
Poacher, Warty, 255
poacher, windowtail. *See* Northern Spearnose Poacher
Podothecus accipenserinus (Sturgeon Poacher), 265
pogy. *See* Shiner Perch
pointed-nosed sole. *See* English Sole
pollacks. *See* **CODS**
pollock, Alaska. *See* Walleye Pollock
pollock, Pacific. *See* Walleye Pollock
Pollock, Walleye, 72, 73, 74–75
pollock, wall-eye. *See* Walleye Pollock
Polypera greeni. See Liparis greeni
Pomfret, Pacific, 100

POMFRETS (Bramidae), 100
  Pacific Pomfret, 100
Pompano, Pacific, 99
popeye sole. *See* C-O Sole
Porichthys notatus (Plainfin Midshipman),
  252–254
Poroclinus rothrocki (whitebarred
  Prickleback), 113
potatohead. *See* Giant Wrymouth
Prickleback, Black, 119
prickleback, black-and-white. *See* Bluebarred
  Prickleback
Prickleback, Bluebarred, 113–114
prickleback, cockscomb. *See* High Cockscomb
prickleback, decorated. *See* Decorated
  Warbonnet
Prickleback, Longsnout, 112
prickleback, mosshead. *See* Mosshead
  Warbonnet
prickleback, Pacific snake. *See* Snake
  Prickleback
prickleback, Pacific. *See* Snake Prickleback
Prickleback, Pearly, 122
Prickleback, Ribbon, 117
Prickleback, Rock, 118
PRICKLEBACKS (Stichaeidae), 112–125
  Arctic Shanny, 116
  Black Prickleback, 119
  Bluebarred Prickleback, 113–114
  Daubed Shanny, 115
  Decorated Warbonnet, 124–125
  High Cockscomb, 120–121
  Longsnout Prickleback, 112
  Matcheek Warbonnet, 122–123
  Mosshead Warbonnet, 122
  Pearly Prickleback, 122
  Ribbon Prickleback, 117
  Rock Prickleback, 118
  Slender Cockscomb, 121
  Slender Eelblenny, 116
  Snake Prickleback, 114–115
  Stout Eelblenny, 116
  Whitebarred Prickleback, 113
Prickleback, Snake, 114–115
Prickleback, Whitebarred, 113
Pricklebreast Poacher, 255
Prickly Sculpin, 214
priestfish. *See* Blue Rockfish
Prionace glauca (Blue Shark), 27
Prowfish, 140–141
PROWFISHES (Zaproridae), 140–141
  Prowfish, 140–141

Psettichthys melanostictus (Sand Sole),
  304
Pseudopentaceros wheeleri (North Pacific
  Armorhead), 101
Psychrolutes paradoxus (Tadpole Sculpin),
  233
Psychrolutes sigalutes (Soft Sculpin), 234
Pteroplatytrygon violacea (Pelagic Stingray),
  40
Ptilichthyidae. *See* **QUILLFISHES**
Ptilichthys goodei (Quillfish), 138
Puget Sound Rockfish, 169
Puget Sound Sculpin, 206
Puget Sound smelt. *See* Longfin Smelt
Pygmy Poacher, 260
pygmy sea-poacher. *See* Pygmy Poacher

qualla. *See* Chum Salmon
Quillback Rockfish, 149–151
Quillfish, 138
QUILLFISHES (Ptilichthyidae), 138
  Quillfish, 138
quinnat salmon. *See* Chinook Salmon

rabbitfish. *See* Spotted Ratfish
Radulinus asprellus (Slim Sculpin), 227
Radulinus boleoides (Darter Sculpin), 228
Radulinus taylori (Spinynose Sculpin), 218
Ragfish, 100
RAGFISHES (Icosteidae), 100
  Ragfish, 100
Rainbow Smelt, 53
rainbow trout, 55, 66–67
Rainbow Trout, (Steelhead), 55, 66–67
Raja binoculata (Big Skate), 35
Raja rhina (Longnose Skate), 34
Rajidae. *See* **SKATES**
rasher. *See* Vermilion Rockfish
rasphead rockfish. *See* Yelloweye Rockfish
Ratfish, Atlantic, 41
Ratfish, Spotted, 40–42
ratfish. *See* Spotted Ratfish
Ray, Bat, 39
ray, electric. *See* Pacific Electric Ray
Ray, Pacific Electric, 37–38
ray, Pacific torpedo. *See* Pacific Electric Ray
RAYS, EAGLE (Myliobatidae), 39
RAYS, ELECTRIC (Torpedinidae), 37–38
Red Brotula, 77–78
red devil. *See* Dwarf Wrymouth
red, genuine. *See* Vermilion Rockfish
Red Gunnel, 131

Red Irish Lord, 248–249
red rockfish. *See* Yelloweye Rockfish
red salmon. *See* Sockeye Salmon
red sculpin. *See* Red Irish Lord
red snapper. *See* Yelloweye Rockfish
Red spotted char. *See* Dolly Varden
Redstripe Rockfish, 180
redtail perch. *See* Redtail Surfperch
redtail seaperch. *See* Redtail Surfperch
Redtail Surfperch, 94
redtail. *See* Redtail Surfperch
red-throated trout. *See* Cutthroat Trout
REQUIEM SHARKS (Carcharhinidae), 27
    Blue Shark, 27
Rex Sole, 302–303
Rhacochilus vacca. See Damalichthys vacca
Rhamphocottus richardsonii (Grunt Sculpin),
    239
Rhinogobiops nicholsii (Blackeye Gobi),
    102–103
Ribbed Sculpin, 225
RIBBONFISHES (Trachipteridae), 84
    King-of-the-Salmon, 84
Ribbon Prickleback, 117
Ribbon Snailfish, 275
RIGHTEYE FLOUNDERS (Pleuronectidae),
    287, 291–308
    Arrowtooth Flounder, 293
    Butter Sole, 297
    C-O Sole, 306–307
    Curlfin Sole, 308
    Dover Sole, 301–302
    English Sole, 300–301
    Flathead Sole, 295
    Forkline Sole, 301
    Pacific Halibut, 291–292, 294
    Petrale Sole, 294
    Rex Sole, 302–303
    Rock Sole, 298–299
    Sand Sole, 304
    Slender Sole, 296
    Starry Flounder, 305–306
    Yellowfin Sole, 298
Rimicola muscarum (Kelp Clingfish), 284
Ringtail Snailfish, 274
River Lamprey, 18, 20
roaring bullhead. *See* Plainfin Midshipman
rock blenny. *See* Rock Prickleback
Rock Greenling, 186–187
Rock Prickleback, 118
Rock Sole, 298–299
rock-eel. *See* Rock Prickleback

ROCKFISH AND OTHER SCORPIONFISHES
    (Scorpaenidae), 147–148
    Black Rockfish, 146, 158–159
    Blue-blotched Rockfish, 161
    Blue-sided Rockfish, 161
    Blue Rockfish, 160–161
    Bocaccio, 165
    Brown Rockfish, 152
    Canary Rockfish, 170–171
    Chilipepper, 166
    China Rockfish, 155–156
    Copper Rockfish, 148–149
    Dark Dusky Rockfish, 162–163
    Grass Rockfish, 153–154
    Greenstriped Rockfish, 181
    Light Dusky Rockfish, 163–164
    Puget Sound Rockfish, 169
    Quillback Rockfish, 149–151
    Redstripe Rockfish, 180
    Rosy Rockfish, 174
    Shortspine Thornyhead, 183
    Silvergray Rockfish, 166–167
    Splitnose Rockfish, 179
    Stripetail Rockfish, 182
    Sunset Rockfish, 173
    Tiger Rockfish, 175–176
    Undetermined Juvenile Rockfish, 182
    Undetermined Rockfish, 161
    Vermilion Rockfish, 172–173
    Widow Rockfish, 167–168
    Yelloweye Rockfish, 11, 177–178
    Yellowtail Rockfish, 157–158
rockfish, banded. *See* Tiger Rockfish
rockfish, bass. *See* Black Rockfish
Rockfish, Black, 146, 158–159
rockfish, blackbanded. *See* Tiger Rockfish
Rockfish, Blue, 160–161
rockfish, blue-blotched. *See* Blue Rockfish
rockfish, blue-sided. *See* Blue Rockfish
Rockfish, Brown, 152
Rockfish, Canary, 170–171
Rockfish, China, 155–156
rockfish, Chinese. *See* China Rockfish
Rockfish, Copper, 148–149
Rockfish, Dark Dusky, 162–163
rockfish, dark. *See* Dark Dusky Rockfish
rockfish, fantail. *See* Canary Rockfish
rockfish, goldeneye. *See* Yelloweye Rockfish
Rockfish, Grass, 153–154
rockfish, greenstripe. *See* Greenstriped
    Rockfish
Rockfish, Greenstriped, 181

Rockfish, Light Dusky, 163–164
rockfish, lobe-finned. *See* Shortspine
Thornyhead
rockfish, lobe-jawed. *See* Splitnose Rockfish
rockfish, orange. *See* Canary Rockfish
rockfish, orange-spotted. *See* Quillback
Rockfish
Rockfish, Puget Sound, 169
Rockfish, Quillback, 149–151
rockfish, rasphead. *See* Yelloweye Rockfish
rockfish, red. *See* Yelloweye Rockfish
Rockfish, Redstripe, 180
Rockfish, Rosy, 174
rockfish, salmon. *See* Bocaccio
rockfish. *See* Yelloweye Rockfish
rockfish, shortspine. *See* Silvergray Rockfish
rockfish, shortspine channel. *See* Shortspine
Thornyhead
rockfish, short-spined. *See* Silvergray
Rockfish
Rockfish, Silvergray, 166–167
rockfish, silvergrey. *See* Silvergray Rockfish
rockfish, speckled. *See* Quillback Rockfish
rockfish, spinycheek. *See* Shortspine
Thornyhead
rockfish, spinyheaded. *See* Shortspine
Thornyhead
Rockfish, Splitnose, 179
rockfish, strawberry. *See* Greenstriped
Rockfish
rockfish, striped. *See* Greenstriped Rockfish
Rockfish, Stripetail, 182
Rockfish, Sunset, 173
Rockfish, Tiger, 175–176
rockfish, turkey red. *See* Yelloweye Rockfish
Rockfish, Undetermined Juvenile, 182
Rockfish, Undetermined, 161
Rockfish, Vermilion, 172–173
Rockfish, Widow, 167–168
rockfish, yellow-backed. *See* Copper Rockfish
rockfish, yellow-backed. *See* Quillback
Rockfish
Rockfish, Yelloweye, 11, 177–178
rockfish, yellow. *See* China Rockfish
rockfish, yellow spotted. *See* China Rockfish
rockfish, yellowstripe. *See* China Rockfish
rockfish, yellowstriped. *See* China Rockfish
Rockfish, Yellowtail, 157–158
rockfish, yellow-tail. *See* Yellowtail Rockfish
Rockhead, 255, 269
rocklings. *See* **CODS**
rockweed blenny. *See* Rockweed Gunnel

Rockweed Gunnel, 126–127
ronquil. *See* Northern Ronquil
Ronquil, Alaskan, 107–108
Ronquil, Northern, 106–107
RONQUILS (Bathymasteridae), 106–108
Northern Ronquil, 106–107
Alaskan Ronquil, 107–108
Searcher, 108
Ronquilus jordani (Northern Ronquil),
106–107
Rosylip Sculpin, 213
Rosy Rockfish, 174
Roughback Sculpin, 230
roughscale sole. *See* Rock Sole
rough sole. *See* Slender Sole
Roughspine Sculpin, 226
round-headed sculpin. *See* Mosshead Sculpin
round-nosed sole. *See* Petrale Sole
rubber sole. *See* Dover Sole
Ruscarius meanyi (Puget Sound Sculpin), 206

Sablefish, 184–185
SABLEFISHES (Anoplopomatidae), 184–185
Sablefish, 184–185
Skilfish, 184–185
Sacramento River salmon. *See* Chinook
Salmon
Sacramento sturgeon. *See* White Sturgeon
Saddleback Gunnel, 130–131
Saddleback Sculpin, 209
saddled blenny. *See* Saddleback Gunnel
Saffron Cod, 75
Sailfin Sculpin, 237–238
Sailfish, Slimy, 275
sailor fish. *See* Sailfin Sculpin
sailorfish. *See* Sailfin Sculpin
Salmo clarki clarki. See Cutthroat Trout
Salmo gairdneri. See Oncorhynchus mykiss
SALMON AND TROUT (Salmoninae), 55–70
Atlantic Salmon, 70
Chinook Salmon, 55, 62–63, 66
Chum Salmon, 56, 58–59, 68
Coho Salmon, 64–66
Cutthroat Trout, 68
Dolly Varden, 69
Pink Salmon, 56–57, 68
Sockeye Salmon, 60–61
Steelhead (Rainbow Trout), 66–67
Salmon, Atlantic, 70
salmon, blackmouth. *See* Chinook Salmon
salmon, blueback. *See* Sockeye
Salmonsalmon, calico. *See* Chum Salmon

Salmon, Chinook, 55, 62–63, 66
salmon, chub. *See* Chinook Salmon
Salmon, Chum, 56, 58–59, 68
Salmon, Coho, 64–66
salmon, Columbia River. *See* Chinook Salmon
salmon, dog. *See* Chum Salmon
salmon, fall. *See* Chum Salmon
salmon, Gardiner's. *See* Steelhead (Rainbow Trout)
salmon, humpback. *See* Pink Salmon
salmon, keta. *See* Chum Salmon
salmon, king. *See* Chinook Salmon
Salmon, Pink, 56–57, 68
salmon, quinnat. *See* Chinook Salmon
salmon, red. *See* Sockeye Salmon
salmon rockfish. *See* Bocaccio
salmon, Sacramento River. *See* Chinook Salmon
Salmon Shark, 25
salmon, silver. *See* Coho Salmon
Salmon, Sockeye, 60–61
salmon, spring. *See* Chinook Salmon
salmon trout. *See* Steelhead (Rainbow Trout)
Salmoninae. *See* **SALMON AND TROUT**
Salmo salar (Atlantic Salmon), 70
salvation fish. *See* Eulachon
Salvelinus malma (Dolly Varden), 69
sand dab, Catalina. *See* Speckled Sanddab
sanddab, mottled. *See* Pacific Sanddab
Sanddab, Pacific, 288
Sanddab, Speckled, 289
Sandfish, Pacific, 89–90
sandfish. *See* Pacific Sandfish
sand-fish. *See* Pacific Sandfish
SANDFISHES (Trichodontidae), 89–90
sand flounder. *See* Sand Sole
SAND FLOUNDERS (Paralichthyidae), 287–290
  California Halibut, 287, 290
  Pacific Sanddab, 288
  Speckled Sanddab, 289
SAND LANCES (Ammodytidae), 53–54
  Pacific Sand Lance, 54
sandlance, Arctic. *See* Pacific Sand Lance
Sand Lance, Pacific, 54
sand-lance. *See* Pacific Sand Lance
sand lance, stout. *See* Pacific Sand Lance
sandlaunce. *See* Pacific Sand Lance
Sandpaper Skate, 36–37
Sand Sole, 304
Sarda chiliensis (Pacific Bonito), 144
Sardine, Pacific, 46–47

sardines. *See* **HERRINGS**
Sardinops sagax (Pacific Sardine), 46
Sawback Poacher, 255
saw-finned stickleback. *See* Threespine Stickleback
scaly-finned sole flounder. *See* Butter Sole
scalyfin sole. *See* Butter Sole
Scalyhead Sculpin, 204–205
Sciaenidae. *See* **Drums and Croakers**
Scissortail Sculpin, 226
Scomber japonicus (Pacific Chub Mackerel), 143
Scombridae. *See* **MACKERELS**
Scorpaenichthys marmoratus (Cabezon), 200, 241–242
Scorpaenidae. *See* **ROCKFISH AND OTHER SCORPIONFISHES**
scrapcod. *See* Walleye Pollock
Sculpin, Antlered, 247
Sculpin, Bald, 212
sculpin, bandeye. *See* Longfin Sculpin
Sculpin, Bigmouth, 244
Sculpin, Blackfin, 232
Sculpin, Blob, 234
Sculpin, Bonehead, 202
Sculpin, Buffalo, 195, 245–246
Sculpin, Calico, 211
sculpin, cirriated. *See* Fluffy Sculpin
sculpin, comb. *See* Northern Sculpin
Sculpin, Coralline, 203
Sculpin, Coastrange, 214
Sculpin, Crested, 236
Sculpin, Darter, 228
Sculpin, Dusky, 221
Sculpin, Eyeshade, 238
sculpin, filamented. *See* Threadfin Sculpin
sculpin, flathead. *See* Smoothhead Sculpin
Sculpin, Fluffy, 208–209
Sculpin, Fringed, 224
sculpin, giant marbled. *See* Cabezon
sculpin, giant. *See* Cabezon
sculpin, globe-headed. *See* Mosshead Sculpin
Sculpin, Great, 243
Sculpin, Grunt, 239–240
Sculpin, Highbrow, 226
Sculpin, Leister, 247
sculpin, lesser filamented. *See* Spotfin Sculpin
Sculpin, Longfin, 216–217
sculpin, long-rayed. *See* Threadfin Sculpin
Sculpin, Manacled, 215
Sculpin, Mosshead, 212
sculpin, mossy. *See* Calico Sculpin

Sculpin, Northern, 220
Sculpin, Pacific Staghorn, 251
Sculpin, Padded, 201
sculpin, plumose. *See* Scalyhead Sculpin
Sculpin, Prickly, 214
Sculpin, Puget Sound, 206
sculpin, red. *See* Red Irish Lord
sculpin, red Irish lord. *See* Red Irish Lord
Sculpin, Ribbed, 225
sculpin, Richardson's. *See* Grunt Sculpin
Sculpin, Rosylip, 213
sculpin, rosy-lipped. *See* Rosylip Sculpin
Sculpin, Roughback, 230
Sculpin, Roughspine, 226
sculpin, round-headed. *See* Mosshead Sculpin
Sculpin, Scissortail, 226
SCULPINS (Cottoidea), 200–251
 Antlered Sculpin, 247
 Bald Sculpin, 212
 Bigmouth Sculpin, 244
 Blackfin Sculpin, 232
 Blob Sculpin, 234
 Bonehead Sculpin, 202
 Brown Irish Lord, 250
 Buffalo Sculpin, 195, 245–246
 Cabezon, 200, 241–242
 Calico Sculpin, 211
 Coralline Sculpin, 203
 Coastrange Sculpin, 214
 Crested Sculpin, 236
 Darter Sculpin, 228
 Dusky Sculpin, 221
 Eyeshade Sculpin, 238
 Fluffy Sculpin, 208–209
 Fringed Sculpin, 224
 Great Sculpin, 243
 Grunt Sculpin, 239–240
 Highbrow Sculpin, 226
 Leister Sculpin, 247
 Longfin Sculpin, 216–217
 Manacled Sculpin, 215
 Mosshead Sculpin, 212
 Northern Sculpin, 220
 Pacific Staghorn Sculpin, 251
 Padded Sculpin, 201
 Prickly Sculpin, 214
 Puget Sound Sculpin, 206
 Red Irish Lord, 248–249
 Ribbed Sculpin, 225
 Rosylip Sculpin, 213
 Roughback Sculpin, 230
 Roughspine Sculpin, 226

Saddleback Sculpin, 209
Sailfin Sculpin, 237–238
Scalyhead Sculpin, 204–205
Scissortail Sculpin, 226
Sharpnose Sculpin, 210
Shorthorn Sculpin, 244
Shortmast Sculpin, 238
Silverspotted Sculpin, 235
Slim Sculpin, 227
Slimy Sculpin, 214
Smoothead Sculpin, 202–203
Snubnose Sculpin, 219
Soft Sculpin, 234
Spectacled Sculpin, 226
Spinyhead Sculpin, 231
Spinynose Sculpin, 218
Spotfin Sculpin, 222
Tadpole Sculpin, 233
Thornback Sculpin, 229
Thorny Sculpin, 225
Threadfin Sculpin, 223
Tidepool Sculpin, 207
Unidentified Sculpin, 225
Sculpin, Saddleback, 209
Sculpin, Sailfin, 237–238
Sculpin, Scalyhead, 204–205
Sculpin, Sharpnose, 210
Sculpin, Shorthorn, 244
Sculpin, Shortmast, 238
sculpin, silverspot. *See* Silverspotted Sculpin
Sculpin, Silverspotted, 235
Sculpin, Slim, 227
Sculpin, Slimy, 214
Sculpin, Smoothead, 202–203
Sculpin, Snubnose, 219
Sculpin, Soft, 234
Sculpin, Spectacled, 226
Sculpin, Spinyhead, 231
Sculpin, Spinynose, 218
Sculpin, Spotfin, 222
sculpin, staghorn. *See* Pacific Staghorn
 Sculpin
Sculpin, Tadpole, 233
Sculpin, Taylor's. *See* Spinynose Sculpin
Sculpin, Thornback, 229
Sculpin, Thorny, 225
Sculpin, Threadfin, 223
Sculpin, Tidepool, 207
Sculpin, Unidentified, 225
sculpin, white-spotted. *See* Scalyhead Sculpin
Scyliorhinidae. *See* **CATSHARKS**
Scytalina cerdale (Graveldiver), 139

Scytalinidae. *See* **GRAVELDIVERS**
sea char. *See* Dolly Varden
sea lamprey. *See* Pacific Lamprey
sea trout. *See* Cutthroat Trout
Seabass, White, 99
SEA CHUBS (Kyphosidae), 98
   Halfmoon, 98
seaperch, blue. *See* Striped Seaperch
sea-perch, brown. *See* Kelp Perch
sea-perch, dusky. *See* Pile Perch
sea-perch, kelp. *See* Kelp Perch
seaperch, pile. *See* Pile Perch
seaperch, redtail. *See* Redtail Surfperch
seaperch, shiner. *See* Shiner Perch
Seaperch, Striped, 95–96
Seaperch, White, 91
sea-poacher, black-finned. *See* Blackfin
   Poacher
sea-poacher, black-tipped. *See* Blacktip
   Poacher
sea-poacher, deep-pitted. *See* Rockhead
sea-poacher, four-horned. *See* Fourhorn
   Poacher
sea-poacher, pygmy. *See* Pygmy Poacher
sea-poacher, smooth. *See* Smooth
   Alligatorfish
sea-poacher, sturgeon-like. *See* Sturgeon
   Poacher
sea-poacher, windowtailed. *See* Northern
   Spearnose Poacher
Searcher, 108
searcher, bluefin. *See* Alaskan Ronquil
Sebastes auriculatus (Brown Rockfish), 152
Sebastes brevispinis (Silvergray Rockfish),
   166–167
Sebastes caurinus (Copper Rockfish),
   148–149
Sebastes ciliatus (Dark Dusky Rockfish),
   162–163
Sebastes crocotulus (Sunset Rockfish), 173
Sebastes diploproa (Splitnose Rockfish), 179
Sebastes elongatus (Greenstriped Rockfish),
   181
Sebastes emphaeus (Puget Sound Rockfish),
   169
Sebastes entomelas (Widow Rockfish),
   167–168
Sebastes flavidus (Yellowtail Rockfish),
   157–158
Sebastes goodei (Chilipepper), 166
Sebastes maliger (Quillback Rockfish),
   150–151

Sebastes melanops (Black Rockfish),
   158–159
Sebastes miniatus (Vermilion Rockfish),
   172–173
Sebastes mystinus (Blue Rockfish), 160–161
Sebastes nebulosus (China Rockfish), 155
Sebastes nigrocinctus (Tiger Rockfish),
   175–176
Sebastes paucispinis (Bocaccio), 165
Sebastes pinniger (Canary Rockfish), 170–171
Sebastes proriger (Redstripe Rockfish), 180
Sebastes rastrelliger (Grass Rockfish),
   153–154
Sebastes rosaceus (Rosy Rockfish), 174
Sebastes ruberrimus (Yelloweye Rockfish),
   177–178
Sebastes saxicola (Stripetail Rockfish), 182
Sebastes sp. (Undetermined Juvenile
   Rockfish), 182
Sebastes variabilis (Light Dusky Rockfish),
   163–164
Sebastolobus alascanus (Shortspine
   Thornyhead), 183
Sebastolobus altivelis (Longspine
   Thornyhead), 183
Seriola lalandi (Yellowtail Jack), 142
seven eleven perch. *See* Shiner Perch
seven-gill shark. *See* Broadnose Sevengill
   Shark
Shad, American, 47
shad. *See* American Shad
shads. *See* **HERRINGS**
Shanny, Arctic, 116
Shanny, Daubed, 115
Shark, Basking, 28
Shark, Blue, 27
Shark, Bluntnose Sixgill, 21–23
shark, bone (Atlantic). *See* Basking Shark
Shark, Broadnose Sevengill, 21–22
shark, brown. *See* Brown Catshark
Shark, Common Thresher, 31
Shark, (Great) White, 26
Shark, Leopard, 31
shark, mackerel. *See* Salmon Shark
shark, mud. *See* Bluntnose Sixgill Shark and
   Pacific Spiny Dogfish
Shark, Pacific Angel, 32
Shark, Pacific Sleeper, 27
Shark, Salmon, 25–26
shark, seven-gill. *See* Broadnose Sevengill
   Shark
shark, shovelnose. *See* Bluntnose Sixgill Shark

shark, six-gilled. *See* Bluntnose Sixgill Shark
shark, six-gill. *See* Bluntnose Sixgill Shark
Shark, Soupfin, 30
shark, spotted cow. *See* Broadnose Sevengill Shark
SHARKS, ANGEL, 32
SHARKS, BASKING, 28
SHARKS, COW, 21–23
SHARKS, DOGFISH, 29–30
SHARKS, HOUND, 30–31
SHARKS, MACKEREL, 25–26
SHARKS, REQUIEM, 27
SHARKS, SLEEPER, 27
SHARKS, THRESHER, 31
Sharpnose Sculpin, 210
Shiner Perch, 97–98
shiner seaperch. *See* Shiner Perch
shiner surfperch. *See* Shiner Perch
shiner, yellow. *See* Shiner Perch
shiner. *See* Shiner Perch
shore liparid. *See* Tidepool Snailfish
Shortfin Eelpout, 81–82
Shortfin Mako, 26
shortfinned sole. *See* Dover Sole
Shorthorn Sculpin, 244
Shortmast Sculpin, 238
SHORTNOSE CHIMAERAS (Chimaeridae), 40–42
Spotted Ratfish, 40–42
shortspine channel rockfish. *See* Shortspine Thornyhead
shortspine rockfish. *See* Silvergray Rockfish
short-spined rockfish. *See* Silvergray Rockfish
Shortspine Thornyhead, 183
shorttail snailfish. *See* Showy Snailfish
shovelnose shark. *See* Bluntnose Sixgill Shark
Showy Snailfish, 278
silver perch. *See* Silver Surfperch
SILVERSIDES (Atherinopsidae), 82
Topsmelt, 82
Jacksmelt, 82
silver salmon. *See* Coho Salmon
silver smelt. *See* Surf Smelt
Silver Surfperch, 93
Silvergray Rockfish, 166–167
silvergrey rockfish. *See* Silvergray Rockfish
silverspot sculpin. *See* Silverspotted Sculpin
Silverspotted Sculpin, 235
six-gill cowshark. *See* Bluntnose Sixgill Shark
six-gilled shark. *See* Bluntnose Sixgill Shark
six-gill shark. *See* Bluntnose Sixgill Shark
Skate, Alaska, 33

Skate, Aleutian, 33
Skate, Big, 33, 35–36
skate, black. *See* Sandpaper Skate
Skate, Longnose, 34
skate, long-nose. *See* Longnose Skate
skate, Pacific barndoor. *See* Big Skate
skate, Pacific great. *See* Big Skate
Skate, Sandpaper, 36–37
SKATES (Rajidae), 33–37
Longnose Skate, 34
Sandpaper Skate, 36–37
Big Skate, 33, 35–36
Skidegate sole. *See* Butter Sole
Skilfish, 184–185
Skipjack Tuna, 144
SLEEPER SHARKS (Somniosidae), 27
Pacific Sleeper Shark, 27
Sleeper Goby, 102
slender cling-fish. *See* Kelp Clingfish
Slender Cockscomb, 121
Slender Eelblenny, 116
slender flounder. *See* Slender Sole
Slender Sole, 296
slime eel. *See* Pacific Hagfish
slime sole. *See* Dover Sole
Slim Sculpin, 227
Slimy Snailfish, 275
slippery sole. *See* Dover Sole
Slipskin Snailfish, 274
smelt, Columbia River. *See* Eulachon
Smelt, Longfin, 50
smelt, long-finned. *See* Longfin Smelt
Smelt, Night, 50
smelt, Pacific. *See* Longfin Smelt
smelt, Puget Sound. *See* Longfin Smelt
Smelt, Rainbow, 53
SMELTS (Osmeridae), 49–53
Capelin, 49, 52–53
Eulachon, 49–51
Longfin Smelt, 50
Night Smelt, 50
Rainbow Smelt, 53
Surf Smelt, 51–52
smelt, silver. *See* Surf Smelt
Smelt, Surf, 51–52
Smelt, Whitebait, 49
Smooth Alligatorfish, 262
Smoothead Sculpin, 202–203
Smootheye Poacher, 259
Smooth Lumpsucker, 280
smooth poacher. *See* Smooth Alligatorfish
smooth sea-poacher. *See* Smooth Alligatorfish

SNAILFISHES (Liparidae), 270–279
    Lobefin Snailfish, 271
    Marbled Snailfish, 276–277
    Ribbon Snailfish, 275
    Ringtail Snailfish, 274
    shorttail snailfish. *See* Showy Snailfish
    Showy Snailfish, 278
    Slimy Snailfish, 275
    Slipskin Snailfish, 274
    Spotted Snailfish, 272
    Tadpole Snailfish, 279
    Tidepool Snailfish, 273
    Variegated Snailfish, 277
Snailfish, Lobefin, 271
Snailfish, Marbled, 276–277
Snailfish, Ribbon, 275
Snailfish, Ringtail, 274
snailfish, shorttail. *See* Showy Snailfish
Snailfish, Showy, 278
Snailfish, Slimy, 275
Snailfish, Slipskin, 274
Snailfish, Spotted, 272
Snailfish, Tadpole, 279
Snailfish, Tidepool, 273
Snailfish, Variegated, 277
Snake Prickleback, 114–115
Snubnose Sculpin, 219
Sockeye Salmon, 60–61
soft flounder. *See* Pacific Sanddab
Soft Sculpin, 234
sole flounder, scaly-finned. *See* Butter Sole
Sole Sand, 304
sole, arrowtooth. *See* Arrowtooth Flounder
sole, Bellingham. *See* Butter Sole
sole, broadfin. *See* Rock Sole
Sole, Butter, 297
sole, California. *See* English Sole
Sole, Cape. *See* Petrale Sole
sole, Chinese. *See* Dover Sole
Sole, C-O, 306–307
sole, common. *See* English Sole
Sole, Curlfin, 308
Sole, Dover, 301–302
Sole, English, 300–301
Sole, Flathead, 295
Sole, Forkline, 301
sole, French. *See* Arrowtooth Flounder
sole, fringe. *See* Sand Sole
sole, lemon. *See* English Sole
sole, longfin. *See* Rex Sole
sole, longfinned. *See* Rex Sole
Sole, Northern Rock, 299

sole, paper. *See* Flathead Sole
Sole, Petrale, 294
sole, pointed-nosed. *See* English Sole
sole, popeye. *See* C-O Sole
Sole, Rex, 302–303
Sole, Rock, 298–299
sole, rough. *See* Slender Sole
sole, roughscale. *See* Rock Sole
sole, round-nosed. *See* Petrale Sole
sole, rubber. *See* Dover Sole
sole, scalyfin. *See* Butter Sole
sole, scaly-finned. *See* Butter Sole
sole, shortfinned. *See* Dover Sole
sole, Skidegate. *See* Butter Sole
Sole, Slender, 296
sole, slime. *See* Dover Sole
sole, slippery. *See* Dover Sole
sole, whitebellied. *See* Rock Sole
Sole, Yellowfin, 298
Somniosidae. *See* **SLEEPER SHARKS**
Somniosus pacificus (Pacific Sleeper Shark),
    27
Soupfin Shark (Tope), 30
spanstickle. *See* Threespine Stickleback
speckled rockfish. *See* Quillback Rockfish
Speckled Sanddab, 289
Spectacled Sculpin, 226
Sphyraena argentea (California Barracuda), 83
Sphyraenidae. *See* **BARRACUDAS**
Spiny Dogfish. *See* Pacific Spiny Dogfish
spinycheek rockfish. *See* Shortspine
    Thornyhead
spinycheek starnose. *See* Spinycheek
    Starsnout
Spinycheek Starsnout, 255–256
spinyheaded rockfish. *See* Shortspine
    Thornyhead
Spinyhead Sculpin, 231
Spinynose Sculpin, 218
Spirinchus starksi (Night Smelt), 50
Spirinchus thaleichthys (Longfin Smelt), 50
Splitnose Rockfish, 179
splittail perch. *See* Pile Perch
spookfish. *See* Spotted Ratfish
Spotfin Sculpin, 222
Spotfin Surfperch, 93
spot flounder. *See* C-O Sole
spotted cow shark. *See* Broadnose Sevengill
    Shark
Spotted Cusk-eel, 79
spotted flounder. *See* Sand Sole
spotted Irish lord. *See* Red Irish Lord

Spotted Ratfish, 40–42
Spotted Snailfish, 272
spring salmon. *See* Chinook Salmon
spurdog. *See* Pacific Spiny Dogfish
Squalidae. *See* **DOGFISH SHARKS**
Squalus suckleyi (Pacific Spiny Dogfish), 29–30
Squatina californica (Pacific Angel Shark), 32
Squatinidae. *See* **ANGEL SHARKS**
staghorn sculpin. *See* Pacific Staghorn Sculpin
starnose, bigeye. *See* Bigeye Poacher
starnose, blackfin. *See* Blackfin Poacher
starnose, gray. *See* Gray Starsnout
starnose, spinycheek. *See* Spinycheek Starsnout
Starry Flounder, 305–306
starsnout, bigeye. *See* Bigeye Poacher
starsnout, blackfin. *See* Blackfin Poacher
Starsnout, Gray, 256–257
star-snout, gray. *See* Gray Starsnout
Starsnout, Spinycheek, 255–256
Steelhead (Rainbow Trout), 66–67
steelhead trout. *See* Steelhead (Rainbow Trout)
Stellerina xyosterna (Pricklebreast Poacher), 255
Stichaeidae. *See* **PRICKLEBACKS**
Stichaeus punctatus (Arctic Shanny), 116
stickleback, common. *See* Threespine Stickleback
stickleback, eastern. *See* Threespine Stickleback
stickleback, European. *See* Threespine Stickleback
stickleback, New York. *See* Threespine Stickleback
STICKLEBACKS (Gasterosteidae), 85–86. *See also* **TUBESNOUTS**
Threespine Stickleback, 85–86
stickleback, saw-finned. *See* Threespine Stickleback
Stickleback, Threespine, 85–86
stickleback, three-spined. *See* Threespine Stickleback
stickleback, three-spine. *See* Threespine Stickleback
stickleback, two-spine. *See* Threespine Stickleback
STINGRAYS (Dasyatidae), 40
Pelagic Stingray, 40
Stingray, Pelagic, 40
Stout Eelblenny, 116

stout sand lance. *See* Pacific Sand Lance
strawberry rockfish. *See* Greenstriped Rockfish
Striped Kelpfish, 109–110
striped rockfish. *See* Greenstriped Rockfish
Striped Seaperch, 95–96
Stripetail Rockfish, 182
Stromateidae. *See* **BUTTERFISHES**
Stromateidae. *See* **MEDUSAFISHES**
STURGEONS (Acipenseridae), 43–44
Green Sturgeon, 44
White Sturgeon, 43–44
Sturgeon Poacher, 265
sturgeon, Columbia. *See* White Sturgeon
Sturgeon, Green, 44
sturgeon-like sea-poacher. *See* Sturgeon Poacher
sturgeon, Oregon. *See* White Sturgeon
sturgeon, Pacific. *See* White Sturgeon
sturgeon, Sacramento. *See* White Sturgeon
Sturgeon, White, 43–44
Sunfish, Ocean, 101
Sunset Rockfish, 173
Surfperch, Calico, 95
SURFPERCHES (Embiotocidae), 90–98
California Tule Perch, 90
Calico Surfperch, 95
Kelp Perch, 96–97
Pile Perch, 92
Redtail Surfperch, 94
Shiner Perch, 97–98
Silver Surfperch, 93
Spotfin Surfperch, 93
Striped Seaperch, 95–96
Walleye Surfperch, 94
White Seaperch, 91
surfperch, kelp. *See* Kelp Perch
surfperch, pile. *See* Pile Perch
Surfperch, Redtail, 94
surfperch, shiner. *See* Shiner Perch
Surfperch, Silver, 93
Surfperch, Spotfin, 93
Surfperch, Walleye, 94
surfperch, white. *See* White Seaperch
Surf Smelt, 51–52
swaive. *See* Eulachon
Symphurus atricaudus (California Tonguefish), 290
Synchirus gilli (Manacled Sculpin), 215
Syngnathidae. *See* **PIPEFISHES**
Syngnathus griseolineatus. *See* *Syngnathus leptorhynchus*

Syngnathus leptorhynchus (Bay Pipefish), 88
Synodontidae. *See* **LIZARDFISHES**
Synodus lucioceps (California Lizardfish), 83

tadpole liparid. *See* Tadpole Snailfish
Tadpole Sculpin, 233
Tadpole Snailfish, 279
Taylor's sculpin. *See* Spinynose Sculpin
Thaleichthys pacificus (Eulachon), 50
Theragra chalcogramma (Walleye Pollock), 74
Thornback Sculpin, 229
Thornyhead, Longspine, 183
Thornyhead, Shortspine, 183
Thorny Sculpin, 225
Threadfin Sculpin, 223
Threespine Stickleback, 85–86
three-spined stickleback. *See* Threespine Stickleback
three-spine stickleback. *See* Threespine Stickleback
three-toothed lamprey. *See* Pacific Lamprey
THRESHER SHARKS (Alopiidae), 31
  Common Thresher Shark, 31
Thunnus alalunga (Albacore), 144
Thymallinae. *See* **SALMON AND TROUT**
tiddler. *See* Threespine Stickleback
Tidepool Sculpin, 207
Tidepool Snailfish, 273
Tiger Rockfish, 175–176
TILEFISHES (Malacanthidae), 98
  Ocean Whitefish, 98
TOADFISHES (Batrachoididae), 252–254
  Plainfin Midshipman, 252–254
Tomcod, Pacific, 73, 74
tomcod. *See* Pacific Tomcod
tomcods. *See* **CODS**
Tonguefish, California, 290
TONGUEFISHES (Cynoglossidae), 290
  California Tonguefish, 290
Tope (Soupfin Shark), 30
Topsmelt, 82
Torpedinidae. *See* **ELECTRIC RAYS**, 37–38
Torpedo californica (Pacific Electric Ray), 38
Trachipteridae. *See* **RIBBONFISHES**
Trachipterus altivelis (King-of-the-Salmon), 84
Trachurus symmetricus (Jack Mackerel), 142
Triakidae. *See* **HOUND SHARKS**
Triakis semifasciata (Leopard Shark), 31
Trichodon trichodon (Pacific Sandfish), 89–90

Trichodontidae. *See* **SANDFISHES**
tridentate lamprey. *See* Pacific Lamprey
TRIGGERFISHES (Balistidae), 145
  Finescale Triggerfish, 145
Triggerfish, Finescale, 145
Triglops forficatus (Scissortail Sculpin), 226
Triglops macellus (Roughspine Sculpin), 226
Triglops metopias (Highbrow Sculpin), 226
Triglops pingeli. See Triglops pingelii
Triglops pingelii (Ribbed Sculpin), 225
Triglops scepticus (Spectacled Sculpin), 226
trout, Clark's. *See* Cutthroat Trout
trout, coastal cut-throat. *See* Cutthroat Trout
trout, coastal cutthroat. *See* Cutthroat Trout
trout, coastal rainbow. *See* Steelhead (Rainbow Trout)
trout, coast cutthroat. *See* Cutthroat Trout
Trout, Cutthroat, 68
trout, rainbow, 55, 66–67
trout, red-throated. *See* Cutthroat Trout
trout, salmon. *See* Steelhead (Rainbow Trout)
trout, sea. *See* Cutthroat Trout
trout. *See* Cutthroat Trout
trout. *See* **SALMON AND TROUT**
trout, steelhead. *See* Steelhead (Rainbow Trout)
true cod. *See* Pacific Cod
true hakes. *See* **CODS**
Tubenose. *See* Tubesnout
Tubenose Poacher, 261
TUBESNOUTS (Aulorhynchidae), 87.
  See also **STICKLEBACKS**
  Tubesnout, 87
tubesnout poacher. *See* Tubenose Poacher
Tubesnout, 87
tube-snout. *See* Tubesnout
Tuna, Skipjack, 144
turkey red rockfish. *See* Yelloweye Rockfish
two-spine stickleback. *See* Threespine Stickleback
tyee. *See* Chinook Salmon

Undetermined Juvenile Rockfish, 182
Undetermined Rockfish, 161
Unidentified Sculpin, 225
Unknown Lycodapine Eelpout, 82

Variegated Snailfish, 277
Vermilion Rockfish, 172–173
VIVIPAROUS BROTULAS (Bythitidae), 77–78
  Red Brotula, 77–78

wachna. *See* Pacific Tomcod
Walleye Pollock, 72, 73, 74–75
wall-eye Pollock. *See* Walleye Pollock
Walleye Surfperch, 94
Warbonnet, Decorated, 124–125
Warbonnet, Mosshead, 122–123
Warty Poacher, 255
water hare. *See* Spotted Ratfish
Wattled Eelpout, 82
western brook char. *See* Dolly Varden
western brook lamprey. *See* River Lamprey
western lamprey. *See* River Lamprey
western river lamprey. *See* River Lamprey
whisker cod. *See* Pacific Cod
White Croaker, 99
white perch. *See* White Seaperch
White Seabass, 99
White Seaperch, 91
White Sturgeon, 43–44
white surfperch. *See* White Seaperch
Whitebait Smelt, 49
white-barred blenny. *See* Whitebarred
  Prickleback
Whitebarred Prickleback, 113
whitebellied sole. *See* Rock Sole
whitefishes. *See* **SALMON AND TROUT**
Whitefish, Ocean, 98
Whitespotted Greenling, 105, 191–193
whiting, Pacific. *See* Pacific Hake
whiting. *See* Walleye Pollock
whitings. *See* **CODS**
Widow Rockfish, 167–168
windowtail poacher. *See* Northern Spearnose
  Poacher
window-tailed sea-poacher. *See* Northern
  Spearnose Poacher
Wolf-eel, 133–135

WOLFFISHES (Anarhichadidae), 133–135
  Wolf-eel, 133–135
Wrymouth, Dwarf, 137
Wrymouth, Giant, 136–137
WRYMOUTHS (Cryptacanthodidae), 136–137
  Dwarf Wrymouth, 137
  Giant Wrymouth, 136–137

Xeneretmus latifrons (Blacktip Poacher), 259
Xeneretmus leiops (Smootheye Poacher), 259
Xeneretmus triacanthus (Bluespotted
  Poacher), 259
Xererpes fucorum. See Apodichthys fucorum
Xiphister atropurpureus (Black Prickleback),
  119
Xiphister mucosus (Rock Prickleback), 118

yellow-backed rockfish. *See* Copper Rockfish
yellow-backed rockfish. *See* Quillback Rockfish
Yelloweye Rockfish, 11, 177–178
Yellowfin Sole, 298
Yellow Irish Lord, 250
yellow rockfish. *See* China Rockfish
yellow shiner. *See* Shiner Perch
yellow spotted rockfish. *See* China Rockfish
yellowstriped rockfish. *See* China Rockfish
yellowstripe rockfish. *See* China Rockfish
Yellowtail Jack, 142
Yellowtail Rockfish, 157–158
yshuh. *See* Eulachon

Zaniolepis latipinnis (Longspine Combfish),
  198–199
Zaprora silenus (Prowfish), 140–141
Zaproridae. *See* **PROWFISHES**
Zoarcidae. *See* **EELPOUTS**

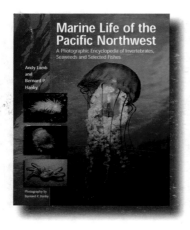

Padded Sculpin

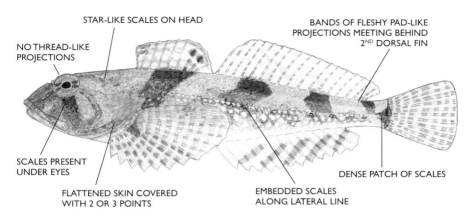

NO THREAD-LIKE PROJECTIONS

STAR-LIKE SCALES ON HEAD

BANDS OF FLESHY PAD-LIKE PROJECTIONS MEETING BEHIND 2ND DORSAL FIN

SCALES PRESENT UNDER EYES

FLATTENED SKIN COVERED WITH 2 OR 3 POINTS

EMBEDDED SCALES ALONG LATERAL LINE

DENSE PATCH OF SCALES

SPECIES: *Artedius fenestralis*

OTHER COMMON NAMES: Incorrect: bullhead

MAXIMUM RECORDED SIZE: 14 cm (5.5 in)

DISTRIBUTION: Southern California to the Aleutian Island chain, Alaska

HABITAT: Most often spotted by divers exploring jetty and piling habitat, the cryptically coloured Padded Sculpin also lurks among eelgrass growing intertidally or slightly deeper. However, this species does live at depths to 60 m (200 ft). Look very carefully to find it, for this usually motionless sculpin is very difficult to spot, and once disturbed darts headlong for nearby shelter.

Peering into the water, the dockside observer may notice the gray Padded Sculpin resting among the barnacles and mussels growing upon the pilings, but this often stationary and irregularly marked creature blends beautifully with any background it has chosen. Seaside strollers should look for the Padded Sculpin along the rocky shore, either in tidepools or beneath adjacent rocks.

COMMENTS: During winter, the gravid female Padded Sculpin deposits small clusters of purple or gray eggs on the bottom, under rocks.

A small, slow-moving creature, the unwelcome Padded Sculpin primarily represents a bait-thieving annoyance to wharf-bound anglers who use small fish, shrimp or other items to tempt more desirable quarry.

Smoothhead Sculpin

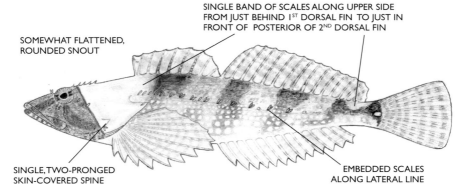

SINGLE BAND OF SCALES ALONG UPPER SIDE FROM JUST BEHIND 1ST DORSAL FIN TO JUST IN FRONT OF POSTERIOR OF 2ND DORSAL FIN

SOMEWHAT FLATTENED, ROUNDED SNOUT

SINGLE, TWO-PRONGED SKIN-COVERED SPINE

EMBEDDED SCALES ALONG LATERAL LINE

SPECIES: *Artedius lateralis*
OTHER COMMON NAMES: flathead sculpin. Incorrect: bullhead
MAXIMUM RECORDED SIZE: 14 cm (5.5 in)
DISTRIBUTION: Northern Baja California, Mexico, to the Aleutian Island chain, Alaska
HABITAT: One of many small sculpins a diver may encounter, the well-camouflaged Smoothhead Sculpin lurks at less than 14 m (46 ft). At the start or finish of a shore dive, look for this species in the shallows. Look closely, though, because it is difficult to locate among seaweed-covered rocks or upon encrusted vertical pilings.

In tidepools or under moist rocks left exposed by the receding tide, the variably hued Smoothhead Sculpin is difficult to see because its irregular banded colouration blends too well with its background.
COMMENTS: In winter each gravid female Smoothhead Sculpin lays small clusters of adhesive, cherry-red, yellow, or orange eggs under rocks.

B. Male guarding nest. Bernard P. Hanby photograph

Generally dismissed as a tiny, bait-stealing nuisance by the pier-fishing crowd, the unpopular Smoothhead Sculpin often grabs any hooked offering and charges off into the pilings.

NOTE: Most abundant in California, the Bonehead Sculpin, *Artedius notospilotus* (sometimes called the Bonyhead Sculpin), might be encountered by readers as far north as Oregon. It is very similar to the Smoothhead Sculpin.